Delfim F. Leão is Professor of Classics at the University of Coimbra. His co-edited books include *Symposion and Philanthropia in Plutarch*, *Nomos, Kosmos and Dike in Plutarch* and *Law and Drama in Ancient Greece*.

P. J. Rhodes is Honorary Professor of Ancient History at Durham University and author and editor of many books, including *Ancient Democracy and Modern Ideology*, *The Greek City States: A Sourcebook*, *A History of the Classical Greek World, 478–323 B.C.* and *A Short History of Ancient Greece* (also published by I.B.Tauris).

'In the early sixth century B.C., Solon of Athens implemented a series of major reforms which laid the groundwork for classical Athenian democracy. He also enacted a large set of laws, which remained the basis of the Athenian legal system through the fourth century and beyond. Now two internationally recognized experts on Greek law, government, and literature have teamed up to produce this fine new edition of Solon's laws, which will be an indispensable resource for anyone interested in Solon's reforms or in ancient Greek law. With up-to-date texts, highly readable translations, and full accounts of recent scholarship – especially on problems of authenticity – Leão and Rhodes will quickly replace the current standard edition of Ruschenbusch (1966), which has long been recognized as inadequate. This is classical scholarship at its best.'

Michael Gagarin, James R. Dougherty, Jr., Centennial Professor Emeritus of Classics, University of Texas at Austin

'Delfim Leão and Peter Rhodes have together produced a new and masterly edition of the fragments of Solon's laws. It expands the number of fragments that appear in the German edition of Eberhard Ruschenbusch (1966) and in his posthumously published translation and notes (2010, curated by K. Bringmann). Texts are in Greek and idiomatic English and accompanied by concise commentary with up-to-date bibliography. Historians (generalist, classical, legal) and their students now have the opportunity to examine in English (and in Greek for those who can) the historical sources that focus on Solon, the most distinguished lawmaker of ancient Athens. Not only can they now study the broad spectrum of Athenian law in the early sixth century BCE (for example, homicide and other private offences; public offences such as tyranny; family law; economic matters; religious regulations, and political institutions), but also the difficulties of the ancient sources themselves (for instance, how can we be sure we have Solon's laws — and not forgeries?). Leão and Rhodes are excellent guides, offering stimulating discussions of diverse aspects, including the publication and survival of the laws, the use of figurative language in them, the economic and social effects of prostitution in Athens, and the penalties for different offences.'

Adele C. Scafuro, Professor of Classics, Brown University

THE LAWS OF SOLON

A New Edition with Introduction, Translation and Commentary

DELFIM F. LEÃO
AND P. J. RHODES

Revised paperback edition published in 2016 by
I.B.Tauris & Co. Ltd
London • New York
www.ibtauris.com

First published in hardback in 2015 by I.B.Tauris & Co. Ltd

Copyright © 2015, 2016 Delfim F. Leão and P. J. Rhodes

The right of Delfim F. Leão and P. J. Rhodes to be identified as the author of this work has been asserted by the author in accordance with the Copyright, Designs and Patents Act 1988.

All rights reserved. Except for brief quotations in a review, this book, or any part thereof, may not be reproduced, stored in or introduced into a retrieval system, or transmitted, in any form or by any means, electronic, mechanical, photocopying, recording or otherwise, without the prior written permission of the publisher.

ISBN: 978 1 78453 668 8
eISBN: 978 0 85773 930 8

A full CIP record for this book is available from the British Library
A full CIP record is available from the Library of Congress

Library of Congress Catalog Card Number: available

CONTENTS

Preface	IX
Guide for the user	XI
Introduction	1

FRAGMENTS

Private wrongs	11
Homicide and wounding (frs. 1–22)	11
Amnesty for *atimoi* (fr. 22/1)	35
Offences against property (frs. 23–5)	36
Moral offences (frs. 26–31)	42
Verbal offences (frs. 32–3)	49
Compensation for damage (frs. 34–5)	53
Enforcement of property rights (fr. 36)	55
Offences against the community	57
Tyranny / overthrowing the constitution (fr. 37)	57
Activist citizenry and political neutrality (fr. 38)	59
Procedure	67
Limitation of self-help (fr. 39)	67
Appeal (fr. 39/1)	67
Prosecution by *ho boulomenos* (fr. 40)	69
Proofs (frs. 41–4)	70
Voting (fr. 45)	73
Time limit for payment of restitutions and fines (fr. 46)	73

VI THE LAWS OF SOLON

Family law	75
Inheritance (fr. 47a)	75
Marriage between brother and sister (fr. 47b)	75
Engyesis and legitimate offspring (fr. 48)	76
Inheritance (frs. 49–54)	78
Care for elderly parents (frs. 55–7)	92
Adoption (fr. 58)	97
Unidentifiable content (fr. 59)	101
Neighbours	103
Distance between properties (frs. 60–2)	103
Sharing of water (fr. 63)	105
Rights concerning natural fertilisers (?) (fr. 64)	106
Economic matters	107
Measures, weights, [coinage] (fr. 64/1)	107
Exports (fr. 65)	108
Limit to land acquisition (frs. 66–66/1)	109
Seisachtheia (fr. 67)	112
Rate of interest (fr. 68)	113
Ban on enslavement for debt (fr. 69)	113
Amnesty for *atimoi* (fr. 70)	114
Sumptuary laws	115
Dowry restrictions (fr. 71)	115
Funeral restrictions (fr. 72)	116
Ban on the trade in perfumes (fr. 73)	121
Paederasty (fr. 74)	122
Constitution, institutions	127
Rights of citizens (frs. 74/1–3)	127
Areopagus and council of four hundred (frs. 74/4–5)	130
Grants of citizenship (fr. 75)	132
Associations (fr. 76)	133
Assessment and property classes (frs. 77–8)	135
Naukrariai (frs. 79–80)	135

Assembly (fr. 80/1)	136
Religion	139
Regulations for offerings (frs. 80/2–82)	139
Calendar of sacrifices (frs. 83–6)	140
Parasitein / eating at public expense (frs. 87–9)	143
Rewards for victors in games (fr. 89/1)	144
Varia (frs. 90–2)	146
Entrenchment of the laws (fr. 93)	149
Unusable, doubtful, spurious	151
From the orators (frs. 94–122)	151
From comedy (frs. 123–7)	181
From Solon's poetry (?) (frs.128–30)	187
Confusion with other legislators (frs. 131–5)	188
Misinterpretation of laws (frs. 136–8)	189
Unusable collective quotations (frs. 139–42)	189
Varia (frs. 143–/154)	192
Bibliography	197
Index of fragments	202
Index of source texts	207

PREFACE

E. Ruschenbusch's Σόλωνος νόμοι of 1966 was an austere publication, in which an introduction was followed simply by the Greek and Latin texts of the fragments and by indexes, with no translation into a modern language or commentary. We therefore set out to provide an edition which would include translations and commentaries in English. After we had formed our plans Ruschenbusch died, but it emerged that he had resumed work on German translations of and commentaries on the fragments, and *Solon: Das Gesetzeswerk — Fragmente*, containing some of the fragments but not all, was edited by K. Bringmann from his papers and published in 2010. Since this was incomplete, and there were several points on which Ruschenbusch's judgment might be questioned, we decided to persevere with our plans, and we offer the results here.

We thank Alex Wright and his staff at I.B.Tauris, for accepting our complex book and helping us with the production of it; Mickael Silva at the University of Coimbra, for converting our computer files into files from which the book could be printed; and Prof. A. C. Scafuro and, particularly, Prof. S. C. Todd, for reading the book in proof, detecting errors and pointing us to improvements. And we thank each other, for friendly and stimulating collaboration. One of us has had the primary responsibility for each of the fragments, but we have read and commented on each other's drafts, and we accept joint responsibility for what is printed here.

GUIDE FOR THE USER

Since Ruschenbusch's numbering has been standard for half a century, we have retained that as far as possible. However, we have added some texts which he did not include, and have moved a few texts to a different place in the collection (as he himself in *Gesetzeswerk* added a few texts and moved a few texts). We have therefore used the following notation:

an addition to Ruschenbusch's numbering includes a slash:
    e.g. after Fr. 4 **Fr. 4/1a, Fr. 4/1b**,
    and after Fr. 5d **Fr. 5/e**;
a fragment in *Gesetzeswerk* but not in *Nomoi* is marked in the lemma with an asterisk: e.g. ***Fr. 1c**;
a fragment not in *Gesetzeswerk* or in *Nomoi* is marked in the lemma with an obelus: e.g. **†Fr. 4/1a**;
when a fragment has been transposed, Ruschenbusch's number is added in the lemma in parentheses: e.g. **Fr. 22/1 (fr. 70 Ruschenbusch)**,
    and a cross reference is given at the point where Ruschenbusch placed the fragment.

We have sometimes printed a longer or shorter passage of text than was printed by Ruschenbusch, and where we have judged it necessary we have printed a revised text. In our *apparatus criticus* we have been more selective than Ruschenbusch, largely limiting ourselves to points where the meaning is seriously affected. Since many of our texts are epigraphic or papyrological, we have in all texts used {braces} rather than [square brackets] to mark editorial deletions.

Whether speeches and other works were written by the man to whom they are attributed does not matter for the purposes of this collection, if they were written at the time when and for the context for which they purport to be written: for the Demosthenic corpus we have followed MacDowell, *Demosthenes the Orator*.

In the Bibliography we give details of all books cited, apart from standard reference works and editions of ancient texts; some we cite by a shorter version of their title (which should cause no difficulty), and we give below the more drastic abbreviations which we use for some frequently-cited books:

Ruschenbusch, *Kleine Schriften zur griechischen Rechtsgeschichte*: *Kleine Schriften*.
—— *Solon: Das Gesetzeswerk — Fragmente*: *Gesetzeswerk*.
—— Σόλωνος νόμοι: *Nomoi*.
—— *Untersuchungen zur Geschichte des athenischen Strafrechts*: *Untersuchungen*.

Boegehold, *The Athenian Agora*, xxviii. *The Lawcourts at Athens*: *Agora* xxviii.
Gagarin, *Drakon and Early Athenian Homicide Law*: *Drakon*.
Harrison, *The Law of Athens*: *L.A.*
Lipsius, *Das attische Recht und Rechtsverfahren*: *A.R.*
MacDowell, *The Law in Classical Athens*: *L.C.A.*
Rhodes, *A Commentary on the Aristotelian Athenaion Politeia*: *Comm. Ath. Pol.*
Stroud, *The Axones and Kyrbeis of Drakon and Solon*: *Axones and Kyrbeis*.
Stroud, *Drakon's Law on Homicide*: *Drakon's Law*.

We give full details of articles cited at their first mention after each subject-sub-heading (i.e. the headings printed with capital initial and lower-case, e.g. **Homicide and wounding**), and a shorter citation thereafter.

Ancient texts and collections of texts, and standard works of reference, are abbreviated as in the fourth edition (2012) of the *Oxford Classical Dictionary*; periodicals as in *L'Anneé Philologique* with the usual anglophone divergences (principally, *AJP* etc. for *AJPh* etc.). We use the following additional abbreviations:

Aeschin. II. *F.L.*: *De Falsa Legatione*.
Antiph. *Tetr.*: *Tetralogies*.
Dem. XIX. *F.L.*: *De Falsa Legatione*.
Hesych.: Hesychius.
Lex. Rhet. Cant.: *Lexicon Rhetoricum Cantabrigiense*.
Lib. *Decl.*: *Declamationes*.
Plut. *Comp. Sol. Publ.*: *Comparison of Solon and Publicola*.

INTRODUCTION

Ruschenbusch in the introductory chapters of *Nomoi* took the background for granted and focused on the following issues: the survival of Solon's laws (1–14), the relationship of *kyrbeis* and *axones* (14–22), the *axones* as physical objects (23–4), the extent of the text on the *axones* (25), the scope of Solon's laws (25–6), the organisation of Solon's laws (27–31), the locations in Athens of the *axones* (31–2), the survival of Solon's laws as a body of current law (32–6), the lack of subsequent changes to the text on the *axones* (36–7), the date of the *axones*' destruction (37–8), the transmission of Solon's laws (39–52) and the effect of the orators and comedians on that transmission (53–8). We think it better to take less for granted, and we discuss first the legislation of Draco and Solon and the publication of their laws (1–6) and secondly the subsequent history of their laws and of the monuments on which they were inscribed (6–8).

One striking feature of Greece in the archaic period was an increasing provision of written laws, inscribed on stone or on some other durable material. In contrast to some scholars in recent decades, we do not believe that the purpose of publishing written laws was primarily symbolic rather than to make the texts publicly available,[1] or that it was intended to repress the citizens rather than to enable them.[2] For Solon's laws we have his own statement (fr. 36. 18–20 West *ap. Ath. Pol.* 12. iv) that he 'wrote laws for bad and good [i.e. the lower and upper classes] alike, fitting

---

[1] E.g. J. H. Whitley, 'Cretan Laws and Cretan Literacy', *AJA*² ci 1997, 635–61; K.-J. Hölkeskamp, '(In)schrift und Monument: Zum Begriff des Geszetzes im archaischen und klassischen Griechenland', *ZPE* cxxxii 2000, 73–96.

[2] E.g. Steiner, *The Tyrant's Writ*; W. Eder, 'The Politicial Significance of the Codification of Law in Archaic Societies: An Unconventional Hypothesis', in Raaflaub (ed.), *Social Struggles in Archaic Rome*², 239–67.

straight justice to each'. When laws on particular matters were published individually, as is the case with many of our surviving early laws, that was presumably done in order to address a particular perceived need.[3] When a substantial body of law was produced, as was the case in Athens perhaps with Draco and certainly with Solon, the perceived need will have been not to solve a particular problem but to make available over a range of issues a statement of what the law was and how it was to be enforced. Gagarin stresses that written laws could preserve a substantial body of details as oral laws could not; and against Hölkeskamp he rightly maintains that, even if Solon did not engage in systematic 'codification', the body of laws which he produced can reasonably be regarded as a 'code'.[4]

The earliest surviving inscribed Greek law is from Drerus, in Crete, probably *c.* 650–600, and limits a man's tenure of the office of *kosmos* to one year in ten (M&L 2). In Athens Draco's legislation was placed in Ol. xxxix = 624/3–621/0, and probably in the year 621/0.[5] Solon's archonship and legislation were in the chronographic tradition dated 594/3.[6] These dates are not beyond doubt, and have indeed been doubted, but they are the best dates available to us and there is no good basis for alternative dates.

The laws of Draco, and the laws of Solon and Draco together, are mentioned for the first time by the fifth-century comedian Cratinus:

πρὸς τοῦ Σόλωνος καὶ Δράκοντος οἷσι νῦν
φρύγουσιν ἤδη τὰς κάχρυς τοῖς κύρβεσιν

In the name of Solon and Draco, on whose *kyrbeis* they now roast the barley

(Cratinus fr. 300 Kassel & Austin *ap.* Plut. *Sol.* 25. ii)

---

[3] Cf. R. Thomas, 'Writing, Law and Written Law', in Gagarin & Cohen (edd.), *The Cambridge Companion to Ancient Greek Law*, 41–60 at 54.

[4] Gagarin, *Writing Greek Law*, 67–92. Solon's laws a 'code', *op. cit.*, 74–5; contr. K.-J. Hölkeskamp, 'What Is a Code? Solon's Laws between Complexity, Compilation and Contingency', *Hermes* cxxxiii 2005, 280–93.

[5] See Stroud, *Drakon's Law*, 66–70; Rhodes, *Comm. Ath. Pol.* 109.

[6] See T. J. Cadoux, 'The Athenian Archons from Kreon to Hypsichides', *JHS* lxviii 1948, 70–123 at 93–9; Rhodes, *Comm. Ath. Pol.* 120–2. Some, such as Hignett, *A History of the Athenian Constitution*, 316–21, have dated Solon's legislation much later, and after the troubles over the archonship which in the chronographic tradition followed his archonship and legislation.

The *anagrapheis* appointed in 410/09 'to write up the laws of Solon' (Lys. XXX. *Nicomachus* 2) published in 409/8 'the law of Draco about homicide' (*IG* i³ 104. 4–6 = fr. 5a); and the restored democracy of 403 was to be based on the *nomoi* of Solon and the *thesmoi* of Draco (Andoc. I. *Myst.* 81). According to *Ath. Pol.* 7. i, Plut. *Sol.* 17. i, Solon's laws superseded all Draco's laws except those on homicide. While it is unlikely that other laws of Draco physically survived, there was a tradition that Draco had produced laws in other areas, which were uniformly severe. Stroud assembled the evidence for measures with which Draco was credited, and took an optimistic view of the Athenians' ability to preserve the memory of laws annulled at the beginning of the sixth century.[7] At the other extreme, there have been sceptics who have doubted even the existence of Draco,[8] and others who have accepted Draco but have doubted whether he produced any laws except on homicide.[9] Ruschenbusch suggested that Draco's homicide law was in effect a general criminal law for offences against persons, but that an offence such as theft would reach a court only when the victim exercised his right of self-help by killing the offender, and that there were no other laws of Draco.[10] We remain uncertain whether there were other laws of Draco (see commentary on fr. 1).

Ath. Pol. treated Draco (4) after the attempted *coup* of Cylon (1). Cylon was an Olympic victor in 640 (Euseb. Arm. p. 92 Karst), and made his attempt in an Olympic year (Thuc. I. 126. iv–vi), which must therefore be one of the years 636/5, 632/1, 628/7, 624/3 (if in 640 he had rushed back from Olympia to stage his *coup* that would probably have been remembered). The episode ended with the killing of Cylon's supporters when it had been understood that their lives would be spared (Hdt. V. 71. ii, Thuc. I. 126. xi). Gagarin stresses that Draco's law did not directly address the particular problems arising from the killing of Cylon's supporters; but since the legislation of Draco followed soon afterwards, and included legislation on homicide, he allows that there

---

[7] Stroud, *Drakon's Law*, 75–82. C. Carey, 'In Search of Drakon', *CCJ* lix 2013, 29–51, supports the view that there were laws of Draco in areas other than homicide, but argues that they were not uniformly severe.

[8] E.g. Beloch, *Griechische Geschichte*², I. ii. 358–62.

[9] E.g. Hignett, *A History of the Athenian Constitution*, 307–8.

[10] Ruschenbusch, 'φόνος', *Historia* ix 1960, 129–54 at 147–52 = his *Kleine Schriften*, 32–53 at 47–51; *Gesetzeswerk*, 24–6.

should be some connection between the two,[11] and that is something which we take seriously.

After its account of the Cylonian affair *Ath. Pol.* moves to *stasis* between upper and lower classes and the plight of a category of dependent peasants called *hektemoroi* (2), and then digresses to the 'ancient constitution' and the development of the archonship (3). Whatever was originally supplied about the laws of Draco was replaced by a reviser with an anachronistic 'constitution of Draco' (4). Then the author rounds off what has been said in 2–3 and embarks on an extensive treatment of Solon (5–12). Solon was appointed archon and reconciler (5. ii). He banned enslavement for debt and he brought in the *seisachtheia*, seen by the author as a cancellation of all debts but perhaps rather to be interpreted as the cancellation of the obligations of the *hektemoroi* (6. i: see on fr. 67). We then read of his establishing a constitution and enacting other laws, superseding those of Draco except on homicide; the laws were inscribed on *kyrbeis* and the Athenians swore to adhere to them (7. i–iii). Constitutional measures included the four property classes as a basis for political rights (7. iii–iv), the appointment of the archons from an elected short list (8. i–ii), the council of four hundred and the duties of the Areopagus (8. iii–iv), and the law against neutrality (8. v). Other measures mentioned are reforms in judicial procedure (9. i) and what the author believes to be a reform of measures, weights and coinage (10). Various laws are cited by Plutarch and other writers, and the fragments collected in this volume, for which as far as possible we follow the arrangement of Ruschenbusch, indicate the range of Solon's laws.

Draco was presumably given a special commission to enact laws, but whatever his status was he was not archon, since there is no reason to doubt the assignment of his laws to the archonship of Aristaechmus (*Ath. Pol.* 4. i: probably part of the original text, not of the reviser's material). Solon's special commission was combined with the office of archon, and probably the chronological distinctions of *Ath. Pol.* 10. i and Plut. *Sol.* 16 result simply from the misinterpretation of a distinction between different areas of activity.[12] Various oaths

---

[11] Gagarin, *Drakon*, 20–1, *Writing Greek Law*, 93–109.
[12] Rhodes, *Comm. Ath. Pol.* 120–2, 163–4.

to uphold Solon's laws are mentioned: by 'the Athenians', apparently in advance, to keep to his laws for ten years (Hdt. I. 29. ii); by 'all', apparently afterwards, to keep to his laws for a hundred years (*Ath. Pol.* 7. i–ii); by the council, apparently afterwards, to keep to his laws (Plut. *Sol.* 25. iii). Herodotus links his oath with Solon's leaving Athens for ten years so that he could not be pressed to change his laws (Hdt. I. 29. i), which *Ath. Pol.* 11. i and Plut. *Sol.* 25. vi – 28. i report separately but with agreement on the ten years. Probably we should follow Herodotus in envisaging an oath sworn in advance to accept whatever laws Solon might enact, and in linking this with Solon's leaving Athens.[13]

Solon's laws were inscribed on monuments called *kyrbeis* by *Ath. Pol.* 7. i but *axones* by Plut. *Sol.* 25. i–ii. As noted above, Cratinus referred to the *kyrbeis* of Solon and Draco; and *kyrbeis* were mentioned in connection with the sacrificial calendar which formed part of the code of laws revised at the end of the fifth century (Lys. XXX. *Nicomachus* 17, 18, 20; cf. *Agora* xix L 4a. 87[14]). However, the inscribed homicide law was copied from at least two *axones* (*IG* i³ 104. 10, 56 = fr. 5a), and Plutarch and others cite laws of Solon as e.g. the eighth law on the thirteenth *axon* (Plut. *Sol.* 19. iv = fr. 70). On the basis of his view (which we doubt) that a small amount of text was omitted at the beginning of the homicide law inscribed in 409/8 (fr. 5a), Ruschenbusch reckoned that Draco's first *axon* contained *c.* 2,300 characters ≈ 1.84 Teubner pages of *c.* 1,250 characters, and that Solon's 16–24 *axones* contained 30–45 Teubner pages.

The significance of the two terms has been disputed both in antiquity and by modern scholars.[15] The meaning of *kyrbis* is uncertain; an *axon* should be an axle or something which revolves on an axle. We agree with Ruschenbusch and Andrewes, against Stroud, that the two terms were applied to the same set of objects, probably revolving wooden beams of square section, set vertically (Ruschenbusch, against

---

[13] Rhodes, *Comm. Ath. Pol.* 135, 169.
[14] On the inscription see S. D. Lambert, 'The Attic Genos Salaminioi and the Island of Salamis', *ZPE* cxix 1997, 85–106 at 92).
[15] Modern discussions include Ruschenbusch, *Nomoi*, 14–24; A. Andrewes, 'The Survival of Solon's *Axones*', in φόρος . . . *Meritt*, 21–8; Stroud, *Axones and Kyrbeis*; Rhodes, *Comm. Ath. Pol.* 131–5.

Andrewes and Stroud) in a frame, and accommodating an extensive text more compactly than could be done on a wall or a series of *stelai*.[16] *Ath. Pol.* 7. i states that they were placed in the Stoa of the Basileus (in the north-west of the agora), but that was built after the time of Solon;[17] their first home was the acropolis according to Anaximenes *FGrH* 72 F 13, Poll. VIII. 128. For their subsequent history see below.

We believe, as Ruschenbusch did, that Solon's *axones* survived long enough to be copied and studied, as the *axones* containing Draco's homicide law survived to be copied in 409/8 (the list by Hesychius Illustrius of Aristotle's works included one in five books on the *axones* of Solon[18]), and that, despite the tendency in fourth-century Athens to attribute all current laws to Draco and Solon, those who wanted to do so could make the distinction and could find out which were the laws of Solon. As pointed out by Scafuro, it is likely that some laws had a Solonian kernel but, without being superseded, were later modified in some respects.[19] From the fact that *Ath. Pol.* and Plut. *Sol.* overlap substantially but each have material which the other lacks, Rhodes has argued that behind both there lies a treatise on Solon which was able to make use both of his poems and of his laws.[20] Solon undoubtedly made changes in Athens' institutions, and if there were laws of Draco in areas other than homicide he will have made changes there; but it is likely that much of the work, first of Draco and afterwards of Solon, will have involved not changing the laws but simply making a clear and publicly accessible statement of what the law was;[21] and later Greeks may have been mistaken when they thought, for instance, that the measures and weights [and, they supposed, coins] of Solon differed from those used by Athens before (see on fr. 64/1). We agree with Ruschenbusch that Solon will not have produced a *Verfassungsgrundgesetz*, a fundamental law of the

---

[16] See the drawings in Ruschenbusch, *Nomoi*, 24; Rhodes, *Aristotle, The Athenian Constitution*, 123 fig. 1.

[17] It is dated *c*. 500 or after 480–479 by Camp, *The Athenian Agora: Site Guide*⁵, 75–81.

[18] Rose, *Aristotelis Qui Ferebantur Librorum Fragmenta*, 16.

[19] A. C. Scafuro, 'Identifying Solonian Laws', in Blok & Lardinois (edd.), *Solon of Athens*, 175–96.

[20] Rhodes, *Comm. Ath. Pol.* 28, 88, 118.

[21] Cf. C. Carey, 'In Search of Drakon', *CCJ* lix 2013, 29–51.

constitution,²² such as that provided by Ptolemy I for Cyrene probably in 321/0 (*SEG* ix 1), but we do nevertheless believe that, at any rate where he did make changes, Solon will have enacted laws concerning political institutions, and we have therefore added fragments on (for instance) the property classes and eligibility for office which were not included in Ruschenbusch's collection.

It is likely enough that Draco's and Solon's *axones* were indeed originally placed on the acropolis. They are said to have been moved from there to 'the *bouleuterion* and the agora', by Ephialtes (Anaximenes *FGrH* 72 F 13), or to 'the *prytaneion* and the agora', without any mention of by whom or when (Poll. VIII. 128). Wilamowitz saw this as simply a metaphorical way of saying that the government of the state was made more democratic, and Ruschenbusch was among those who followed him on that;²³ but Jacoby in his commentary on Anaximenes was prepared to accept it as a literal statement.

Whatever may have been done by Ephialtes, it is likely that by the end of the fifth century the *axones* were housed in the Stoa of the Basileus, as stated by *Ath. Pol.* 7. i: in 409/8 the *anagrapheis* of the new code of laws were instructed to take over Draco's homicide law from the *basileus* and to set up their *stele* in front of the Stoa (fr. 5a. 4–8), and Andocides states of laws approved in 403/2 that they were to be inscribed 'in the stoa' (Andoc. I. *Myst.* 82, 85).²⁴ It has indeed been suggested that the Stoa was built in order to house the *axones*.²⁵ J. L. Shear (accepting as genuine the documents in Andoc. I. *Myst.*) has discussed both texts and buildings with reference to the democratic restorations of 410 and 403, and has argued that between 410 and 403 republished laws were placed on *stelai*, mostly in the two annexes added to the front of the Stoa and in the area in front of the Stoa, while the calendar of sacrifices as revised between 403 and 399 was

---

²² *Nomoi*, 25–6.

²³ Wilamowitz, *Aristoteles und Athen*, i. 45 n. 7; Ruschenbusch, *Nomoi*, 21–2.

²⁴ Against the authenticity of the 'decree of Teisamenus' quoted in §§83–4, which ends by stating that such laws were to be inscribed 'on the wall, where they were inscribed before', see M. Canevaro & E. M. Harris, 'The Documents in Andocides' *On the Mysteries*', *CQ*² lxii 2012, 98–129, esp. 110–6.

²⁵ E.g. T. L. Shear, jr., 'ἰσονόμους τ' Ἀθήνας ἐποιησάτην: The Agora and the Democracy', in Coulson *et al.* (edd.), *The Archaeology of Athens and Attica under the Democracy*, 225–48 at 240–1.

on slabs joined to form a continuous sheet of stone, placed inside the Stoa against the north wall on a ledge.[26] Whatever happened to the *axones* then, they were at some time moved to the *prytaneion*: they are mentioned as being there by Polemon, of the early second century (fr. 48 *FHG*, printed also at Eratosthenes *FGrH* 241 F 37c, *ap.* Harp. α 166 Keaney ἄξονι), and later by Plut. *Sol.* 25. i, Paus. I. 18. iii.

We believe that the *axones* survived substantially intact to the end of the fifth century, and were available to be used by the *anagrapheis* appointed in 410/09 to republish the laws (Lys. XXX. *Nicomachus* 2). However the Thirty in 404 set about annulling laws of Solon which offered scope for dispute (*Ath. Pol.* 35. ii), we doubt if they presumed physically to defile or destroy his *axones* rather than simply to modify the texts which had been produced by the *anagrapheis*; and, similarly, before the late fifth century, modifications of the laws will have been made by enacting and inscribing new decrees, not by altering the *axones*.[27] As we have stated above, we believe that the *axones* still in the fourth century remained available to be studied, and that those who wished to distinguish between laws of Solon and later laws were able to do so. The passage from Cratinus which we have quoted is to be read as a metaphorical suggestion the the *axones / kyrbeis* had become obsolete, not as a literal suggestion that they were being used for firewood.

They were seen by Eratosthenes in the third century and by Polemon in the early second, but by the time of Plutarch (*c.* A.D. 100) only meagre fragments survived, and already in the hellenistic period it was possible to argue over whether the *axones* and *kyrbeis* were the same or different, what their physical form(s) was or were, and, if they were different objects, whether they differed in content.

However, it is an undeniable fact that fourth-century Athenians, taking their lead from the decision to base the restored democracy of 403 on the *thesmoi* of Draco and the *nomoi* of Solon, did tend to attribute to Draco and Solon all their current laws, even those which were clearly more recent (e.g. frs. 94, 98). Once Athens had the code of laws as revised between 410 and 399, the *axones* will have been of antiquarian interest only, and those who were interested in their

---

[26] J. L. Shear, *Polis and Revolution*, 85–96, 240–6.
[27] Ruschenbusch, *Nomoi*, 36–7.

content are likely to have consulted transcriptions of them and books about them rather than the original objects. Ruschenbusch argued that, while they still existed in the early second century, they had been destroyed by the time of Didymus, in the mid first century (*ap.* Harp. o 14 Keaney ὁ κάτωθεν νόμος and other lexica), or even of Apollodorus, in the later second century (*FGrH* 244 F 107);[28] but in reaching that conclusion he perhaps placed too much trust in the text of fragments transmitted in the lexica.

But Solon was remembered as one of the Seven Wise Men (e.g. Pl. *Prt.* 343 A) and one of the lawgivers of archaic Greece, and so it is not surprising that we have references to his laws, more reliable in some cases than in others, by a variety of later writers, including Cicero (first century B.C.: frs. 4b, 38c, 72a–b), Gellius (second century A.D.: frs. 23a, 38b), Lucian (second century A.D.: frs. 39, 55b, 97c) and Libanius (fourth century A.D.: frs. 39, 55b, 97c).

---

[28] Ruschenbusch, *Nomoi*, 37–8.

FRAGMENTS

PRIVATE WRONGS

Homicide and wounding

Fr. 1a: *Ath. Pol.* 7. i
πολιτείαν δὲ κατέστησε καὶ νόμους ἔθηκεν ἄλλους, τοῖς δὲ Δράκοντος θεσμοῖς ἐπαύσαντο χρώμενοι πλὴν τῶν φονικῶν.
[Solon] established a constitution and enacted other laws, and they ceased using the ordinances of Draco except those on homicide.

Fr. 1b: Plut. *Sol.* 17. i
πρῶτον μὲν οὖν τοὺς Δράκοντος νόμους ἀνεῖλε πλὴν τῶν φονικῶν ἅπαντας διὰ τὴν χαλεπότητα καὶ τὸ μέγεθος τῶν ἐπιτιμίων· μία γὰρ ὀλίγου δεῖν ἅπασιν ὥριστο ζημία τοῖς ἁμαρτάνουσι, θάνατος.
First [Solon] annulled all the laws of Draco except those on homicide, because of their severity and the greatness of the penalties: for one penalty was stipulated for virtually all offenders, death.

*Fr. 1c: Ael. *V.H.* VIII. 10
ἐπεὶ δὲ ἡρέθη, τά τε ἄλλα ἐκόσμησε τὴν πόλιν καὶ δὴ καὶ τοὺς νόμους τοὺς νῦν ἔτι φυλαττομένους συνέγραψεν αὐτοῖς. καὶ τότε ἐπαύσαντο οἱ Ἀθηναῖοι χρώμενοι τοῖς Δράκοντος· ἐκαλοῦντο δὲ ἐκεῖνοι θεσμοί. μόνους δὲ ἐφύλαξαν τοὺς φονικοὺς αὐτοῦ.
When [Solon] was appointed, he adorned the city in other ways and in particular he drafted the laws which are still kept now. And then

the Athenians ceased using those of Draco: these were called *thesmoi* [ordinances]. They kept only his homicide laws.

*Fr. 1d: Georgius Cedrenus, *Historiarum Compendium* (i. 145. 18–20 Bekker) ἐν τούτοις τοῖς ἄρχουσιν ἐνομοθέτει Ἀθηναίων πρῶτος Δράκων ὀνόματι. μετ' αὐτὸν δὲ Σόλων τοῦ Δράκοντος τοὺς νόμους ἠθέτει. In the period of these archons [*sc.* who followed the kings] the first of the Athenians to enact laws was the man called Draco. After him Solon deleted the laws of Draco.

Since Solon is said to have retained Draco's law on homicide, Ruschenbusch began his collection with the fragments of Draco's homicide law.

That law is known to have occupied at least two *axones* (fr. 5a). Whether it was in fact Draco's only law, or there were indeed others which were superseded by laws of Solon, continues to be debated. Ruschenbusch, *Gesetzeswerk*, in commenting on fr. 1 argued that there were none: (i) the entrenchment clause in fr. 22 protects only the homicide law; (ii) if there were other laws they would have been similarly protected and Solon would have breached that protection; (iii) Solon similarly protected his laws (fr. 93); (iv) by the fourth century there was no genuine tradition on Draco and Solon, and no trace of other laws of Draco survived; (v) the only other laws seriously attributed to Draco are on theft (frs. 140–1) and on idleness (fr. 66/1), both are problematic, and both invoke the death penalty, which Ruschenbusch believed was not introduced until later (arguing that Draco's only penalty was *atimia* — which might in fact result in death: so too Gagarin, *Drakon*, 116–21). However, for the possibility at this date of execution by the authorities see on fr. 16. From the provisions for lawful homicide in Dem. XXIII. *Aristocrates* 22, 53, 60, fr. 19a, Dem. XXIV. *Timocrates* 113, he inferred that Draco's law covered offences against the person, but except when they led to the killing of the offender (and a court had to pronounce the killing lawful) the injured party could resort to self-help without obtaining a judicial verdict.

It is certainly true that we do not have reliable evidence for other laws of Draco — which is not surprising if they were superseded after less than thirty years. But Ruschenbusch himself believed that despite the entrenchment clause the homicide law was modified later; similarly Solon's laws were modified later; and, if Solon was given a special commission to enact new laws, that could explicitly or implicitly have overridden any entrenchment clause of Draco. Gagarin, *Early Greek Law*, 76, raises that question but does not answer it. We think the question whether there were other laws of Draco is better left open. For laws on idleness see fr. 66/1, on theft frs. 140–1. See also Stroud, *Drakon's Law*, 77–82; Gagarin, *Drakon*, 116–21, 'The Thesmothetai and the Earliest Athenian Tyranny Law', *TAPA* cxi 1981, 71–7 at 73.

Later texts commonly refer to the *thesmoi* ('ordinances') of Draco and the *nomoi* ('laws') of Solon (e.g. Andoc. I *Myst.* 81, decree *ap.* 83, *Ath. Pol.* 4. i contr. 6. i, 7. i), but in fr. 36. 21 West *ap. Ath. Pol.* 12. iv Solon himself refers to his laws as *thesmoi*.

Altogether in classical Athens there were five categories of homicide and courts for dealing with them (fr. 4/1b cf. Dem. XXIII. *Aristocrates* 63–79). In *Nomoi*, on the basis of fr. 5a, Ruschenbusch limited his fragments of Draco's law to unwilling homicide, with some matters which he thought applicable both to willing and to unwilling (frs. 3–18), and lawful homicide (frs. 19–21); in *Gesetzeswerk* he added unknown and non-human killers (frs. 21a–d), on the basis of the *prytaneion*'s inclusion in fr. 22/1. However, while fr. 2 shows that the Areopagus was not a homicide court in Draco's laws, fr. 5a shows that Draco did recognise a distinction between willing and unwilling homicide, and we think it likely that all the categories and (with the exception of the Areopagus) the courts for dealing with them figured in his law (cf. Boegehold, *Agora* xxviii, 43–4).

Ruschenbusch had strong views on the development of Athenian homicide law, and believed that there were several changes later than Draco and Solon: the specification of penalties (including death) other than *atimia* and the wrath of the gods, proclamation against the killer not merely by the kin of the deceased but by the *basileus*, the transformation of *aidesis* from acceptance of blood money in all cases to an act of forgiveness for unwilling homicide, the introduction of the second pair of speeches (seen as occurring when the prosecutor's *diomosia* no longer settled the factual qustion), the transfer of willing homicide from the *ephetai* to the Areopagus (which he dated after Solon but before 508), the development of exile from a normal consequence of *atimia* into a formal penalty which could be imposed, the introduction of a *graphe traumatos*, and the introduction of *endeixis* to accompany an *apagoge* which he saw as losing its original character of self-help (*Gesetzeswerk*, 20–4, with his *Untersuchungen* and articles reprinted in his *Kleine Schriften*).

However, much of that depends on assumptions about what ought to have happened rather than evidence of what did happen, and has been answered strongly by Hansen, *Apagoge, Endeixis and Ephegesis*, 113–8. It is credible that, as institutions were strengthened and developed, rights of self-help and the *atimia* of offenders were replaced by punishments fixed by law or assessed by a court and inflicted by the authorities; but fr. 16 suggests that even in the time of Draco execution by the authorities was a possible alternative to killing by an aggrieved citizen, while self-help still persisted in some circumstances in the fourth century (as in some of the sub-categories of lawful homicide, frs. 19–21/1). On our interpretation of fr. 5a Draco already prescribed different procedures, and possibly different outcomes, for willing and unwilling homicide.

After Draco willing homicide was transferred to the Areopagus, and where one change is certain other changes are possible: for instance, the killing of metics (fr. 5/e) cannot have been added to the list of cases tried at the Palladium until a distinct category of metics was created (perhaps not until the mid fifth century: J. Watson, 'The Origin of Metic Status at Athens', *CCJ* lvi 2010, 259–78), and some of the sub-categories of lawful homicide may be later additions. However, we agree with Hansen that there is no justification for postulating as many and as great changes as were postulated by Ruschenbusch. We have accordingly added to Ruschenbusch's list of fragments 4/1a–b (willing homicide), 5/e (*Ath. Pol.* on trials at the Palladium), 16b (*endeixis*), 21/1 (*Ath. Pol.* on trials at the Delphinium) and 21/2a–b (trials at Phreatto).

Fr. 2: Plut. *Sol.* 19. iii
οἱ μὲν οὖν πλεῖστοι τὴν ἐξ Ἀρείου πάγου βουλήν, ὥσπερ εἴρηται, Σόλωνα συστήσασθαί φασι, καὶ μαρτυρεῖν αὐτοῖς δοκεῖ μάλιστα τὸ μηδαμοῦ τὸν Δράκοντα λέγειν μηδ' ὀνομάζειν Ἀρεοπαγίτας, ἀλλὰ τοῖς ἐφέταις ἀεὶ διαλέγεσθαι περὶ τῶν φονικῶν.

Most people say that it was Solon who instituted the council of the Areopagus, as I have stated (19. i), and it seems particularly to be evidence in support of this that Draco never mentions the Areopagites by name, but always in matters of homicide refers to the *ephetai*.

Plutarch goes on to cite Solon's amnesty law (fr. 22/1), which does mention the Areopagus by name, and he suggests that perhaps Solon was referring to cases which would have been tried by the Areopagus under his own laws, but leaves the problem unsolved. The best solution is that the Areopagus did exist before Solon, but was then concerned with major offences against the state, not with homicide (see on fr. 22/1).

Fr. 3: Phot. α 1753 Theodoridis
ΑΝΔΡΑΦΟΝΩΝ· οὕτως Σόλων ἐν τοῖς ἄξοσιν <ἀντὶ> τῶν ἀνδροφόνων ἀεί φησιν.

Perhaps ΑΝΔΡΟΚΟΝΟΙ, cf. Hesych. α 4753 Latte *et al.* ἀνδροκόνοι, Theodoridis.   <ἀντὶ> Reizenstein.

ANDRAPHONON ['killers']: This form is always used in the *axones* by Solon rather than *androphonon*.

Ruschenbusch assumed this to be derived from a work on the *axones*, and remarks that the form *androphonos* is used in frs. 16–18 but that the form with *alpha* must have been used several times in the *axones* to have prompted this comment. He does not consider what we believe to be a possiblity, that the documents inserted in Dem. XXIII. *Aristocrates* have not preserved Solon's spelling.

Fr. 4a: Diog. Laert. I. 59
ἐρωτηθεὶς διὰ τί κατὰ πατροκτόνου νόμον οὐκ ἔθηκε, διὰ τὸ ἀπελπίσαι ἔφη.

On being asked why he had not enacted a law against patricide, [Solon] replied, because he had not expected [*sc.* the deed to occur].

Fr. 4b: Cic. Rosc. Am. 70
Eius porro civitatis sapientissimum Solonem dicunt fuisse, eum qui leges quibus hodie quoque utuntur scripserit. Is, cum interrogaretur cur nullum supplicium constituisset in eum qui parentem necasset, respondit se id neminem facturum putasse.

They say that the wisest man in that state [*sc.* Athens] was Solon, who wrote the laws which they still use today. When he was asked why he had not fixed any punishment for one who killed his parent, he replied that he had thought nobody would do that.

Fr. 4c: Orosius, V. 16. xxiii–xxiv

Publicius siquidem Malleolus servis adnitentibus matrem suam interfecit, damnatus parricidii insutusque in culleum et in mare proiectus est. Inpleveruntque Romani et facinus et poenam, unde et Solo Atheniensis decernere non ausus fuerat, dum fieri posse non credit.

One Publicius Malleolus with the help of his slaves killed his own mother, was condemned for patricide, sewn up in a leather sack and thrown into the sea. The Romans devised both the crime and the penalty, since Solon the Athenian had not dared to decide this because he did not believe that it could happen.

Fr. 4/d (fr. 136 Ruschenbusch, but printed at this point in *Gesetzeswerk*): Sext. Emp. *Pyr.* III. 211

ὁ Σόλων Ἀθηναίοις τὸν περὶ τῶν ἀκρίτων νόμον ἔθετο, καθ' ὃν φονεύειν ἑκάστῳ τὸν ἑαυτοῦ παῖδα ἐπέτρεψεν.

Solon enacted for the Athenians the law about things not subject to trial, in accordance with which he allowed any man to kill his own child.

If killing is in general unlawful, no special law is needed to forbid killing one's own parent or child, unless one thinks that that deserves a special punishment. However, a problem over enforcement would arise in Athens, where prosecutions for homicide had to be brought by the next of kin, since often when a parent or child was killed the killer would be the only person qualified to prosecute: see Ruschenbusch, 'δικαστήριον πάντων κύριον', *Historia* vi 1957, 257–74 at 264–5 = his *Kleine Schriften*, 23–4. A possible remedy was the use of another charge: in the fourth century Diodorus was accused of killing his father, and Androtion entered a *graphe asebeias* against Diodorus' uncle for associating with him as a patricide, but the prosecution failed (Dem. XXII. *Androtion* 2, XXIV. *Timocrates* 7).

Fr. 4/d misunderstands this, and supposes that such killing was 'not subject to trial', i.e. lawful. Ruschenbusch in this connection cites texts which refer to *agrapha adikemata*, acts which were considered wrong but were not forbidden by any law: schol. Pl. *Resp.* VIII. 565 c, *Lex. Rhet. Cant* (74. 4–19 *Lexica Graeca Minora*) and *Suda* (ει. 221 Adler) εἰσαγγελία refer to discussions of this in 'the diatribes of the sophists'; and these and other texts claim that the procedure of *eisangelia* was available not only for specified major offences against the state but also for *agrapha demosia adikemata*, 'unwritten public offences', a tradition which is accepted by Rhodes, *The Athenian Boule*, 162–4, but rejected by Hansen, *Eisangelia*, 16–20.

†Fr. 4/1a: Dem. XXIII. *Aristocrates* 22

ΝΟΜΟΣ ΕΚ ΤΩΝ ΦΟΝΙΚΩΝ ΝΟΜΩΝ ΤΩΝ ΕΞ ΑΡΕΙΟΥ ΠΑΓΟΥ· δικάζειν δὲ τὴν βουλὴν τὴν ἐν Ἀρείῳ πάγῳ φόνου καὶ τραύματος ἐκ προνοίας καὶ πυρκαιᾶς καὶ φαρμάκων ἐάν τις ἀποκτείνῃ δούς.

LAW FROM THE HOMICIDE LAWS FROM THE AREOPAGUS: The council of the Areopagus shall judge premeditated homicide and wounding and arson and poison if one kills by giving it.

†**Fr. 4/1b:** *Ath. Pol.* 57. iii–iv
εἰσὶ δὲ φόνου δίκαι καὶ τραύματος, ἂν μὲν ἐκ προνοίας ἀποκτείνῃ ἢ τρώσῃ, ἐν Ἀρείῳ πάγῳ, καὶ φαρμάκων, ἐὰν ἀποκτείνῃ δούς, καὶ πυρκαϊᾶς· ταῦτα γὰρ ἡ βουλὴ μόνα δικάζει (**fr. 4/1b**). τῶν δ' ἀκουσίων καὶ βουλεύσεως, κἂν οἰκέτην ἀποκτείνῃ τις ἢ μέτοικον ἢ ξένον, οἱ ἐπὶ Παλλαδίῳ (**fr. 5/e**). ἐὰν δ' ἀποκτεῖναι μέν τις ὁμολογῇ, φῇ δὲ κατὰ τοὺς νόμους, οἷον μοιχὸν λαβὼν ἢ ἐν πολέμῳ ἀγνοήσας ἢ ἐν ἄθλῳ ἀγωνιζόμενος, τούτῳ ἐπὶ Δελφινίῳ δικάζουσιν (**fr. 21/1**). ἐὰν δὲ φεύγων φυγὴν ὧν αἴδεσίς ἐστιν αἰτίαν ἔχῃ ἀποκτεῖναι ἢ τρῶσαί τινα, τούτῳ δ' ἐν Φρεάτου δικάζουσιν· ὁ δ' ἀπολογεῖται προσορμισάμενος ἐν πλοίῳ (**fr. 21/2b**). δικάζουσι δ' οἱ λαχόντες ταῦ[τ<α να΄>] ἄ[νδρε]ς, πλὴν τῶν ἐν Ἀρείῳ πάγῳ γιγνομένων, εἰσάγει δ' ὁ βασιλεύς, καὶ δικάζουσιν ἐν ἱερ[ῷ] καὶ ὑπαίθριοι, καὶ ὁ βασιλεὺς ὅταν δικάζῃ περιαιρεῖται τὸν στέφανον. ὁ δὲ τὴν αἰτίαν ἔχων τὸν μὲν ἄλλον χρόνον εἴργεται τῶν ἱερῶν, καὶ οὐδ' εἰς τὴν ἀγορὰν ν[όμος] ἐμβαλεῖν αὐτῷ· τότε δ' εἰς τὸ ἱερὸν εἰσελθὼν ἀπολογεῖται. ὅταν δὲ μὴ εἰδῇ τὸν ποιήσαντα, τῷ δράσαντι λαγχάνει. δικάζει δ' ὁ βασιλεὺς καὶ οἱ φυλοβασιλεῖς καὶ τὰς τῶν ἀψύχων καὶ τῶν ἄλλων ζῴων (**fr. 21b**).
ταῦ[τ<α να΄>] ἄ[νδρε]ς Stroud.

Lawsuits for homicide and wounding, if a man has killed or wounded from forethought, are held on the Areopagus, and for poison if one kills by giving it, and arson: these are the only cases which the council tries. For unwilling homicide, and planning [*sc.* when somebody else did the deed], and if anybody kills a slave or metic or foreigner, those at the Palladium try the case. If somebody admits that he has killed but claims that he has done so in accordance with the laws, for instance when catching an adulterer or killing [*sc.* an Athenian] in war without recognising him or [*sc.* a fellow competitor] when competing in the games, for him they hold the trial at the Delphinium. If a man has gone into exile for a killing for which reconciliation is possible and is accused of killing or wounding somebody, for him the trial is at Phreatus': he makes his defence moored offshore in a boat. These cases are judged by fifty-one men appointed by lot, apart from those held at the Areopagus; the *basileus* is the introducer, they try the case in a sanctuary and in the open air, and the *basileus* when he pronounces the verdict takes off his crown. The man under accusation for the rest of the time [*sc.* until the trial] is excluded from the sanctuaries, and it is not lawful for him to intrude into the agora; but then he enters the sanctuary and makes his defence. When one does not know who did the deed, one enters a case against 'the doer'; the *basileus* and the *phylobasileis* judge also cases of inanimate objects and other creatures.

Many of the texts of Athenian lawcourt speeches as transmitted have documents inserted in them, whose status is open to dispute (the most palpably false are those in Dem. XVIII. *Crown*). For a systematic attempt to establish and apply criteria for distinguishing genuine from false documents see Canevaro, *The Documents in the Attic Orators*, who at pp. 37–76 defends all the laws included in Dem. XXIII. *Aristocrates*. (When a document has to be judged false, that does not necessarily mean that it is a baseless invention: the invention may be based on genuine knowledge of the Athenian law, but we cannot automatically assume that that is so.)

Fr. 4/1a, which in Demosthenes' version begins his series of extracts from the homicide law, must be post-Draconian, since the Areopagus did not appear in Draco's law (fr. 2). The Areopagus was trying homicide cases by the time of Ephialtes' reform in 462/1 (Philoch. *FGrH* 328 F 64. b. α, cf. Aesch. *Eum*.), and if we can rely on this detail in the story of Pisistratus' facing a charge of homicide (*Ath. Pol.* 16. viii), which of course is not certain, it must have been given that role by Solon: thus Gagarin, *Drakon*, 136–7. We therefore include it in our collection. If fr. 4/1a is an accurate quotation, *Ath. Pol.* in fr. 4/1b has transposed a prescription of what should happen into a description of what does happen, and sometimes by rearrangement has improved the clarity (Rhodes, *Comm. Ath. Pol.* 641–2).

The whole extract from *Ath. Pol.* printed here lists the five categories of homicide and courts for dealing with them which existed in classical Athens (cf. Dem. XXIII. *Aristocrates* 63–79, in the same order except that unknown and non-human killers come before exiles accused of another killing). We believe that these categories were already recognised, and apart from the Areopagus the courts to deal with them already existed, in Draco's law (cf. on fr. 1). What is said about *ephetai* and Areopagus, the *basileus* and the exclusion of the accused applies to all cases of homicide, and again apart from the involvement of the Areopagus there is no reason why it should not go back to Draco and Solon — after which the author seems to realise that he has omitted one category, and adds a condensed note on that.

Fr. 5a: *IG* i³ 104
ἔδοχσεν τêι βουλêι καὶ τôι δέμοι. Ἀκα[μ]αντὶς
ἐπ[ρ]υτάνευε· [Δ]ιό[γ]-

νετος ἐγραμμάτευε· Εὐθύδικος [ἐ]πεστάτε. [..]ε[...]άνες
εἶπε· τὸ[ν]
5 Δράκοντος νόμον τὸμ περὶ τô φό[ν]ο ἀναγρα[φ]σά[ν]τον
οἱ ἀναγραφε-
ς τὸν νόμον παραλαβόντες παρὰ τô β[α]σ[ι]λ̣έ[ος με[τ[ὰ
τô γραμμ]ατέο-
ς τês βουλês ἐστέλει λιθίνει καὶ κα[τ]α[θ]ένṭ[ον
πρόσ]θε[ν] τês στο-
ᾶς τês βασιλείας· οἱ δὲ πολεταὶ ἀπομι[σθο]σ[άντον κατὰ
τὸν ν]όμο-
ν· οἱ δὲ ἑλλενοταμίαι δόντον τὸ ἀρ[γ]ύ[ρ]ι[ον.]   vacat
10 πρôτος ἄχσον.
καὶ ἐὰμ μὲ᾽ κ [π]ρονοί[α]ς̣ [κ]ṭ[ένει τίς τινα,
φεύγ]ε[ν. δ]ι-
κάζεν δὲ τὸς βασιλέας αἴṭιο[ν] φόν[ο] Ε[―――¹⁷―――]
Ε [β]ολ-
εύσαντα· τὸς δὲ ἐφέτας διαγν[ô]ν̣[α]ι̣. [αἰδέσασθαι δ᾽ ἐὰμ
μὲν πατὲ]ρ ê̂-
ι ê̂ ἀδελφὸ[ς], ê̂ hυες, hάπαντ[α]ς ê̂ τὸν κọ[λύοντα κρατêν.
ἐὰν δὲ μὲ] họῦ-
15 τοι ôσ̣ι, μέχρ᾽ ἀνεφ[σι]ότετος καὶ [ἀνεφσιô, ἐὰν hάπαντες
[αἰδέσ]ας̣-
θαι ἐθέλοσι, τὸν κο[λύ]οντα̣ [κ]ρα[τêν. ἐὰν δὲ τούτον μεδὲ
hês ê̂ι, κτ]ε-
νει δὲ ἄκο[ν], γνôσι δὲ hοι̣ [πε]ντ[έκοντα καὶ hês hοι
ἐφέται ἄκοντ]α̣
κτêναι, ἐσέṣθ[ο]ν δὲ ḥ[οι φ]ρ̣[άτορες ἐὰν ἐθέλοσι δέκα·
τούτος δ]ὲ ḥọ-
ι πεντέκο[ν]τ[α καὶ] hês ἀρ̣[ι]σ̣τ̣[ίνδεν hαιρέσθον. καὶ hοι
δὲ πρ]ότε[ρ]-
20 ον κτέ[ν]α[ντ]ε[ς ἐν] τô[ιδε τôι θεσμôι ἐνεχέσθον.
προειπên δ]ὲ τôι κ-
τέν̣ạν̣[τι ἐν ἀ]γορ[ᾶι μέχρ᾽ ἀνεφσιότετος καὶ ἀνεφσιô· συνδιόκ]εν
δὲ [κ]ἀνεφσιὸς καὶ ἀνεφσιôν παῖδας καὶ γαμβρὸς καὶ πενθερὸ]ς κ-
αὶ φρ[ά]τ[ο]ρ̣[ας ――――³⁶――――] αἴτι-
ος [ê̂]ι φόν[ο ―――²⁶――― τὸς πεντέκοντ]α καὶ
25 h[ένα ――――⁴²――――] φόνο

hέλοσ[ι ————————35———————— ἐὰν δ]έ [τ]ις τ-
ὸ[ν ἀν]δρ[οφόνον κτένει ἒ αἴτιος ἒι φόνο, ἀπεχόμενον
ἀγορᾶ]ς ἐφο-
ρί[α]ς κ[α]ὶ [ἄθλον καὶ hιερὸν Ἀμφικτυονικὸν, hόσπερ
τὸν Ἀθεν]αῖον κ-
[τένα]γ[τα, ἐν τοῖς αὐτοῖς ἐνέχεσθαι· διαγιγνόσκεν δὲ τὸς]
ἐ[φ]έτα[ς]. (fr. 18a)

after which only a few letters can be read at the beginnings and ends of lines as far as l. 58; most noteworthy are

36   ΕΙΣΕ ἐλεύθ-
ε[ρ]ος ἒι. κα[ὶ ἐὰν φέροντα ἒ ἄγοντα βίαι ἀδίκος
εὐθὺς] ἀμυνόμενο-
ς κτέ[ν]ει, ν[επoινὲ τεθνάναι. (fr. 19a)
and
56 [δεύτ]ερος [ἄχσον.]

which with the text continuing from it seems to have been treated in the same way as ll. 10–11.

Letters underlined were seen by earlier scholars but could not be seen by Stroud. 4 [Ἀθ]ε[νοφ]άνες U. Köhler, *Hermes* ii 1867, 27–36, [Χσ]ε[νοφά]νες A. Kirchhoff, *IG* i¹ 61, and there are other possibilities.   10 πρδτος ἄχσον is in larger letters than the surrounding text, and the line which we number 11 continues from that on a slightly lower level, so that there is a blank space between ll. 9 and 11.   12 ἒ [τὸν αὐτόχερα ἒ τὸν βου]λ|εύσαντα H. J. Wolff, *Traditio* iv 1946, 71–8, before Stroud's edition, ε[ἴτε τὸν αὐτόχερα εἴτ]ε *vel sim.* Stroud, ἒ[ναι ἒ χειρὶ ἀράμενον] ἒ G. Thür, *JJP* xx 1990, 152 cf. Antiph. VI. *Chor.* 16.   13–23 restored from law *ap.* Dem. XLIII. *Macartatus* 57, where the text of 20–3 precedes that of 13–20, and 14–16 is omitted. 26–9 restored from Dem. XXIII. *Aristocrates* 38–42 with law *ap.* 37 (28 as restored has 52 letters and 29 as restored has 51 letters).   36–8 restored from Dem. XXIII. 60 with law.

3   Resolved by the council and the people. Acamantis was the prytany; Diognetus was the secretary; Euthydicus was the chairman. —phanes proposed:

4   Draco's law about homicide the *anagrapheis* ['writers-up'] of the laws shall write up on a stone *stele*, taking it over from the *basileus* and the secretary of the council, and shall place in front of the Stoa. The *poletai* shall make the contract in accordance with the law; the *hellenotamiai* shall provide the money.

10   First *axon*.

11 And if anybody kills anybody not from forethought, he shall be exiled. The *basileis* shall pronounce responsible for homicide [?the one who himself killed or the one] who planned it; the *ephetai* shall decide it.

13 There shall be reconciliation, if there are a father or brother or sons, to be granted by all, or the objector shall prevail. If these do not exist, then as far as cousinhood and cousin, if they are all willing to grant reconciliation, or the objector shall prevail. If none of these exists but he killed unwillingly and the fifty-one *ephetai* decide that he killed unwillingly, let ten members of the phratry allow him to enter if they are willing: these shall be chosen by the fifty-one on the basis of good birth.

19 And those who killed previously shall be liable to this ordinance.

20 There shall be a proclamation against the killer in the agora by those as far as cousinhood and cousin; there shall join in the prosecution cousins and cousins' sons and brothers-in-law and fathers-in-law and phratry members. – – –

23 – – – is responsible for homicide – – – the fifty-one – – – convict of homicide – – –

26 If anybody kills a killer, or is responsible for his being killed, when he is keeping away from a frontier market and Amphictyonic contests and rites, he shall be liable to the same things as if he had killed an Athenian; the *ephetai* shall decide – – –

36 – – – he is a free man. And if he kills a man by defending immediately when he is forcibly and unjustly taking and removing, that man shall have been killed without penalty – – –

56 Second *axon*.

57 – – –

Fr. 5b: law *ap.* Dem. XLIII. *Macartatus* 57

προειπεῖν τῷ κτείναντι ἐν ἀγορᾷ ἐντὸς ἀνεψιότητος καὶ ἀνεψιοῦ· συνδιώκειν δὲ καὶ ἀνεψιοὺς καὶ ἀνεψιῶν παῖδας καὶ γαμβροὺς καὶ πενθεροὺς καὶ φράτερας καὶ ἀνεψιοὺς καὶ ἀνεψιῶν παῖδας καὶ γαμβροὺς καὶ πενθεροὺς καὶ φράτερας. αἰδέσασθαι δέ, ἐὰν μὲν πατὴρ ᾖ ἢ ἀδελφὸς ἢ υἱεῖς, ἅπαντας ἢ τὸν κωλύοντα κρατεῖν. ἐὰν δὲ τούτων μηδεὶς ᾖ, κτείνῃ δὲ ἄκων, γνῶσι δὲ οἱ πεντήκοντα καὶ εἷς, οἱ ἐφέται, ἄκοντα κτεῖναι, ἐσέσθων οἱ φράτερες, ἐὰν ἐθέλωσι, δέκα· τούτους δὲ οἱ πεντήκοντα καὶ εἷς ἀριστίνδην αἱρείσθων. καὶ οἱ πρότερον κτείναντες ἐν τῷδε τῷ θεσμῷ ἐνεχέσθων.

καὶ ἀνεψιοὺς καὶ ἀνεψιῶν παῖδας καὶ γαμβροὺς καὶ πενθεροὺς καὶ φράτερας edd., cf. inscription: καὶ ἀνεψιοῦ· συνδιώκειν δὲ καὶ ἀνεψιῶν παῖδας καὶ γαμβροὺς καὶ ἀνεψιοὺς καὶ πενθεροὺς καὶ ἀνεψιαδοῦς καὶ φράτερας MSS.   αἰδέσασθαι δέ edd., cf. inscription: ἐὰν αἰδέσασθαι δεῖ MSS.   ἅπαντας edd., cf. inscription: πάντας MSS.

There shall be a proclamation against the killer in the agora by those as far as cousinhood and cousin; there shall join in the prosecution cousins and cousins' sons and brothers-in-law and fathers-in-law and phratry members. There shall be reconciliation, if there are a father or brother or sons, to be granted by all, or the objector shall prevail. If none of these exists but he killed unwillingly and the fifty-one *ephetai* decide that he killed unwillingly, let ten members of the phratry allow him to enter if they are willing: these shall be chosen by the fifty-one on the basis of good birth. And those who killed previously shall be liable to this ordinance.

Fr. 5c: *Anecd. Bekk.* i. 401. 18–24
ΑΝΕΨΙΑΔΟΙ· . . . καὶ Δημοσθένης ἐν τῷ περὶ τοῦ Ἁγνίου κλήρου παρατίθεται νόμον ἐν ᾧ γέγραπται "καὶ πενθεροὺς καὶ ἀνεψιαδοῦς". καὶ Λυσίας δέ. λέγεται καὶ ἀνεψιότης. Δημοσθένης καὶ Σόλωνος νόμους παρατίθεται ἐν τῷ περὶ Ἁγνίου κλήρου, ἐν οἷς ἐστὶν ἡ ἀνεψιότης.

ANEPSIADOI ['cousins' sons']: . . . And Demosthenes in the speech about the estate of Hagnias cites a law in which is written, 'and fathers-in-law and cousins' sons'. And Lysias. 'Cousinhood' also is mentioned: Demosthenes cites laws of Solon in the speech on Hagnias' estate in which 'cousinhood' appears.

Fr. 5d: Poll. III. 28
Δημοσθένης (XLIII. *Macartatus* 63) δὲ τῆς "ἀνεψιότητος" εἴρηκε καὶ Σόλων.
Demosthenes has mentioned 'cousinhood' and Solon.

†**Fr. 5/e:** *Ath. Pol.* 57. iii (part of **fr. 4/1b**)
τῶν δ' ἀκουσίων καὶ βουλεύσεως κἂν οἰκέτην ἀποκτείνῃ τις ἢ μέτοικον ἢ ξένον, οἱ ἐπὶ Παλλαδίῳ.
For unwilling homicide, and planning [*sc.* when somebody else did the deed], and if anybody kills a slave or metic or foreigner, those at the Palladium try the case.

Draco's homicide law was treated by later commentators as part of Solon's code, but it remained physically distinct, and in the late fifth and fourth centuries Athenians referred to the *thesmoi* of Draco and the *nomoi* of Solon (cf. fr. 1). We learn from Lys. XXX. *Nicomachus*, esp. 2–5, that Nicomachus was one of a board of *anagrapheis* who were appointed in 410/09 to write up the laws of Solon, that they had still not finished when the Thirty came to power in 404, and that they were reappointed on the restoration of the democracy and worked again, particularly on the religious calendar, from 403/2 to 400/399. Andoc. I. *Myst.* 81–2 with decree of Teisamenus *ap.* 83–4 (but on the decree see p. 7 n. 24) tells us that the restored democracy was to be based on the laws of Solon and the ordinances of Draco. It appears that what was intended, and what led to the work's taking longer than expected, was that the *anagrapheis* should in fact republish all the laws valid under the late-fifth-century democracy, and this gave Nicomachus' prosecutor the opportunity to accuse him of departing from his brief by making additions and subtractions. Since Solon was believed to have replaced all of Draco's laws of 621/0 except that on homicide (fr. 1), it may well be that despite the silence of Lys. XXX Draco was coupled with Solon in 410/09 as in 403/2. The inscription giving us fr. 5a records in the opening lines a specific instruction to the *anagrapheis* in 409/8 to republish Draco's law on homicide (and A. B. Gallia, 'The Republication of Draco's Law on Homicide', CQ^2 liv 2004, 451–60, considers why there might have been a specific instruction in this case).

The law is quoted from a 'first *axon*' (10), followed by a 'second *axon*' (56). Solon's laws too were published on *axones* or *kyrbeis* (cf. Introduction, pp. 5–6). Some have doubted whether Draco's laws were published on *axones* and what we have is in fact Draco's law (e.g. T. J. Figueira, 'The Strange Death of Draco on Aegina', in *Nomodeiktes* ... *M. Ostwald*, 287–304 at 291–5).

The law as quoted begins with the word *kai*, 'and' or perhaps 'even' (11), and proceeds to deal with killing 'not from forethought' (11) or 'unwillingly' (17). Some, including Stroud, *Drakon's Law*, 34–40, Gagarin, *Drakon*, believe that if the word is translated 'even' this can indeed be the beginning of Draco's law (and Gagarin argues that what survives applies implicitly both to 'willing' and to 'unwilling' homicide); others, including M&L and Rhodes, *Comm. Ath. Pol.* 111–2, believe that Draco's law cannot have begun so abruptly and the beginning must have been omitted, presumably because a more recent law had supplanted it; Ruschenbusch argued that a short clause has been omitted which read (e.g.) ἐὰν ἐκ προνοίας κτένει τίς τινα, χρῆσθαι αὐτὸν hοίος ἂν ἐθέλει, τὰ δὲ χρήματα αὐτô ἄτιμα ἔναι, 'If anybody kills anybody from forethought, one may treat him as one wishes, and his property shall be *atima*', but it may well be that the missing material on willing homicide was more extensive than that. In the classical period 'willing' homicide was tried by the Areopagus, but probably in Draco's law that too was tried by the *ephetai* (*Ath. Pol.* 57. iii: see frs. 2, 22/1): we suggest in the commentary on fr. 4/1 that these trials may have been transferred to the Aropagus by Solon.

There is disagreement also whether 'not from forethought' and 'unwillingly' are synonymous (e.g. MacDowell, *Athenian Homicide Law*, 59–60, and his *Demosthenes, Against Meidias*, 258–9, Gagarin, *Drakon*, 46–7), with which we agree (notice particularly Arist. *M.M.* 1188 B 25–39), or the latter is a sub-category within the former (e.g. Stroud, *Drakon's Law*, 40–1); on the difference between 'willing' and 'unwilling' homicide see also Rickert, ἑκών *and* ἄκων *in Early Greek Thought;* E. M. Harris, 'More Thoughts on Open Texture in Athenian Law', in Leão *et al.* (edd.), *Nomos*, 241–62 at 245–51, revised at his *The Rule of Law in Action in Democratic*

Athens, 182–9. We use the terms 'willing' and 'unwilling': it may not always have been uncontroversial which side of the line an act which caused death but had not been intended to cause death should fall.

The killer is to *pheugein*: most scholars, we think rightly, take this to mean that he is to be exiled, but a few (most recently Pepe, *Phonos*, 22–30) see the text as proceeding in chronological order and the meaning as that he is to stand trial. The *basileis* have to *dikazein*, and the *ephetai* have to *diagnonai* (11–13). Most probably this means that the *ephetai* decide the verdict and the *basileis* formally pronounce the outcome (Stroud, *Drakon's Law*, 42–5, MacDowell, *Athenian Homicide Law*, 38, Gagarin, *Drakon*, 47–8), but some have seen it as the *basileis*' task to initiate rather than conclude the process (for instance, G. Thür, e.g. 'Law of Procedure in Attic Inscriptions', in *Law, Rhetoric and Comedy* . . . *D. M. MacDowell*, 33–49 at 36–8, Ruschenbusch). *Basileis* (plural) might refer to successive holders of the position of *basileus*, one of the nine archons, in successive years (Stroud, *Drakon's Law*, 45–6, Ruschenbusch); but that would be an abnormal usage, the court to try homicide attributed to animals and inanimate objects comprised the *basileus* and the *phylobasileis*, the heads of Athens' four old tribes (*Ath. Pol.* 57. iv), and we agree with M&L and the majority of recent discussions that they are probably what is meant here (MacDowell, 87–8, is agnostic; for a very different view of 11–13 see W. Schmitz, '"Drakonische Strafen": Die Revision der Gesetz Drakons durch Solon und die Blutrache in Athen', *Klio* lxxxiii 2001, 7–38). The *ephetai* (13) number fifty-one (17): it is perhaps more likely than not that at any rate in early Athens they were members of the Areopagus, but this remains uncertain (cf. MacDowell, *Athenian Homicide Law*, 48–57, Stroud, *Drakon's Law*, 47–9, Rhodes, *Comm. Ath. Pol.* 646–8; L. Gagliardi, 'Ruolo e competenze degli efeti da Draconte all' età degli oratori', *Dike* xv 2012, 33–71, accepts that for early Athens but returns to the older view that in the classical period they were ordinary jurors). They also tried cases for killing non-citizens, for lawful homicide and for a second homicide alleged against a man already exiled for a first (fr. 4/1b). *Bouleusis* is planning an act performed by somebody else, in this context presumably an act of unwilling homicide, as in Antiph. VI. *Chorus Member*, where the speaker seems to have been accused of 'killing by having planned', and replies that he did not kill either by his own act or by planning (§16: cf. *Ath. Pol.* 57. iii; MacDowell, 60–9; E. M. Harris, 'How to Kill in Attic Greek", *Symposion 1997* [*AGR* xiii 2001], 75–88 = his *Democracy and the Rule of Law*, 391–404; Ruschenbusch). Fr. 5/e shows that those accused of killing somebody other than an Athenian were tried at this court too.

Ath. Pol. 57. iii refers to men subject to exile in cases where 'reconciliation (*aidesis*) is possible', and in the inscription ll. 13–20 spell out the conditions for granting reconciliation to an unwilling killer, by concentric circles of men related to the victim. If they exist, it must be granted by his father, brother(s) and sons, who must be unanimous. If there are none of them, by the wider family 'as far as cousinhood and cousin', with 'cousinhood' usually interpreted as sons of cousins, i.e. cousins once removed (fr. 72/d, cf. MacDowell, 18), though I. Kidd, 'The Case of Homicide in Plato's *Euthyphro*', in *Owls for Athens* . . . *Dover*, 213–21 at 216–7, argues for 'cousinhood, i.e. cousin'. If there are none of them either, then the killer may be 'allowed to enter [Attica]' by ten members of the phratry, the notional kinship-group, to which the victim belonged, to be chosen *aristinden* by the *ephetai*: *aristinden* normally means 'on the basis of good birth' (e.g. *Ath. Pol.* 3. vi); MacDowell, *Athenian Homicide Law*, 124, is agnostic as to what it might mean in practice in this context. Ruschenbusch thought that

Draco envisaged reconciliation as the norm, for willing as well as unwilling homicide, and a case tried in court as the exception. The clause making these rules retrospective (19–20) will have become redundant after a generation, but Stroud, *Drakon's Law*, 50–1, notes that in 409/8 the *anagrapheis* punctiliously retained it.

The law then moves backwards to deal with the procedure to be followed before the trial, beginning with a proclamation in the agora by the victim's family as defined above (20–1), and including also among those to share in the prosecution his brothers-in-law and fathers-in-law (21–3). On the various proclamations in cases of homicide see MacDowell, *Athenian Homicide Law*, 23–7. Another clause which can be restored deals with those who kill an exiled killer who is duly avoiding places which he is required to avoid (26–8: fr. 18). Another clause deals with one sub-category of lawful homicide, killing in defence against violent seizure of person or property (37–8: fr. 19).

That the court for these categories was the court at the Palladium (fr. 5/e) is mentioned also by Dem. XXIII. *Aristocrates* 71. Trials there go back at any rate to the late fifth century (Ar. fr. 602 Kassel & Austin), and we see no reason why the different locations for the different categories should not be ancient. The Palladium was probably south-east of the acropolis and west of the temple of Olympian Zeus (Travlos, *Pictorial Dictionary of Ancient Athens*, 412–6, identifies here 'The Lawcourt ἐπὶ Παλλαδίῳ', where the physical remains are of the fourth or third century but that building may have replaced one of the sixth or fifth century). Boegehold, *Agora* xxviii, 47–8 cf. 139–46, argues that there was another Palladium at Phalerum and homicide trials were held there; but against that see Sourvinou-Inwood, *Athenian Myths and Festivals*, 246–62.

Fr. 6: Dem. XXIII. *Aristocrates* 72

τί οὖν ὁ νόμος κελεύει; τὸν ἁλόντ' ἐπ' ἀκουσίῳ φόνῳ ἔν τισιν εἰρημένοις χρόνοις ἀπελθεῖν τακτὴν ὁδὸν καὶ φεύγειν, ἕως ἂν αἰδέσηταί τις τῶν ἐν γένει τοῦ πεπονθότος. τηνικαῦτα δ' ἥκειν δέδωκεν ἔστιν ὃν τρόπον, οὐχ ὃν ἂν τύχῃ, ἀλλὰ καὶ θῦσαι καὶ καθαρθῆναι καὶ ἄλλ' ἄττα διείρηκεν, ἃ χρὴ ποιεῖν, ὀρθῶς, ὦ ἄνδρες Ἀθηναῖοι, πάντα ταῦτα λέγων ὁ νόμος.

What then does the law command? The man convicted of willing homicide shall within a stated time depart by a specified route and go into exile, until he is granted reconciliation by somebody among the kin of the victim. Then the law has given him the right to come — in a certain way, not any casual way, but to sacrifice and be purified, and it has specified other things which he must do; and the law is right, men of Athens, to say all these things.

As Ruschenbusch argues, the need for a trial (at the *prytaneion*) for homicide by unknown killers and non-human killers (frs. 21a–d) makes sense only if killers were already at this date considered polluted: cf. Parker, *Miasma*, 66–70, 114–27, 130–43; but contr. MacDowell, *Athenian Homicide Law*, 1–5, 141–50, Gagarin, *Drakon*, 164–7. See also on fr. 21.

Fr. 7: see fr. 153

Fr. 8: *Anecd. Bekk.* i. 82. 17–18
ΑΝΥΠΟΔΗΜΑΤΟΣ· ἐν τοῖς Ἀθηναίων νόμοις καὶ τοῖς Ἀρεοπαγιτικοῖς.
ANYPODEMATOS ['barefoot']: In the laws of Athens and those concerning the Areopagus.

Ruschenbusch accepted this as a gloss on the *axones*, and referred it to the litigants' *diomosia*, sworn standing over the entrails of a boar, a ram and a bull (Dem. XXIII. *Aristocrates* 67–8, not mentioning the barefoot requirement).

Fr. 9: see fr. 154

Fr. 10: Poll. IX. 61
κἂν τοῖς Δράκοντος νόμοις ἔστιν "ἀποτίνειν εἰκοσάβοιον".
And in the laws of Draco there occurs 'make a twenty-ox payment'.

Ruschenbusch notes that, while Solon reckoned in drachmae (e.g. fr. 26), Draco like Homer reckoned in oxen (twenty oxen, Hom. *Od.* I. 430–1). If one ox was equivalent to 5 drachmae (fr. 92), twenty oxen were equivalent to 100 drachmae, the highest level of fine attested for Solon's laws (frs. 26, 65), so Ruschenbusch took this to be a payment of blood money leading to reconciliation. Heitsch, *Aidesis im attischen Strafrecht*, 12, saw this as a fixed payment introduced to supersede earlier negotiable payments.

Fr. 11: Phot. π 1009 Theodoridis
ΠΟΙΝΑΝ ΚΑΙ ΑΠΟΙΝΑΝ· τὸ λυτροῦν· Σόλων.
ποίναν, ἄποιναν, λύτρον MSS.
POINAN AND *APOINAN* ['to take / exact blood money']: To ransom: Solon.

For commentary see after fr. 12.

Fr. 12: *Anecd. Bekk.* i. 428. 9–10, *Suda* α 3716 Adler
ΑΠΟΙΝΑ· λύτρα ἃ δίδωσί τις ὑπὲρ φόνου ἢ σώματος· οὕτω Σόλων ἐν νόμοις.
APOINA: Ransom, which a man pays for homicide or body [*sc.* wounding]: thus Solon in his laws.

Cf. *apoinan* in law *ap.* Dem. XXIII. *Aristocrates* 28, with elucidation §33: these words will refer to the payment of blood money leading to reconciliation. The terms appear frequently in Homer, where they can refer either to a ransom for a living captive (e.g. *poine* Hom. *Il.* III. 290, *apoina Il.* I. 13) or to blood money for a dead man (e.g. *poine Il.* IX. 633, *apoina Il.* XXIV. 137).

Fr. 13: Dem. XXIII. *Aristocrates* 82
ΝΟΜΟΣ· ἐάν τις βιαίῳ θανάτῳ ἀποθάνῃ, ὑπὲρ τούτου τοῖς προσήκουσιν εἶναι τὰς ἀνδροληψίας ἕως ἂν ἢ δίκας τοῦ φόνου ὑπόσχωσιν ἢ τοὺς ἀποκτείναντας ἐκδῶσι. τὸ δὲ ἀνδρολήψιον εἶναι μέχρι τριῶν, πλέον δὲ μή.
τὸ δὲ ἀνδρολήψιον MacDowell, cf. §§83–4: τὴν δὲ ἀνδροληψίαν MSS.
LAW: If anybody dies by a violent death, it shall be permitted to his relatives to seize men until they submit to justice for the killing or give up the killers. The seizure may extend to three men but not further.

This was interpreted in Demosthenes' elucidation, §§82–5, and in the lexica as referring to cases in which an Athenian was killed by a non-Athenian outside Attica; but Ruschenbusch argues persuasively that that is not credible, but that this is an early law, already misunderstood in the fourth century, which refers to killing in Athens by an Athenian (cf. his 'φόνος', *Historia* ix 1960, 129–54 at 140–2 = his *Kleine Schriften*, 41–3).

Fr. 14: Dem. XX. *Leptines* 158
ἐν τοίνυν τοῖς περὶ τούτων νόμοις ὁ Δράκων φοβερὸν κατασκευάζων καὶ δεινὸν τό τιν' αὐτόχειρ' ἄλλον ἄλλου γίγνεσθαι, καὶ γράφων χέρνιβος εἴργεσθαι τὸν ἀνδροφόνον, σπονδῶν, κρατήρων, ἱερῶν, ἀγορᾶς, πάντα τἆλλα διελθὼν οἷς μάλιστ' ἄν τινας ᾤετ' ἐπισχεῖν τοῦ τοιοῦτόν τι ποιεῖν, ὅμως οὐκ ἀφείλετο τὴν τοῦ δικαίου τάξιν, ἀλλ' ἔθηκεν ἐφ' οἷς ἐξεῖναι ἀποκτιννύναι, κἂν οὕτω τις δράσῃ καθαρὸν διώρισεν εἶναι.
In the laws about these matters Draco made it a fearful and terrible thing that one man should be the killer of another, and by writing that the killer should be kept away from all lustral basins, libations, mixing bowls, sanctuaries, the agora, and going through all the other things which he thought would particularly restrain men from such behaviour, he nevertheless did not take away the rule of justice, but he laid down the circumstances in which it is permissible to kill, and if anybody acts in that way Draco ruled that he should be pure.

This refers to the *prorrhesis* made in the agora by the relatives of the deceased (fr. 51. 20–1, law *ap.* Dem. XLIII. *Macartatus* 57, cf. *Antiph.* VI. *Chorus Member* 25, [Dem.] XLVII. *Evergus*

& Mnesibulus 69) and by the *basileus* when the charge had been lodged with him (*Ath. Pol.* 57. ii, Antiph. VI. *Chorus Member* 36–8). The summary formulation εἴργεσθαι τῶν νομίμων (e.g. Antiph. VI. *Chorus Member* 35) means 'be excluded from the things specified in the laws' (e.g. MacDowell, *L.C.A.* 111); we can add exclusion from speaking to other people and entering their houses (Soph. *O.T.* 236–41, Hdt. III. 52. i–ii); and this exclusion is best explained as due to the pollution associated with a killer (cf. on fr. 6).

Fr. 15a: Dem. XXIII. *Aristocrates* 69
καὶ τῷ μὲν διώκοντι ὑπάρχει ταῦτα, τῷ δὲ φεύγοντι τὰ μὲν τῆς διωμοσίας ταὐτά, τὸν πρότερον δ' ἔξεστιν εἰπόντα λόγον μεταστῆναι, καὶ οὔθ' ὁ διώκων οὔθ' οἱ δικάζοντες οὔτ' ἄλλος ἀνθρώπων οὐδεὶς κύριος κωλῦσαι.

That is what is available to the prosecutor [*sc.* he swears the *diomosia*, will be disgraced if proved wrong, but if the accused is found guilty he will be punished not by the prosecutor but by the state]; and for the defendant the rules about the *diomosia* are the same, but it is permissible for him to withdraw after delivering his first speech, and neither the prosecutor nor the judges nor any other man has the right to prevent him.

Fr. 15b: see fr. 95/1

Ruschenbusch's fr. 15b is not necessarily connected with 15a, and therefore does not confirm the antiquity of this right of withdrawal. Ruschenbusch himself thought the two pairs of speeches were not instituted until *c.* 430, and if that is right the formulation of fr. 15a does not reflect Draco's law, though it is still possible that a right of withdrawal was included in Draco's law.

Fr. 16/a: Dem. XXIII. *Aristocrates* 28
ΝΟΜΟΣ· τοὺς δ' ἀνδροφόνους ἐξεῖναι ἀποκτείνειν ἐν τῇ ἡμεδαπῇ καὶ ἀπάγειν, ὡς ἐν τῷ ἄξονι ἀγορεύει, λυμαίνεσθαι δὲ μή, μηδὲ ἀποινᾶν, ἢ διπλοῦν ὀφείλειν ὅσον ἂν καταβλάψῃ. εἰσφέρειν δὲ <εἰς> τοὺς ἄρχοντας ὧν ἕκαστοι δικασταί εἰσι τῷ βουλομένῳ· τὴν δ' ἡλιαίαν διαγιγνώσκειν.
<α'> ἄξονι Cobet. δὲ <εἰς> Dilts: δ' <ἐ>ς Schelling, δὲ MSS.

LAW: Killers may be killed in our own territory or subjected to *apagoge*, as it says on the *axon*, but not maltreated and not have blood money exacted from them, or there shall be a penalty of double the harm done. Whoever wishes may bring the matter to the officials who have jurisdiction in each matter; the *eliaia* shall decide.

28   THE LAWS OF SOLON

†Fr. /16b: law *ap.* Dem. XXIII. *Aristocrates* 51
ΝΟΜΟΣ· "φόνου δὲ δίκας μὴ εἶναι κατὰ τῶν τοὺς φεύγοντας ἐνδεικνύντων, ἐάν τις κατίη ὅποι μὴ ἔξεστιν." ὁ μὲν νόμος ἐστὶν οὗτος Δράκοντος, ὦ ἄνδρες Ἀθηναῖοι, καὶ οἱ ἄλλοι δέ, ὅσους ἐκ τῶν φονικῶν νόμων παρεγραψάμην.
LAW: 'There shall not be trials for homicide of those who make an *endeixis* against exiles, if one returns to where it is not permitted.' This law is of Draco, men of Athens, like the others which I have transcribed from the homicide laws.

Demosthenes elucidates the law of fr. 16/a in §§29–33, and that of fr. /16b (the point of which is that a man who secures the death of a returned exile by making an *endeixis* will not be guilty of *bouleusis*) in §§51–2. The part referring to *ho boulomenos* and the *eliaia* must be Solonian or later, but reference to an *axon* should guarantee the antiquity of the first part (cf. Glotz, *La Solidarité de la famille*, 319–21; Ruschenbusch, *Untersuchungen*, 37 = his *Kleine Schriften*, 94). *Androphonoi* will be men convicted by a court, either willing killers who may be put to death, or unwilling killers who have failed to depart into exile or have returned from exile or without reconciliation. Ruschenbusch, believing that there was not yet a death penalty (cf. on fr. 1), supposed that *apagein* means place under private arrest, in order to exact payment, but Hansen compares the reference to *endeixis* in fr. /16b, and argues persuasively that such men could already be brought to the authorities by *endeixis* or *apagoge* (*Apagoge, Endeixis and Ephegesis*, 113–8), in which case execution by the authorities will already have been at any rate a possible alternative to *atimia* resulting in killing by the next of kin of the deceased. Cf. fr. 23/1 = 113, where anybody who steals at night may either be killed or be subjected to *apagoge*. Attribution to Draco in fr. /16b is of course no more reliable than attribution by the orators of other laws to Solon, but in fr. 16/a *apagein* should be part of the text from the *axon*, and frs. 16/a and /16b stand and fall together.

On *apagoge* and *endeixis*, haling before the authorities or pointing out to the authorities offenders who if they admit their guilt are liable to summary punishment, see *Ath. Pol.* 52. i and Hansen, *op. cit.* Demosthenes states in §31 that the *thesmothetai* were the relevant officials for men exiled for homicide, and *Ath. Pol.* says that they are the *eisagousa arche* (the authority introducing the case into court) for 'some of the *endeixeis*'. Stroud, *Drakon's Law*, 54–6, argues against restoring a version of fr. 16/a in fr. 5a. 30–1.

Fr. 17: Dem. XXIII. *Aristocrates* 44
ΝΟΜΟΣ· ἐάν τίς τινα τῶν ἀνδροφόνων τῶν ἐληλυθότων, ὧν τὰ χρήματα ἐπίτιμα, πέρα ὅρου ἐλαύνῃ ἢ φέρῃ ἢ ἄγῃ, τὰ ἴσα ὀφείλειν ὅσα περ ἂν ἐν τῇ ἡμεδαπῇ δράσῃ.
LAW: If anybody drives, raids and carries off beyond the frontier property of any of the killers who have departed, which is not confiscated, he shall owe the same as if he did it in our own land.
Demosthenes elucidates the law in §§45–6. This is a supplementary provision for those who have gone into exile after trial at the Palladium: such men retained ownership of their property,

whereas the property of those convicted of willing killing was confiscated (cf. Theophr. *Nomoi* fr. 9 Szegedy-Maszak *ap.* Harp. o 42 Keaney ὅτι οἱ ἁλόντες; also Lys. I. *Murder of Eratosthenes* 50, Dem. XXI. *Midias* 43, *Ath. Pol.* 47. ii).

Fr. 18a: *IG* i³ 104. 26–9 (part of **fr. 5a**)

[ἐὰν δ]έ [τ]ις τ-
ὁ[ν ἀν]δρ[οφόνον κτένει ἒ αἴτιος ἒ̂ι φόνο, ἀπεχόμενον ἀγορᾶ]ς ἐφο-
ρί[α]ς κ̣[α]ὶ [ἄθλον καὶ ἱερὸν Ἀμφικτυονικὸν, hόσπερ τὸν
 Ἀθεν]αῖον κ-
[τένα]ν̣[τα ἐν τοῖς αὐτοῖς ἐνέχεσθαι· διαγιγνόσκεν δὲ τὸς]
ἐ[φ]έτα[ς].

Fr. 18b: law *ap.* Dem. XXIII. *Aristocrates* 37
ΝΟΜΟΣ· ἐὰν δέ τις τὸν ἀνρδοφόνον κτείνῃ ἢ αἴτιος ᾖ φόνου, ἀπεχόμενον ἀγορᾶς ἐφορίας καὶ ἄθλων καὶ ἱερῶν Ἀμφικτυονικῶν, ὥσπερ τὸν Ἀθηναῖον κτείναντα ἐν τοῖς αὐτοῖς ἐνέχεσθαι· διαγιγνώσκειν δὲ τοὺς ἐφέτας.
LAW: If anybody kills a killer, or is responsible for his being killed, when he is keeping away from a frontier market and Amphictyonic contests and rites, he shall be liable to the same things as for killing an Athenian; the *ephetai* shall decide.

Demosthenes elucidates the law in §§38–41. He understands 'Amphictyonic' with rites only; K. Latte, perhaps correctly, argues that it should be understood both with 'contests' and with 'rites' (*RE* xvi. 286–7); Ruschenbusch followed him on that, but less plausibly took 'amphictyonic' to refer not to the Delphic or any other amphictyony but to joint festivals celebrated by people living near the frontier. Ruschenbusch was right, however, to maintain that 'as for killing an Athenian' does not imply that a man convicted of unwilling killing, who might in the future achieve reconciliation and return to Athens, was deprived of his citizenship: 'in our own land' in fr. 17 and 'as for killing an Athenian' here are both ways of insisting that such an exile remains himself under the protection of Athenian homicide law.

Fr. 19a: *IG* i³ 104. 37–8 (part of **fr. 5a**)
κạ[ὶ ἐὰν φέροντα ἒ ἄγοντα βίαι ἀδίκος
 εὐθὺς] ἀμυνόμενο-
ς κτέ[ν]ει, ν[εποινὲ τεθνάναι.
And if he kills a man by defending immediately when he is forcibly and unjustly taking and removing, that man shall have been killed without penalty.

Ruschenbusch printed ll. 33–8, but the earlier lines cannot be reconstructed sufficiently to merit inclusion here.

Fr. 19b: Dem. XXIII. *Aristocrates* 60
ΝΟΜΟΣ· καὶ ἐὰν φέροντα ἢ ἄγοντα βίᾳ ἀδίκως εὐθὺς ἀμυνόμενος κτείνῃ, νηποινεὶ τεθνάναι.
LAW: And if he kills a man by defending immediately when he is forcibly and unjustly taking and removing, that man shall have been killed without penalty.

Demosthenes continues by elucidating the law. For commentary see after fr. 21/1.

Fr. 20: law *ap.* Dem. XXIII. *Aristocrates* 53
ΝΟΜΟΣ· ἐάν τις ἀποκτείνῃ ἐν ἄθλοις ἄκων ἢ ἐν ὁδῷ καθελὼν ἢ ἐν πολέμῳ ἀγνοήσας ἢ ἐπὶ δάμαρτι ἢ ἐπὶ μητρὶ ἢ ἐπ' ἀδελφῇ ἢ ἐπὶ θυγατρὶ ἢ ἐπὶ παλλακῇ ἣν ἂν ἐπ' ἐλευθέροις παισὶν ἔχῃ, τούτων ἕνεκα μὴ φεύγειν κτείναντα.
LAW: If anybody kills unwillingly in games or when catching [*sc.* a man waylaying him] on the road or [*sc.* an Athenian] in war without recognising him or [*sc.* lying] with his wife or mother or sister or daughter or a concubine whom he has with the objective of free children, he shall not be exiled if he has killed for these reasons.

Demosthenes elucidates the law in §§53–6. For commentary see after fr. 21/1.

Fr. 21: Dem. IX. *Philippic iii.* 43–4
οἱ Ἀθηναῖοι ... Ζελείτην τινά, Ἄρθμιον, δοῦλον βασιλέως (ἡ γὰρ Ζέλειά ἐστι τῆς Ἀσίας) ὅτι τῷ δεσπότῃ διακονῶν χρυσίον ἤγαγεν εἰς Πελοπόννησον, οὐκ Ἀθήναζε, ἐχθρὸν αὐτῶν ἀνέγραψαν καὶ τῶν συμμάχων αὐτὸν καὶ γένος, καὶ ἀτίμους. τοῦτο δ' ἐστὶν οὐχ ἣν οὑτωσί τις ἂν φήσειεν ἀτιμίαν· τί γὰρ τῷ Ζελείτῃ τῶν Ἀθηναίων κοινῶν εἰ μὴ μεθέξειν ἔμελλεν; ἀλλ' οὐ τοῦτο λέγει· ἀλλ' ἐν τοῖς φονικοῖς γέγραπται νόμοις, ὑπὲρ ὧν ἂν μὴ δίδῳ δίκας φόνου δικάσασθαι, ἀλλ' εὐαγὲς ᾖ τὸ ἀποκτεῖναι, "καὶ ἄτιμος", φησίν, "τεθνάτω". τοῦτο δὴ λέγει, καθαρὸν τὸν τούτων τινὰ ἀποκτείναντα εἶναι.

ἀλλ' οὐ τοῦτο λέγει om. S, Harp. α 258 Keaney ἄτιμος.   δίδῳ δίκας: δίκας om. A, Y^{ac}, δίκην Harp.   ἀλλ' εὐαγὲς ᾖ τὸ ἀποκτεῖναι om. S^{ac}, Y^{ac}, Harp.

The Athenians ... wrote up that a man of Zelea, Arthmius, a slave of the King (for Zelea is in Asia), because in ministering to his master he brought gold to the Peloponnese, not to Athens, was to be an enemy of themselves and the allies, himself and his issue, and *atimoi*. This is not what one might generally call *atimia;* for what would it matter to a man of Zelea if he could not share in what is common to the Athenians? It does not mean this; but it has been written in the homicide laws, among the matters for which a man does not have to render justice for homicide but the killing is holy, 'and a man who is *atimos*', it says, 'may be killed'. This means that a man who has killed one of these is pure.

For commentary see after fr. 21/1.

†**Fr. 21/1:** *Ath. Pol.* 57. iii (part of **fr. 4/1b**)
ἐὰν δ' ἀποκτεῖναι μέν τις ὁμολογῇ, φῇ δὲ κατὰ τοὺς νόμους, οἷον μοιχὸν λαβὼν ἢ ἐν πολέμῳ ἀγνοήσας ἢ ἐν ἄθλῳ ἀγωνιζόμενος, τούτῳ ἐπὶ Δελφινίῳ δικάζουσιν.

If somebody admits that he has killed but claims that he has done so in accordance with the laws, for instance when catching an adulterer or killing [*sc.* an Athenian] in war without recognising him or [*sc.* a fellow competitor] when competing in the games, for him the trial is at the Delphinium.

On lawful homicide see MacDowell, *Athenian Homicide Law*, 70–81. The Delphinium was south of the temple of Olympian Zeus: see Travlos, *Pictorial Dictionary of Ancient Athens*, 83–90; Boegehold, *Agora* xxviii, 48–9 with 135–9. It is mentioned also by Dem. XXIII. *Aristocrates* 74. Since fr. 19a shows that Draco's law specified at least one situation in which a man could kill with impunity, it is likely that other situations attested, though perhaps not all of them, were included in Draco's law. Killing an adulterer or an *atimos* was willing homicide, so too was killing a raider or a highwayman (for the interpretation of the latter cf. Harp. o 2 Keaney ὁδός), killing an Athenian in war was willing but under a misapprehension as to the vicitm's identity, killing a fellow-competitor in the games was an unintended consequence of an intended act. Other instances of lawful killing can be added: death resulting from treatment by a doctor (an unintended consequence of an intended act: Antiph. IV. *Tetr. iii*, γ. 5), killing anybody who was stealing at night (willing: Dem. XXIV. *Timocrates* 113), killing in self-defence against an attacker, where it was at least desirable to show that the attacker had struck the first blow (willing: Antiph. IV. *Tetr. iii*. δ. 3). On the other hand, the accidental killing at the games of somebody other than a fellow competitor was not lawful (Antiph. III. *Tetr. ii*, Plut. *Per.* 36. v).

As always, a trial would be held only if somebody prosecuted: if it was agreed that the killing was lawful there would presumably be no prosecution; but there would be a trial if a man was accused of unlawful homicide, willing or unwilling, and admitted that he had killed but claimed that he had done so lawfully (cf. MacDowell, *Athenian Homicide Law*, 70–3).

The clause concerning those caught in unlawful intercourse (fr. 20) refers both to rapists and to seducers: cf. frs. 26-7, and see E. M. Harris, 'Did the Athenians Regard Seduction as a Worse Crime than Rape?', *CQ*² xl 1990, 370-7 = his *Democracy and the Rule of Law*, 283-93[-95], cf. 'Did Rape Exist in Classical Athens?', *Dike* vii 2004, 41-83 = his *Democracy and the Rule of Law*, 297-332. It mentions both a *damar* (an early word), i.e. a wife acquired by a marriage based on *engye*, a formal promise by the woman's father to her husband (cf. Hdt. VI. 130. ii), and a *pallake*, i.e. a concubine with the objective of free children, who seems to have been a long-term partner not formally acquired either by *engye* or by *epidikasia* after her father's death: her children will have been free, but they will have been not *gnesioi* but *nothoi* (cf. fr. 48b and Poll. III. 21), who had limited rights of inheritance in the absence of *gnesioi* (perhaps no rights in the fourth centutry) and were probably excluded from citizenship. See in general Harrison, *LA*. i. 3–15, 61–8; and on citizenship MacDowell, 'Bastards as Athenian Citizens', *CQ*² xxvi 1976, 88–91 (admitted), Rhodes, 'Bastards as Athenian Citizens', *CQ*² xxviii 1978, 89–92 (excluded).

We believe that pollution was already attached to homicide in the time of Draco (cf. on fr. 6). Demosthenes in fr. 21 when writing of lawful homicide states not only that such a killer is not to be punished but also that he is *euages*, 'holy', and *katharos*, 'pure' (cf. fr. 14, Dem. XXIII. *Aristocrates* 55). The anti-tyranny law of 337/6 uses *hosios*, 'righteous' (*Agora* xvi 73. 10–11), Plato suggests that lawful killing is non-polluting (*Euthyphr.* 4 B–C), the decree of Demophantus *ap.* Andoc. I. *Myst.* 97 uses *hosios* and *euages*. As for homicide and pollution in general, earlier evidence is lacking, but the presumption must be that already in the time of Draco, while unlawful homicide was polluting, lawful was not. See J. W. Hewitt, 'The Necessity of Ritual Purification after Justifiable Homicide', *TAPA* xli 1910, 99–113; MacDowell, *Athenian Homicide Law*, 128–9; Parker, *Miasma*, 366–9.

The decree against Arthmius (fr. 21) is one of a number of putative fifth-century documents of which we first have evidence in the fourth century: it is cited also, with variations in wording, in Dem. XIX. *F.L.* 271–2, Aeschin. III. *Ctesiphon* 258, Din. II. *Aristogeiton* 24–5, and it was inscribed on a bronze *stele* on the acropolis, apparently visible there at the time of these speeches. Whether it is a genuine survival or a later reconstruction does not matter here (we believe in reconstruction, but by that do not mean baseless invention; for reconstruction see C. Habicht, 'Falsche Urkunden zur Geschichte Athens im Zeitalter der Perserkriege', *Hermes* lxxxix 1961, 1–35; for survival see Meiggs, *The Athenian Empire*, 508–12). What does matter here is Demosthenes' interpretation, that when *atimia* denotes outlawry (cf. fr. 37) anybody who kills the *atimos* will be holy and pure.

*Fr. 21a: Dem. XXIII. *Aristocrates* 76
τέταρτον τοίνυν ἄλλο πρὸς τούτοις τὸ ἐπὶ πρυτανείῳ. τοῦτο δ' ἐστίν, ἐὰν λίθος ἢ ξύλον ἢ σίδηρος ἤ τι τοιοῦτον ἐμπεσὸν πατάξῃ, καὶ τὸν μὲν βάλοντ' ἀγνοῇ τις, αὐτὸ δ' εἰδῇ καὶ ἔχῃ τὸ τὸν φόνον εἰργασμένον, τούτοις ἐνταῦθα λαγχάνεται.

The fourth court in addition to these is that at the *prytaneion*. This is if a stone or a piece of wood or iron or something of that kind falls and hits anybody, and it is not known who threw it but one knows and has the object which caused the death, and a case is entered against these there.

*Fr. 21b: *Ath. Pol.* 57. iv (part of fr. 4/1b)
ὅταν δὲ μὴ εἰδῇ τὸν ποιήσαντα, τῷ δράσαντι λαγχάνει. δικάζει δ' ὁ βασιλεὺς καὶ οἱ φυλοβασιλεῖς καὶ τὰς τῶν ἀψύχων καὶ τῶν ἄλλων ζῴων.

When one does not know who did the deed, one enters a case against 'the doer'; the *basileus* and the *phylobasileis* also judge cases of inanimate objects and other creatures.

*Fr. 21c: Poll. VIII. 120
τὸ ἐπὶ πρυτανείῳ δικάζει περὶ τῶν ἀποκτεινάντων κἂν ὦσιν ἀφανεῖς, καὶ περὶ τῶν ἀψύχων καὶ τῶν ἐμπεσόντων καὶ ἀποκτεινάντων. προειστήκεσαν δὲ τούτου τοῦ δικαστηρίου φυλοβασιλεῖς, οὓς ἔδει τὸ ἐμπεσὸν ἄψυχον ὑπερορίσαι.

The court at the *prytaneion* tries cases against those who have killed if they are unidentified, and against inanimate objects which have fallen and killed somebody. This court was presided over by *phylobasileis*, who had to cast the fallen inanimate object beyond the frontier.

*Fr. 21d: *Lexicon Patmense ad* Dem. XXIII. *Aristocrates* 76 (149. 1–7 *Lexica Graeca Minora*)
ΕΠΙ ΠΡΥΤΑΝΕΙΩΙ· ἐν τούτῳ τῷ δικαστηρίῳ δικάζονται φόνου ὅταν ὁ μὲν ἀνῃρημένος δῆλος ᾖ ζητεῖται δὲ ὁ τὸν φόνον δράσας, καὶ ἀποφέρει τὴν γραφὴν πρὸς τὸν βασιλέα, καὶ ὁ βασιλεὺς διὰ τοῦ κήρυκος κηρύττει καὶ ἀπαγορεύει τόνδε τὸν ἀνελόντα τὸν δεῖνα μὴ ἐπιβαίνειν ἱερῶν καὶ χώρας Ἀττικῆς. ἐν τῷ αὐτῷ δὲ τούτῳ δικαστηρίῳ κἄν τι ἐμπεσὸν πατάξῃ τινὰ καὶ ἀνέλῃ τῶν ἀψύχων, δικάζεται τούτῳ καὶ ὑπερορίζεται.

AT THE *PRYTANEION*: In this court cases of homicide are tried when it is clear who has been killed but the one who did the killing is sought. And the written charge is submitted to the *basileus*, and the *basileus* through the herald proclaims and forbids the killer of so-and-so to set foot on the sanctuaries and land of Attica. In this same court, if any inanimate object has fallen, hit somebody and killed him, a trial is held for this and it is cast beyond the frontier.

For the attribution to Draco's law of the different categories of and trials for homicide see on fr. 1. Ruschenbusch omitted these fragments from *Nomoi*, but added them in

Gesetzeswerk, on the grounds that fr. 22/1 shows the *prytaneion* in use as a homicide court before Solon. In this court the *basileus* and *phylobasileis* apparently acted without the *ephetai* (the inclusion of this among the *ephetai*'s courts by Harp. ε 173 Keaney ἐφέται cf. Poll. VIII. 125 seems mistaken): this was presumably because no human being was on trial and no decision had to be made as to the intentions behind and the lawfulness of the act. The ritual casting of the animal or inanimate object beyond the frontier supports the view that already at this date homicide was seen as incurring pollution (cf. on frs. 6, 21).

On the *prytaneion* see Boegehold, *Agora* xxviii, 50 with 148–50: for the most recent suggestion of a site to the east of the acropolis, see G. Kavvadias & A. P. Matthaiou, in Ἀθηναίων ἐπίσκοπος . . . *H. B. Mattingly*, 51–72.

†Fr. 21/2a: Dem. XXIII. *Aristocrates* 77–8
ἔτι τοίνυν πέμπτον δικαστήριον ἄλλο θεάσασθ' οἷον ὑπερβέβηκε, τὸ ἐν Φρεαττοῖ. ἐνταῦθα γάρ, ὦ ἄνδρες Ἀθηναῖοι, κελεύει δίκας ὑπέχειν ὁ νόμος, ἐάν τις ἐπακουσίῳ φόνῳ πεφευγώς, μήπω τῶν ἐκβαλόντων ᾐδεσμένων, αἰτίαν ἔχῃ ἑτέρου φόνου ἑκουσίου. . . . εἶθ' ὁ μὲν ἐν πλοίῳ προσπλεύσας λέγει τῆς γῆς οὐχ ἁπτόμενος, οἱ δ' ἀκροῶνται καὶ δικάζουσιν ἐν τῇ γῇ. κἂν μὲν ἁλῷ, τὴν ἐπὶ τοῖς ἑκουσίοις φόνοις δίκην ἔδωκε δικαίως, ἐὰν δ' ἀποφυγῇ, ταύτης μὲν ἀθῷος ἀφίεται, τὴν δ' ἐπὶ τῷ πρότερον φόνῳ φυγὴν ὑπέχει.
φυγὴν: δίκην A, deleted Dobree.

Now see how he has transgressed another, fifth, court, that at Phreatto. For there, men of Athens, the law orders trials to be held if anybody is in exile for unwilling homicide, and those who exiled him have not yet granted reconciliation, and is accused of another, willing, homicide. . . . Then he sails up in a boat and speaks without touching the land, while they listen and judge on the land. And if he is convicted, he rightly pays the penalty for willing homicide, but if he is acquitted, he is released without penalty from that but still suffers the exile for the previous homicide.

†Fr. 21/2b: *Ath. Pol.* 57. iii (part of **fr. 4/1b**)
ἐὰν δὲ φεύγων φυγὴν ὧν αἴδεσίς ἐστιν αἰτίαν ἔχῃ ἀποκτεῖναι ἢ τρῶσαί τινα, τούτῳ δ' ἐν Φρεάτου δικάζουσιν· ὁ δ' ἀπολογεῖται προσορμισάμενος ἐν πλοίῳ.

If a man has gone into exile for a killing for which reconciliation is possible and is accused of killing or wounding somebody, for him the trial is at Phreatus': he makes his defence moored offshore in a boat.

This court is located at Piraeus by Paus. I. 28. xi; for these cases *Anecd. Bekk.* i. 311. 17–22 has a court 'at Zea' followed by a court 'at Phreatto'. However, A. L. Boegehold, 'Ten Distinctive Ballots: The Law Court in Zea', *CSCA* ix 1976, 7–19, cf. *Agora* xxviii, 49–50 with 146–8, has argued from ballots found there that in the fourth century there was an ordinary court at Zea, with which the court in Phreatto or of Phreatus (which rarely had to meet) was mistakenly identified.

Fr. 22: law *ap.* Dem. XXIII. *Aristocrates* 62
λέγε τὸν μετὰ ταῦτα νόμον. "ὃς ἂν ἄρχων ἢ ἰδιώτης αἴτιος ᾖ τὸν θεσμὸν συγχυθῆναι τόνδε ἢ μεταποιήσῃ αὐτόν, ἄτιμον εἶναι καὶ παῖδας {ἀτίμους} καὶ τὰ ἐκείνου."
ἀτίμους deleted Taylor.
Read the law after this. 'Any official or private citizen who is guilty of abolishing this ordinance or alters it shall be *atimos* and his children and his property.'

Demosthenes continues by elucidating the law. This is an entrenchment clause, reinforcing the law by threatening penalties for those who attempt to annul or change it: see D. M. Lewis, 'Entrenchment-Clauses in Attic Decrees', in φόρος . . . B. D. Meritt, 81–9 = his *Selected Papers in Greek and Near Eastern History*, 136–49, not mentioning this fragment or fr. 93, the entrenchment of Solon's laws; E. M. Harris, 'Solon and the Spirit of the Laws in Archaic and Classical Greece', in Blok & Lardinois (edd.), *Solon of Athens*, 290–318 at 309–12 = his *Democracy and the Rule of Law* 22–4. This is not explicitly attributed by Demosthenes to the homicide law, but it is presented as the sequel to the extracts from the homicide law which have preceded it, and the use of *thesmos* encourages belief in its antiquity. However, Ruschenbusch wrote, 'Für die Differenzierung Archon / Privatmann habe ich keine Erklärung'. It occurs in some of the later instances (*IG* ii² 43. *A*. 51–3; *IG* i³ 63. 1–5 restored, cf. *IG* i³ 46. 20–6), where the distinction is between an individual who makes a proposal in the assembly and an official who permits discussion of and voting on that proposal. That scenario is hard to envisage for Draco, but easier to envisage for Solon, if we accept his creation of the council of four hundred to perform *probouleusis* for the assembly (fr. 74/5: *Ath. Pol.* 8. iv, Plut. *Sol.* 19. i–ii). Since Demosthenes' extracts from the homicide law begin with fr. 4/1, which specifies the Areopagus as the court for willing homicide and must therefore be post-Draconian, it is possible that this entrenchment clause too, though ancient, is post-Draconian.

Amnesty for *atimoi*

Fr. 22/1 (fr. 70 Ruschenbusch): Plut. *Sol.* 19. iv
ὁ δὲ τρισκαιδέκατος ἄξων τοῦ Σόλωνος τὸν ὄγδοον ἔχει τῶν νόμων οὕτως αὐτοῖς ὀνόμασι γεγραμμένον· "ἀτίμων· ὅσοι ἄτιμοι

ἦσαν πρὶν ἢ Σόλωνα ἄρξαι ἐπιτίμους εἶναι, πλὴν ὅσοι ἐξ Ἀρείου πάγου ἢ ὅσοι ἐκ τῶν ἐφετῶν ἢ ἐκ πρυτανείου καταδικασθέντες ὑπὸ τῶν βασιλέων ἐπὶ φόνῳ ἢ σφαγαῖσιν ἢ ἐπὶ τυραννίδι ἔφευγον ὅτε ὁ θεσμὸς ἐφάνη ὅδε."

The thirteenth *axon* of Solon has as the eighth of its laws written as follows in these very words: 'Of *atimoi*: As many as were *atimoi* before the archonship of Solon shall be *epitimoi* [with rights], except those who from the Areopagus or the *ephetai* or the *prytaneion* were condemned by the *basileis* for homicide or wounding (?), or were in exile for tyranny, when this ordinance was revealed.'

Ruschenbusch placed this as fr. 70 because he linked it with the ban for the future on enslavement of debtors (cf. 69), and saw in the *atimoi* made *epitimoi* debtors currently enslaved for default. However, we do not know what offences could lead to *atimia* in the period between Draco and Solon. Ruschenbusch himself suggested elsewhere that under Draco's laws all convicted offenders were *atimoi* ('φόνος, *Historia* ix 1960, 129–54 at 147–52 = his *Kleine Schriften*, 47–51), and even that the same was true of Solon's laws, with fines being a commutation of that *atimia* (*Untersuchungen*, 11–15 = his *Kleine Schriften*, 77–80). *Atimoi* are not the same as slaves, and this fragment is better not linked with the *seisachtheia*.

The exceptions are clearer. In the classical period the Areopagus tried cases of willing homicide and wounding (perhaps wounding with a weapon, not necessarily limited to cases in which there was an intention to kill: MacDowell, *L.C.A.* 123–4); *sphagai* is normally taken to be massacre e.g. in a political upheaval (e.g. Gagarin, *Drakon*, 129 n. 49), though Ruschenbusch suggests that it is used here as a predecessor of the classical *trauma*; the *ephetai* in various courts tried other categories of killing; the *prytaneion* was used for homicide by an unknown person and by non-human agents (Dem. XXIII. *Aristocrates* 76; *Ath. Pol.* mentions these cases without specifying the court); and the plural *basileis* will be the *phylobasileis*, the heads of the old tribes, who formally pronounced the outcome of homicide trials (cf. fr. 5). In Draco's law the Areopagus was not mentioned. It is best to read this passage as chiastic, with the Areopagus concerned with tyranny (cf. fr. 37) and the *ephetai* and the *prytaneion* with homicide and wounding: thus *inter alios* Ruschenbusch, *Historia* ix 1960, 129–54 at 132–5 = his *Kleine Schriften*, 34–7; Gagarin, *Drakon*, 125–32. It is surprising in view of the information in frs. 21a–d that men could be made *atimoi* as a result of a trial in the *prytaneion*; the best explanation that has been suggested is that the *prytaneion* is included here because its cases included those of unidentified human killers (e.g. MacDowell, *Athenian Homicide Law*, 88–9; Gagarin, *Drakon*, 131 n. 57).

Offences against property

For the Athenian law of theft in general see Cohen, *Theft in Athenian Law*.

Fr. 23a: Gell. *N.A.* XI. 18. v

Solo . . . sua lege in fures non, ut Draco antea, mortis sed dupli poena vindicandum existimavit.

Solon . . . in his law against thieves thought they should be punished not, as Draco had thought previously, by death but by twofold <restitution>.

Whatever may have been the penalties envisaged under Draco's laws (cf. on fr. 1), Athens' subsequent laws in fact prescribed the death penalty for thieves caught ἐπ' αὐτοφώρῳ and prosecuted by *apagoge*, and allowed killing by the victim for nocturnal theft (fr. 113, cf. *Ath. Pol.* 52. i, Lys. XIII. *Agoratus* 86, etc.). For twofold restitution cf. frs. 23c, d.

Fr. 23b: Poll. VIII. 22

τὰ μέντοι προστιμήματα Σόλων ἐπαίτια καλεῖ.
ἐπάτεια II.

However, Solon calls the additional assessments *epaitia*.

There is no other Athenian instance of ἐπαίτια in any possibly relevant sense except in fr. 23d (§105): there it seems to mean the property in question (Lipsius, *A.R.* 440–1 n. 79, after Reiske), though in that case it misrepresents the Athenian law, and if that is what it means Pollux has misunderstood it (thus Ruschenbusch); however, M. Kaser, 'Der altgriechische Eigentumsschutz', ZRG lxiv 1944, 134–205 at 146 n. 34, considered Pollux' interpretation possible (cf. Cohen, *Theft in Athenian Law*, 62–3 n. 82).

Fr. 23c: Lys. X. *Theomnestus i*, 15–20

καί μοι ἀνάγνωθι τούτους τοὺς νόμους τοὺς Σόλωνος τοὺς παλαιούς. (16) ΝΟΜΟΣ· "δεδέσθαι δ' ἐν τῇ ποδοκάκκῃ ἡμέρας δέκα τὸν πόδα, ἐὰν {μὴ} προστιμήσῃ ἡ ἡλιαία." ἡ ποδοκάκκη αὕτη ἐστίν, ὦ Θεόμνηστε, ὃ νῦν καλεῖται ἐν τῷ ξύλῳ δεδέσθαι. εἰ οὖν ὁ δεθεὶς ἐξελθὼν ἐν ταῖς εὐθύναις τῶν ἕνδεκα κατηγοροίη, ὅτι οὐκ ἐν τῇ ποδοκάκκῃ ἐδέδετο ἀλλ' ἐν τῷ ξύλῳ, οὐκ ἂν ἠλίθιον αὐτὸν νομίζοιεν; **(fr. 23c)** λέγε ἕτερον νόμον. (17) ΝΟΜΟΣ· "ἐπεγγυᾶν δ' ἐπιορκήσαντα τὸν Ἀπόλλω. δεδιότα δὲ δίκης ἕνεκα δρασκάζειν." τοῦτο τὸ ἐπιορκήσαντα ὀμόσαντά ἐστι, τό τε δρασκάζειν ὃ νῦν ἀποδιδράσκειν ὀνομάζομεν. **(fr. 95/1)** "ὅστις δὲ ἀπίλλει τῇ θύρᾳ, ἔνδον τοῦ κλέπτου ὄντος." τὸ ἀπίλλειν τοῦτο ἀποκλῄειν νομίζεται, καὶ μηδὲν διὰ τοῦτο διαφέρου. **(fr. 25)** (18) "τὸ ἀργύριον στάσιμον εἶναι ἐφ' ὁπόσῳ ἂν βούληται ὁ δανείζων." τὸ στάσιμον τοῦτό ἐστιν, ὦ βέλτιστε, οὐ ζύγῳ ἱστάναι ἀλλὰ τόκον πράττεσθαι ὁπόσον ἂν βούληται. (**fr. 68**) ἔτι δ' ἀνάγνωθι τουτουὶ τοῦ νόμου τὸ τελευταῖον. (19) "ὅσαι δὲ πεφασμένως πωλοῦνται" (**fr. 30b**) καὶ "οἰκῆος καὶ δουλῆς τὴν βλαβὴν εἶναι ὀφείλειν. (**fr. 34a**) πρόσεχε τὸν νοῦν· τὸ μὲν πεφασμένως ἐστὶ φανερῶς, πωλεῖσθαι δὲ βαδίζειν, τὸ δὲ οἰκῆος θεράποντος. (20) πολλὰ δὲ τοιαῦτα καὶ ἄλλα ἐστίν, ὦ ἄνδρες δικασταί.

(16) often emended to match fr. 23d. ἡμέρας δέκα: ἡμέρας πέντε Taylor; πόδα <καὶ νύκτας ἴσας> Sauppe; {μὴ} deleted Auger. Carey's O.C.T. keeps to the manuscripts apart from deleting μὴ; Todd's commentary considers that 'a useful corrective to the consensus', but notes that, while the texts of laws inserted in Demosthenes' speeches are suspect (cf. on fr. 23d), the argument that what we have in this fragment cannot be a law about theft, because fr. 25 is 'the' law about theft, is insecure — but that if this is not a version of the law of fr. 23d its negative μὴ may be authentic, referring to a statutory penalty to which the *eliaia* could add. Although it is not certain that this extract is not concerned with theft, there is nothing in the text to indicate that it is concerned with theft, and the only positive reason to believe that it is concerned with theft is the assumption that it is a version of the law of fr. 23d. (17) δίκης ἕνεκα <μὴ> δρασκάζειν Hillgruber. ἀπίλλει, ἀπίλλειν codd.: ἀπείλλει, ἀπείλλειν Lipsius. (18) εἶναι: θεῖναι Francken, τιθέναι Zakas. (19) δούλης τὴν βλάβην Schott: βλάβης τὴν δούλην MSS. εἶναι deleted Taylor καὶ βλάβης ... εἶναι obelised Ruschenbusch.

And read for me these ancient laws of Solon. (16) LAW: 'He shall be bound in the foot-clasp for ten days by his foot, if the *eliaia* makes that additional assessment.' This foot-clasp, Theomnestus, is what is now called being bound in the stocks [*literally*, in the wood]. If then the man who was bound on being released accused the Eleven in their *euthynai* that he had been bound not in the foot-clasp but in the stocks, would they not think he was stupid? Read another law. (17) LAW: 'He shall give a guarantee after oath-taking by Apollo. If he is afraid because of justice, he shall abscond.' 'Oath-taking' means swearing, and 'abscond' is what we call run away. 'Whoever debars by means of the door, when the thief is inside.' This 'debar' means shut out; do not argue on account of that. (18) 'The silver is to be placed on the basis of whatever amount the lender wishes.' 'Placed', my good fellow, means not weighed on a balance, but let out at whatever rate of interest he wishes. And now read the last part of this law. (19) 'Those women who promenade manifestly' and 'it shall be permitted to owe the damage of a houseman and a female slave.' Give your mind to this: 'manifestly' is openly, 'promenade' is walk, 'of a houseman' is of a domestic slave. (20) There are many other things of this kind, men of the jury.

Podokakke is probably a version of ποδοκατοχή, 'foot-clasp' [Didymus *ap.* Harp. π 76 Keaney ποδοκάκκη], and the purpose was to humilate the offender by confining him thus in public (Todd, cf. Dem. XXIV. *Timocrates* 114).

This text and fr. 23d (§105) use *eliaia* (inscriptions show that the word was not aspirated at Athens), while Demosthenes in §114 uses *dikasterion*. On Solon's court, to which appeals could be made, see *Ath. Pol.* 9. i, Plut. *Sol.* 18. vi–vii (both of which use *dikasterion*), with Rhodes, *Comm. Ath. Pol.* 160–1. M. H. Hansen accepts (but aspirates) the name *eliaia* for Solon's court but distinguishes this body from the assembly: 'The Athenian Heliaia from Solon to Aristotle', *C&M* xxxiii 1981–2, 9–47. If *eliaia* was used in this law, that might suggest that the function of the *eliaia* was not limited to the hearing of appeals; cf. on fr. 30/1. On *eliaia* and *dikasterion* in the classical period see Boegehold, *Agora* xxviii, 3–6, concluding that the two words 'are in most senses synonymous'.

Lysias cites this and other laws to illustrate wording which is archaic but not problematic in his own time, and we may assume that this was an ancient law (whether unaltered or later modified but not in this respect: cf. Introduction, p. 6, and commentary on fr. 52), and could well have been a law of Solon.

Fr. 23d: Dem. XXIV. *Timocrates* 105 (part of frs. 111–4)

ΝΟΜΟΙ ΚΛΟΠΗΣ, ΚΑΚΩΣΕΩΣ ΓΟΝΕΩΝ, ΑΣΤΡΑΤΕΙΑΣ· "ὅ τι ἄν τις ἀπολέσῃ, ἐὰν μὲν ἀπολάβῃ, τὴν διπλασίαν καταδικάζειν, ἐὰν δὲ μή, τὴν δεκαπλασίαν πρὸς τοῖς ἐπαιτίοις. δεδέσθαι δ' ἐν τῇ ποδοκάκκῃ τὸν πόδα πενθ' ἡμέρας καὶ νύκτας ὅσας, ἐὰν προστιμήσῃ ἡ ἡλιαία· προστιμᾶσθαι δὲ τὸν βουλόμενον, ὅταν περὶ τοῦ τιμήματος ᾖ."
δεκαπλασίαν MSS: διπλασίαν Heraldus, cf. §§114, 115. See commentary.
Cf. §103: λεγόντων γὰρ τῶν νόμων οὓς ἔθηκε Σόλων, οὐδὲν ὅμοιος ὢν τούτῳ νομοθέτης, ἐάν τις ἁλῷ κλοπῆς καὶ μὴ τιμηθῇ θανάτου, προστιμᾶν αὐτῷ δεσμόν.
Cf. §114: εἰ δέ τις ἰδίαν δίκην κλοπῆς ἁλοίη, ὑπάρχειν μὲν αὐτῷ διπλάσιον ἀποτεῖσαι τὸ τιμηθέν, προστιμῆσαι δ' ἐξεῖναι τῷ δικαστηρίῳ πρὸς τῷ ἀργυρίῳ δεσμὸν τῷ κλέπτῃ, πενθ' ἡμέρας καὶ νύκτας ἴσας, ὅπως ὁρῶεν ἅπαντες αὐτὸν δεδεμένον. (Restated in different words in §115.)
LAWS ABOUT THEFT, MALTREATMENT OF PARENTS, SHIRKING MILITARY SERVICE: 'What a man has lost, if he has recovered it, [the thief] shall be sentenced to twofold restitution, if not, tenfold in addition to the *epaitia* [= the property in question?]. He shall be bound in the foot-clasp by his foot for five days and as many nights, if the *eliaia* makes that additional assessment; whoever wishes may propose the additional assessment, when the assessment is being considered.'

Cf. §103: For the laws enacted by Solon, a lawgiver in no way like this one [sc. Timocrates], say that if a man is convicted of theft and the death penalty is not assessed he may be subjected to the additional assessment of being bound.

Cf. §114: But if a man was convicted of theft in a private suit, he was liable to repay the assessed amount twofold, and it was possible for the court in addition to the money to make an additional assessment of being bound for the thief, for five days and the same number of nights, so that all should see him bound. (Restated in different words in §115.)

On the laws inserted in speeches of the orators see in general on fr. 4/1. In this case Canevaro (*The Documents in the Attic Orators*, 157–73, and 'Thieves, Parent Abusers, Draft Dodgers ... and Homicide?', *Historia* lxii 2013, 25–47), argues that the documents in §105 were not present in the early version of the speech on which the stichometry was based, and are not authentic Athenian laws. Demosthenes' own words mention a requirement of twofold restitution and the possibility of an additional assessment of five days and nights' confinement, which we think (though Canevaro does not) means confinement in the stocks. They do not mention tenfold restitution, or *epaitia* (on which see fr. 23b). Tenfold restitution has usually been removed by emendation: tenfold restitution was required of stolen sacred property (§111) and from officials convicted in their *euthynai* (§112, *Ath. Pol.* 54. ii), and Cohen, *Theft in Athenian Law*, 62–8, considers it possible though not certain here. However, if the law in §105 is a later forgery there is no point in emending the manuscripts' text in the light of other evidence.

'Whoever wishes' is one of the suspect features of §105: the penalty would be proposed by the prosecutor; in the *dike klopes* (cf. §114) the prosecutor would be the injured party; a *graphe klopes*, with prosecution by 'whoever wishes', is clearly attested only in Dem. XXII. *Androtion* 26–7 among the remedies available for theft, but that if it existed may have been available only for theft of public property (Cohen, *Theft in Athenian Law*, 44–9, cf. MacDowell, *L.C.A.* 149). But Gagarin, *Early Greek Law*, 75 with n. 109, accepts §105 as authentic and tries to justify this clause.

The only part of fr. 23 which we can be reasonably sure gives us part of Solon's law of theft is what Demosthenes himself says in §§103–15 in fr. 23d.

Fr. 23/1: Dem. XXIV. *Timocrates* 113 (part of **frs. 111–4**)
καίτοι γ' ὁ Σόλων, ὦ ἄνδρες δικασταί, ᾧ οὐδ' ἂν αὐτὸς Τιμοκράτης φήσειεν ὅμοιος νομοθέτης εἶναι, οὐχ ὅπως ἀσφαλῶς κακουργήσουσι φαίνεται παρασκευάζων τοῖς τοιούτοις ἀλλ' ὅπως ἢ μὴ ἀδικήσουσι ἢ δώσουσι δίκην ἀξίαν, καὶ νόμον εἰσήνεγκεν, εἰ μέν τις μεθ' ἡμέραν ὑπὲρ πεντήκοντα δραχμὰς κλέπτοι, ἀπαγωγὴν πρὸς τοὺς ἕνδεκ' εἶναι, εἰ δέ τις νύκτωρ ὁτιοῦν κλέπτοι, τοῦτον ἐξεῖναι καὶ ἀποκτεῖναι καὶ τρῶσαι διώκοντα καὶ ἀπαγαγεῖν τοῖς ἕνδεκα, εἰ βούλοιτο. τῷ δ' ἁλόντι, ὧν αἱ ἀπαγωγαί εἰσιν, οὐκ ἐγγυητὰς καταστήσαντι ἔκτισιν εἶναι τῶν κλεμμάτων, ἀλλὰ θάνατον τὴν ζημίαν.

Yet Solon, men of the jury, whom not even Timocrates himself can claim to resemble as a lawgiver, far from enabling them to commit crimes in safety can be seen to have prepared for such men that they should either not do wrong or pay a worthy penalty. He introduced a law that if anybody by day steals more than fifty drachmae he may be brought by *apagoge* to the Eleven, and if anybody by night steals anything at all one may pursue him and kill or wound him, or bring him by *apagoge* to the Eleven if one wishes. The man convicted of offences which are subject to *apagoge* is not allowed to present guarantors for the repayment of what is stolen, but the punishment is death.

We accept the procedure of *apagoge* as Solonian (cf. fr. 16), so Ruschenbusch's fr. 113 becomes our fr. 23/1.

Fr. 24: Poll. VIII. 34
Σόλων μέντοι τὸ κλέμμα κλέπος ἐν τοῖς νόμοις ὠνόμασεν.
However, Solon called *klemma* ('thing stolen') *klepos* in his laws.

The form *klepos* is not found anywhere else (unless by emendation, cf. fr. 25, below). Presumably Pollux like Lysias had access to laws which were certainly ancient and could well have been Solonian.

Fr. 25: Lys. X. *Theomnestus i*, 17 (part of **fr. 23c**)
(15 καί μοι ἀνάγνωθι τούτους τοὺς νόμους τοὺς Σόλωνος τοὺς παλαιούς.)
"ὅστις δὲ ἀπίλλει τῇ θύρᾳ, ἔνδον τοῦ κλέπτου ὄντος." τὸ ἀπίλλειν τοῦτο ἀποκλῄειν νομίζεται, καὶ μηδὲν διὰ τοῦτο διαφέρου.
(15 And read for me the ancient laws of Solon.)
'Whoever debars by means of the door, when the thief is inside.'
This 'debar' means shut out; do not argue on account of that.

Cf. fr. 23c. Here again the law is quoted for the sake of an archaic word whose meaning is not problematic (cf. fr. 36); and again we may assume that this was from an ancient law (whether unaltered or later modified but not in this respect), which could well have been a law of Solon. Todd *ad loc.* argues that the purpose of the clause was most probably to prevent a thief caught inside the house he was robbing from being rescued by his accomplices; for an alternative explanation he is tempted by fr. 24 and Dobree on this passage to emend κλέπτου to κλέπους, 'while the object stolen is inside', and to suppose that the reference is to a search of the suspect's house for the stolen property (cf. Lipsius, *A.R.* 440 with n. 78, and Pl. *Leg.* XII. 954 A–B).

Moral offences

There were laws protecting marriage as an institution and laws that were intended to prevent situations that might put it in danger, either when marriage was already a consummated fact, or when it was only a project for the near future, as happened with rape and adultery.

Fr. 26: Plut. *Sol.* 23. i
ἐὰν δ' ἁρπάσῃ τις ἐλευθέραν γυναῖκα καὶ βιάσηται, ζημίαν ἑκατὸν δραχμὰς ἔταξε.
If a man seized a free woman and had sexual intercourse by force with her, he fixed a fine of a hundred drachmae.

Fr. 27 (= fr. 52b): Hesych. β 466 Latte *et al.*
ΒΙΝΕΙΝ· παρὰ Σόλωνι τὸ βίᾳ μίγνυσθαι. τὸ δὲ κατὰ νόμον ὀπύειν.
BINEIN ['have sexual relations']: in Solon, means to have sexual intercourse by force. Legitimate intercourse is *opyein*.

Fr. 26 deals with cases of rape committed upon women with free status (ἐλευθέραν γυναῖκα), and the aspect that indicates rape is that the sexual intercourse is forced (βιάσηται), i.e. without the woman's consent. Hesychius also stresses the use of force (βίᾳ), implying that the sexual intercourse was not legitimised by marriage (in the latter case, the term used should be ὀπύειν). Ruschenbusch, *Gesetzeskwerk*, 57, considers fr. 27 to be a gloss from the *axones*. According to Plutarch the penalty consisted of a monetary fine. On the equivalence between the price of animals and drachmae, see fr. 92 (and commentary to fr. 65).

    E. M. Harris, 'Did Rape Exist in Classical Athens? Further Reflections on the Laws about Sexual Violence', *Dike* vii 2004, 41–83, = his *Democracy and the Rule of Law*, 297–332, argues that Attic law was more concerned with safeguarding the honour of the *oikos* and the power of the *kyrios* to keep his control over the women under his responsibility than with the personal situation of a female victim of sexual abuse. Therefore, if the aggressor could not be accused of *hybris* (because he had no intent of humiliating the victim), and if he was ready to reach an agreement with the family of the woman, the case could be resolved with some indulgence. At any rate, even if there was not a specific term to designate rape (which is usually referred to with words such as *hybris*, *bia* or *biazein*, *aischynein*, *atiman* or *atimazein*), Solon's law shows that there were specific penalties for specific kinds of sexual offence. Thus Leão, 'Sólon e a legislação em matéria de direito familiar', *Dike* viii 2005, 8–9 n. 6. The question of the woman's consent is better understood when taken together with the law on adultery (frs. 28a–c). See also Gagarin, *Early Greek Law*, 65; Manfredini & Piccirilli, *Plutarco. La vita di Solone*[5], 242–3.

Fr. 28a: Plut. *Sol.* 23. i
μοιχὸν μὲν γὰρ ἀνελεῖν τῷ λαβόντι δέδωκεν.
In fact, he gave to the captor [the right] to kill an adulterer caught [in the act].

Fr. 28b: *Dig.* XLVIII. 5. xxiv

Vlpianus libro primo de adulteriis. Quod ait lex 'in filia adulterum deprehenderit', non otiosum videtur: voluit enim ita demum hanc potestatem patri competere, si in ipsa turpitudine filiam de adulterio deprehendat. Labeo quoque ita probat, et Pomponius scripsit in ipsis rebus Veneris deprehensum occidi: et hoc est quod Solo et Draco dicunt ἐν ἔργῳ.

Ulpian in the first book *On adultery*: in so far as the law says 'caught the adulterer lying with the daughter', it should not be taken as indifferent. In fact it means precisely that the father has this power [*sc.* to kill the adulterer], if he catches the daughter in flagrant infamy of adultery. Labeo shares this same opinion, and Pomponius writes that the one caught in the very act of love can be killed. This is what Solon and Draco mean by ἐν ἔργῳ ('in the act').

Fr. 28c: Lucian *Eunuchus* 10

εἰ δὲ μὴ ψεύδονται οἱ περὶ αὐτοῦ λέγοντες, καὶ μοιχὸς ἑάλω ποτέ, ὡς ὁ ἄξων φησίν, ἄρθρα ἐν ἄρθροις ἔχων.

Unless those who speak about him are lying, he was once caught in adultery, as the *axon* says, limbs on limbs.

Fr. 28a states that an adulterer (*moichos*) caught *in flagrante* could be killed with impunity, a clause that possibly belonged already to the homicide law of Draco (see commentary after fr. 21/1). If one compares this capital penalty with the fine of 100 drachmae, mentioned in fr. 26 (Plut. *Sol.* 23.i), to punish rape, it seems quite probable, as is generally understood, that the Athenians considered adultery a more serious crime than rape (e.g. MacDowell, *L.C.A.* 124–5). This fact caused perplexity already to Plutarch (*Sol.* 23.ii), who says that this way of acting was ἄλογον. At any rate, the penalty of 100 drachmae was the highest level of fine attested for Solon's legislation. Draco reckoned in oxen (fr. 10), while Solon reckoned in drachmae, probably by using standard weights of silver and not coinage, which seems not to have existed in Athens until the middle of the sixth century (see commentary on fr. 64/1). On the equivalence between oxen, goats and drachmae, see fr. 92 (and commentary on fr. 65).

The crime of *moicheia* (which we translate 'adultery') was quite wide-ranging for the Athenians, and could involve illegitimate sexual intercourse with most of the women included in the *oikos*. Fr. 29a makes it clear that a man engaged with a prostitute could not be considered a *moichos*. The law *ap.* Dem. XXIII. *Aristocrates* 53 (= fr. 20), even if it is mainly directed not to *moicheia* but to cases of homicide not subject to a penalty of exile, nevertheless identifies the situations that might allow lawful killing of an adulterer: when the *moichos* was caught *in flagrante* 'with his wife or mother or sister or daughter or a concubine whom he has with the objective of free children'. Ruschenbusch, *Gesetzeswerk*, 61, suggests that ἐν ἔργῳ in fr. 28b may be a quotation from the law, while ἄρθρα ἐν ἄρθροις in fr. 28c is a concretisation of what it implied. Contrary to rape, where the use of force was implied (fr. 26), with *moicheia* what was in question was the seduction and moral corruption of the women and the honour of the *oikos* (a feeling well expressed in Lys. I. *On the killing of Eratosthenes* 32-3). Fr. 20 also calls attention to a more practical reason for the severity of the law (ἢ ἐπὶ παλλακῇ ἣν ἂν ἐπ' ἐλευθέροις παισὶν ἔχῃ): the ability to identify the exact paternity of children, which would be much more difficult if there was a relationship with a *moichos*.

Rape and adultery are a much debated question: e.g. Harrison, *L.A.* i. 32–6; Cohen, *Law, Sexuality and Society*, 98–132; C. Carey, 'Rape and Adultery in Athenian Law', *CQ*² xlv 1995, 407–17; M. Galaz, 'Delitos sexuales en la Atenas clásica', in Leão *et al.* (edd.), *Nomos*, 175–98. Because rape is a kind of abuse that affects the honour of the victims and of their *oikos*, it would be possible, at least in theoretical terms, to make a public accusation for *hybris* (*graphe hybreos*). So Harris, 'Did the Athenians Regard Seduction as a Worse Crime than Rape?', *CQ*² xl 1990, 370–7 at 373–4 = his *Democracy and the Rule of Law*, 287–8, together with Carey, *CQ*² xlv 1995, although the latter calls attention to the fact that there is no extant example of such a case. In those kinds of process (*agones timetoi*) for which the law did not specify clearly the nature of the crime and the penalty to be applied, it would be possible for the injured party to suggest the penalty — death included. So if rape gave rise to a *graphe hybreos*, if the prosecutor suggested the death penalty and if the court decided in favour of this, rape could, *theoretically*, lead to the death of the offender. At any rate, this does not change the traditional understanding of the problem, that adultery was perceived as a more serious crime than rape: it is one thing to have the legal possibility of considering rape as an act of *hybris*, whose punishment could, in an extreme case, lead to the death penalty; it is a very different thing to state by law, from the beginning, that the *moichos* could be legally killed if caught *in flagrante*. Besides this, the fact that Solon fixed a pecuniary fine for the rapist makes fr. 26 fall within the range of the *agones atimetoi*, thereby avoiding the need for a *graphe hybreos*. On the distinction between *agones timetoi* and *agones atimetoi*, see Harrison, *L.A.* ii. 80-2.

Fr. 29a: [Dem.] LIX. *Against Neaera* 67

τόν τε νόμον ἐπὶ τούτοις παρεχόμενος, ὃς οὐκ ἐᾷ ἐπὶ ταύτῃσι μοιχὸν λαβεῖν ὁπόσαι ἂν ἐπ' ἐργαστηρίου καθῶνται ἢ πωλῶνται ἀποπεφασμένως ...

In addition to this, he presented the law that does not allow taking as an adulterer the man who has affairs with women who sit in a brothel or who promenade manifestly ...

Fr. 29b: Lys. X. *Theomnestus i.* 19 (part of **fr. 23c**)

(15 καί μοι ἀνάγνωθι τούτους τοὺς νόμους τοὺς Σόλωνος τοὺς παλαιούς.)

"ὅσαι δὲ πεφασμένως πωλοῦνται". . . . πρόσεχε τὸν νοῦν· τὸ μὲν "πεφασμένως" ἐστὶ φανερῶς, "πωλεῖσθαι" δὲ βαδίζειν.
(15 And read for me these ancient laws of Solon.)
'Those women who promenade manifestly'. . . . Give your mind to this: 'manifestly' is openly, 'promenade' is walk.

Fr. 30a: Plut. *Sol.* 23. i
κἂν προαγωγεύῃ, δραχμὰς εἴκοσι, πλὴν ὅσαι πεφασμένως πωλοῦνται, λέγων τὰς ἑταίρας· αὗται γὰρ ἐμφανῶς φοιτῶσι πρὸς τοὺς διδόντας.
If a man procures [a free woman] he is fined twenty drachmae, with the exception of those who promenade manifestly, meaning the *hetairai*: these go in fact openly to those who pay them their price.

Fr. 30b = fr. 29b

Fr. 29a makes it clear that the man who seeks the services of a professional prostitute is not liable to the rules about *moicheia*. As is suggested by frs. 29b and 30a, the expression πεφασμένως πωλοῦνται used to define the activity of the *hetairai* is probably Solonian. In fact it is in accordance with the ability to coin metaphorical terms, which is said to be characteristic of the legislator, as can be seen in the way he decided to label his first emblematic reform, by naming it the 'shaking-off of burdens' (*seisachtheia*) — a linguistic practice which, according to an ironical comment by Plut. *Sol.* 15. ii, the Athenians adopted very quickly. On the interpretation of the *seisachtheia* and on enslavement for debt, see frs. 67, 69a–c.

According to fr. 30a, Solon forbade the procuring (*proagogeia*) of free women, prescribing a fine of twenty drachmae, a lesser penalty than the hundred drachmae prescribed for rape (fr. 26). The fine was not applied when the prostitution was voluntary — admittedly a distinction that would not always be easy to establish, if the *kyrios* was the one responsible for this kind of sexual exploitation. Solon did not forbid voluntary prostitution, but attention must be paid to the different situation of *hetairai* and *pallakai*: the first received their payment from any client, while the latter were concubines and part of the *oikos*, to the point of being protected by the laws dealing with *moicheia* (as mentioned in the context of lawful homicide of an adulterer, fr. 20) and of having free children from with the *kyrios*. See commentary after fr. 21/1.

†Fr. 30/c: Aeschin. I. *Timarchus* 13–14
ἐκ γὰρ τοῦ πράττεσθαί τιν' ὧν οὐ προσῆκεν, ἐκ τούτου νόμους ἔθεντο οἱ παλαιοί. διαρρήδην γοῦν λέγει ὁ νόμος, ἐάν τινα ἐκμισθώσῃ ἑταιρεῖν πατὴρ ἢ ἀδελφὸς ἢ θῖος ἢ ἐπίτροπος ἢ ὅλως

τῶν κυρίων τις, κατ' αὐτοῦ μὲν τοῦ παιδὸς οὐκ ἐᾷ γραφὴν εἶναι, κατὰ δὲ τοῦ μισθώσαντος καὶ τοῦ μισθωσαμένου, τοῦ μὲν ὅτι ἐξεμίσθωσε, τοῦ δὲ ὅτι, φησίν, ἐμισθώσατο. καὶ ἴσα τὰ ἐπιτίμια ἑκατέρῳ πεποίηκε, καὶ μὴ ἐπάναγκες εἶναι τῷ παιδὶ ἡβήσαντι τρέφειν τὸν πατέρα μηδὲ οἴκησιν παρέχειν, ὃς ἂν ἐκμισθωθῇ ἑταιρεῖν· ἀποθανόντα δὲ θαπτέτω καὶ τἆλλα ποιείτω τὰ νομιζόμενα (**fr. 57/b**).

καὶ τίνα ἕτερον νόμον ἔθηκε φύλακα τῶν ὑμετέρων παίδων; τὸν τῆς προαγωγείας, τὰ μέγιστα ἐπιτίμια ἐπιγράψας ἐάν τις ἐλεύθερον παῖδα ἢ γυναῖκα προαγωγεύῃ.

For because various things were happening which were not proper, because of this the ancients enacted their laws. The law says explicitly, if anybody is hired out for prostitution by father or brother or uncle or guardian or generally by any of those with authority over him, it does not allow a prosecution against the boy himself, but against the man who hired him out and the man who took him on hire, the first because he hired him out, the second, it says, because he took him on hire; and it has made the penalties equal for each. And it is not obligatory for the boy when he has grown up to support his father or provide a home for him, if he has been hired out for prostitution; but when he has died the son must bury him and perform the other customary rites.

And what other law has he enacted as a guardian of your children? The law on procuring, imposing the greatest penalties if anybody procures a free child or woman.

Fr. 30/d (fr. 116 Ruschenbusch): Aeschin. I. *Timarchus* 183
ὁ δὲ Σόλων ὁ τῶν νομοθετῶν ἐνδοξότατος . . . καὶ τὰς προαγωγοὺς καὶ τοὺς προαγωγοὺς γράφεσθαι κελεύει, κἂν ἁλῶσι θανάτῳ ζημιοῦν.

Solon the most distinguished of the lawgivers . . . And he orders a *graphe* (public suit) against female and male procurers, and if they are convicted the death penalty.

A series of laws is cited in the opening sections of Aeschin. I. *Timarchus*, which we consider in general here. (However, we ignore the inserted documents, which are found only in one set of late manuscripts and are generally regarded as later compilations: see, e.g., E. Drerup,

'Über die bei den attischen Rednern eingelegten Urkunde', *JAW* Supp. xxiv 1898, 221–366 at 305–8; Fisher, *Aeschines, Against Timarchos*, 68. This means not that they necessarily have no basis at all in Athenian law, but that they cannot be relied on as genuine laws and used as evidence for what is not attested elsewhere: cf. on fr. 4/1.) There are laws on hiring out and procuring (fr. 30/c–d), on *hybris* against children and slaves (fr. 30/1), on priority in the assembly for older speakers (fr. 80/1b), on disqualifications for men who had prostituted themselves (fr. 103), a DOKIMASIA RHETORON to prevent unworthy men from speaking in the assembly (fr. 104a); and a new law on the presiding tribe in the assembly (Aeschin. I. *Timarchus* 33–4 cf. III. *Ctesiphon* 4). While the last is said to be recent, the others are said to be ancient, and Fisher *ad locc.* suggests that they could go back to Solon.

The fourth century was a time when various earlier documents were rediscovered or, we think more likely in most cases, reconstructed, and put to political use (cf. on frs. 21–21/1): Aeschines in 348 read out the decree of Miltiades, the decree of Themistocles and the ephebic oath (Dem. XIX. *F.L.* 303), and possibly the Greek oath of 479 (cf. Theopomp. *FGrH* 115 F 153), and in 330 he referred to Arthmius of Zelea (cf. on fr. 21/1). However, the citation here of laws said still to be valid is not on the same level as the citation as *exempla* of decisions in past crises. In some of these instances Aeschines had the law read out, and it is best to accept that all of these, including the law cited here, were genuine laws. We follow Fisher in thinking that most of these laws, apart from that on the *graphe hetaireseos* and that on the *dokimasia rhetoron*, could go back to Solon (which is not to rule out later modification: cf. Introduction, p. 6, and commentary on fr. 52), and we therefore print them as such in our collection.

Hiring out a boy would be dealt with by a *graphe hetaireseos*, procuring (which we believe was included in Solon's laws) by a *graphe proagogeias*: see Harrison, *L.A.* i. 37–8, Fisher *ad loc.* Plutarch (fr. 30a) has a penalty of twenty drachmae for procuring; Fisher wonders if these were or became *agones timetoi*, with the penalty assessed by the court (cf. *hybris*, fr. 30/1). On the reduced familial obligation of a son hired out for prostitution, see Leão, 'Paidotrophia et gerotrophia dans les lois de Solon', *RHD* lxxxix 2011, 457–72 at 469.

†Fr. 30/1a: Aeschin. I. *Timarchus* 15
καὶ ποῖον ἄλλον [sc. νόμον]; τὴν τῆς ὕβρεως, ὃς ἑνὶ κεφαλαίῳ ἅπαντα τὰ τοιαῦτα συλλαβὼν ἔχει. ἐν ᾧ διαρρήδην γέγραπται, ἐάν τις ὑβρίζῃ εἰς παῖδα (ὑβρίζει δὲ δή που ὁ μισθούμενος) ἢ ἄνδρα ἢ γυναῖκα, ἢ τῶν ἐλευθέρων ἢ τῶν δούλων, ἢ ἐὰν παράνομόν τι ποιῇ εἰς τούτων τινά, γραφὰς ὕβρεως εἶναι πεποίηκεν καὶ τίμημα ἐπέθηκεν ὅ τι χρὴ παθεῖν ἢ ἀποτεῖσαι. λέγε τὸν νόμον.

And what other law? The law on *hybris*, which sums up all these things in one statement. Here it has been written explicitly, 'If anybody commits *hybris* against a child (and surely one who hires commits *hybris*) or man or woman, whether free or slave, or if anybody commits anything unlawful against any of these', it has created *graphai* (public suits) *hybreos* and has imposed an assessment of what the offender should suffer or pay. Read the law.

For *hybris*, which tended to involve arrogance and attacks on the honour of others, see in particular D. M. MacDowell, '*Hybris* in Athens', *G&R*² xxiii 1976, 14–31, and his *Demosthenes, Against Meidias*, 18–23; Fisher on fr. 30/1a, and his *Hybris*, 76–82; D. L. Cairns, '*Hybris*, Dishonour and Thinking Big', *JHS* cxvi 1996, 1–51. In keeping with his view of the development of Athenian law, Ruschenbusch believed that the law on and *graphe* for *hybris* were not Solonian, but were an innovation of the Periclean period, to fill gaps in the law on offences against the person, and through assessment to supersede Solonian penalties which by then were unrealistically low ('ὕβρεως γραφή: Ein Fremdkörper im athenischen Recht des 4. Jahrhunderts v. Chr.', *ZRG* lxxxii 1965, 302–9 = his *Kleine Schriften*, 67–74); cf. M. Gagarin, 'The Athenian Law Against *Hybris*', in *Arktouros* . . . *B. M. W. Knox*, 229–36. However, as with fr. 30/c–d, we follow MacDowell *ad loc.* and Fisher, *Hybris*, 36–82, in believing that Aeschines' law on *hybris* could go back to Solon. But the law quoted in Dem. XXI. *Midias* is not genuine, and we print that as fr. 98/1.

'Commits anything unlawful', in both fr. 30/1a and fr. 98/1, has caused problems (Harris sees it not as a quotation but as a gloss by Aeschines), but it appears also in a different law inserted in Dem. XLIII. *Macartatus* 75 (= fr 51c), for which both ὑβριστής and παρανομώτεροι are used in the elucidation in §§76–8, and (perhaps with a broader meaning than 'contrary to written law') that is better accepted as a genuine phrase in the law. H. van Wees, 'The "Law of *Hybris*" and Solon's Reform of Justice', in *Sociable Man* . . . *N. Fisher*, 117–44, sees in it a sign that this is part of a more general law instituting the procedure of *graphe* (cf. on fr. 40) for offences against the person, and instituting the *eliaia* not only as an appeal court but also as a court of first instance (cf. on fr. 23c).

Fr. 31a: Plut. *Sol.* 23. ii
ἔτι δ' οὔτε θυγατέρας πωλεῖν οὔτ' ἀδελφὰς δίδωσι, πλὴν ἂν μὴ λάβῃ παρθένον ἀνδρὶ συγγεγενημένην.
Besides this, he does not allow anyone to sell a daughter or a sister, unless it is discovered that she has already had intercourse with a man and is no longer a virgin.

Fr. 31b: Plut. *Sol.* 13. iv–v
ἅπας μὲν γὰρ ὁ δῆμος ἦν ὑπόχρεως τῶν πλουσίων. ἢ γὰρ ἐγεώργουν ἐκείνοις ἕκτα τῶν γινομένων τελοῦντες, ἑκτημόριοι προσαγορευόμενοι καὶ θῆτες, ἢ χρέα λαμβάνοντες ἐπὶ τοῖς σώμασιν, ἀγώγιμοι τοῖς δανείζουσιν ἦσαν, οἱ μὲν αὐτοῦ δουλεύοντες, οἱ δ' ἐπὶ τὴν ξένην πιπρασκόμενοι. πολλοὶ δὲ καὶ παῖδας ἰδίους ἠναγκάζοντο πωλεῖν – οὐδεὶς γὰρ νόμος ἐκώλυε – καὶ τὴν πόλιν φεύγειν διὰ τὴν χαλεπότητα τῶν δανειστῶν.

In fact, all the common people were indebted to the rich. For they either worked the land and gave them a sixth of the produce (for which reason they were called *hektemoroi* and *thetes*), or they had to take loans on the security of their persons, being liable to seizure by their creditors; some became slaves at home, while others were sold out of the country. Many were even forced to sell their own children — no law forbade that practice — and leave the city, owing to the severity of their creditors.

These two dispositions complete frs. 30a–b and 30/c–d, in the sense that they also deal with prostitution, but they differ in the fact that the procurer in this case is not a stranger, but the legal *kyrios* of the victim. Plutarch (fr. 31b) connects this social problem with the economic situation of Attica, and this justification is plausible. He also interprets the term *polein* in the current meaning of 'sell', in this case 'sell into slavery'. Despite this, the verb appeared in the dispositions concerning the activity of *hetairai* (frs. 30a–b), and Lysias (X. *Theomnestus i.* 19 = fr. 29b) explains that the term πωλεῖσθαι was equivalent to βαδίζειν, in the sense of 'walking in search of a client'. So Ruschenbusch, *Untersuchungen*, 42 and n. 127, 50 and n. 162 = his *Kleine Schriften*, 97 and n. 127, 102 and n. 162; others, like Gagarin, *Early Greek Law*, 68, interpret the clause as a law against 'selling members of one's own family into slavery'. That explanation is in accordance with Plutarch's understanding of the law, but the occurrence of the term *polein* favours, in this context, the idea that the law deals with a situation of procuring members of one's own family. Before Solon, free women (and possibly young boys – see fr. 30/c and fr. 57a) had no legal protection against this kind of sexual exploitation. At any rate, the law keeps a strong link with the honour of the *oikos*: women who had sexual intercourse with a man before marriage were not protected by this disposition, because the loss of virginity would affect their capacity to find a suitable marriage. Even if concealed, illegitimate sexual intercourse with a supposed virgin could be exposed by a subsequent pregnancy. Fr. 31a may reflect this situation rather than the idea of catching the woman in the act.

On the much-debated topic of *hektemoroi* / *hektemorioi* (glossed here as *thetes* by Plutarch and as *pelatai* by *Ath. Pol.*), see commentary on fr. 67.

Verbal offences

Fr. 32a: Plut. *Sol.* 21. i–ii
ἐπαινεῖται δὲ τοῦ Σόλωνος καὶ ὁ κωλύων νόμος τὸν τεθνηκότα κακῶς ἀγορεύειν. καὶ γὰρ ὅσιον τοὺς μεθεστῶτας ἱεροὺς νομίζειν, καὶ δίκαιον ἀπέχεσθαι τῶν οὐχ ὑπαρχόντων, καὶ πολιτικὸν ἀφαιρεῖν τῆς ἔχθρας τὸ ἀίδιον. ζῶντα δὲ κακῶς λέγειν ἐκώλυσε πρὸς ἱεροῖς καὶ δικαστηρίοις καὶ ἀρχείοις καὶ θεωρίας οὔσης ἀγώνων, ἢ τρεῖς δραχμὰς τῷ ἰδιώτῃ, δύο δ' ἄλλας ἀποτίνειν εἰς τὸ δημόσιον ἔταξε.

Praise is given also to the law of Solon that forbids speaking ill of the dead in public. In fact, it is pious to consider the deceased as sacred, just to leave in peace the absent and urbane to put an end to everlasting enmities. He forbade also speaking ill of the living in sanctuaries, in courts, in public offices, and while attending the games, prescribing that [the transgressor] should pay three drachmae to the person offended and two more drachmae into the public treasury.

Fr. 32b: Lys. X. *Theomnestus i.* 6–12
(6) ἴσως τοίνυν, ὦ ἄνδρες δικασταί, περὶ τούτων μὲν οὐδὲν ἀπολογήσεται, ἐρεῖ δὲ πρὸς ὑμᾶς ἅπερ ἐτόλμα λέγειν καὶ πρὸς τῷ διαιτητῇ, ὡς οὐκ ἔστι τῶν ἀπορρήτων, ἐάν τις εἴπῃ τὸν πατέρα ἀπεκτονέναι· τὸν γὰρ νόμον οὐ ταῦτ' ἀπαγορεύειν, ἀλλ' ἀνδροφόνον οὐκ ἐᾶν λέγειν. (7) ἐγὼ δὲ οἶμαι ὑμᾶς, ὦ ἄνδρες δικασταί, οὐ περὶ τῶν ὀνομάτων <δεῖν> διαφέρεσθαι ἀλλὰ τῆς τούτων διανοίας ... (8) οὐ γὰρ δήπου, ὦ Θεόμνηστε, εἰ μέν τίς σε εἴποι πατραλοίαν ἢ μητραλοίαν, ἠξίους ἂν αὐτὸν ὀφλεῖν σοι δίκην, εἰ δέ τις εἴποι ὡς τὴν τεκοῦσαν ἢ τὸν φύσαντα ἔτυπτες, ᾤου ἂν αὐτὸν ἀζήμιον δεῖν εἶναι, ὡς οὐδὲν τῶν ἀπορρήτων εἰρηκότα. (9) ἡδέως δ' ἄν σου πυθοίμην ...· εἴ τίς σε εἴποι ῥῖψαι τὴν ἀσπίδα, ἐν δὲ τῷ νόμῳ εἴρηται, ἐάν τις φάσκῃ ἀποβεβληκέναι, ὑπόδικον εἶναι, οὐκ ἂν ἐδικάζου αὐτῷ, ἀλλ' ἐξήρκει ἄν σοι ἐρριφέναι τὴν ἀσπίδα λέγοντι οὐδέν σοι μέλειν; οὐδὲ γὰρ τὸ αὐτό ἐστι ῥῖψαι καὶ ἀποβεβληκέναι. ... (12) καὶ αὐτὸς μὲν Θέωνι κακηγορίας ἐδικάσω εἰπόντι σε ἐρριφέναι τὴν ἀσπίδα. καίτοι περὶ μὲν τοῦ ῥῖψαι οὐδὲν <ἐν> τῷ νόμῳ εἴρηται, ἐὰν δέ τις εἴπῃ ἀποβεβληκέναι τὴν ἀσπίδα, πεντακοσίας δραχμὰς ὀφείλειν κελεύει.
Θέωνι: Λυσιθέῳ Frohberger

It is also possible, men of the jury, that he will argue against those points and that he will repeat to you what he had the audacity to state before the arbitrator also — that it is not to pronounce one of the forbidden words to declare that 'someone has killed the father', because the law does not forbid this, but only 'does not concede the use of the word "murderer" '. (7) In what concerns me, men of the jury, I think that the debate should concern not the words by themselves but their meaning ... (8) You certainly, Theomnestus, would expect to get satisfaction from someone who called you a 'father-beater' or a 'mother-beater', but not even you would argue that someone who said that you 'struck the persons who engendered and begot you' was not liable to penalty, just because he did not use a forbidden word. (9) I should also appreciate it if you could tell me this ... if someone declared that you 'cast your shield' — according to the terms of the law, 'if someone says that a man has thrown it away, that person can be brought to trial' —, would you not charge him? If you were said to have cast your shield, would you be glad to dismiss that accusation, just because to cast the shield and to throw it away is not the same? ... (12) But you have yourself prosecuted Theon for slander, simply because he said that you have cast your shield. But there is nothing in the law about casting, while it states that 'if someone says that a man has thrown away his shield, the law prescribes a penalty of five hundred drachmae'.

†Fr. 32c: Dem. XXI. *Midias* 32
ἂν μὲν τοίνυν ἰδιώτην ὄντα τιν' αὐτῶν ὑβρίσῃ τις ἢ κακῶς εἴπῃ, γραφὴν ὕβρεως καὶ δίκην κακηγορίας ἰδίαν φεύξεται.
If anybody commits *hybris* against or speaks ill of any of them as a private individual, he will stand trial on a public charge for *hybris* or in a private suit for speaking ill.

Fr. 33a: Plut. *Sol.* 21. i (part of **fr. 32a**)
ὁ κωλύων νόμος τὸν τεθνηκότα κακῶς ἀγορεύειν.
The law that forbids speaking ill of the dead in public.

Fr. 33b: *Lex. Rhet. Cant.* (78. 18–23 *Lexica Graeca Minora*)
ΚΑΚΗΓΟΡΙΑΣ ΔΙΚΗ· ἐάν τις κακῶς εἴπῃ τινὰ τῶν κατοιχομένων, κἂν ὑπὸ τῶν ἐκείνου παίδων ἀκούσῃ κακῶς, πεντακοσίας καταδικασθεὶς ὦφλε· τῷ δημοσίῳ <διακοσίας>, τριακοσίας δὲ τῷ ἰδιώτῃ. Ὑπερείδης δὲ ἐν τῷ κατὰ Δωροθέου χιλίαις μὲν ζημιοῦσθαι <ἐὰν> τοὺς κατοιχομένους κακηγορήσαντάς φησι, πεντακοσίαις δέ, <ἐὰν> τοὺς ζῶντας.
<διακοσίας> Lipsius   τριακοσίας Hermann: τριάκοντα MS.   <ἐὰν> x2 Sauppe.
KAKEGORIAS DIKE ['private suit for speaking ill']: if someone speaks ill of any dead person, even if he in turn is ill spoken of by the sons of the deceased, if he is condemned he has to pay five hundred drachmae:

two hundred to the state and three hundred to the private individual. But Hyperides says, in the speech against Dorotheus, that the fine would be of one thousand drachmae, if the victims of speaking ill are dead, and of five hundred drachmae if the victims are still alive.

A personal offence could be either physical or verbal, and Solon established by law a protection against verbal offences, that is against slander. The dispositions concerning this topic were intended to prevent attacks on the reputation of the dead (frs. 32a and 33a), who were now protected by a many-sided shelter, which combined religious (ὅσιον τοὺς μεθεστῶτας ἱεροὺς νομίζειν) and ethical (δίκαιον ἀπέχεσθαι τῶν οὐχ ὑπαρχόντων) implications, as stated in fr. 32a. Plutarch adds also a pragmatic factor (πολιτικὸν ἀφαιρεῖν τῆς ἔχθρας τὸ ἀίδιον): by forbidding speaking ill against the dead, he also intended to put an end to previous enmities, thus preventing them from continuing to affect the community. In fr. 32c, Demosthenes quotes the law on *hybris* (for which see fr. 30/1) and on speaking ill in close connection. See Freeman, *The Work and Life of Solon*, 26–7; MacDowell, *Demosthenes, Against Meidias*, 250.

According to fr. 32a, the law defined, with regard to the living, the moments and places where the *kakegoria* was punishable: sanctuaries, courts, public offices and games, certainly because of the fact that the public visibility of slander would harm the victim more severely. As for the dead, Solon's law forbade 'speaking ill in public' (ἀγορεύειν), which means that it could involve any place. Despite the argumentation of Lysias' speech (fr. 32b), it is probable that the *dike kakegorias* was applicable only when certain expressions or words (τὰ ἀπόρρητα, 'forbidden words') were uttered in such circumstances. The exact nature of the verbal offences punished by Solon's law is not known, but they probably corresponded to (or at least included) the kind of expressions mentioned by Lysias: 'murderer' (ἀνδροφόνος), 'father-beater' (πατραλοία), 'mother-beater' (μητραλοία), and 'someone who has thrown away his shield' (ἀποβεβληκέναι τὴν ἀσπίδα), as a public sign of cowardice. MacDowell, *L.C.A.* 127, finds it plausible that the specifications of slander mentioned in fr. 32b may be a sign that Solon's law concerning speaking ill of the living had been superseded. See also Wallace, 'The Athenian Law against Slander', *Symposion 1993* (*AGR* x 1994), 115–6. Archilochus composed a poem (fr. 5 West) in which he mocks the idea of having left his shield in the hands of the enemy (τί μοι μέλει ἀσπὶς ἐκείνη;), because, by acting like this, he managed to save his life (ἐξεσάωσα), while keeping the possibility of buying an even better shield in the future (ἐξαῦτις κτήσομαι οὐ κακίω).

In fr. 32a Plutarch says that, for a crime of *kakegoria* against a living person, Solon prescribed a fine of five drachmae, of which three should be paid to the victim of the slander (τῷ ἰδιώτῃ) and the two remaining to the public treasury (εἰς τὸ δημόσιον). Lysias (fr. 32b) speaks of a penalty of five hundred drachmae, but does not state how they should be paid. According to Demetrius of Phalerum, five drachmae were equivalent to one ox (fr. 92 = Plut. *Sol.* 23. iii), a price that Plutarch considers very low in comparison with the prices of his own time. If the penalty of five hundred drachmae is accepeted as equivalent to five drachmae in the time of Solon, and if the same proportion for dividing the fine was kept in the future, then three hundred drachmae were destined to the individual (or to his family, if the victim of speaking ill was dead already) and two hundred to the state, as implied by fr. 33b (although the text is disputed). Even if the suit is private (a *dike kakegorias*), the public interest resulting from the necessity of avoiding the effects of slander within the whole community justifies that the state should receive two fifths of the fine. See MacDowell, *L.C.A.* 126-9; Ruschenbusch, *Gesetzeswerk*, 64-5.

For the principle that one should not speak ill of the dead cf. e.g. Hom. *Od.* XXII. 412, Eur. *Phoen.* 1663, Dem. XL. *Boeotus ii.* 49, Diog. Laert. I. 70 (Chilon of Sparta). Sourvinou-Inwood, *'Reading' Greek Death*, 369–72, accepts fr. 32a as a Solonian law reflecting new attitudes towards death. J. H. Blok, in Blok & Lardinois (edd.), *Solon of Athens*, 218, wonders whether it is a 'social prescription' rather than a law. A. H. Sommerstein conjectured ten dr. in the time of Solon for speaking ill of the dead ('Comedy and the Unspeakable', in *Law, Rhetoric and Comedy . . . D. M. MacDowell*, 205–22 at 217 n. 13).

Compensation for damage

Fr. 34a: Lys. X. *Theomnestus i.* 19 (part of **fr. 23c**)
(15 καί μοι ἀνάγνωθι τούτους τοὺς νόμους τοὺς Σόλωνος τοὺς παλαιούς.)
"οἰκῆος καὶ δουλῆς τὴν βλάβην εἶναι ὀφείλειν". πρόσεχε τὸν νοῦν· . . . τὸ δὲ οἰκῆος θεράποντος.
δούλης τὴν βλάβην Schott: βλάβης τὴν δούλην MSS.   εἶναι deleted Taylor   καὶ βλάβης . . . εἶναι obelised Ruschenbusch.
(15 And read for me these ancient laws of Solon.)
'It shall be permitted to owe the damage of a houseman and a female slave' . . . Give your attention to this . . . 'of a houseman' is of a domestic slave.

Fr. 34b: Ammon. *Diff.* 345
<οἰκότριψ> καὶ <οἰκέτης> διαφέρει. οἰκότριψ μὲν γὰρ ὁ ἐν τῇ οἰκίᾳ διατρεφόμενος ὃν ἡμεῖς θρεπτὸν καλοῦμεν, οἰκέτης δὲ καὶ δοῦλος ὁ ὠνητός. παρὰ δὲ Σόλωνι ἐν τοῖς ἄξοσιν οἰκεὺς κέκληται ὁ οἰκότριψ.
ἄξοσιν Stephanus: ἄζωσιν MSS.
Oikotrips and *oiketes* have different meanings. *Oikotrips* is in fact the slave bred in the house, whom we call *threptos*; *oiketes* is the bought slave. In the *axones* of Solon, an *oikotrips* is called *oikeus*.

Fr. 34/c (fr. 119 Ruschenbusch): Hyp. III. *Athenogenes* 21
διαιτητὴς ἡμῖν γενέσθω ὁ νόμος, ὃν οὐχ οἱ ἐρῶντε[ς ο]ὐδ' οἱ ἐπιβουλεύοντες τοῖς [ἀλλο]τρίοις ἔθεσαν, ἀλλ' ὁ δημοτικώτα[τος] Σόλων· ὃς εἰδὼς ὅτι πολλαὶ ὠναὶ [ποιοῦν]ται ἐν τῇ πόλει ἔθηκε

νόμον δίκαι[ον, ὡς] παρὰ πάντων ὁμολογ[ε]ῖται, τὰς ζη[μίας ἃς ἂν] ἐργάσωνται οἱ οἰκέται, καὶ τὰ ἀ[ναλώμ]ατα διαλύειν τὸν δεσπότην παρ' ᾧ [ἂν ἐργάσ]ωνται οἱ οἰκέται, εἰκότως, καὶ γὰρ ἐάν τι ἀγ]αθὸν πράξῃ ἢ ἐργασίαν εὕρ[ῃ] ὁ ο[ἰκέτης το]ῦ κεκτημένου αὐτὸν γ[ίγ]νετ[αι. σὺ δὲ τὸν] νόμον ἀφεὶς περὶ συνθ[ήκων παραβαινο]μένων διαλέγῃ (**fr. 99** follows).

[ποιοῦν]ται Jensen (*addenda*), approved Whitehead: [γί(γ)νον]ται Weil ἀ[δικήμ]ατα Wyse, Jensen originally, approved Whitehead: ἀ[ναλώμ]ατα Revillout, Jensen (*addenda*).

Let the law be our arbitrator which was made neither by lovers nor by men who scheme for what is not their own, but by the most democratic Solon. He knew that there are many sales in the city, and enacted a law agreed by all to be just, that the crimes perpetrated by slaves and their offences shall be discharged by the owner for whom they work. And this is fair, for, if a slave achieves anything good or devises business, that is credited to the man who owns him. But you are neglecting the law and talking about a broken contract.

Fr. 35: Plut. *Sol.* 24. iii
ἔγραψε δὲ καὶ βλάβης τετραπόδων νόμον, ἐν ᾧ καὶ κύνα δάκνοντα παραδοῦναι κελεύει κλοιῷ τριπήχει δεδεμένον· τὸ μὲν ἐνθύμημα χάριεν πρὸς ἀσφάλειαν.

He also wrote a law concerning damage caused by animals, in which he prescribed that a dog which had bitten anyone must be surrendered tied up with a leash three cubits long. This was a clever device for promoting safety.

The text of fr. 34a has been the object of much dispute, dealing with the nature of the damage (*blabe*) inflicted and the kind of compensation that ought to be paid to (or by) the owner of the slaves. For detailed *app. crit.* see Ruschenbusch, *Gesetzeswerk*, 43 and 69, and Carey's Oxford Text. The archaic wording used in fr. 34a and the reference to the *axones* in fr. 34b both confirm that this disposition is Solonian. As rendered here, fr. 34a suggests that the owner of a slave (either man or woman) is responsible for the damage caused by that slave. Fr. 34b implies that in the *axones* the term *oikeus* was equivalent to οἰκότριψ, in the sense of a 'slave bred in the house'. In fr. 34/c a law attributed generally to Solon states that a loss or damage attributed to a slave should be compensated by the owner of the slave at the time when the wrong was committed. Even if the text is disputed, the word used here to define the slave is probably οἰκέτης, the same term used in fr. 34b to denote a 'bought slave'. Taken together, those dispositions would suggest that Solon intended to define primarily the obligations of a *kyrios* towards slaves reared at home. In *Nomoi*, 116, Ruschenbusch considered fr. 34/c not Solonian, but fr. 34b, added in Ruschenbusch, *Gesetzeswerk*, together with fr. 34a, makes the authenticity of that disposition less improbable. See also Harrison, *L.A.* i. 173–4; MacDowell, *L.C.A.* 81.

Fr. 35 is probably part of wider legislation on damage caused by animals (βλάβης τετραπόδων νόμος). The law transmitted by Plutarch deals more directly with dangerous dogs, and he interprets the disposition as a preventive measure for promoting security. The existence of the kind of practice described in this legislation is known from other sources (e.g. Eupolis fr. 172. 16 Kassel & Austin; Ar. *Vesp.* 894–7; Xen. *Hell.* II. iv. 41, III. iii. 11) and the law is generally accepted as Solonian. Gagarin, *Early Greek Law*, 64–5 n. 58, envisages the possibility that it may be apocryphal, although he is more interested in stressing the fact that it belongs to the set of laws which, like those of Zaleucus and Charondas, 'fix precise penalties for certain offenses'. The main difficulty with this disposition lies in the interpretation of κλοιός, understood either as a wooden dog-collar that prevented the animal from biting, or as a kind of fetter intended to control the movements of the dog. See Manfredini & Piccirilli, *Plutarco. La vita di Solone*^{5}, 252. In their translation of this passage, Dillon & Garland, *Ancient Greece: Social and Historical Documents*, 82, suggest that παραδοῦναι implies 'to deliver the dog to the victim', but Plutarch is more plausible in suggesting the preventive effect of the device. I. Calero Secall, 'Plutarco y su interpretación de leyes griegas concernientes a la familia y propiedad', in Ferreira *et al.* (edd.), *Nomos, Kosmos and Dike in Plutarch*, 62–3, thinks instead that Plutarch misunderstood the law and that παραδοῦναι is to be interpreted as the obligation to 'deliver the dog to the victim', as a kind of *actio noxalis*. It is however bizarre to perceive the delivering of a ferocious dog to the victim of the biting as a proper pecuniary compensation. There is however the possibility that the intention would be to allow the victim the satisfaction of personally having the dog destroyed.

Enforcement of property rights

Fr. 36a: Schol. Hom. *Il.* XXI. 282
ΕΡΧΘΕΝΤ' ΕΝ ΜΕΓΑΛΩΙ· . . . Κράτης "εἰλθέντ' ἐν μεγάλῳ"· εἴλλειν γάρ φησιν εἶναι τὸ εἴργειν, ὥστε τὴν τῆς κωλύσεως δίκην ἐξούλης καλεῖσθαι· καὶ παρατίθεται Σόλωνος ἐν ε΄ ἄξονι· "ΕΞΟΥΛΗΣ· ἐάν τις ἐξείλλῃ, ὧν ἄν τι<ς> δίκην νικήσῃ, ὁπόσου ἂν ἄξιον ᾖ, εἰς δημόσιον ὀφείλειν καὶ τῷ ἰδιώτῃ, ἑκατέρῳ ἴσον".
ε΄ ἄξονι: ἐννεάξονι MS.   τι<ς> Helck.   ὀφείλειν Ruschenbusch: ὀφλάνει MS.
ERCHTHENT' EN MEGALOI = ['pent in the great']: . . . Crates reads (?) *eilthent' en megaloi* [= 'shut in the great']. *Eillein* ['shut in'] is here equivalent to *eirgein* ['enclose'], just as the private indictment against obstruction is called *dike exoules*. The disposition is presented also in Solon's fifth *axon*: '*EXOULES*: if someone obstructs the access to the property that anybody has won by a lawsuit, then the same amount is owed to the state and to the private individual, the same to each of them'.

Fr. 36b: *P. Oxy.* ii. 221 (Schol. Hom. *Il.*) col. xiv. 9–16 (*ad Il.* XXI. 282, ἐρχθέντ' ἐν μεγάλῳ)
Κράτης [δὲ "εἰλθέ]ντα", ἵν' ᾖ ἐρχθέντα· καὶ τὴν [ἐξούλης] δίκην ἐντεῦθεν· ἐπιτίθη[σι δὲ καὶ Σ]όλωνος ἐκ ε΄ ἄξονος· "ΕΞΟΥ[ΛΗΣ· ἐάν τι]ς ἐξείλλῃ, ὧν ἄν <τις> δίκην [νικήσῃ, ὁπόσ]ου ἂν ἄξιον ᾖ, εἰς δημόσι[ον ὀφείλε]ιν καὶ τῷ ἰδιώτῃ, ἑκατέρῳ [ἴσον"].
ἐπιτίθησι Ruschenbusch: ἐκτίθησι pap.   <τις> Ruschenbusch.   ὁπόσ]ου Ruschenbusch: ὅσ]ου P. Oxy.   ὀφείλε]ιν Ruschenbusch: ὀφλε]ῖν P. Oxy.

Crates reads (?) *eilthenta* ['shut in'] as equivalent to *erchthenta* ['pent']: just like the *dike exoules* here. The disposition is presented also in Solon's fifth *axon*: 'EXOULES: if someone obstructs the access to the property that anyone has won by a lawsuit, then whatever it is worth is owed to the state and to the private individual, the same to each of them'.

This disposition has a procedural nature and is intended to create conditions for the execution of a judgment, one of the areas that presented difficulties in legal practice. The use of a *dike exoules* depended on certain conditions, which seem to be present already in Solon's legislation: first, the existence of a previous court decision that had adjudicated to the plaintiff the rights to the property in dispute (ὧν ἄν τις δίκην νικήσῃ); besides this, it was also necessary that a previous attempt to claim those rights over the property had not succeeded (ἐάν τις ἐξίλλῃ). By bringing a *dike exoules*, the plaintiff would turn into a kind of state's agent, and in consequence the defendant was accused of harming not only the private person but also the whole citizen body. Because of this, the amount of the property in dispute (ὁπόσου ἂν ἄξιον ᾖ) had to be paid double: one share to the individual plaintiff and another to the public treasury. On the *dike exoules*, see Harrison, *L.A.* i. 217–21; MacDowell, *L.C.A.* 153–4; Gagarin, *Early Greek Law*, 74; Todd, *The Shape of Athenian Law*, 144–5. M. Gagarin, 'Legal Procedure in Solon's Laws', in Blok & Lardinois (edd.), *Solon of Athens*, 265–6, maintains that the *dike exoules* was a procedural innovation, through which Solon aimed at strengthening the role of individual litigants in a legal process.

The explicit reference to the fifth *axon* is a strong argument in support of the Solonian origin of the law. Ruschenbusch, *Nomoi*, 52 n. 138, identifies the Crates of frs. 36a–b as Crates from Athens (first century B.C.); Stroud, *Axones and Kyrbeis*, 29, argues instead that the author of this commentary on *Il.* XXI. 282 is Crates of Pergamum (second century B.C.).

OFFENCES AGAINST THE COMMUNITY

Tyranny / overthrowing the constitution

See in general M. Ostwald, 'The Athenian Legislation Against Tyranny and Subversion', *TAPA* lxxxvi 1955, 103–28; Rhodes, *Comm. Ath. Pol.*, 156, 220–3.

Fr. 37a: *Ath. Pol.* 16. x
ἦσαν δὲ καὶ τοῖς Ἀθηναίοις οἱ περὶ τῶν τυράννων νόμοι πρᾶοι κατ' ἐκείνους τοὺς καιροὺς οἵ τε ἄλλοι καὶ δὴ καὶ ὁ μάλιστα καθήκων πρὸς τῆς τυραννίδος <κατάστασιν>. νόμος γὰρ αὐτοῖς ἦν ὅδε· "θέσμια τάδε Ἀθηναίων καὶ πάτρια· ἐάν τινες τυραννεῖν ἐπανιστῶνται ἐπὶ τυραννίδι ἢ συγκαθιστῇ τὴν τυραννίδα, ἄτιμον εἶναι καὶ αὐτὸν καὶ γένος."
<κατάστασιν> Kaibel & Wilamowitz. τυραννεῖν deleted and ἐπὶ τυραννίδι retained N. C. Conomis, Ἑλληνικά xvi 1958–9, 10, cf. *Agora* xvi 73; τυραννεῖν retained and ἐπὶ τυραννίδι deleted Kenyon, cf. decree *ap.* Andoc. I. *Myst.* 97; ἐπὶ τυραννίδι transposed to after πάτρια Heichelheim, in Balogh with Heichelheim, *Political Refugees in Ancient Greece*, 91 n. 20. <τις> συγκαθιστῇ Herwerden & Leeuwen, and other suggestions have been made, but perhaps the author is here giving excerpts from a fuller text.
At those times [*sc.* those of Pisistratus] the Athenians' laws about tyrants were mild in general, and particularly the one about the establishment of the tyranny. For their law was as follows: 'These are ordinances and traditions of the Athenians: if any men rise up for a tyranny or one joins in establishing the tyranny, both he and his issue shall be *atimoi*.'

Fr. 37b: *Ath. Pol.* 8. iv
βουλὴν . . . τὴν δὲ τῶν Ἀρεοπαγιτῶν ἔταξεν . . . τοὺς ἐπὶ καταλύσει τοῦ δήμου συνισταμένους ἔκρινεν, Σόλωνος θέντος νόμον εἰσαγγελίας περὶ αὐτῶν.
The council . . . of the Areopagites he appointed . . . it judged those who combined for the overthrow of the *demos*, Solon having enacted the law of *eisangelia* about them.

Fr. 37c: Plut. *Comp. Sol. Publ.* 2. iv
τὸ δὲ μισοτύραννον ἐν τῷ Ποπλικόλᾳ σφοδρότερον· εἰ γάρ τις ἐπιχειροίη τυραννεῖν, ὁ μὲν ἁλόντι τὴν δίκην ἐπιτίθησιν, ὁ δὲ καὶ πρὸ τῆς κρίσεως ἀνελεῖν δίδωσι.
The hostility to tyranny of Publicola was sterner: for if any one attempted to become tyrant, the one [*sc.* Solon] prescribed justice when he was convicted, but the other [*sc.* Publicola] allowed men to kill him even before a trial.

Our sources mention a series of laws against setting up a tyranny / overthrowing the *demos* = democratic constitution:

(*a*)   Solon's amnesty law excluded 'those who from the Areopagus ... were in exile for tyranny when this ordinance was revealed' (fr. 22/1).

(*b*)   Solon prescribed *eisangelia* to the Areopagus against such men (fr. 37b).

(*c*)   Fr. 37a is cited to show the mildness of the law in the time of Pisistratus.

(*d*)   Fear of tyranny is said to have been Cleisthenes' reason for introducing ostracism (*Ath. Pol.* 22. iii–iv etc.).

(*e*)   Andoc. I. *Myst.* 95 quotes a law 'on the *stele* in front of the *bouleuterion*' as Solon's law, and §§96–7 contain what purports to be a decree of Demophantus in 410/09 (fr. 94).

(*f*)   This was one of the offences specified in the consolidated *nomos eisangeltikos* of the fourth century (Hyp. IV. *Euxenippus* 7–8, cf. Poll. VIII. 52, *Lex .Rhet. Cant.* εἰσαγγελία [74. 4–19 *Lexica Graeca Minora*]).

(*g*)   A law of Eucrates in 337/6 added to existing clauses the suspension of the Areopagus if a tyranny were established or the democracy overthrown (*IG* ii^3 320).

Although 'tyranny' and 'overthrowing the *demos*' are both used in *g*, from the end of the fifth century the chief threat to the democracy was seen as oligarchy, and the emphasis was on overthrowing the democracy; but before then the chief threat was seen as tyranny, and despite the wording of fr. 37b the focus will have been on that. We believe that the word *demokratia* was coined not long before Aesch. *Supp.* 604, probably of 463; but in any case the formulation 'overthrowing the *demos*' is unlikely before the reforms of Cleisthenes in 508/7. Fr. 22/1 confirms that men were exiled 'for tyranny', probably by the Areopagus, before the archonship of Solon; in fr. 37b *Ath. Pol.* is probably reporting Solon's law but using the language of the author's time rather than the language of the law — but Hansen, *Eisangelia*, 17–19 cf. 56–7, argues that *Ath. Pol.* reflects only contemporary debate, not knowledge of a law of Solon.

In fr. 37a θέσμια ... πάτρια probably signals the reaffirmation of an ancient law: the original can hardly be later than Solon (Ostwald, noting the absence of the term *eisangelia*, supposed it to be a law of Draco; M. Gagarin, 'The Thesmothetai and the Earliest Athenian Tyranny Law', *TAPA* cxi 1981, 71–7, immediately after the affair of Cylon); there are various occasions when it might have been reaffirmed (Ostwald suggested *c.* 510 after the expulsion of Hippias; Gagarin, by Solon), but we can only guess.

Ath. Pol.'s πρᾶοι in fr. 37a is based on a misunderstanding of *atimia*, which originally denoted outlawry but later was used to denote the loss of civic rights; and Plutarch in making

Solon milder than Publicola (fr. 37 c) seems to have been influenced by that: *e* and *g* above both allow offenders to be killed with impunity; cf. the decree, probably a fourth-century reconstruction, against Arthmius of Zelea (Dem. IX. *Phil. iii.* 41–6 and other texts: see fr. 21), which combined *atimos* and *polemios* and which prompted Demosthenes to comment on the different senses of *atimia* and to use the further gloss *echthros*.

Probably there was a law of Solon which allowed the killing of men who attempted to set up a tyranny and provided for *eisangelia* to the Areopagus against those accused of that: cf. what Solon says in his poetry about the fate of a man who becomes tyrant (fr. 33. 5–7 West). *Eisangelia* as known in the fourth century perhaps goes back to Ephialtes' taking such trials from the Areopagus in 462/1 (*Ath. Pol.* 25. i–ii with Rhodes, *Comm. Ath. Pol. ad loc.*, cf. Plut. *Cim.* 15. ii–iii, *Per.* 9. v); but *Ath. Pol.*'s reference to *eisangelia* in fr. 37b may echo the word used by Solon in this connection. Ruschenbusch, *Untersuchungen*, 73–4 = his *Kleine Schriften*, 116–7, suggested that it was the original term for any verbal denunciation to the authorities.

Activist citizenry and political neutrality

Fr. 38a: *Ath. Pol.* 8. v

ὁρῶν δὲ τὴν μὲν πόλιν πολλάκις στασιάζουσαν, τῶν δὲ πολιτῶν ἐνίους διὰ τὴν ῥαθυμίαν ἀγαπῶντας τὸ αὐτόματον, νόμον ἔθηκεν πρὸς αὐτοὺς ἴδιον, ὃς ἂν στασιαζούσης τῆς πόλεως μὴ θῆται τὰ ὅπλα μηδὲ μεθ' ἑτέρων, ἄτιμον εἶναι καὶ τῆς πόλεως μὴ μετέχειν.

Seeing that, while the city was involved frequently in strife, some of the citizens, owing to indifference, were content with what chance would bring them, he enacted a law specifically to deal with them: 'If someone, when the city is facing strife, does not place his arms at the disposal of either side, he shall become *atimos* and shall have no share in the city.'

Fr. 38b: Gell. *N.A.* II. 12. i

In legibus Solonis illis antiquissimis, quae Athenis axibus ligneis incisae sunt quasque latas ab eo Athenienses, ut sempiternae manerent, poenis et religionibus sanxerunt (**fr. 93b**), *legem esse Aristoteles* (**fr. 38a**) *refert scriptam ad hanc sententiam: 'Si ob discordiam dissensionemque seditio atque discessio populi in duas partes fiet et ob eam causam irritatis animis utrimque arma capientur pugnabiturque, tum qui in eo tempore in eoque casu civilis discordiae non alterutrae parti sese adiunxerit, sed solitarius separatusque a communi malo civitatis secesserit, is domo, patria fortunisque omnibus careto, exul extorrisque esto.'*

Among those very old laws of Solon, which were inscribed at Athens on wooden tablets, and which, when he had enacted them, the Athenians made irrevocable by penalties and sacred oaths so that they should last for ever, Aristotle states that there was a law written with this significance: 'If, because of discord and dissension, there arises sedition and strife which produces a division of the people into two parties, and if because of that each side, moved by incensed feelings, decides to take arms and fight, then if anybody, in such a time and situation of civil discord, does not adhere to one of the factions, but chooses to stay by himself and away from the common affliction of the state, let him be deprived of his house, country and all his properties, and be exiled and banished.'

Fr. 38c: Cic. *Att.* X. 1. ii
Ego vero Solonis ... legem neglegam, qui capite sanxit, si quis in seditione non alterius utrius partis fuisset.
I shall in fact disregard ... a law of Solon, which made it a capital offence for someone not to adhere to either side in times of strife.

Fr. 38d: Plut. *Sol.* 20. i
τῶν δ' ἄλλων αὐτοῦ νόμων ἴδιος μὲν μάλιστα καὶ παράδοξος ὁ κελεύων ἄτιμον εἶναι τὸν ἐν στάσει μηδετέρας μερίδος γενόμενον. βούλεται δ' ὡς ἔοικε μὴ ἀπαθῶς μηδ' ἀναισθήτως ἔχειν πρὸς τὸ κοινόν, ἐν ἀσφαλεῖ τιθέμενον τὰ οἰκεῖα καὶ τῷ μὴ συναλγεῖν μηδὲ συννοσεῖν τῇ πατρίδι καλλωπιζόμενον, ἀλλ' αὐτόθεν τοῖς τὰ βελτίω καὶ δικαιότερα πράττουσι προσθέμενον συγκινδυνεύειν καὶ βοηθεῖν μᾶλλον ἢ περιμένειν ἀκινδύνως τὰ τῶν κρατούντων.
Among his other laws, particularly peculiar and surprising is the one prescribing that 'he who in strife does not take either side shall become *atimos*'. It seems that the goal is to avoid apathy and indifference towards common interests, by putting one's private affairs in safety and glorying in not having shared the disgrace and the sickness of the country. On the contrary, they should immediately support the better and more righteous cause, face the same perils and provide assistance, instead of waiting safely for the dispositions of the winners.

Fr. 38e: Plut. *De Sera* 550 c
παραλογώτατον δὲ τὸ τοῦ Σόλωνος, ἄτιμον εἶναι τὸν ἐν στάσει πόλεως μηδετέρᾳ μερίδι προσθέμενον μηδὲ συστασιάσαντα.

Particularly unreasonable is [the law] of Solon prescribing that 'he who when the city is in strife does not attach himself to or strive with either side shall become *atimos*'.

Fr. 38f: Plut. *Praec. Ger. Reip.* 823 F
ἀπορήσει δὲ καὶ θαυμάσει τί παθὼν ἐκεῖνος ὁ ἀνὴρ ἔγραψεν ἄτιμον εἶναι τὸν ἐν στάσει πόλεως μηδετέροις προσθέμενον.
It will cause difficulty (?) and surprise to understand what induced him to decree that 'he who when the city is in strife does not attach himself to either side shall become *atimos*'.

Fr. 38g: Diog. Laert. I. 58
καὶ πρῶτος τὴν συναγωγὴν τῶν ἐννέα ἀρχόντων ἐποίησεν εἰς τὸ συνειπεῖν, ὡς Ἀπολλόδωρός φησιν ἐν δευτέρῳ Περὶ νομοθετῶν. ἀλλὰ καὶ τῆς στάσεως γενομένης οὔτε μετὰ τῶν ἐξ ἄστεως, οὔτε μετὰ τῶν πεδιέων, ἀλλ' οὐδὲ μετὰ τῶν παράλων ἐτάχθη.
Solon was the first to bring together the nine archons, so that they could talk with each other, as Apollodorus states in the second book of *On Legislators*. When the civil strife came, he did not adhere to those of the city, or to those of the plain, or to those of the coast.

*Fr. 38h: Alexander of Aphrodisias *in Arist. Top.* II. 109 B 13 (*Comm. in Arist. Graeca* II. ii, p. 139. 33)
ὁμοίως καὶ τὸ "στάσεως οὐ μετέχει" διττόν· ἢ γὰρ ὅτι <οὐ> χρὴ νοσούσῃ τῇ πατρίδι συννοσεῖν, καθὼς ἠξίου Σόλων· πολιτικοῦ γὰρ τὸ μὴ ἀπάγειν αὐτὸν τῆς κοινῆς συμφορᾶς καὶ οὕτως ἂν καταπαῦσαί τι τῆς στάσεως ἴσως, εἰ φαίνοιτο συνάγων καὶ ἐν τοῖς αὐτοῖς ὤν· ἢ πάλιν ὅτι κατάρχειν οὐ χρὴ τῆς στάσεως καὶ ἡγεμόνα γίνεσθαι.
<οὐ> Wallies.

The same ambiguity occurs with the expression 'does not take part in strife': in fact, it may imply that it is not necessary to suffer together with a suffering country, just as Solon has required: it is befitting to a citizen not to withdraw himself from the common misfortune, and so to contribute to putting an end to what causes the strife, if he makes it clear that he joins the group and is present among the others; but it may also imply that it is not necessary to lead the strife and become a leader.

*Fr. 38i: Nicephorus Gregoras, *Historia Byzantina* IX. 7 (i, p. 427. 4 Schopen) (*Corpus Scriptorum Historiae Byzantinae* XXV. i)
εἰ δὲ καὶ ἡμεῖς τῷ γηραιῷ κατὰ τὸ εἰκὸς προσκείμενοι βασιλεῖ ῥοθίοις τισὶν ἐνετύχομεν τοῦ χειμῶνος ἐκείνου, καινὸν οὐδέν. οὔτε γὰρ δίκαιον ἦν, ἡμᾶς μηδεμιᾷ προσκεῖσθαι μερίδι, τοῦ Σόλωνος τοῦτο προτρέποντος· καὶ πρός γε τῶν εἰκότων αὖ, τοῦ ποιμένος παταχθέντος δεινὰ παθεῖν κατὰ τὸ ἀνάλογον ἅπαν τὸ ποίμνιον.
And if we also, when adhering to the aged ruler, encountered as would be likely some of the waves of his storm, that would constitute no novelty. Neither would it be just for us to adhere to neither side, as Solon urged; and in addition it would again be likely that if the shepherd were stricken the whole herd would suffer harm in the same way.

*Fr. 38j: Cantacuzenus, *Historia* IV. 13 (iii, p. 87 Schopen) (*Corpus Scriptorum Historiae Byzantinae* II. iii)
καὶ τῶν Λυκούργου νόμων πάντων ἀμελήσαντες, ἑνὸς μόνου τῶν Σόλωνος ἐξέχονται τοῦ Ἀθηναίου ἀκριβῶς, ὃς ἀτίμους ποιεῖ τῶν πολιτῶν τοὺς ἐν στάσει μηδεμιᾷ μερίδι προσκειμένους.
And, neglecting all the laws of Lycurgus, they cling punctiliously to one single law of Solon the Athenian, who makes *atimoi* those citizens who, in strife, involve themselves with neither side.

*Fr. 38k: Plut. *De Soll. An.* 965 E
Ruschenbusch, *Gesetzeswerk* 76, presents part of this as a 'new' fragment, but the text quoted there has no obvious relevance to the discussion. The relevant passage occurs a few lines before and is here presented as fr. 38/l.

†Fr. 38/l: Plut. *De Soll. An.* 965 D
πάλαι γὰρ ὁ Σόλωνος ἐκλέλοιπε νόμος, τοὺς ἐν στάσει μηδετέρῳ μέρει προσγενομένους κολάζων.
Solon's law has long fallen into disuse which punished those who in strife gave support to neither side.

†Fr. 38/m: Lysias XXXI. *Philon* 27
ἀκούω δ' αὐτὸν λέγειν ὡς, εἴ τι ἦν ἀδίκημα τὸ μὴ παραγενέσθαι ἐν ἐκείνῳ τῷ καιρῷ, νόμος ἂν ἔκειτο περὶ αὐτοῦ διαρρήδην, ὥσπερ καὶ περὶ τῶν ἄλλων ἀδικημάτων. οὐ γὰρ οἴεται ὑμᾶς γνώσεσθαι

ὅτι διὰ τὸ μέγεθος τοῦ ἀδικήματος οὐδεὶς περὶ αὐτοῦ ἐγράφη νόμος. τίς γὰρ ἄν ποτε ῥήτωρ ἐνεθυμήθη ἢ νομοθέτης ἤλπισεν ἁμαρτήσεσθαί τινα τῶν πολιτῶν τοσαύτην ἁμαρτίαν;
People tell me that he argues that, if it was a crime not to be present at that time of emergency, there should be a law dealing explicitly with that, as happens with all the other crimes. He does not expect you to understand that the magnitude of the crime is the very reason why no law was written concerning this crime. Is there any orator who would have envisaged or legislator who would have expected that any of the citizens could be responsible for such a serious offence?

Among the legislation attributed to Solon the law against political neutrality has attracted a great deal of attention on the part of modern scholars, because it apparently contradicts the conciliatory nature of the legislator. For a conspectus of the main trends of analysis in what concerns this regulation see Walter, *An der Polis teilhaben*, 195–6 n. 104. In fact, this law already had a reputation for strangeness in antiquity, as is clearly stated by Plutarch (frs. 38d–f). Against the authenticity of the law, see K. von Fritz, 'Nochmals das solonische Gesetz gegen Neutralität im Bürgerzwist', *Historia* xxvi 1977, 245–7; E. Gabba, 'Da qualche considerazione generale al caso della legge sull'impossibile neutralità (*AP* 8.5)', in Maddoli (ed.), *L'Athenaion Politeia di Aristotele, 1891-1991*, 101–11. E. David, 'Solon, Neutrality and Partisan Literature of Late Fifth-Century Athens', *MH* xli 1984, 129–38, suggests that the law was invented within Theramenes' circle; C. Pecorella Longo, 'Sulla legge "soloniana" contro la neutralità', *Historia* xxxvii 1988, 374–9, thinks that the law was forged probably between 410 and 403 by the oligarchic faction, but not necessarily by Theramenes' partisans.

One factor which has to be taken into account is the meaning that should be attributed to the term *stasis*. Ruschenbusch, *Nomoi*, 83 n. on frs. 38a–g, states that the primitive meaning of *stasiazein* was to fight against an external enemy ('sich in einem Kriege gegen einen äußeren Feind befinden'). With this interpretation the difficulties would be eliminated because Solon's intent would be simply to stimulate his fellow citizens to unite against an external threat. In the same note, Ruschenbusch nevertheless evokes the sole passage, in his poetry, where Solon uses this term (fr. 4. 19 West: στάσιν ἔμφυλον). The context where this expression occurs clearly favours, by contrast, the meaning 'internal agitation' or 'civil war', in the sense that the menace that the city was then facing was a direct consequence of the citizens' behaviour, not corresponding to an external danger. Theognis (51 West) implies also that *stasis* is internal strife. At any rate, in Ruschenbusch, *Gesetzeswerk*, 76, all the testimonies concerning this disposition are taken to be non-Solonian ('alle Stücke sind ohne eigenständigen Wert').

In its essentials, fr. 38a (*Ath. Pol.* 8. v) is in accordance with Plutarch's testimony, although it refers to the idea of collaborating actively in a moment of *stasis* with the expression θῆται τὰ ὅπλα, which has sometimes been interpreted as a legal term used in contexts related to the practice of civic rights, but that possibility is not always clearly supported by the texts. Basically, the expression means 'rest arms, i.e. halt, with arms in an easy position but ready for action' (LSJ τίθημι, A. II). Therefore θῆται τὰ ὅπλα should be understood in the sense of assuming a position, but not necessarily with the obligation of taking up arms, although the military inspiration of the metaphor seems undeniable. See J. Goldstein, 'Solon's Law for an Activist Citizenry', *Historia* xxi 1972, 543–5; R. Develin, 'Solon's Law on *Stasis*', *Historia* xxvi 1977, 507–8; Rhodes, *Comm. Ath. Pol.* 157-8. P. E. van 'T Wout, 'Solon's Law on *Stasis*: Promoting Active Neutrality', *CQ*[2] lx 2010, 289–301, maintains that, according to *Ath. Pol.*, the law on *stasis* advocates neutrality, instead of penalising it, but the argumentation is not convincing. The same can be said about W. Schmitz, 'Athen — Eine wehrhafte Demokratie? Überlegungen zum Stasisgesetz Solons und zum Ostrakismos', *Klio* xciii 2011, 23–51, who argues that this law can be interpreted as an appeal to participate in the voting process and not to take up arms in a context of civil strife.

It is possible that the expression θῆται τὰ ὅπλα was already present in the original version of Solon's law, because he seems to have some kind of predilection for the use of figurative language, visible, for example, in the way he resorted to the term *seisachtheia* ('shaking-off of burdens') to name the bulk of his emergency measures (cf. Plut. *Sol.* 15. ii and commentary on fr. 69c). It is an ingenuous suggestion of B. Lavagnini, 'Solone e il voto obbligatorio', *RFIC*[3] xxv 1947, 81–93 at 92–3, that the way Plutarch (*Sol.* 30. vii) describes Solon's reaction to Pisistratus' first coup somehow echoes the law under discussion. The author of *Ath. Pol.* is more self-restrained (*Ath. Pol.* 14. ii); the episode is amplified in Diodorus (IX. 20. i), Aelian (VIII. 16) and Diogenes Laertius (I. 49–50), who presents the more romantic version. Even taking into account the risk of exaggeration, there are not enough reasons to disregard the whole episode as a simple forgery. On this, see Leão, 'A *Sophos* in Arms: Plutarch and the Tradition of Solon's Opposition to the Tyranny of Peisistratus', in Ferreira *et al.* (edd.), *Philosophy in Society*, 129–38.

According to fr. 38a, Solon prescribed that anyone who had remained neutral in civil strife should be punished with *atimia* (ἄτιμον εἶναι). Plutarch agrees on this essential point, but does not specify that the *atimos* would lose the right of participating in the life of the *polis* (καὶ τῆς πόλεως μὴ μετέχειν). This supplementary element may not be innocuous, and its interpretation derives ultimately from the way *atimia* is understood. During the sixth and the first part of the fifth century, *atimia* corresponded probably to a state of outlawry, according to which the *atimos* could suffer maltreatment, lose his property or even be killed with impunity (cf. on fr. 37). The penalty mentioned in fr. 38a and implied by the law of Solon would correspond then to the primitive and harsher version of *atimia*, applicable to crimes of their extreme gravity, which would put in danger the safety of the community as a whole, as happened with cases of high treason (see frs. 21 and 37a–c). Even so, there still remains the problem of how to interpret the expression καὶ τῆς πόλεως μὴ μετέχειν. One possibility is to understand this clause as an explanatory note due to the author of the *Ath. Pol.*, in order to give the concept of *atimia* a meaning closer to the times of Solon, because in the fourth century *atimia* was somehow milder. If this interpretation is accepted, the implication is that the expression καὶ τῆς πόλεως μὴ μετέχειν was not part of the original law of Solon, simply because it was unnecessary, since this sanction was already implied in a state of generalized proscription. This is the basic idea sustained by L. Piccirilli, 'Aristotele e l'*atimia* (*Athen. Pol.*, 8.5)', *ASNP*[4] vi 1976, 739–61. At any rate, apart from the severity of *atimia* in the times of Solon, the addition of that comment by the author of the *Ath. Pol.* would give no further guidance to the readers of the fourth century on the implications of the penalty ἄτιμον εἶναι at the beginning of the sixth century, as remarked by Rhodes, *Comm. Ath. Pol.* 158–9. Even so, Plutarch mentions the law against neutrality several times, but does not include the clause presented in fr. 38a.

The testimonies of Cicero and Gellius tend to be devalued by scholars, as mere rhetorical interpretations of Solon's regulation. Cicero gave as equivalent to the penalty stated by Solon (ἄτιμον εἶναι) the Latin words *capite sanxit* (fr. 38c), generally understood as corresponding to a situation of *deminutio capitis* and thereby somehow comparable to the notion of *atimia* by the time the *Ath. Pol.* was written (Lavagnini, RFIC³ xxv 1947, 82–3 n. 1). On the other hand, it is possible that the Latin expression may also imply the death penalty (Piccirilli, ASNP⁴ vi 1976, 756–7), and in that case Cicero could have had an interpretation of *atimia* closer to its original connotation. The same can be said of Gellius, whose testimony is usually seen as rhetorical amplification because of the way he understood ἄτιμον εἶναι: *is domo, patria fortunisque omnibus careto, exsul extorrisque esto* (fr. 38b). In fact, confiscation of property (*fortunisque omnibus careto*) and perpetual exile (*domo, patria . . . careto, exsul, extorrisque esto*) could correspond to some of the harsh consequences of an *atimia* of the proscriptive type. Hence both Cicero and Gellius could be right if they indeed understood *atimia* in a more punitive way and thereby closer to the meaning it had in the time of Solon.

Apart from the difficulty, felt by some scholars, in reconciling the law against political neutrality with the appeasing nature of the legislator, a passage from Lysias' *Against Philon*, a speech written a few years after 403, is the main problem for the authenticity of the law. The fitness of Philon to be included in the council of five hundred is questioned on the grounds that, among other misdeeds, he did not take part in the events of 404/3 that would lead to the deposition of the Thirty and to the democratic restoration. Contrary to that obligation, he chose to flee from Attica, giving no support to any of the parties in conflict (XXXI. *Philon* 14). The plaintiff classifies Philon's behaviour as shameful (fr. 38/m). This seems to imply that there was no law that would punish a citizen who did not take sides in a period of internal strife — an interpretation advanced already by E. Graf, 'Ein angebliches Gesetz Solons', *HG* xlvii 1936, 34–5 — and therefore to cast doubt on the authenticity of the law ascribed to Solon.

Nevertheless one has to consider (*a*) that the plaintiff may not have been acquainted with an ancient law that was perhaps never (or at least only very seldom) activated, or (*b*) that this particular rule may not have been included among the laws revised after the deposition of the Four Hundred. This passage might then not be fatal to the authenticity of the law, even if it is literally interpreted. Besides that, there are still further arguments to be taken into account. First of all, the fact that Lysias' speech *Against Philon* was delivered after the second democratic restoration and that it concerned a case of *dokimasia*, i.e. the verification of the defendant's fitness to occupy a public office. Secondly, that the *dokimasia* in question belongs to the group of cases dealt with after the amnesty of 403 and because of that the plaintiff could not afford to call upon regulations that had been violated during the confusing period of the tyranny of the Thirty. This contingency might be enough to explain why Solon's law (if it was in fact re-enacted) could not be invoked in this specific context (Goldstein, *Historia* xxi 1972, develops this perspective at length). Another, simpler possibility has been advanced already: the law of Solon determined that anyone should be punished with *atimia* if that person, having remained on Attic soil, intended to stay neutral during a time of *stasis*. Philon was accused of having fled from Athens during the period in question, by choosing to live as a metic in another *polis*, an option that, in practical terms, was equivalent to suffering the harsher consequences of being considered *atimos*. Therefore Solon's disposition did not apply in this case and, as the plaintiff stresses, there was not a law designed to punish someone who had voluntarily gone into exile during a period of *stasis*. See Develin, *Historia* xxvi 1977, and also B. Manville, "Solon's Law of Stasis and *Atimia* in Archaic Athens", *TAPA* cx 1980, 213–21. Whatever possibility one may prefer, there are several ways in which the passage from Lysias need not be fatal to the existence of the law under analysis and — most important — to its attribution to Solon. See Rhodes, 'The Reforms and Laws of Solon: An Optimistic View', in Blok & Lardinois (edd.), *Solon of Athens*, 248–60 at 255.

There remains, however, the apparent contradiction between Solon's law against neutrality and his conciliatory nature overall. In fact, although Solon attained the archonship during a period of *stasis*, he repeatedly claims in his poetry to have acted as an impartial mediator between the parties in conflict (e.g. frs. 5. 5–6 and 37. 9–10 West; this may be the explanation for the attitude described in fr. 38g). This balanced outlook was indeed to be expected from someone who came into power in the position of διαλλακτής καὶ νομοθέτης (Plut. *Sol.* 14. iii). But it still cannot be stated of Solon that he is a neutral character, because in other poems he makes it clear that he is aware of the internal tensions of the *polis*, denouncing in a direct and vigorous way the origin of the troubles that afflicted his homeland (e.g. fr. 4. 19, 26–9; fr. 36. 15–17). So the ideas expressed in his poetry cannot be used to prevent the attribution to him of the law against political neutrality.

Fr. 38d, although underlining the peculiar character of the law in question, provided already a very plausible explanation for its creation: to avoid political apathy. In fact, neutrality in civil dissension, motivated either by simple egoism or by careful strategy, may turn into an important factor of social disequilibrium. It makes it possible, for example, that a small (but well organised) group may be able to reach power and dominate political affairs, a scenario that is not so easily fulfilled when citizens decide to fight for their rights and for their identity. It is reasonable to suppose that it was already the popular reaction that had prevented Cylon and his followers from being successful in their attempt to seize power. In Pisistratus' case, his personal bodyguard granted him the basis to implement tyranny in Athens, but he also had to count on the apathy of a part of the citizen body, together with some popular and external support. The whole picture gains coherence if we imagine Solon enacting a law to promote an activist citizenry before starting his voluntary *apodemia*, and fighting to put it into practice (after his return to Athens and not long before dying), by providing his example in the way he foresaw Pisistratus' intentions and reacted against his first coup. V. Bers, 'Solon's Law Forbidding Neutrality and Lysias 31', *Historia* xxiv 1975, 493–8, suggests that this law was among Solon's first dispositions, in order to force his fellow citizens to clarify their political preferences and evaluate the support he could count on. This hypothesis has its attractions, but it also faces a strong difficulty, because with such a decision Solon might have simply deepened internal divisions, when his goal should have been precisely the opposite. The enactment of this law in a later period (immediately before starting his ten-year *apodemia*) would therefore be much more appropriate.

A. Maffi, 'De la Loi de Solon à la loi d'Ilion, ou comment défendre la démocratie', in Bertrand (ed.), *La Violence dans les mondes grec et romain*, 138, is inclined to accept the law as Solonian, and calls attention to the parallel represented by the fourth-century Eretrian law against tyranny and oligarchy, according to which citizens were invited to take arms in order to restore democracy; there were sanctions for those who decided not to get involved. For the Eretrian law see D. Knoepfler, 'Loi d'Érétrie contre la tyrannie et l'oligarchie', *BCH* cxxv 2001, 195–238, and cxxvi 2002, 149–204, cf. *SEG* li 1105. Knoepfler accepts the possibility that this law may have been influenced by Athenian legislation.

PROCEDURE

Limitation of self-help

Fr. 39: Lib. *Decl.* XIX. 7
παρελθὼν γὰρ ἀναγνώσομαι μὲν τοὺς νόμους τοὺς Σόλωνος, οἳ τὸν Ἀθηναῖον Ἀθήνησι κρίνουσιν, οὐκ ἄκριτον ἐγχειρίζουσιν ἀνομίᾳ τυράννων.

Having come forward I shall read you the laws of Solon, which have Athenians judged in Athens, and do not allow hands to be laid on them without a trial, in the lawless manner of tyrants.

In general it is true that the laws of Athens from Draco onwards required recourse to judicial procedure rather than self-help, and at any rate from Solon onwards stipulated either fixed or assessed penalties rather than unlimited revenge. However, certain categories of intentional killing were recognised as lawful (see frs. 19b, 20, 21 and commentary on fr. 37), and by *apagoge* individuals could take certain kinds of offender to the authorities (cf. frs. 16/a–b, 23/1).

Appeal

†Fr. 39/1a: *Ath. Pol.* 9. i
δοκεῖ δὲ τῆς Σόλωνος πολιτείας τρία ταῦτ' εἶναι τὰ δημοτικώτατα· πρῶτον μὲν καὶ μέγιστον τὸ μὴ δανείζειν ἐπὶ τοῖς σώμασιν (**fr. 69a**), ἔπειτα δὲ τὸ ἐξεῖναι τῷ βουλομένῳ τιμωρεῖν ὑπὲρ τῶν ἀδικουμένων (**fr. 40a**), τρίτον δέ, <ᾧ> μάλιστά φασιν ἰσχυκέναι τὸ πλῆθος, ἡ εἰς τὸ δικαστήριον ἔφεσις.
<ᾧ> Herwerden & Leeuwen.

These seem to be the most democratic features of Solon's constitution: first and greatest, that there should be no loans on the security of the person; next, that it should be possible for whoever wished to seek redress for those who were wronged; third, what is said to have done most to strengthen the masses, appeal to the lawcourt.

†**Fr. 39/1b (fr. 138a Ruschenbusch):** Plut. *Sol.* 18. ii–iii
οἱ δὲ λοιποὶ πάντες ἐκαλοῦντο θῆτες, οἷς οὐδεμίαν ἄρχειν ἔδωκεν ἀρχήν, ἀλλὰ τῷ συνεκκλησιάζειν καὶ δικάζειν μόνον μετεῖχον τῆς πολιτείας. ὃ κατ᾽ ἀρχὰς μὲν οὐδέν, ὕστερον δὲ παμμέγεθες ἐφάνη. τὰ γὰρ πλεῖστα τῶν διαφόρων ἐνέπιπτεν εἰς τοὺς δικαστάς· καὶ γὰρ ὅσα ταῖς ἀρχαῖς ἔταξε κρίνειν, ὁμοίως καὶ περὶ ἐκείνων εἰς τὸ δικαστήριον ἐφέσεις ἔδωκε τοῖς βουλομένοις.
All the others [*sc.* not assigned to the higher property classes] were called *thetes*, and he did not give them the right to hold any office, but they shared in the constitution merely by joining in the assembly and by judging. At the beginning this was nothing, but later it was shown to be very great. For most disputes fell to the *dikastai*: for the cases which he appointed the officials to judge, likewise concerning them he granted the right of appeal to the lawcourt to those who wished.

†**Fr. 39/1c (fr. 138b Ruschenbusch):** Plut. *Comp. Sol. Publ.* 2. ii
καὶ τοῖς φεύγουσιν δίκην ἐπικαλεῖσθαι τὸν δῆμον, ὥσπερ ὁ Σόλων τοὺς δικαστάς, ἔδωκε.
And to those defending lawsuits he [*sc.* Publicola] granted the right to invoke the *demos* as Solon did to invoke the *dikastai*.

It appears that before Solon lawsuits were tried either by the Areopagus (or other homicide courts) or by individual officials, and that Solon granted a right of *ephesis* — which in general denotes the removal of a case from one plane to another (Ruschenbusch, 'ἔφεσις — Ein Beitrag zur griechischen Rechtsterminologie', *ZRG* lxxviii 1961, 386–90 = his *Kleine Schriften*, 54–8; Harrison, *L.A.* ii. 72–4), but in this context means 'appeal' (MacDowell, *L.C.A.* 30–2), from the verdict of an individual official to a lawcourt. *Ath. Pol.* and Plutarch both use the word *dikasterion*, but it has often been thought that Solon's court was called *eliaia* (the word was not aspirated in Athens); and, because cognate words in other dialects denote the assembly, that this court was a judicial session of the whole assembly (for these questions see on fr. 23c).

Probably appeals were rare at first but became more frequent over time, until in the end officials stopped giving verdicts where the penalty exceeded a low limit, and instead after a preliminary enquiry (*anakrisis*) referred cases automatically to a *dikasterion* in which they presided: probably in the end a law standardised the new procedure, and that may have happened about the time of Ephialtes' reform in 462/1 (Rhodes, *Comm. Ath. Pol.* 318–9; but H. T. Wade-Gery thought of an abrupt reform by Ephialtes ('Themistokles' Archonship', *BSA* xxxvii 1936/7, 263–70 = his *Essays in Greek History*, 171–9; and *Essays*, 180–200), while R. Sealey ('Ephialtes', *CP* lix 1964, 11–22 at 14–18 = his *Essays in Greek Politics*, 46–52) and MacDowell (*L.C.A.* 32–3) doubted if there was ever a change in the law.

Prosecution by *ho boulomenos*

Fr. 40a: *Ath. Pol.* 9. i (part of **fr. 39/1a**)
δοκεῖ δὲ τῆς Σόλωνος πολιτείας τρία ταῦτ' εἶναι τὰ δημοτικώτατα·
... ἔπειτα δὲ τὸ ἐξεῖναι τῷ βουλομένῳ τιμωρεῖν ὑπὲρ τῶν ἀδικουμένων.

These seem to be the most democratic features of Solon's constitution: ... next, that it should be possible for whoever wished to seek redress for those who were wronged.

Fr. 40b: Plut. *Sol.* 18. vi–vii
ἔτι μέντοι μᾶλλον οἰόμενος δεῖν ἐπαρκεῖν τῇ τῶν πολλῶν ἀσθενείᾳ, παντὶ λαβεῖν δίκην ὑπὲρ τοῦ κακῶς πεπονθότος ἔδωκε· καὶ γὰρ καὶ πληγέντος ἑτέρου καὶ βιασθέντος ἢ βλαβέντος, ἐξῆν τῷ δυναμένῳ καὶ βουλομένῳ γράφεσθαι τὸν ἀδικοῦντα καὶ διώκειν, ὀρθῶς ἐθίζοντος τοῦ νομοθέτου τοὺς πολίτας ὥσπερ ἑνὸς μέρη <σώματος> συναισθάνεσθαι καὶ συναλγεῖν ἀλλήλοις. τούτῳ δὲ τῷ νόμῳ συμφωνοῦντα λόγον αὐτοῦ διαμνημονεύουσιν· ἐρωτηθεὶς γάρ, ὡς ἔοικεν, ἥτις οἰκεῖται κάλλιστα τῶν πόλεων, "ἐκείνην", εἶπεν, "ἐν ᾗ τῶν ἀδικουμένων οὐχ ἧττον οἱ μὴ ἀδικούμενοι προβάλλονται καὶ κολάζουσι τοὺς ἀδικοῦντας".
<σώματος> Coraes.

However, since he thought there was still more need to support the weakness of the many, he gave to all the right to exact justice for the one who suffered harm: for, when another man was struck or subjected to violence or harmed, it was possible for one who was able and willing to indict and prosecute the wrongdoer, since the lawgiver rightly accustomed the citizens like parts of one body to feel and grieve with one another. And it is recorded that he spoke in conformity with this law: for it appears that he was asked which city was best administered, and replied, 'The one in which those who are not wronged no less than those who are wronged denounce and punish the wrongdoers'.

In classical Athens there was a fundamental distinction between *dikai* or private suits, in which only the injured party or his or her closest competent relative might prosecute, and *graphai* or public suits, in which any citizen in full possession of his rights who wished, *ho boulomenos*, might prosecute (cf. *Ath. Pol.* 53. i, 59. ii–iii, v, 67. i; and see Lipsius, *A.R.* 238–46, Harrison, *L.A.* ii. 75–8, and commentary on fr. 30/1). Presumably before Solon prosecution was always limited to the injured party, and the best explanation of this distinction is that prosecution by *ho boulomenos* was first allowed in cases where the injured party was unable for legal or personal reasons to prosecute on his own account (Glotz, *La Solidarité de la famille*, 369–82; Ruschenbusch, *Untersuchungen*, 47–53 = his *Kleine Schriften*, 100–4); but it was needed also in such cases as overthrowing the constitution (fr. 37), where the injured party was the state as a whole, not an individual who could prosecute on his own account.

Proofs

Fr. 41a: Gal. *Linguarum Hippocratis Explicatio, prooemium* (xix. 66 Kuhn)
νομίζω δέ σοι τὰ ὑπὸ Ἀριστοφάνους ἀρκέσειν τὰ ἐκ τῶν Δαιταλέων ὡδέ πως ἔχοντα (fr. 233 Kassel & Austin)·
"πρὸς ταῦτα σὺ λέξον Ὁμηρείους γλώττας, τί καλοῦσι κόρυμβα (Hom. *Il.* IX. 241);"
προβάλλει γὰρ ἐν ἐκείνῳ τῷ δράματι ὁ ἐκ τοῦ δήμου τῶν Δαιταλέων πρεσβύτης τῷ ἀκολάστῳ υἱεῖ πρῶτον μὲν τὰ κόρυμβα τί ποτ' ἐστὶν ἐξηγήσασθαι. μετὰ δὲ τοῦτο·
"τί καλοῦσιν ἀμενηνὰ κάρηνα (Hom. *Od.* X. 521, etc.);"
κἀκεῖνος μέντοι ἀντιπροβάλλει τῶν ἐν τοῖς Σόλωνος ἄξοσιν γλῶτταν εἰς δίκας διαφερούσας ὡδί πως·
"ὁ μὲν οὖν σὸς, ἐμὸς δὲ οὗτος ἀδελφὸς φρασάτω, τί καλοῦσιν ἰδυίους;"
εἶτ' ἐφεξῆς προβάλλει·
"τί ποτέ ἐστιν ὀπυίειν (**fr. 52c**);"
ἐξ ὧν δῆλον ὡς ἡ γλῶττα παλαιόν ἐστιν ὄνομα τῆς συνηθείας ἐκπεπτωκός.
κόρυμβα Poll. II. 109: κόρυβα Galen.   τὸ ὀπυίειν Dindorf: τὸ εὐποιεῖν Galen.

I think what is said by Aristophanes in the *Banqueters* will be sufficient for you, which runs like this:
'In addition to this you must expound Homeric expressions: what do they mean by *korymba* ['high point']?'
For in that drama the old man from the deme Daitaleis challenges his dissolute son first to explain what *korymba* means. After that:
'What do they mean by *amenena karena* ['fleeting heads']?'
He then challenges him in turn on expressions in Solon's *axones* relating to various lawsuits, like this:
'Your son and my brother, tell me, what is meant by *idyioi* ['witnesses']?'
Then he challenges next:
'What is *opyiein* ['marry']?'

From which it is clear that the expression is an ancient name which has fallen out of currency.

Fr. 41b: Phot. ι 36 Theodoridis
ΙΔΥΟΥΣ· τοὺς μάρτυρας· οὕτως Σόλων.
IDYOUS: Witnesses; thus Solon.

Fr. 41c: Eustathius *ad* Hom. *Il.* XVIII. 501 (1158. 23)
ὅτι δὲ ἰδύους καὶ Δράκων καὶ Σόλων τοὺς μάρτυράς φησιν, Αἴλιος Διονύσιος ἱστορεῖ (151 Schwabe).
That both Draco and Solon call witnesses *idyoi*, Aelius Dionysius reports.

Fr. 42: *Anecd. Bekk.* i. 242. 19–22
ΔΟΞΑΣΤΑΙ· κριταί εἰσιν οἱ διαγιγνώσκοντες πότερος εὐορκεῖ τῶν κρινομένων. κελεύει γὰρ Σόλων τὸν ἐγκαλούμενον, ἐπειδὰν μήτε συμβόλαια ἔχῃ μήτε μάρτυρας, ὀμνύναι, καὶ τὸν εὐθύνοντα δὲ ὁμοίως.
DOXASTAI (Antiph. V. *Herodes* 94): They are judges who determine which of the men between whom they are deciding is swearing truly. For Solon orders the man who is accused, when he has no tokens or witnesses, to swear; and the accuser likewise.

Fr. 43: Hesych. α 907 Latte *et al.*
ΑΓΧΙΣΤΙΝΔΗΝ ΟΜΝΥΩΝ· ἐγγὺς τῶν βωμῶν. παρὰ Σόλωνι.
ἀγχιστίνδην Ruschenbusch: ἀγχιστίδην MS., ἀγχιστάδην Latte.
ANCHISTINDEN OMNYON ['swearing in accordance with relationship']: Near the altars. In Solon.

Fr. 44a: Hesych. τ 1298 Latte *et al.*
ΤΡΕΙΣ ΘΕΟΙ· παρὰ Σόλωνι ἐν τοῖς ἄξοσιν ὅρκῳ τέτακται· ἔνιοι κατὰ τὸ Ὁμηρικόν.
TREIS THEOI ['three gods']: In Solon, in the *axones*, appointed for an oath; some explain with reference to Homer (Hom. *Il.* XV. 367: oath by Gaia, Ouranos, Styx).

Fr. 44b: Poll. VIII. 142
τρεῖς θεοὺς ὀμνύναι κελεύει Σόλων· ἱκέσιον, καθάρσιον, ἐξακεστῆρα.

Solon orders one to swear by three gods, of supplication, purification, appeasement.

†Fr. 44/1: [Dem.] XLVI. *Stephanus ii.* 7–8
[*sc.* οἱ νόμοι] ἀκοὴν δ' οὐκ ἐῶσι ζῶντος μαρτυρεῖν, ἀλλὰ τεθνεῶτος, τῶν δὲ ἀδυνάτων καὶ ὑπερορίων ἐκμαρτυρίαν γεγραμμένην ἐν τῷ γραμματείῳ· καὶ ἀπὸ τῆς αὐτῆς ἐπισκήψεως τήν τε μαρτυρίαν καὶ ἐκμαρτυρίαν ἀγωνίζεσθαι ἅμα. . . . ΝΟΜΟΣ· "ἀκοὴν εἶναι μαρτυρεῖν τεθνεῶτος, ἐκμαρτυρίαν δέ ὑπερορίου καὶ ἀδυνάτου."
[*sc.* The laws] do not allow the testimony of a living man by hearsay, but they do allow that of a deceased man; and of those who are incapable or abroad they allow a testimony-statement (*ekmartyria*) written on the tablet, and they allow testimonies and testimony-statements to be tried on the same *episkepsis* at the same time. . . . LAW: 'It is possible to submit testimony by hearsay of a deceased man and a testimony-statement of a man who is abroad or incapable [presumably one who is physically unable to attend the court].'

†Fr. 44/2: [Dem.] XLVI. *Stephanus ii.* 9–10
μαρτυρεῖν γὰρ οἱ νόμοι οὐκ ἐῶσιν αὐτὸν αὑτῷ οὔτ' ἐπὶ ταῖς γράφαις οὔτ' ἐπὶ ταῖς δίκαις οὔτ' ἐν ταῖς εὐθύναις. . . . ΝΟΜΟΣ· "τοῖν ἀντιδίκοιν ἐπάναγκες εἶναι ἀποκρίνασθαι ἀλλήλοις τὸ ἐρωτώμενον, μαρτυρεῖν δὲ μή."
The laws do not allow a man to give testimony himself for himself, whether in *graphai* or *dikai* or *euthynai*. . . . LAW: 'Opposing litigants are required to answer one another's questions [not confirmed in the text of the speech] but not to give testimony.'

Ruschenbusch groups under this heading fragments relating to matters of proof. Frs. 41, 43 and 44 are certainly derived from the *axones*, and fr. 42 appears to be so also.

Idyoi (fr. 41) are witnesses to a will or a solemn agreement. Antiphon, arguing that a homicide case ought to be tried by a different procedure, called on the jurors to take cognisance of the case now but to be *dikastai* of it later, to be *doxastai* of the truth now and judges of it later — and fr. 42 uses a law of Solon to give a mistaken explanation, that *doxastai* are men who have to decide between the rival oaths of contending parties. (*Symbolaia* are tokens, *sc.* of an agreement: see Gauthier, *Symbola*, 72–3, 87.) Fr. 43 refers to the *diomosia* sworn by the next of kin (as defined in Draco's law, fr. 5a) against a man accused of homicide (cf. Antiph. V. *Herodes* 11–12, [Dem.] XLVII. *Evergus & Mnesibulus* 72). Fr. 44 refers to the swearing of an oath by three gods: *Hikesios* (e.g. Aesch. *Supp.* 616), *Katharsios* (e.g. Hdt. I. 44. ii) and *Exakesterios* (Hesych. ε 3525 Latte *et al.* ἐξακεστήριος) are all cult titles of Zeus.

We print as frs. 44/1 and 44/2 two further items which Ruschenbusch, *Gesetzeswerk*, 81–2, considered 'wohl unter die Soloniana gehöhren', concerning admissible forms of testimony: hearsay allowed only from dead men who can no longer give testimony themselves, testimony-statements from men who through illness or absence from Attica cannot attend the court as other witnesses can (fr. 44/1), and litigants not allowed to appear as witnesses in their own cases (fr. 44/2). By the time of Demosthenes written statements of testimony, to which the witnesses were simply asked to assent in court, had replaced statements of testimony made orally in court: oral statements still Lys. XVI. *Mantitheus* 8 (*c.* 390), law requiring written statements [Dem.] XLV. *Stephanus i.* 44 (*c.* 350); change *c.* 390 e.g. Ruschenbusch, 'Drei Beiträge zur öffentlichen Diaita in Athens', in *Symposion 1982* (*AGR* v 1989) 31–40 at 34–5 = his *Kleine Schriften*, 174–5; 370's e.g. Bonner & Smith, *Administration of Justice*, i. 353–62. *Ekmartyriai* from men unable to attend the court will have been comparable to other statements of testimony except that these witnesses will not have been asked to assent to the statement. We do not know what arrangments, if any, were made for such witnesses earlier; and, indeed, we do not know how early the other refinements of the rules about testimony were made. See Lipsius, *A.R.* 886–8, Harrison, *L.A.* ii. 145–7.

Voting

Fr. 45: Schol. Hom. *Il.* XXI. 260
ΨΗΦΙΔΕΣ· οὐχ ὑφ' Ὁμήρου αἱ ψηφῖδες πεποίηνται, ἀλλ' ἔστιν ἡ λέξις Ἀττική· οὕτως γὰρ καὶ ἐν τοῖς ἄξοσιν.
PSEPHIDES ['pebbles']: *Psephides* were not a creation of Homer, but the expression is Athenian: it is found thus in the *axones* also.

Psephides in the *axones* will have been pebbles used for voting, *psephoi* in later Athenian usage. On voting in the Athenian courts see for the fifth century Ar. *Vesp.* 987–94, for the fourth century *Ath. Pol.* 68. ii – 69, with Lipsius, *A.R.* 920–6, Harrison, *L.A.* ii. 164–6. What is not found in Homer is the counting of votes to determine which side has the greater support: J. A. O. Larsen, 'The Origin and Significance of the Counting of Votes', *CP* xliv 1949, 164–81, argued that in Athens it was first used by the Areopagus, and was extended to the people, or at any rate to the *eliaia* (cf. on fr. 23) by Solon; A. L. Boegehold, 'Toward a Study of Athenian Voting Procedure', *Hesperia* xxxii 1963, 366–74, argued that the original purpose was simply to achieve an accurate count and the advantage of a secret ballot was appreciated only later.

Time limit for payment of restitutions and fines

Fr. 46: Hesych. τ 1437 Latte *et al.*
ΤΡΙΤΑΙΑ· παρὰ Σόλωνι μὴ πλείω εἶναι τριταίας τὴν ἔκτισιν (?).
ἔκτισιν Ruschenbusch: κτίστην cod.

TRITAIA ['third day']: In Solon the payment (?) is not to be beyond the third day.

There were time limits for making payments required by a court verdict, though in cases of payment to an individual the two parties could agree to extend the limit: a man who failed to pay on time was *hyperemeros*, and this state of failure was *hyperemeria*: see Lys. XXIII. *Pancleon* 14, [Dem.] XLVII. *Evergus & Mnesibulus* 49–51, Isae fr. 10 Sauppe *ap.* Harp. υ 7 Keaney ὑπερήμεροι. If Ruschenbusch's attractive emendation is right, this fragment shows that Solon required some payments to be made by the third day from the court's verdict. See Lipsius, *A.R.* 944–52, Harrison, *L.A.* ii. 185–90.

FAMILY LAW

Inheritance

*Fr. 47a: *Ath. Pol.* 9. ii
ἔτι δὲ καὶ διὰ τὸ μὴ γεγράφθαι τοὺς νόμους ἁπλῶς μηδὲ σαφῶς, ἀλλ' ὥσπερ ὁ τῶν κλήρων καὶ ἐπικλήρων, ἀνάγκη πολλὰς ἀμφισβητήσεις γίγνεσθαι.
And also because the laws were not written in a simple and a clear way, but like the law on inheritances and heiresses, it results necessarily that many ambiguities arise.

Solon's laws may have seemed obscure or not clear enough to a late-fifth-century audience, much more used to litigation, but this does not imply that Solon wanted consciously to produce ambiguous legislation. ἀμφισβητήσεις and other words with the same root (cf. *Ath. Pol.* 35. ii = fr. 49d) are used often by Aristotle and *Ath. Pol.* to refer generally to 'disputes' and 'ambiguities'. For other occurrences, see Rhodes, *Comm. Ath. Pol.* 103, 163, 440–1. On *amphisbetesis* in a case dealing with dispute concerning ownership and inheritance rights, see Harrison, *LA.* i. 215–6; on *amphisbetesis* referring specifically to *epikleroi*, see Karabélias, *L'Épiclérat attique*, 128–34.

After adding this new fr. 47a, Ruschenbusch, *Gesetzeswerk*, 83–6, provides an outline of the main arguments dealing with inheritance, testaments and adoption, which occupy a major part in Solon's regulations concerning family law and are dealt with in the next sections.

Marriage between brother and sister

Fr. 47b: Philo, *De Specialibus Legibus* III. 22
ὁ μὲν οὖν Ἀθηναῖος Σόλων ὁμοπατρίους ἐφεὶς ἄγεσθαι τὰς ὁμομητρίους ἐκώλυσεν, ὁ δὲ Λακεδαιμονίων νομοθέτης ἔμπαλιν τὸν ἐπὶ ταῖς ὁμογαστρίοις γάμον ἐπιτρέψας τὸν πρὸς τὰς ὁμοπατρίους ἀπεῖπεν.
In fact, Solon the Athenian allowed marriage with a paternal half-sister, but forbade it with a maternal half-sister; but the Spartan legislator

prescribed the opposite, permitting marriage with women born of the same mother, but prohibiting it with those born of the same father.

Athenian law admitted marriage between close relatives under certain circumstances. It was not legal to marry a woman to direct ascendants or descendants (grandfather, father, son and grandson); also she could not marry a brother, or a half-brother when they shared the same mother (ὁμομητρίους). According to fr. 47b, Solon allowed half-brothers and half-sisters to marry when they shared the same father (ὁμοπατρίους), and the custom is confirmed in later times by other sources (e.g. Dem. LVII. *Eubulides* 20, Plut. *Them.* 32. ii). In fr. 47b, Philo states that Spartan law had exactly the opposite practice, although this information is not confirmed by any other source. In Athens, a woman could also marry an adopted brother, an uncle, cousin or any other more distant male relative. Diog. Laert. I. 56 (= fr. 131) mentions a law of Solon forbidding the marriage of a guardian to the mother of the orphans under his care, but this regulation is probably spurious. See Harrison, *L.A.* i. 21–5; MacDowell, *L.C.A.* 86–7; *Spartan Law*, 82; Gagarin, *Early Greek Law*, 67. There is a different interpretation of the Athenian practice in Ruschenbusch, *Gesetzeswerk*, 86–8, who sees Theophrastus as the possible source of Philo. For a general approach to the problem of incest in Athens, see Karabélias, *Études d'histoire juridique et sociale de la Grèce ancienne*, 83–102, esp. 91–5 with references to the Solonian law.

Engyesis and legitimate offspring

Fr. 48a: Poll. III. 33
Ἰσαῖος (fr. XXVI Thalheim) δὲ καὶ ἐπικληρῖτιν, ὥσπερ καὶ Σόλων.
Isaeus also calls [the *epikleros* ('heiress')] *epikleritis*, as does Solon also.

Pollux says that Isaeus uses the work *epikleritis* as equivalent to *epikleros* and that the same was true of Solon. The first part of the testimony is confirmed by other sources (e.g. *Etym. Magn.* ἐπίδικος), which state that Isaeus uses the word *epikleritis* in the speech *Against Lysibius*, but Pollux is the only one to make the connection with Solon. On the other hand, the testimonies dealing with Solon and the *epikleros* never use the term *epikleritis*. More details in Ruschenbusch, *Gesetzeswerk*, 89. Karabélias, *L'Épiclérat attique*, 16, considers that the word *epikleritis* (which he compares with *perikleritis*) was 'd'usage restreint dans le monde attique', and he considers (17–18) that the term *epikleros* goes back at least to Solon.

Fr. 48b: law *ap.* [Dem.] XLVI. *Stephanus ii.* 18
ΝΟΜΟΣ· ἣν ἂν ἐγγυήσῃ ἐπὶ δικαίοις δάμαρτα εἶναι ἢ πατὴρ ἢ ἀδελφὸς ὁμοπάτωρ ἢ πάππος ὁ πρὸς πατρός, ἐκ ταύτης εἶναι παῖδας γνησίους. ἐὰν δὲ μηδεὶς ᾖ τούτων, ἐὰν μὲν ἐπίκληρός τις ᾖ, τὸν κύριον ἔχειν, ἐὰν δὲ μὴ ᾖ, ὅτῳ ἂν ἐπιτρέψῃ, τοῦτον κύριον εἶναι.

LAW: The woman who is betrothed for a lawful marriage, by her father or brother born of the same father or by her grandfather on her father's side, shall have her children as *gnesioi*. If there is none of these relatives and if she is an *epikleros*, her *kyrios* shall have her as his wife, but if she is not [*epikleros*], then the man entitled shall act as her *kyrios*.

The passage mentions several important aspects of family law and the preoccupation with preserving the integrity of an *oikos*, although its correct understanding depends on certain characteristics of Athenian law. First, it is necessary to take into consideration the social position of women (and children), who, in the eyes of the law, could not act autonomously, and because of that depended legally on a *kyrios* (the 'head' or 'master' of the house). Until marriage, the *kyrios* would normally be the father of the young woman, and after that the husband would fulfil this function. Before the marriage, there should be a formal agreement between the former *kyrios* and the man who would play this role in the future, in order to recognise and legitimise the transfer of a woman from her original *oikos* to that of the husband. This formal act is usually known as *engyesis* or *engye*. There was no technical word to denote the concept of marriage by itself, but the terms mentioned derive from the verb that usually occurs in such contexts — as happens in fact in the passage under analysis (ἐγγυήσῃ), thus denoting the official nature of the procedure. See MacDowell, *L.C.A.* 84 and 87. The use of the term *damar* to define a wife acquired by a marriage based on *engye* is visible also in the disposition on lawful homicide (fr. 20); being an early word, it reinforces the authenticity of the law in both cases.

As pointed out by fr. 48b, the bride's father should perform the procedure of *engye*, but if that was not possible (if he had already died), the function should be fulfilled by a brother begotten of the same father or by the grandfather on her father's side (cf. Pl. *Leg.* VI. 774 E). The transfer or the 'giving in marriage' (*ekdosis*) of the woman to her new *kyrios*, together with the dowry, consolidated the public and official union of the couple, thus granting that their descendants would be considered legitimate (*paides gnesioi*); otherwise they would be *nothoi*. On the rights and legal limitations of *nothoi* see fr. 20, fr. 49a, fr. 49/g, frs. 50a–b and fr. 57 with commentary.

Nevertheless, the situation must also be considered in which these male relatives were no longer alive or simply did not exist: in such circumstances, the woman would become *epikleros*, 'heiress'. In a case like this, the simplest solution would be to marry the *epikleros* to the nearest kin, usually an uncle on her father's side. If this solution was not possible, she had to submit to the wish of the *kyrios* determined by her father (regularly by will) in order to deal with this situation. A *kyrios* designated under these circumstances would work as a kind of guardian, and would play a role equivalent to that of the normal *kyrios*: oversee the patrimony, protect and look after the woman, and in due time give her in marriage, according to the usual procedure of *engyesis*. Further details in Biscardi, *Diritto greco antico*, 108–12; Ruschenbusch, 'Bemerkungen zum Erbtochterrecht in den solonischen Gesetzen', *Symposion 1988* (*AGR* vii 1990), 15–20 = his *Kleine Schriften*, 193–6; *Gesetzeswerk*, 90–4. For a comprehensive approach to the *epikeros* in Athenian law, see Karabélias, *L'Épiclérat attique*.

Despite the relative clarity of the global interpretation of fr. 48b, it nevertheless presents some passages which are the subject of much debate. This is the case with two apparently similar provisions: τὸν κύριον ἔχειν and τοῦτον κύριον εἶναι. The first probably implies that the man legally in a position to claim to be the *kyrios* of the *epikleros* should marry her ('shall have her as his wife'); for the second, much depends on the way the preceding expression ὅτῳ ἂν ἐπιτρέψῃ is interpreted. Taken exactly as it is in the passage, it seems that the subject of the verb ἐπιτρέψῃ is the woman herself and, in that case, this could imply the odd consequence that the woman had the possibility of choosing her *kyrios*. Other recurrent suggestions are ὁ πατήρ and ὁ ἄρχων: the first would imply that, if the woman was not *epikleros*, the father could designate a *kyrios* for her by will; the second, that the formal *kyrios* was defined by an *epidikasia* before the archon. See Harrison, *LA*. i. 20–1; Karabélias, *L'Épiclérat attique*, 77 n. 82. Ruschenbusch, *Gesetzeswerk*, 90 and 93, thinks that the word omitted is ὁ θεσμός ('das Gesetz').

Inheritance

Fr. 49a: law *ap.* [Dem.] XLVI. *Stephanus ii.* 14
ΝΟΜΟΣ· ὅσοι μὴ ἐπεποίηντο, ὥστε μήτε ἀπειπεῖν μήτ' ἐπιδικάσασθαι, ὅτε Σόλων εἰσῄει τὴν ἀρχήν, τὰ ἑαυτοῦ διαθέσθαι εἶναι ὅπως ἂν ἐθέλῃ, ἂν μὴ παῖδες ὦσι γνήσιοι ἄρρενες, ἂν μὴ μανιῶν ἢ γήρως ἢ φαρμάκων ἢ νόσου ἕνεκα, ἢ γυναικὶ πειθόμενος, ὑπὸ τούτων του παρανοῶν, ἢ ὑπ' ἀνάγκης ἢ ὑπὸ δεσμοῦ καταληφθείς.
πειθόμενος: perhaps πιθόμενος Rhodes (cf. fr. 49d).   παρανοῶν Wesseling: παρανόμων MSS.
LAW: Those citizens who had not been adopted and thereby may neither renounce [the inheritance] nor claim their rights in an *epidikasia*, when Solon entered on his archonship shall be allowed to bequeath their own property as they wish, as long as they do not have male legitimate children, and their intellect was not disturbed by insanity, senility, drugs, sickness or by the manipulation of a woman, or forced by necessity or imprisonment.

Fr. 49b: Plut. *Sol.* 21. iii–iv
εὐδοκίμησε δὲ καὶ τῷ περὶ διαθηκῶν νόμῳ. πρότερον γὰρ οὐκ ἐξῆν, ἀλλ' ἐν τῷ γένει τοῦ τεθνηκότος ἔδει τὰ χρήματα καὶ τὸν οἶκον καταμένειν· ὁ δ' ᾧ βούλεταί τις ἐπιτρέψας, εἰ μὴ παῖδες εἶεν αὐτῷ, δοῦναι τὰ αὐτοῦ, φιλίαν τε συγγενείας ἐτίμησε μᾶλλον καὶ χάριν ἀνάγκης, καὶ τὰ χρήματα κτήματα τῶν ἐχόντων ἐποίησεν. οὐ μὴν ἀνέδην γε πάλιν οὐδ' ἁπλῶς τὰς δόσεις ἐφῆκεν, ἀλλ' εἰ μὴ

νόσων οὕνεκεν ἢ φαρμάκων ἢ δεσμῶν ἢ ἀνάγκῃ κατασχεθεὶς ἢ γυναικὶ πειθόμενος.

He became also highly popular because of the law concerning wills. In fact, before his time it was not possible to make wills, and therefore the possessions and the house had to remain with the family of the deceased. By allowing a man to transfer his property to whom he wished, on the condition that he had no children, [Solon] gave preference to friendship over kinship, and to affection over necessity, making a man's possessions in fact his own property. At any rate, he did not permit all kinds of donations, without any control or restraint, but only when they were not made under the effect of sickness, drugs, imprisonment or necessity, or under the manipulation of a woman.

Fr. 49c: Plut. *Quaest. Rom.* 265 E
Σόλων γράψας τὰς δόσεις κυρίας εἶναι τῶν τελευτώντων, πλὴν εἰ μή τις ἀνάγκῃ συνεχόμενος ἢ γυναικὶ πειθόμενος.
Solon prescribed that the donations of the deceased were valid, unless the donation was forced by necessity or made under the manipulation of a woman.

Fr. 49d: *Ath. Pol.* 35. ii
καθεῖλον ... καὶ τῶν Σόλωνος θεσμῶν ὅσοι διαμφισβητήσεις εἶχον, καὶ τὸ κῦρος ὃ ἦν ἐν τοῖς δικασταῖς κατέλυσαν, ὡς ἐπανορθοῦντες καὶ ποιοῦντες ἀναμφισβήτητον τὴν πολιτείαν, οἷον περὶ τοῦ δοῦναι τὰ ἑαυτοῦ, ᾧ ἂν ἐθέλῃ, κύριον ποιήσαντες καθάπαξ· τὰς δὲ προσούσας δυσκολίας, "ἐὰν μὴ μανιῶν ἢ γήρως <ἕνεκα> ἢ γυναικὶ πιθόμενος", ἀφεῖλον ὅπως μὴ ᾖ τοῖς συκοφάνταις ἔφοδος.
μανιῶν ἢ γήρως <ἕνεκα> Wyse (cf. fr. 49a): μανιῶν ἢ γηρῶν papyrus, μανιῶν ἢ γήρως Blass, Ruschenbusch.   πιθόμενος papyrus: πειθόμενος Wyse, Ruschenbusch (cf. fr. 49a).

They removed ... also those of the statutes of Solon that were open to ambiguities, and abolished the authority residing in the jurors, by revising the constitution and making it unambiguous, as happened with the allowance to a man to give his property to whoever he liked, thus making the act valid absolutely: they thereby removed the difficulties attached to 'except in consequence of insanity or of senility or under the manipulation of a woman', in order not to leave any opening for the action of sycophants.

Fr. 49/e = fr. 58/c (fr. 121a Ruschenbusch): [Dem.] XLIV. *Leochares* 67

τὸ δὲ πάντων μέγιστον καὶ γνωριμώτατον ὑμῖν· ὁ γὰρ τοῦ Σόλωνος νόμος οὐδὲ διαθέσθαι τὸν ποιητὸν ἐᾷ τὰ ἐν τῷ οἴκῳ οἷ ἂν ποιηθῇ. εἰκότως, οἶμαι. τῷ γὰρ κατὰ νόμον εἰσποιηθέντι ἐπὶ τὰ ἑτέρου οὐχ οὕτως ὡς περὶ τῶν ἰδίων κτημάτων βουλευτέον ἐστίν, ἀλλὰ τοῖς νόμοις ἀκολούθως, περὶ ἑκάστου τῶν γεγραμμένων, ὡς ὁ νόμος λέγει· "ὅσοι μὴ ἐπεποίηντο", φησί, "ὅτε Σόλων εἰσῄει τὴν ἀρχήν, ἐξεῖναι αὐτοῖς διαθέσθαι ὅπως ἂν ἐθέλωσιν", ὡς τοῖς γε ποιηθεῖσιν οὐκ ἔξον διαθέσθαι.

What is most important of all and best known to you: the law of Solon does not allow an adopted son even to bequeath the property of the household into which he has been adopted. Reasonably, I think: for somebody who has been adopted in accordance with the law into the property of another ought not to decide about it as he would about his own possessions, but in conformity with the laws, following each of the things written as the law states. 'Those who had not been adopted', it says, 'when Solon entered on his archonship shall be permitted to bequeath as they wish', implying that those who had been adopted were not permitted to bequeath.

Fr. 49/f (fr. 121b Ruschenbusch): Dem. XLVIII. *Olympiodorus* 56

Ὀλυμπιόδωρος μὲν οὑτοσὶ τοιοῦτός ἐστιν ἄνθρωπος, οὐ μόνον ἄδικος ἀλλὰ καὶ μελαγχολᾶν δοκῶν ἅπασιν τοῖς οἰκείοις καὶ τοῖς γνωρίμοις τῇ προαιρέσει τοῦ βίου, καὶ ὅπερ Σόλων ὁ νομοθέτης λέγει παραφρονῶν, ὡς οὐδεὶς πώποτε παρεφρόνησεν ἀνθρώπων, γυναικὶ πειθόμενος πόρνῃ. καὶ ἄκυρά γε ταῦτα πάντα ἐνομοθέτησεν εἶναι ὁ Σόλων ὅ τι ἄν τις γυναικὶ πειθόμενος πράττῃ, ἄλλως τε καὶ τοιαύτῃ.

This Olympiodorus is that kind of man, not only unjust but judged by all his family and acquaintances from the direction of his life to be of an evil disposition, and, as the lawgiver Solon says, out of his mind as nobody ever was, because he is under the manipulation of a woman who is a prostitute. And Solon made it a law that everything which anybody does under the manipulation of a woman should be invalid, particularly a woman of that kind.

Fr. 49/g (fr. 121c Ruschenbusch): Dem. XX. *Leptines* 102
ἐμοὶ δ', ὦ ἄνδρες Ἀθηναῖοι, δοκεῖ Λεπτίνης (καί μοι μηδὲν ὀργισθῇς· οὐδὲν γὰρ φλαῦρον ἐρῶ σε) ἢ οὐκ ἀνεγνωκέναι τοὺς Σόλωνος νόμους ἢ οὐ συνιέναι. εἰ γὰρ ὁ μὲν Σόλων ἔθηκεν νόμον ἐξεῖναι δοῦναι τὰ ἑαυτοῦ ᾧ ἄν τις βούληται, ἐὰν μὴ παῖδες ὦσι γνήσιοι, οὐχ ἵν' ἀποστερήσῃ τοὺς ἐγγυτάτω γένει τῆς ἀγχιστείας ἀλλ' ἵν' εἰς τὸ μέσον καταθεὶς τὴν ὠφέλειαν ἐφάμιλλον ποιήσῃ τὸ ποιεῖν ἀλλήλους εὖ, σὺ δὲ τοὐναντίον εἰσενήνοχας, μὴ ἐξεῖναι τῷ δήμῳ τῶν αὑτοῦ δοῦναι μηδενὶ μηδέν, πῶς σέ τις φήσει τοὺς Σόλωνος ἀνεγνωκέναι νόμους ἢ συνιέναι;

To my mind, men of Athens (and do not be angry with me, Leptines: I shall not say anything disreputable about you), Leptines either has not read Solon's laws or does not understand them. For if Solon enacted a law that a man should be permitted to give his property to whoever he liked, if he had no legitimate children, not in order to deprive those most closely related of their claim to kinship but to put the benefit in the middle as a prize for doing good to one another, but you on the contrary have introduced [a law] that it should not be permitted to the *demos* to give anything of its own to anybody, how can somebody say that you have read or understand the laws of Solon?

†Fr. 49/h: Phot. α 2316 Theodoridis
ΑΠΕΙΠΕΙΝ· τὸ καμεῖν καὶ ἀπαγορεῦσαι. σημαίνει δὲ καὶ τὸ ἀποκηρῦξαι παῖδα. καὶ δῆλον τοῦτο ἐκ τοῦ νόμου Σόλωνος τοῦ λέγοντος· "μήτ' ἀπειπεῖν †μήτε πείθεσθαι†", τουτέστιν μήτε ἀποκηρῦξαι μήτ' ἄλλον ἐπ' αὐτοῖς θεῖναι.
μήτε πείθεσθαι: μητ' ἐπιθέσθαι Tsantsanoglou.

APEIPEIN ['renounce']: To suffer distress and to make an announcement. It also means to renounce publicly a child. This is clear from the law of Solon, which says, 'Neither renounce †nor be subordinated†', meaning neither renounce publicly nor pass to others (?).

Ruschenbusch rejected frs. 49/e–g as references to fourth-century law rather than to Solon's laws; but since they simply restate and attribute to Solon what is attributed to him in frs. 49a–d they too should be accepted as genuine fragments. Ruschenbusch, *Gesetzeswerk*, 102, is correct in considering that the quotation of Solon's law in fr. 49/h is corrupt, and therefore that the explanation of Photius cannot be taken as accurate. Nevertheless, this is a new reference that derives, at least partially, from a genuine fragment.

According to Plutarch (fr. 49b), before Solon's legislation it was not possible to make wills, and therefore the properties of the deceased passed immediately to the next of kin. By creating this law concerning wills (τῷ περὶ διαθηκῶν νόμῳ), Solon conceded to the owner the legal ability to dispose of his prossessions (τὰ χρήματα κτήματα τῶν ἐχόντων ἐποίησεν). The formal expression is τὰ ἑαυτοῦ διαθέσθαι, used by [Demosthenes] — in fact Apollodorus — when he mentions the law in question (fr. 49a). Not all modern scholars would agree with Plutarch, and some maintain, on the contrary, that Solon simply passed this law in order to make official a practice already current in former times. According to this latter interpretation, the law intended essentially to clarify the controversies and problems deriving from the application of that mechanism. E.g. Ruschenbusch, 'διατίθεσθαι τὰ ἑαυτοῦ: Ein Beitrag zum sogenannten Testamentsgesetz des Solon', ZRG 79 (1962) 307–11 = his *Kleine Schriften*, 59–62; Rubinstein, *Adoption in IV. Century Athens*, 10–11, tends in the same direction. L. Gagliardi, 'Per un'interpretazione della legge di Solone in materia sucessoria', *Dike* v 2002, 5–59, analyses in detail the controversies related to the interpretation of Solon's law, with regard to ancient testimonies and modern scholarship. Although recognising the ambivalence of the sources, he maintains that the 'legge testamentaria' is intended not only to cover the making of wills, but also to normalise the practice of universal donations and adoptions, whether they are made *inter vivos* or by will. For a synthesis of the main arguments in the debate, see Harrison, *L.A.* i. 149–55; Manfredini & Piccirilli, *Plutarco. La vita di Solone*[5], 231–3; Ruschenbusch, *Gesetzeswerk*, 96–102. Suggestions for further reading in Arnaoutoglou, *Ancient Greek Laws*, 2.

It must be underlined that the ability to adopt by will depended on the lack of legitimate offspring, because only a man in those conditions could bequeath his property. Plutarch does not mention (εἰ μὴ παῖδες εἶεν αὐτῷ) the indispensable prerequisite that those children should be legitimate, but this requirement is clearly stated by fr. 49a (cf. also fr. 49/g), ἂν μὴ παῖδες ὦσι γνήσιοι ἄρρενες. This helps to clarify that one of the objectives of the adoption was to prevent the extinction of the *oikos* of the testator. In Athens, the adoption could be done in three ways: during the lifetime of the adopter (commonly known as adoption *inter vivos*); by will (so-called testamentary adoption), stipulating that the beneficiary of the will would become an adopted son (or daughter); or, lastly, in the case that someone died without leaving any legitimate son (natural or adopted) he could become an adopter posthumously, even without having had an active part in the procedure. See Harrison, *L.A.* i. 82–96; Rubinstein *Adoption in IV. Century Athens*, 1–2.

Besides the preliminary condition of not having legitimate offspring of his own, it was also binding, in order to guarantee that the will was valid (fr. 49c: τὰς δόσεις κυρίας εἶναι), that it should have been made voluntarily and with full use of the testator's faculties, therefore under no such pressures as insanity, senility, drugs, sickness or under the manipulation of a woman (cf. frs. 49a–d). Fr. 49/f (γυναικὶ πειθόμενος πόρνῃ) confirms that the expression γυναικὶ πειθόμενος embraces any woman, and not the 'wife' in particular, because there the speaker is mentioning specifically the bad influence of a prostitute. On fr. 49/e, see frs. 58a–c with commentary.

Fr. 49d, despite the information that the Thirty abolished the authority of the jurors (τὸ κῦρος ὃ ἦν ἐν τοῖς δικασταῖς κατέλυσαν), implies only the removal of ambiguities from Solon's laws, which could stimulate the temptation to argue, after a man's death, that his decision might have been made in a state of madness, senility or under manipulation. This would discourage disputes and the activity of sycophants, although it would not necessarily result in a higher degree of justice concerning inheritances. See Rhodes, *Comm. Ath. Pol*, 442 and 443-4.

Fr. 50a: Ar. *Av.* 1660–4
ἐρῶ δὲ δὴ καὶ τὸν Σόλωνός σοι νόμον·
"νόθῳ δὲ μὴ εἶναι ἀγχιστείαν παίδων ὄντων
γνησίων· ἐὰν δὲ παῖδες μὴ ὦσι γνήσιοι, τοῖς
ἐγγυτάτω γένους μετεῖναι τῶν χρημάτων."
I will then cite for you the law of Solon: 'An illegitimate child shall not have right of inheritance, if there are legitimate children; and if there are no legitimate children, the property shall pass to those most closely related.'

Fr. 50b: Dem. XLIII. *Macartatus* 51
ΝΟΜΟΣ· ὅστις ἂν μὴ διαθέμενος ἀποθάνῃ, ἐὰν μὲν παῖδας καταλίπῃ θηλείας, σὺν ταύτῃσιν, ἐὰν δὲ μή, τούσδε κυρίους εἶναι τῶν χρημάτων. ἐὰν μὲν ἀδελφοὶ ὦσιν ὁμοπάτορες· καὶ ἐὰν παῖδες ἐξ ἀδελφῶν γνήσιοι, τὴν τοῦ πατρὸς μοῖραν λαγχάνειν· ἐὰν δὲ μὴ ἀδελφοὶ ὦσιν ἢ ἀδελφῶν παῖδες, <ἀνεψιοὺς πρὸς πατρὸς καὶ παῖδας> ἐξ αὐτῶν κατὰ ταὐτὰ λαγχάνειν· κρατεῖν δὲ τοὺς ἄρρενας καὶ τοὺς ἐκ τῶν ἀρρένων, ἐὰν ἐκ τῶν αὐτῶν ὦσι, καὶ ἐὰν γένει ἀπωτέρω. ἐὰν δὲ μὴ ὦσι πρὸς πατρὸς μέχρι ἀνεψιῶν παίδων, τοὺς πρὸς μητρὸς τοῦ ἀνδρὸς κατὰ ταὐτὰ κυρίους εἶναι. ἐὰν δὲ μηδετέρωθεν ᾖ ἐντὸς τούτων, τὸν πρὸς πατρὸς ἐγγυτάτω κύριον εἶναι. νόθῳ δὲ μηδὲ νόθῃ μὴ εἶναι ἀγχιστείαν μήθ' ἱερῶν μήθ' ὁσίων. (ἀπ' Εὐκλείδου ἄρχοντος.)
For the *app. crit.* see Ruschenbusch, *Gesetzeswerk*, 103, whose text is here adopted. The supplement is Ruschenbusch's own: Dilts in his Oxford Text (2009) simply marks a lacuna, and punctuates to make the reference to Euclides' archonship apply specifically to the final clause.

LAW: If a man dies without having made a will, if he leaves daughters, his property shall be to them; if not, the following relatives shall be entitled to the property: if there are brothers of the same father or legitimate children of brothers, they shall take the part of the father; if there are no brothers or children of brothers, then <the cousins on the father's side and the children> of them shall inherit in the same way. The male relatives and their male descendants shall take precedence, if they are from the same ancestors, even if they are of remoter affinity. If there is nobody on the father's side to the degree of children of cousins, the relatives of the deceased on the maternal side shall inherit in the same way. And if there is nobody on both sides covered by these degrees, then the next of kin on the father's side shall inherit. Neither an illegitimate son nor an illegitimate daughter shall have rights of kinship, either in sacred or in secular affairs. (Effective from the archonship of Euclides.)

Fr. 50/c (fr. 120 Ruschenbusch): Dem. XLIII. *Macartatus* 78
ὁ δὲ νόμος κελεύει ὁ τοῦ Σόλωνος κρατεῖν τοὺς ἄρρενας καὶ τοὺς ἐκ τῶν ἀρρένων.
The law of Solon orders that males and sons of males shall prevail.

Cf. fr. 50b (the law inserted in §51), which includes these words; they are quoted also in Isae. VII. *Apollodorus* 20 and in [Dem.] XLIV *Leochares* 12 (not included by Ruschenbusch in his *testimonia* for fr. 50). Ruschenbusch rejected fr. 50/c as a reference to fourth-century law, not to the laws of Solon; but if fr. 50b is accepted as authentically Solonian, then this fragment must be accepted too, because it simply reiterates, in a more general way, the same principle. This opinion is shared by Karabélias, *L'Épiclérat attique*, 40.

It could happen that a man died without having made a will and without having direct heirs: a child, grandchild or great-grandchild of legitimate birth. If this line of succession was interrupted, then other collateral relatives could claim the inheritance, according to an order of succession deriving from the *anchisteia*. This was the technical term to designate the direct family members of a deceased person (see commentary on fr. 5), despite the fact that parents in the broadest sense could also be referred to as *syngeneia*; however, the first term is more restrictive since it did not include family members beyond 'children of cousins'. In other words, not all the *syngeneis* were *anchisteis*, even though all *anchisteis* were *syngeneis*. See Harrison, *L.A.* i. 143–8.

Among potential heirs could be rather distant relatives, such as uncles or cousins, who might belong to the same *oikos* as the deceased, although family members who did belong to the same *oikos* had priority over others. This implies that the legal incidence of *anchisteia* was broader than the *oikos* and could, in some circumstances, override it, even if, when this happened, the main objective remained to prevent the disappearance of the original *oikos*. This is the situation envisaged by fr. 50b. The essence of the provisions continued to be Solonian, as can be deduced from the testimony of Aristophanes (fr. 50a), even if fr. 50b constitutes an example of the laws that have been subject to revision, as is made clear by the information that this norm was (re)published at the end of the fifth century (to be valid from the archonship of Euclides, 403/2). The law defines precedence in terms of sucession, stipulating that male relatives have priority over the female, and the nearest kin over the remoter family (fr. 50b–50/c).

According to fr. 50b, if a man died intestate (μὴ διαθέμενος ἀποθάνῃ), but with female offspring, his daughter or daughters were the direct heirs of the paternal property. A girl or woman under these conditions was called *epikleros* (cf. frs. 48a–b). The closest translation of this term is 'heiress', even though it must be made clear that an *epikleros* did not own the property in the sense of having the ability to dispose of it freely; she possessed the property until she had a son which would become heir to the property of the father and, therefore, his successor in the *oikos*. The husband of an *epikleros* dealt with a similar situation, in so far as he could administer the possessions of his wife (a situation which, in itself, could be very attractive if the sums involved were large), but only until a son of the couple reached majority. See MacDowell, *L.C.A.* 95–6, 98–9.

Beyond the remarks regarding *epikleroi*, the law in question is especially interesting in that it defines the order in which the other members were entitled to inheritance, if the deceased had no direct descendants as previously indicated. The preferred line was that of the male, starting with the deceased's brother by the same father, and extending to the sons of cousins if one accepts Ruschenbusch's text. On the precise legal limits resulting from this expression, see MacDowell, *L.C.A.* 106–7; see also Karabélias, *L'Épiclérat attique*, 93–9; Ruschenbusch, *Gesetzeswerk*, 104–9. If in the line of the deceased there were no descendants, the same order of succession applied to the maternal side of the deceased. If, however, there was no heir meeting those criteria, then the property could be claimed by the nearest of distant relatives, again with preference for the male line.

The last provision of fr. 50b (νόθῳ δὲ μηδὲ νόθῃ μὴ εἶναι ἀγχιστείαν μήθ' ἱερῶν μήθ' ὁσίων) states that illegitimate children (*nothoi*) were excluded from the whole process by being deprived of the rights of *anchisteia*, both in sacred and in secular affairs. This distinction between the rights of *gnesioi* and *nothoi* (clearly underlined also in fr. 50a) emphasises very sharply the benefits of the official recognition of marriage and of legitimate birth (fr. 48b with commentary). Plut. *Sol.* 22. iv (= fr. 57/a) says that children born from a *hetaira*, and therefore *nothoi*, had no obligation to provide *gerotrophia* to their father. On this see Leão, 'Paidotrophia et gerotrophia dans les lois de Solon', *RHD* lxxxix 2011, 457–72 at 466–7.

Fr. 51a: Plut. *Sol.* 20. iv

καὶ τὸ τρὶς ἑκάστου μηνὸς ἐντυγχάνειν πάντως τῇ ἐπικλήρῳ τὸν λαβόντα.

And that the man who took as wife an heiress should approach her unfailingly thrice a month.

Fr. 51b: Plut. *Amat.* 769 A

τόν τε Σόλωνα μαρτυρεῖ γεγονέναι τῶν γαμικῶν ἐμπειρότατον νομοθέτην, κελεύσαντα μὴ ἔλαττον ἢ τρὶς κατὰ μῆνα τῇ γαμετῇ πλησιάζειν.

And that Solon was a legislator familiar with marital affairs is confirmed by his law prescribing that the man should have sexual intercourse with his wife at least thrice a month.

†Fr. 51/c: Dem. XLIII. *Macartatus* 75

ΝΟΜΟΣ· ὁ ἄρχων ἐπιμελείσθω τῶν ὀρφανῶν καὶ τῶν ἐπικλήρων καὶ τῶν οἴκων τῶν ἐξερημουμένων καὶ τῶν γυναικῶν, ὅσαι μένουσιν ἐν τοῖς οἴκοις τῶν ἀνδρῶν τῶν τεθνηκότων φάσκουσαι κυεῖν. τούτων ἐπιμελείσθω καὶ μὴ ἐάτω ὑβρίζειν μηδένα περὶ τούτους. ἐὰν δέ τις ὑβρίζῃ ἢ ποιῇ τι παράνομον, κύριος ἔστω ἐπιβάλλειν κατὰ τὸ τέλος. ἐὰν δὲ μείζονος ζημίας δοκῇ ἄξιος εἶναι, προσκαλεσάμενος πρόπεμπτα καὶ τίμημα ἐπιγραψάμενος, ὅ τι ἂν δοκῇ αὐτῷ, εἰσαγέτω εἰς τὴν ἡλιαίαν. ἐὰν δ' ἁλῷ, τιμάτω ἡ ἡλιαία περὶ τοῦ ἁλόντος, ὅ τι χρὴ αὐτὸν παθεῖν ἢ ἀποτεῖσαι.

LAW: The archon shall take care of orphans, of heiresses and of the houses left destitute [of heirs], and of those widows who continue in the houses of their deceased husbands, claiming to be pregnant. He shall take charge of these and allow nobody to commit *hybris* against them. If someone commits an act of *hybris* or commits anything unlawful against them, he shall have the authority to impose a fine up to the fixed limit. If the offender seems to him to deserve a more severe penalty, he shall summon the offender, giving him five days' notice, and then bring him before the *eliaia*, stipulating the fine that he thinks is deserved by the offender. And if he is convicted, the *eliaia* shall determine what the offender is to suffer or pay.

†**Fr. 51/d:** *Ath. Pol.* 56. vii

[ἐπιμελεῖτ]αι δὲ καὶ τῶν ὀρφανῶν καὶ τῶν ἐπικλήρων, καὶ τῶν γυναικῶν ὅσαι ἂν τελευτ[ήσαντος τοῦ ἀνδρ]ὸς σκήπτωνται κύειν. καὶ κύριός ἐστι τοῖς ἀδικοῦσιν ἐπιβάλ[λειν ἢ εἰσάγειν εἰς] τὸ δικαστήριον. μισθοῖ δὲ καὶ τοὺς οἴκους τῶν ὀρφανῶν καὶ τῶν ἐπικλ[ήρων, ἕως ἄν τις τετταρ]ακαιδεκέτις γένηται, καὶ τὰ ἀποτιμήματα λαμβάν[ει, καὶ τοὺς ἐπιτρόπους], ἐὰν μὴ διδῶσι τοῖς παισὶ τὸν σῖτον, οὗτος εἰσπράττει.

[The archon] takes care also of orphans, of heiresses and of those widows who after the death of their husbands claim to be pregnant. He has the full authority to fine anyone offending against them or to bring them to court. He lets out the estates of orphans and heiresses until they come to the age of fourteen, and receives the securities [provided by the lessees]. And if the guardians do not provide the maintenance due to the orphans, the archon exacts it from them.

Fr. 51/1 (*testimonium* to frs. 126a–c Ruschenbusch): Dem. XLIII. *Macartatus* 54

ΝΟΜΟΣ· τῶν ἐπικλήρων ὅσαι θητικὸν τελοῦσιν, ἐὰν μὴ βούληται ἔχειν ὁ ἐγγύτατω γένους, ἐκδιδότω ἐπιδοὺς ὁ μὲν

πεντακοσιομέδιμνος πεντακοσίας δραχμάς, ὁ δ' ἱππεὺς τριακοσίας, ὁ δὲ ζευγίτης ἑκατὸν πεντήκοντα, πρὸς οἷς αὐτῆς. ἐὰν δὲ πλείους ὦσιν ἐν τῷ αὐτῷ γένει, τῇ ἐπικλήρῳ πρὸς μέρος ἐπιδιδόναι ἕκαστον. ἐὰν δ' αἱ γυναῖκες πλείους ὦσι, μὴ ἐπάναγκες εἶναι πλέον ἢ μίαν ἐκδοῦναι τῷ γ' ἑνί, ἀλλὰ τὸν ἐγγύτατα ἀεὶ ἐκδιδόναι ἢ αὐτὸν ἔχειν. ἐὰν δὲ μὴ ἔχῃ ὁ ἐγγυτάτω γένους ἢ μὴ ἐκδῷ, ὁ ἄρχων ἐπαναγκαζέτω ἢ αὐτὸν ἔχειν ἢ ἐκδοῦναι. ἐὰν δὲ μὴ ἐπαναγκάσῃ ὁ ἄρχων, ὀφειλέτω χιλίας δραχμὰς ἱερὰς τῇ Ἥρᾳ. ἀπογραφέτω δὲ τὸν μὴ ποιοῦντα ταῦτα ὁ βουλόμενος πρὸς τὸν ἄρχοντα.
γ' ἑνί Herrmann; γένει codd.

LAW: With regard to those heiresses who belong to the class of *thetes*, if the next of kin does not want to marry her, he shall give her in marriage with a dowry of five hundred drachmae if he belongs to the class of *pentakosiomedimnoi*, of three hundred drachmae if he belongs to the *hippeis*, or of one hundred and fifty drachmae if he belongs to the *zeugitai*, in addition to her own personal belongings. If there are several kinsmen of the same degree of kinship, each one of them shall contribute his share to the [dowry of the] heiress. If there are several women, it shall not be necessary for a single kinsman to give in marriage more than one, but the next of kin in each case shall give her in marriage or marry her himself. If the next of kin does not marry her or give her in marriage, then the archon shall compel him to marry her himself or to give her in marriage. If the archon fails to compel him, then he shall incur a fine of a thousand drachmae, consecrated to Hera. Anyone who wishes may denounce to the archon the kinsman who does not carry out this duty.

Fr. 51/2 (fr. 126a Ruschenbusch): Eustathius *ad Hom. Il.* XXI. 450 (1246.13)
θῆσσα γάρ, φησί, ἣν πατὴρ καταλέλοιπε πένης ὤν. αὕτη δέ, φησίν (Ar. Byz. fr. 39 Nauck), ἐπὶ τὸν πλησίον τοῦ γένους πορεύεται κατὰ νόμον ἀναγκάζοντα τοῦτο, καὶ ὁ μὴ αἱρούμενος γῆμαι πέντε μνᾶς ἀποτίνει, ὡς ἔταξε Σόλων. ἐν δὲ τοῖς ἐπικαινισθεῖσι νόμοις μετέδοξε τοῦτο ὡς μικρὸν καὶ ἐγένοντο δέκα μναῖ.

Therefore a *thessa* [*sc.* an *epikleros* of the class of *thetes*], [Aristophanes of Byzantium] says, is the woman left behind by a poor father. That woman, he says, should be sent to the next of kin, in accordance with the law that compels this practice; and if he [*sc.* the next of kin] does not choose to take her in marriage, he shall pay five minas, as was fixed by Solon. In the revised laws, there was a change in this, because the amount was considered too small, and it was made ten minas.

Fr. 51/3 (fr. 126b Ruschenbusch): Diod. Sic. XII. 18. iii
τρίτος δὲ νόμος διωρθώθη ὁ περὶ τῶν ἐπικλήρων, ὁ καὶ παρὰ Σόλωνι κείμενος. ἐκέλευε γὰρ τῇ ἐπικλήρῳ ἐπιδικάζεσθαι τὸν ἔγγιστα γένους, ὡσαύτως δὲ καὶ τὴν ἐπίκληρον ἐπιδικάζεσθαι τῷ ἀγχιστεῖ, ᾧ ἦν ἀνάγκη συνοικεῖν ἢ πεντακοσίας ἐκτῖσαι δραχμὰς εἰς προικὸς λόγον τῇ πενιχρᾷ ἐπικλήρῳ.

A third law [of Charondas] which was corrected was that about *epikleroi*, and is included also in Solon's legislation. In fact, he ordered that the next of kin was to be assigned in marriage (*epidikazein*) to the *epikleros*, just as the *epikleros* was to be assigned in marriage (*epidikazein*) to her next of kin, who had to marry her, or if not to pay five hundred drachmae as a dowry to the needy *epikleros*.

Fr. 52a: Plut. *Sol.* 20. ii–vi
ἄτοπος δὲ δοκεῖ καὶ γελοῖος ὁ τῇ ἐπικλήρῳ διδούς, ἂν ὁ κρατῶν καὶ κύριος γεγονὼς κατὰ τὸν νόμον αὐτὸς μὴ δυνατὸς ᾖ πλησιάζειν, ὑπὸ τῶν ἔγγιστα τοῦ ἀνδρὸς ὀπύεσθαι. καὶ τοῦτο δ' ὀρθῶς ἔχειν τινές φασι πρὸς τοὺς μὴ δυναμένους συνεῖναι, χρημάτων δ' ἕνεκα λαμβάνοντας ἐπικλήρους καὶ τῷ νόμῳ καταβιαζομένους τὴν φύσιν. ὁρῶντες γὰρ ᾧ βούλεται τὴν ἐπίκληρον συνοῦσαν, ἢ προήσονται τὸν γάμον, ἢ μετ' αἰσχύνης καθέξουσι, φιλοπλουτίας καὶ ὕβρεως δίκην διδόντες. εὖ δ' ἔχει καὶ τὸ μὴ πᾶσιν, ἀλλὰ τῶν συγγενῶν τοῦ ἀνδρὸς ᾧ βούλεται διαλέγεσθαι τὴν ἐπίκληρον, ὅπως οἰκεῖον ᾖ καὶ μετέχον τοῦ γένους τὸ τικτόμενον. εἰς τοῦτο δὲ συντελεῖ καὶ τὸ τὴν νύμφην τῷ νυμφίῳ συγκαθείργνυσθαι μήλου κυδωνίου {συγ}κατατραγοῦσαν (**fr. 127a**), καὶ τὸ τρὶς ἑκάστου μηνὸς ἐντυγχάνειν πάντως τῇ ἐπικλήρῳ τὸν λαβόντα (**fr. 51a**). καὶ γὰρ εἰ μὴ γένοιντο παῖδες, ἀλλὰ τιμή τις ἀνδρὸς αὕτη πρὸς σώφρονα γυναῖκα καὶ φιλοφροσύνη, πολλὰ τῶν συλλεγομένων ἑκάστοτε δυσχερῶν ἀφαιροῦσα καὶ ταῖς διαφοραῖς οὐκ ἐῶσα παντάπασιν ἀποστραφῆναι. τῶν δ' ἄλλων γάμων ἀφεῖλε τὰς φερνάς, ἱμάτια τρία καὶ σκεύη μικροῦ τιμήματος ἄξια κελεύσας, ἕτερον δὲ μηδέν, ἐπιφέρεσθαι τὴν γαμουμένην (**fr. 71a**).

{συγ}κατατραγοῦσαν Coraes, cf. fr. 127b

The (law) seems illogical and ridiculous that allows an heiress, when the man under whose power and authority she is legally placed is unable to have sexual intercourse with her, to be married by one of his nearest kin. This disposition is correct, in the opinion of some, for those who are incapable of having intercourse, and take the *epikleroi* to wife only for the sake of their property, commit violence against nature under cover of the law. In fact, seeing that the *epikleros* can consort with whom she pleases, they will either renounce such a marriage or keep it to their shame, suffering the penalty for their greed and disrespect for dignity. It is also a good disposition that the *epikleros* may not choose her consort from all, but that she should choose the man she prefers from among the kinsmen of her husband, so that the offspring is kept within the family and the same lineage. To that purpose also contributes the requirement that 'a bride sould be shut up in a chamber with the bridegroom, after having eaten a quince', and that 'the man who took as wife an heiress should approach her unfailingly three times every month'. For even if children are not born, still this is a gesture of respect and friendship from a husband towards a chaste woman; it precludes many of the displeasures that arise from such cases, and prevents them from coming into conflict because of their differences. In all other marriages, he banned dowries, prescribing that the bride could take with her three garments, household stuff of little value and nothing else.

Fr. 52b (= fr. 27): Hesych. β 466 Latte *et al.*
ΒΙΝΕΙΝ· παρὰ Σόλωνι τὸ βίᾳ μίγνυσθαι. τὸ δὲ κατὰ νόμον ὀπύειν.
BINEIN ('have sexual relations'): in Solon, means to have sexual intercourse by force. Legitimate intercourse is *opyein*.

Fr. 52c: Gal. *Linguarum Hippocratis Explicatio, prooemium* (xix. 66 Kuhn) (part of **fr. 41a**)
κἀκεῖνος μέντοι ἀντιπροβάλλει τῶν ἐν τοῖς Σόλωνος ἄξοσιν γλῶτταν εἰς δίκας διαφερούσας ...
εἶτ' ἐφεξῆς προβάλλει·
"τί ποτέ ἐστιν ὀπυίειν;"
ἐξ ὧν δῆλον ὡς ἡ γλῶττα παλαιόν ἐστιν ὄνομα τῆς συνηθείας ἐκπεπτωκός.
For the *app. crit.* see fr. 41a.

He then challenges him in turn on expressions in Solon's *axones* relating to various lawsuits . . .
Then he challenges next:
'What is *opyiein* ["marry"]?'
From which it is clear that the expression is an ancient name which has fallen out of currency.

The regulation mentioned by Plutarch (fr. 52a) should be taken together with the dispositions of the law *ap*. Dem. XLIII. *Macartatus* 51 (fr. 50b; cf. also frs. 50a and 50/c), defining the order in which relatives were entitled to inheritance, if the deceased had no direct descendants. The preferred line was that of the male, starting with the deceased's brother by the same father, and extended to the son of cousins. Therefore, when Solon determines that the *epikleros* should have as *kyrios* (ὁ κρατῶν καὶ κύριος γεγονὼς κατὰ τὸν νόμον) the next of kin of her deceased father, this would correspond, first, to the paternal uncle and so on up to the degree of a cousin's son. Ruschenbusch, 'Bemerkungen zum Erbtochterrecht in den solonischen Gesetzen', *Symposion 1988* (*AGR* vii 1990), 15–20 at 15–17 = his *Kleine Schriften*, 193–5, analyses one of the possible problems arising from this obligation if the first legal candidate for taking the *epikleros* as wife was married already and had his own children. One logical solution would be to interpret the law not in the sense of forcing the next of kin to marry the *epikleros* himself, but to assure her a suitable marriage, as any *kyrios* had the moral obligation to do.

This explanation receives support from fr. 51/1, although Ruschenbusch, *Nomoi*, 120, places this disposition among the spurious laws (as a testimonium to frs. 126a–c). However A. C. Scafuro, 'Identifying Solonian Laws', in Blok & Lardinois (edd.), *Solon of Athens*, 175–96, is probably right when she argues that there are laws which have at any rate a 'Solonian kernel' and in that sense should be considered genuine (cf. Introduction, p. 6). The use in fr. 51/1 of the Solonian property-classes as reference for the amount to be given as dowry also supports the Solonian origin of the law, even if the dowries are too high for the time of the legislator. Thereby, the kernel of the law may correspond, in Scafuro's terms (p. 190), to the basic statement that 'kinsmen who did not marry poor *epiklêroi* were to dower them', although this does not imply that the original law prescribed such high sums, or even any sums at all. For the same reason, frs. 51/2–3 (considered spurious by Ruschenbusch) are also to be accepted among the laws where a similar Solonian kernel can be identified. Cf. Poll. III. 33; *Suda* θ 371 Adler θῆττα; Ter. *Phorm*. 125-6; 296-7. See Karabélias, *L'Épiclérat attique*, 211-23, for a review of the main interpretations dealing with *thessai* (the poor *epikleroi*). On Solon's general restriction on dowries see fr. 71a.

Fr. 51c and fr. 51d refer most probably to the same law which should also be seen as Solonian in its substance, for the reasons adduced in connection with fr. 51/1. It deals with the archon's duties in taking care of those who were deprived of the protection of their *kyrios*, as happened in such vulnerable situations as those regarding *epikleroi*, orphans, empty *oikoi* and pregnant widows. The 'Solonian kernel' of the law is possibly to be identified with the procedure of legally involving the archon in the enforcement of the obligation to protect these persons against acts of arrogance and attacks on their honour, and in the very nature of the offence. On the Solonian law on *hybris* and the clause τι παράνομον 'anything unlawful' used in fr. 51c (fr. 51d has the more general statement τοῖς ἀδικοῦσιν), see commentary on frs. 30/1a–b, and Rhodes, *Comm. Ath. Pol.* 633–6. Scafuro, 181–2, argues that the original meaning of the clause τι παράνομον could have been 'anything contrary to the social code'.

Fr. 52a approaches a situation deriving from the possibility that the relative who took the *epikleros* as wife might be impotent (αὐτὸς μὴ δυνατὸς ᾖ πλησιάζειν). This contingency would represent a serious obstacle, as it would prevent the achievement of a central purpose behind the special status of an *epikleros*: securing the birth of a legitimate son, descendant in direct line from the *epikleros*' father. The solution would be to marry her to the next nearest of kin. Plutarch seems to imply that the *epikleros* could choose whoever she wanted as her sexual partner (ὁρῶντες γὰρ ᾧ βούλεται τὴν ἐπίκληρον συνοῦσαν), but this is highly questionable, even if she were to make her choice among the men belonging to the family and the same lineage. What is most probable is that the same basic line of precedence was followed as with the relatives entitled to inheritance (cf. fr. 50b wih commentary). The term ὀπύεσθαι used in fr. 52a (ὑπὸ τῶν ἔγγιστα τοῦ ἀνδρὸς ὀπύεσθαι) to define a legitimate marriage is Solonian and occurred in the *axones*, as is clearly stated by frs. 52b–c (cf. frs. 27 and 41a with commentary), but seems to have been misunderstood by Plutarch. See Sondhaus, *De Solonis Legibus*, 25–6; MacDowell, *L.C.A.* 96–7; Manfredini & Piccirilli, *Plutarco. La vita di Solone*[5], 225-6; Ruschenbusch, *Gesetzeswerk*, 114–5, with references to other sources.

Frs. 51a–b, both transmitted by Plutarch, prescribe that the husband of an *epikleros* ought to have sexual intercourse with his wife at least three times every month. This rule clearly aims to improve the probability of having a successful pregnancy and the expected legitimate offspring, but the biographer fails again to understand (or at least to give due importance to) the pragmatism of the regulation, by favouring a moral interpretation of the law, as if it was intended to promote respect and affection between husband and wife. Even if this ethical approach may be pertinent (for a similar consideration, see *Coniugalia Praecaepta* 143 D–E), it does not correspond to the pragmatic essence of Solon's regulation. Plutarch mentions also a norm connected with fertility rites (= fr. 127a), but this is probably not Solonian, even if it might be appropriate in a context dealing with sexual impotence. See Karabélias, *L'Épiclérat attique*, 139–40. For other references to the practice of eating a quince (μήλου κυδωνίου) in similar contexts, see Manfredini & Piccirilli, *Plutarco. La vita di Solone*[5], 226–7, who admit that the law may be genuine and Solonian, in the sense that it would correspond to a proof that the *iustae nuptiae* had already taken place, thus representing the 'regolarità giuridica del matrimonio' and therefore the ability to have *gnesioi* children.

Fr 53: [Dem.] XLVI. *Stephanus ii.* 20
ΝΟΜΟΣ· καὶ ἐὰν ἐξ ἐπικλήρου τις γένηται καὶ ἅμα ἡβήσῃ ἐπὶ δίετες, κρατεῖν τῶν χρημάτων, τὸν δὲ σῖτον μετρεῖν τῇ μητρί.
LAW: If the *epikleros* has a son, two years after having attained puberty he shall have control of the property, on condition that he provides maintenance for his mother.

Fr. 54: Harp. σ 18 Keaney, cf. *Suda* σ 502 Adler, Phot. σ 248 Theodoridis
ΣΙΤΟΣ· Δημοσθένης ἐν τῷ κατ' Ἀφόβου α' (XXVII. 15). σῖτος καλεῖται
ἡ διδομένη πρόσοδος εἰς τροφὴν ταῖς γυναιξὶν ἢ τοῖς ὀρφανοῖς,
ὡς ἐξ ἄλλων μαθεῖν ἐστι καὶ ἐκ τῶν τοῦ Σόλωνος πρώτου ἄξονος
καὶ ἐκ τῆς Ἀριστοτέλους Ἀθηναίων πολιτείας (56. vii).

We print Keaney's text of Harpocration. Ruschenbusch printed πρώτου καὶ <e.g. τετάρτου> τοῦ <e.g. γ'> ἄξονος, 'the first and <e.g. the fourth> [law] of the <e.g. third> *axon*': see his *apparatus criticus*; but in *Gesetzeswerk* he translated a different text.

SITOS: Demosthenes, in the *Against Aphobus i*. The revenue provided for maintenance to women or orphans is called *sitos*, as can be learned from others and especially from Solon's first *axon* and from Aristotle's *Constitution of the Athenians*.

The legal mechanism with regard to *epikleroi* aimed to protect, in immediate terms, the woman who had that status, since it consisted of a way of assuring her a dowry, a husband and maintenance. However, both the *epikleros* and the man who took her in marriage ended up as instruments of a more important goal, that of preventing the extinction of the *epikleros'* original *oikos*. Therefore, when the male child born of an *epikleros* came of age (ἅμα ἡβήσῃ ἐπὶ δίετες), he would become the natural heir and *kyrios* of the mother's patrimony (κρατεῖν τῶν χρημάτων), as successor of his grandfather. However, this new position would not exempt him from responsibilities, particularly in relation to the mother, whose maintenance he had to ensure. Therefore, in practice, the male child had to take the father's role as *kyrios*, a status to which, under normal circumstances, he would end up by having access, thus restoring the regular family order. At any rate, it is doubtful whether he would also have automatically the control of the *epikleros*. See Harrison, *LA*. i. 113 and n. 2. On coming of age in Athens, see *Ath. Pol.* 42. ii, v, with the commentary of Rhodes, *Comm. Ath. Pol.* 503 and 509; Karabélias, *L'Épiclérat attique*, 177–8. Solon fr. 27 West suggests that coming of age occurred around fourteen, although the line (ἥβης †δὲ φάνει† σήματα γεινομένης) does not imply necessarily a single year.

The law transmitted in fr. 53 is anonymous, but its Solonian origin is made clear by fr. 54, which has a direct reference to the *axones* (even if the text of this passage is disputed). The use of the archaic expressions ἡβᾶν ἐπὶ διετές and τὸν σῖτον μετρεῖν in fr. 53 also favours its authenticity. See Ruschenbusch, *Gesetzeswerk*, 117. In fr. 51d the term σῖτος is also used to refer to the maintenance owed to orphans by their guardians. See Scafuro, 188–9.

Care for elderly parents

Fr. 55a: Ar. *Av.* 1353–7
ἀλλ' ἔστιν ἡμῖν τοῖσιν ὄρνισιν νόμος
παλαιὸς ἐν ταῖς τῶν πελαργῶν κύρβεσιν·

"ἐπὴν ὁ πατὴρ ὁ πελαργὸς ἐκπετησίμους
πάντας ποήσῃ τοὺς πελαργιδέας τρέφων,
δεῖ τοὺς νεοττοὺς τὸν πατέρα πάλιν τρέφειν."
But there is among us, the birds, this ancient law written in the *kyrbeis* of the storks: 'When the father stork has brought up all his storklings and made them ready to fly, then must those young support the father in their turn.'

Fr. 55b: Lib. *Decl.* XI. 14
μὴ τοίνυν μηδὲ τὴν ἐμὴν ταυτηνὶ λειτουργίαν διαβαλλέτω τις, ἣ μάχεται μὲν οὐδενὶ τῶν γεγραμμένων νόμων, ὁμολογεῖ δὲ πολλοῖς τε καὶ καλῶς ἔχειν δοκοῦσιν, οὓς ὁ Σόλων τοῖς γονεῦσι βοηθοῦντας τέθεικε, φόβῳ τῆς τιμωρίας καὶ τοὺς οὐ φύσει χρηστοὺς ἀναγκάζων, ἃ δεῖ τοῖς γεγεννηκόσι φέρειν.
And no one should attack my public service here, for it not only contradicts no written laws, but on the contrary is in agreement with many laws considered to be good, which Solon enacted in order to protect parents, thus through the threat of punishment forcing even those who are not worthy by nature to give their parents what is needed.

Fr. 55c: Ael. *N.A.* IX. 1
ὁ λέων ἤδη προήκων τὴν ἡλικίαν καὶ γήρᾳ βαρὺς γεγενημένος θηρᾶν μὲν ἥκιστός ἐστιν, ἀσμένως δὲ ἀναπαύεται ἐν ταῖς ὑπάντροις ἢ λοχμώδεσι καταδρομαῖς, καὶ τῶν θηρίων οὐδὲ τοῖς ἀσθενεστάτοις ἐπιθαρρεῖ, τόν τε αὑτοῦ χρόνον ὑφορώμενος καὶ τὸ τοῦ σώματος ἐννοῶν ἀσθενές. οἱ δὲ ἐξ αὐτοῦ γεγενημένοι θαρροῦντες τῇ τῆς ἡλικίας ἀκμῇ καὶ τῇ ῥώμῃ τῇ συμφυεῖ προΐασι μὲν ἐπὶ θήραν, ἐπάγονται δὲ καὶ τὸν ἤδη γέροντα, ὠθοῦντες αὐτόν· εἶτα ἐπὶ μέσης τῆς ὁδοῦ ἧς ἐλθεῖν δεῖ καταλιπόντες, ἔχονται τῆς ἄγρας αὐτοί, καὶ τυχόντες τοσούτων ὅσα ἀποχρήσει καὶ αὐτοῖς καὶ τῷ γεγεννηκότι σφᾶς, βρυχησάμενοι γενναῖόν τε καὶ διάτορον καλοῦσιν {τὸν πατέρα} ὡς δαιτυμόνα ἑστιάτορες ἐπὶ θοίνην οἱ νέοι τὸν γεγηρακότα, τὸν πατέρα οἱ παῖδες. ... καὶ Σόλων μὲν τοῖς λέουσιν οὐ κελεύει ταῦτα νομοτεθῶν τρέφειν τοὺς πατέρας ἐπάναγκες, διδάσκει δὲ ἡ φύσις, ᾗ νόμων ἀνθρωπικῶν οὐδὲν μέλει· γίνεται δὲ ἄτρεπτος αὕτη νόμος.

{τὸν πατέρα} deleted Hercher.   νομοτεθῶν τρέφειν τοὺς πατέρας ἐπάναγκες deleted Hercher.

After having grown old and become heavy with age, the lion is no longer able to go hunting, but he is happy to rest in a cave or in thick bushes. He does not venture even against the weakest animals, so wary he is of his age and aware of his feeble body. But his offspring go to the hunt, confident in their flourishing youth and full vigour, and they bring along their old father with them, by pushing him forward. When they have travelled half way on the journey they must take, they leave him alone while they themselves engage in the chase. And when they have captured enough for themselves and for their father, they emit a piercing roar and, as does a host inviting the guests to a meal, the young call the old, like the children their father. ... And it is not Solon who legislates to order the lions to maintain their fathers, but nature, which takes no notice of human laws, teaches them: she is an unchangeable law.

Fr. 56/a: Plut. *Sol.* 22. i
ὁρῶν δὲ τὸ μὲν ἄστυ πιμπλάμενον ἀνθρώπων ἀεὶ συρρεόντων πανταχόθεν ἐπ' ἀδείας εἰς τὴν Ἀττικήν, τὰ δὲ πλεῖστα τῆς χώρας ἀγεννῆ καὶ φαῦλα, τοὺς δὲ χρωμένους τῇ θαλάττῃ μηδὲν εἰωθότας εἰσάγειν τοῖς μηδὲν ἔχουσιν ἀντιδοῦναι, πρὸς τὰς τέχνας ἔτρεψε τοὺς πολίτας, καὶ νόμον ἔγραψεν, υἱῷ τρέφειν πατέρα μὴ διδαξάμενον τέχνην ἐπάναγκες μὴ εἶναι.

After considering that the city was being filled with people continuously streaming in from all sides, attracted by the security of Attica, that most of the land was unproductive and of low quality, and that people engaged in seafaring are not disposed to bring merchandise to those who have nothing to offer them in exchange, [Solon] turned his fellow citizens towards crafts and passed a law that a son was not obliged to support a father who had not taught him a craft.

†Fr. 56/b: Vitr. *De Arch.* VI. *praefatio* 3–4
Alexis, qui Athenienses ait oportere ideo laudari, quod omnium Graecorum leges cogunt parentes <ali> a liberis, Atheniensium non omnes nisi eos, qui liberos artibus erudissent. ... Itaque ego maximas infinitasque parentibus ago atque habeo gratias, quod Atheniensium legem probantes me arte erudiendum curaverunt, et ea, quae non potest esse probata sine litteratura encyclioque doctrinarum omnium disciplina.

Alexis says that the Athenians deserve particular praise, because, while the laws of all the Greeks make it obligatory for children to support their parents, those of the Athenians do not grant this mandatory protection to all [parents], but only to those who taught their children a craft. ... For that reason, I feel myself under great and infinite obligations to my parents, for having adopted the practice of the Athenians and taken care to teach me a craft, of a kind that cannot be put into practice without erudition and a global knowledge of science.

†**Fr. 56/c:** Gal. *Adhortatio ad Artes Addiscendas*, 8. i (i. 15 Kuhn)
ἐπαινέσειε δ' ἄν τις καὶ τὸν Ἀθήνησι νομοθέτην, ὃς τὸν μὴ διδάξαντα τέχνην ἐκώλυε πρὸς τοῦ παιδὸς τρέφεσθαι.
One would approve also the lawgiver at Athens who forbade the [father] who had not taught a craft to be maintained by his son.

Fr. 57/a: Plut. *Sol.* 22. iv
ἐκεῖνο δ' ἤδη σφοδρότερον, τὸ μηδὲ τοῖς ἐξ ἑταίρας γενομένοις ἐπάναγκες εἶναι τοὺς πατέρας τρέφειν, ὡς Ἡρακλείδης ἱστόρηκεν ὁ Ποντικός (fr. 146 Wehrli).
But even more severe is that [law] that those born of a prostitute do not even have the obligation to support their parents, as recorded by Heraclides Ponticus.

†**Fr. 57/b:** Aeschin. I. *Timarchus* 13 (part of **fr. 30/c**)
καὶ μὴ ἐπάναγκες εἶναι τῷ παιδὶ ἡβήσαντι τρέφειν τὸν πατέρα μηδὲ οἴκησιν παρέχειν, ὃς ἂν ἐκμισθωθῇ ἑταιρεῖν· ἀποθανόντα δὲ θαπτέτω καὶ τἆλλα ποιείτω τὰ νομιζόμενα.
And it is not obligatory for the boy when he has grown up to support his father or provide a home for him, if he has been hired out for prostitution; but when he has died the son must bury him and perform the other customary rites.

The *anchisteia* conceded to those who were covered by that status the important right to claim the estate of a deceased family member (cf. frs. 50a–50/c with commentary), but it also involved certain obligations regarding the deceased relative. If the death was the result of a homicide, it would fall under the duties of the *anchisteis* to ensure that justice was done (fr. 5a); family members also had obligations of a ritual character, particularly regarding the honour and respect that should be granted to the dead (e.g. frs. 33a–b). However, even before the moment of a relative's death, there was a different kind of responsibility that fell to the *anchisteis*, especially to the most direct descendants with legal responsibilities, such as sons: to assure that they would support the members of the *oikos* in their old age (*gerotrophia*). Hes. *Op.* 185–8 already presents the lack of respect concerning *gerotrophia* as a sign of human degradation. The concern with *gerotrophia* could be one of the motivations for adopting a son, but, for obvious reasons, only *inter vivos*.

At a time when the state was still far from creating a social security system, the certainty of maintenance at a more advanced age was, of course, a guarantee that the parents were eager to get from their children. Taking care of older relatives was, in fact, the natural counterpart to the effort that the parents had themselves made in the way they nurtured their children (*paidotrophia*) and prepared them for life with appropriate learning. Fr. 55a refers by way of parody to this same basic principle of reciprocity, included already in Solon's laws. Despite the obvious comic perspective, the passage of Aristophanes contains the essence of the law concerning the obligation of the children to feed their parents in old age (δεῖ τοὺς νεοττοὺς τὸν πατέρα πάλιν τρέφειν), which worked as a mutual support observed also among animals (cf. fr. 55c).

As illustrated by fr. 56/a, the legal and moral obligation of granting *gerotrophia* could face some restrictions. This law was properly bound up with Solon's concern to encourage trade and crafts, at a time when the economy of Attica needed a strong incentive to overcome its problems. This is in accord with Plut. *Sol.* 24. iv (fr. 75), which states that he promised full integration in the Athenian *polis* to those who were qualified in a *techne* and were ready to settle in Attica together with their families (μετοικιζομένοις ἐπὶ τέχνῃ), thus giving a definite incentive in order to stimulate the economy. In fr. 56/a, Solon is said to have encouraged his fellow citizens to dedicate themselves to handicraft production, as the poor soil of Attica did not have the ability to support a large number of people (τὰ δὲ πλεῖστα τῆς χώρας ἀγεννῆ καὶ φαῦλα). Therefore the strengthening of the economy in the areas of manufacturing would create surplus production that could stimulate trade in order to import necessities. Within the spirit of encouraging production, it is particularly significant that Solon linked the moral obligation of *gerotrophia* to the parents' duty of teaching their children a craft (υἱῷ τρέφειν πατέρα μὴ διδαξάμενον τέχνην ἐπάναγκες μὴ εἶναι). He probably had in mind that *paidotrophia* was not well conducted if the parents had not taught their children a profession that would allow them to earn their living as adults. Consequently, the principle of reciprocity which bound the relationship between *paidotrophia* and *gerotrophia* would no longer apply. Frs. 56b–c refer most probably to the same Solonian law, as was remarked already by K.-L. Weeber, 'Ein vernachlässigtes solonisches Gesetz', *Athenaeum*[2] li 1973, 30–3. On the general principle of reciprocity between relatives, see Dover, *Greek Popular Morality*, 273–5. For the extension of this principle to tragedy, see M. do C. Fialho, '*Paidotrophia* and *Gêrotrophia*: Reciprocity and Disruption in Attic Tragedy', in Harris *et al.* (edd.), *Law and Drama in Ancient Greece*, 108–21.

Pl. *Cri.* 50 D establishes a connection between *paideia* and *trophe*, even if the *technai* implied are music and gymnastics. Solon is certainly thinking of a more practical application of the term, therefore a 'craft' or 'profession', especially manufacturing, although agriculture is not necessarily excluded from the concept (cf. Xen. *Oec.* v. 17, which clearly states that γεωργία 'farming' is the mother and feeder of the other *technai*). Aeschin. I. *Timarchus* 27 (part of fr. 104a) states that Solon did not drive from the assembly the man 'who plies some craft (τέχνην) to support the necessities of his maintenance (τροφῇ)'; although that is of course merely a statement of an exclusion not imposed by Solon, it nevertheless establishes a positive connection between *techne* and *trophe*. On this see also Stroud, *Axones and Kyrbeis*, 5; Manfredini & Piccirilli, *Plutarco. La vita di Solone*[5], 238–9; Ruschenbusch, *Gesetzeswerk*, 122–3.

Fr. 57/a states that the obligation to support parents in old age was binding only on legitimate offspring, therefore not extended to *nothoi* born from a *hetaira*. Ruschenbusch, *Gesetzeswerk*, 121–2, considers the word *hetaira* anachronistic when applied to a law of Solon, because the term occurs for the first time only in Hdt. II. 134. Even if this consideration does not prevent the law from being Solonian, the original regulation should have had a different term for prostitute. The expression ὅσαι πεφασμένως πωλοῦνται ('those who promenade manifestly', cf. frs. 29a–b and 30a) is in accordance with Solon's metaphorical use of language in legal and political issues.

The disposition concerning the moral obligations of *nothoi* is quite balanced, because illegitimate children were heavily penalised in terms of legal powers (cf. fr. 50b with commentary). On the other hand, fr. 57/a accentuates the legal gap that stood between *gnesioi* and *nothoi*, by deepening the degree of exclusiveness distinctive of citizenship status. S. Lape, 'Solon and the Institution of the "Democratic" Family Form', *CJ* xcviii 2002/3, 129–35, envisages this provision as a kind of first step towards the Periclean citizenship law of 451/0, aimed at limiting the privileges of nobility, because aristocrats were the majority of those who had enough resources to allow the maintenance of illegitimate children.

According to fr. 57/b, a son would be exempt from *gerotrophia* if his father had previously hired him out for prostitution (*hetairein*), in so far as the *kyrios* had used his authority not to protect but to exploit his dependant. In such a situation, which would fall in the area of family exploitation, the law required the minor, who meanwhile had become adult, to guarantee simply the burial of the father and the customary funeral rites, certainly because of religious piety. See Fisher, *Aeschines, Against Timarchos*, 137. Although it is not clearly stated that this disposition went back to the time of Solon, it is not unlikely that he inspired it, because he made illegal the prostitution of elements of the *oikos* by the *kyrios*. In the section devoted to Solon's laws concerning women, Plutarch states that he forbade the procuring of free women (*Sol.* 23. i = fr. 30a), and the forced prostitution of daughters and sisters (*Sol.* 23. ii = fr. 31a), but he also states that before Solon no law prevented the exploitation of children in general (*Sol.* 13. iv–v = fr. 31b), and so young boys could also have been covered by his legislation. Besides, the disposition of fr. 57/b fits well the logic of mutual obligations concerning *paidotrophia* and *gerotrophia*. According to Diog. Laert. I. 55 (fr. 104b), Solon stated that a man who failed to provide *gerotrophia* for his parents would become *atimos*, but this penalty is too high and most probably is not Solonian. For more details, see Leão, '*Paidotrophia* et *gerotrophia* dans les lois de Solon', *RHD* lxxxix 2011, 457–72 at 467–70.

Adoption

Fr. 58a: Harp. o 43 Keaney
ὅτι οἱ ποιητοὶ παῖδες ἐπανελθεῖν εἰς τὸν πατρῷον οἶκον οὐκ ἦσαν κύριοι, εἰ μὴ παῖδας γνησίους καταλίποιεν ἐν τῷ οἴκῳ τοῦ

ποιησαμένου, Ἀντιφῶν ἐπιτροπικῷ <κατὰ> Καλλιστράτου (fr. IV / 15 Thalheim) καὶ Σόλων ἐν κα΄ νόμων.

<κατὰ> Sauppe.   For νόμων perhaps read ἀξόνων Ruschenbusch.

That adopted sons were not free to go back to their natural family, unless they could leave legitimate children in the household of their adoptive father. So Antiphon in the speech about guardianship *Against Callistratus*, and so Solon in the twenty-first [*axon*] of the laws.

Fr. 58b: [Dem.] XLIV. *Leochares* 64
ὁ νομοθέτης ἀπεῖπεν τῷ ποιητῷ αὐτῷ ὄντι ποιητὸν υἱὸν μὴ ποιεῖσθαι, τίνα τρόπον διορίσας περὶ τούτων; ὅταν εἴπῃ "υἱὸν γνήσιον ἐγκαταλιπόντα ἐπανιέναι", δηλοῖ δήπου φανερῶς ὅτι οὐ δεῖ ποιεῖσθαι· ἀδύνατον γάρ ἐστιν υἱὸν γνήσιον ἐγκαταλιπεῖν, ἐὰν μὴ γόνῳ γεγονὼς ᾖ τινι.

The legislator did not allow an adopted son to adopt a son in his turn. And in what terms did he define this? When he states that 'he may return [to his natural family] on the condition that he leaves a legitimate son [in the household of the adoptive father]', the legislator clearly denies him the right to adopt: in fact, it is impossible lo leave a legitimate son, if one has no natural children.

Fr. 58/c = fr. 49/e (fr. 121a Ruschenbusch): Dem. XLIV. *Leochares* 67
τὸ δὲ πάντων μέγιστον καὶ γνωριμώτατον ὑμῖν· ὁ γὰρ τοῦ Σόλωνος νόμος οὐδὲ διαθέσθαι τὸν ποιητὸν ἐᾷ τὰ ἐν τῷ οἴκῳ οἷ ἂν ποιηθῇ. εἰκότως, οἶμαι. τῷ γὰρ κατὰ νόμον εἰσποιηθέντι ἐπὶ τὰ ἑτέρου οὐχ οὕτως ὡς περὶ τῶν ἰδίων κτημάτων βουλευτέον ἐστίν, ἀλλὰ τοῖς νόμοις ἀκολούθως, περὶ ἑκάστου τῶν γεγραμμένων, ὡς ὁ νόμος λέγει· "ὅσοι μὴ ἐπεποίηντο", φησί, "ὅτε Σόλων εἰσῄει τὴν ἀρχήν, ἐξεῖναι αὐτοῖς διαθέσθαι ὅπως ἂν ἐθέλωσιν", ὡς τοῖς γε ποιηθεῖσιν οὐκ ἔξον διαθέσθαι.

What is most important of all and best known to you: the law of Solon does not allow an adopted son even to bequeath the property of the household into which he has been adopted. Reasonably, I think: for somebody who has been adopted in accordance with the law into the property of another ought not to decide about it as he would about his own possessions, but in conformity with the laws, following each of the things written as the law states. 'Those who had not been adopted', it says, 'when Solon entered on his archonship shall be permitted to bequeath as they wish', implying that those who had been adopted were not permitted to bequeath.

A man who did not have a son could adopt a boy or more frequently a man to take the place of the legitimate son whom he lacked (cf. frs. 49a–g with commentary). Ruschenbusch, *Gesetzeswerk*, 125, says that the man adopted should usually be at least twenty-five or thirty years old. In principle, he should also have at least one brother, so that the decision to leave his natural family would not put in danger the survival of his original *oikos*. Adopted children (ποιητοὶ παῖδες) enjoyed the same rights as a natural child, but lost, at the same time, the legal prerogatives which bound them to their previous family. It is to this situation that the law of Solon mentioned in frs. 58a–c refers (the number of the *axon* provided in fr. 58a reinforces its authenticity). Once completed, the adoption process could not simply be undone: in order to return legally to his original household, the adopted son had to leave in the *oikos* of the adoptive father a natural child who would occupy the place left vacant. In other words, an adoption by one who has himself been adopted was considered unlawful (cf. Isae. IX. *Astyphilus* 33; X. *Aristarchus* 11). The probable goal of this disposition was to protect the household of the adopter, as well as to prevent the escalating of adoptions. See MacDowell, *L.C.A.* 100–1; Rubinstein, *Adoption in IV. Century Athens*, 57–8; Leão, *Sólon: Ética e política*, 112–3.

UNIDENTIFIABLE CONTENT

Fr. 59: Poll. VI. 156
οἱ γὰρ ὁμογάλακτες ἴδιον τῶν Ἀττικῶν, τὸ δ' ὁμοερκὴς σκληρόν, εἰ καὶ παρὰ Σόλωνι.
The word *homogalaktes* ['foster-brothers'] is typical of the Attic dialect; the word *homoerkes* ['in the same house'] is inappropriate, even if it can be found in Solon.

The content of fr. 59 cannot be defined with certainty, although it may refer to a gloss dealing with the household or with some cult association. Like fr. 59a, it shows nevertheless that Solon's laws attracted the attention of lexicographers, probably because of the archaic nature of its language. See Ruschenbusch, *Gesetzeswerk*, 126.

*Fr. 59a: *Anecd. Oxon.* iii. 193
(p. 195) Σόλων ὁ νομοθέτης ἐν τοῖς ἄξοσι ... ὁμαίμονας.
(p. 193) τοῦ δὲ ὁμαίμου ἢ καὶ ὁμαίμονος, ἀπό τε τῶν βίβλων Ἀριστοφάνους τοῦ γραμματικοῦ (fr. 7 Nauck) καὶ Σόλωνος τοῦ νομοθέτου καὶ τῶν ἄλλων σοφῶν ποιήσομαί σοι τὰς μαρτυρίας.
Solon the legislator in the *axones* ... [mentions] *homaimones* ['of the same blood'].
Concerning the words *homaimos* and *homaimon* I shall bring you the evidence from the books of Aristophanes the grammarian, of Solon, the legislator, and from the other wise men.

Although the content of fr. 59a is not clearly identifiable, a possible context for it could be the rules dealing with marriage between brother and sister (see fr. 47b), where the terms *homopatrioi* and *homometrioi* are used, or even the regulations respecting legitimate offspring (*gnesioi paides*) and *engyesis* (cf. fr. 48b with commentary). The grammarian Aristophanes dealt with these questions in his work on *Kinship* (cf. *Anecd. Oxon.* iii. 194: Ἀριστοφάνης ... ἐν τῷ Συγγενικῷ περὶ διαφορᾶς τῶν ἀδελφῶν διαλαμβάνων), where the reference to Solon's laws would fit well.

NEIGHBOURS

Distance between properties

Fr. 60a: *Dig.* X. 1. xiii
GAIUS LIBRO QUARTO AD LEGEM XII TABULARUM: *Sciendum est in actione finium regundorum illud observandum esse, quod ad exemplum quodammodo eius legis scriptum est, quam Athenis Solonem dicitur tulisse; nam illic ita est:* ἐάν τις αἱμασιὰν παρ' ἀλλοτρίῳ χωρίῳ <οἰκοδομῇ ἢ> ὀφρύγην, τὸν ὅρον μὴ παραβαίνειν· ἐὰν τειχίον, πόδα ἀπολείπειν, ἐὰν δὲ οἴκημα, δύο πόδας, ἐὰν δὲ τάφρον ἢ βόθυνον ὀρύττῃ, ὅσον <ἂν> τὸ βάθος ᾖ, τοσοῦτον ἀπολείπειν· ἐὰν δὲ φρέαρ, ὀργυάν· ἐλάαν δὲ καὶ συκῆν ἐννέα πόδας ἀπὸ τοῦ ἀλλοτρίου φυτεύειν, τὰ δὲ ἄλλα δένδρη πέντε πόδας.
<οἰκοδομῇ ἢ> Paoli. <ἂν> *Mommsen.*
GAIUS, ON THE LAW OF THE TWELVE TABLES, BOOK IV: It should be taken into account that, in an action for the definition of boundaries, that rule must be observed which, to a certain extent, was written according to the law that Solon is said to have passed in Athens. In effect, it runs like this: 'If someone builds a wall or a landfill bordering the land of another, he cannot go beyond the boundary; if it is a masonry wall, he must keep a distance of one foot, and if it is a house, two feet; if he digs a pit or hole, he must keep a distance equal in width to the depth; if a cistern, [he must keep the distance] of a fathom. If he plants an olive-tree or a fig-tree, [he must keep the distance] of nine feet from the bordering land, and with the other trees, five feet.'

Fr. 60b: Plut. *Sol.* 23. vii–viii
ὥρισε δὲ καὶ φυτειῶν μέτρα μάλ' ἐμπείρως, τοὺς μὲν ἄλλο τι φυτεύοντας ἐν ἀγρῷ πέντε πόδας ἀπέχειν τοῦ γείτονος κελεύσας, τοὺς δὲ συκῆν ἢ ἐλαίαν ἐννέα· πορρωτέρω γὰρ ἐξικνεῖται ταῦτα ταῖς ῥίζαις καὶ οὐ πᾶσι γειτνιᾷ τοῖς φυτοῖς ἀσινῶς, ἀλλὰ καὶ τροφὴν παραιρεῖται καὶ βλάπτουσαν ἐνίοις ἀπορροὴν ἀφίησι.

βόθρους δὲ καὶ τάφρους τὸν βουλόμενον ἐκέλευσεν ὀρύσσειν, ὅσον ἐμβάλλει βάθος ἀφιστάμενον μῆκος τἀλλοτρίου.

He has also shown great experience regarding the distance between planted trees, by dictating that whoever planted anything else in a field ought to keep the distance of five feet from the neighbour's land, or of nine feet, if it was a fig tree or an olive tree. In fact, these trees extend their roots farther and their proximity is not harmless to all the plants, because they steal their nourishment and emit exhalations that are sometimes harmful. He also determined that someone who wants to dig a hole or a pit must keep from the bordering land a distance equal in width to the depth.

Fr. 60c: *Anecd. Bekk.* i. 85. 1
βόθυνον οὔ φασι δεῖν λέγειν. ἀλλὰ Σόλων ἔφη ἐν τοῖς νόμοις.
They say that the word *bothynos* ('hole') should not be used. But Solon makes use of it in his laws.

Fr. 61: Hesych. π 3643 Latte *et al.*
ΠΡΟΠΤΟΡΘΙΑ· ἐν τοῖς ἄξοσιν ἡ λέξις φέρεται.
PROPTORTHIA ('projecting branch'): this word is found in the *axones*.

Fr. 62: Plut. *Sol.* 23. viii
καὶ μελισσῶν σμήνη καθιστάμενον, ἀπέχειν τῶν ὑφ' ἑτέρου πρότερον ἱδρυμένων πόδας τριακοσίους.
[He prescribed that someone who wants] to install hives of bees must place them three hundred feet away from those previously set out by another person.

The regulations included in this section may, at a first sight, seem excessive minutiae, but Plutarch (fr. 60b) is correct when he says that with such provisions Solon has shown signs of great experience (μάλ' ἐμπείρως). Indeed, in a system where agricultural land is subdivided into small parcels, any change in existing boundaries of land can lead to major disputes between neighbours. For this reason, it becomes very important to provide the exact definition of some basic rules, such as the space to leave between plantations bordering a neighbour's land. He also reveals accurate practical knowledge, when stating that the distance to be kept between planted trees had to be larger when a certain type of tree was involved (τοὺς δὲ συκῆν ἢ ἐλαίαν ἐννέα), in order to prevent damage to other plants. The disposition regarding the depth and separation between wells expresses the same practical approach, and it most probably aims at avoiding the exhaustion of water sources, a serious risk in areas of low rainfall, as happens in Mediterranean countries.

The same can be said about the definition (fr. 62) of the distance to be preserved between hives of bees (πόδας τριακοσίους), certainly in order to avoid the overcrowding of the explored area, which would be reflected in a lower production of honey. Papazarkadas, *Sacred and Public Land in Ancient Athens*, 265–6 n. 19, maintains that penalties against farmers who tilled the ground too close to the *moriai* were reminiscent of Solon's laws regarding the distance between plantations.

Frs. 60c and 61, which register the use in the *axones* of odd or unusual words, prove that these kinds of regulation weres indeed included in Solon's laws. The dispositions referred to in fr. 60a confirm in general terms the account of Plutarch, besides suggesting the direct influence of Solon on Rome's Law of the Twelve Tables. Manfredini & Piccirilli, *Plutarco. La vita di Solone*[5], 248–9, maintain that Gaius did not have access to the original Solonian text of the law, but only to a corrupted copy.

We do not know what length standard was used in Solon's Athens. The fourth-century Athenian stade (= 600 feet) was 184.98m, which yields 1 foot = 0.31m, 1 cubit (*pechys*, 1½ feet) = 0.46m, 1 fathom (*orgyia*, 6 feet) = 1.85m; the Olympic stade was slightly longer, 192.28m.

Sharing of water

Fr. 63: Plut. *Sol.* 23. vi
ἐπεὶ δὲ πρὸς ὕδωρ οὔτε ποταμοῖς ἐστιν ἀεννάοις οὔτε λίμναις τισὶν οὔτ' ἀφθόνοις πηγαῖς ἡ χώρα διαρκής, ἀλλ' οἱ πλεῖστοι φρέασι ποιητοῖς ἐχρῶντο, νόμον ἔγραψεν, ὅπου μέν ἐστι δημόσιον φρέαρ ἐντὸς ἱππικοῦ, χρῆσθαι τούτῳ (τὸ δ' ἱππικὸν διάστημα τεσσάρων ἦν σταδίων)· ὅπου δὲ πλεῖον ἀπέχει, ζητεῖν ὕδωρ ἴδιον· ἐὰν δ' ὀρύξαντες ὀργυιῶν δέκα βάθος παρ' ἑαυτοῖς μὴ εὕρωσι, τότε λαμβάνειν παρὰ τοῦ γείτονος, ἐξάχουν ὑδρίαν δὶς ἑκάστης ἡμέρας πληροῦντας· ἀπορίᾳ γὰρ ᾤετο δεῖν βοηθεῖν, οὐκ ἀργίαν ἐφοδιάζειν.

Since the country did not have sufficient water sources supplied by ever-flowing rivers, or lakes, or abundant springs, but most people used artificial wells, Solon wrote a law that where there was a public well within the space of a horse race (a horse race is a distance of four stades), use should be made of that; where the distance was greater, it was up to each one to look for water. If, after digging to the depth of ten fathoms on their own land, they did not find water, they could get it from a neighbour's well, filling a water-pot (*hydria*) holding six *choes*, twice a day. For he thought it necessary to give assistance in case of need, without encouraging idleness.

As also with frs. 60–2, this regulation is representative of the importance given to practical land issues in Solon's legislation. Fr. 60b comprises dispositions regarding the depth and separation between private wells; fr. 63 deals also with water resources, but this time in what concerns public wells. Up to a distance of four *stadia* (*c.* 740–770 m), private farmers had free access to the common water supplies; if the distance was greater (with an increased risk of waste during the transportation), each private user had to look for water in his own land. If water was not found up to the depth of ten fathoms (*c.* 18.5–19.2 m) on their own soil, a neighbour's well could be used, up to the limit of a *hydria* holding six *choes*, filled twice a day (2 × 19.7 l). Plato (*Leg.* VII. 843 B – 845 E) provides an illuminating set of regulations dealing with affairs between neighbours, which are probably rooted in the Athenian legal tradition and thereby at least partially in Solon's laws, even if a direct influence cannot be detected. See also Ruschenbusch, *Gesetzeswerk*, 129–30.

Plutarch's final remark emphasises that, with those rules, Solon wanted to promote collaboration within the community, but at the same time intended to prevent idleness (*argia*), by encouraging individual initiative. On the possibly Solonian law concerning the punishment of *argia*, see frs. 66/1a–g with commentary. See also frs. 56–7, on the connection between *paidotrophia* and *gerotrophia*, and the obligation to teach a craft to children.

Rights concerning natural fertilisers (?)

Fr. 64a: *Paroemiogr. Appendix* I. 58 (i. 388)
ΒΟΛΙΤΟΥ ΔΙΚΗΝ· πρὸς τοὺς ἀξίους καὶ ἐπὶ μικροῖς τιμωρίαν ὑπέχειν. ἐν γὰρ τοῖς Σόλωνος ἄξοσιν ὁ νόμος καὶ τοὺς βόλιτον ὑφελομένους κολάζει.
DUNG SUIT: [a proverb] coined for those who suffer deservedly even because of trifles. For in the *axones* of Solon the law punishes also those who have stolen dung.

Fr. 64b: Schol. Ar. *Eq.* 658, *Suda* β 367
ΒΟΛΙΤΟΥ ΔΙΚΗΝ· πρὸς τοὺς ἐπὶ μικροῖς δίκας ὑπέχοντας. ὁ γὰρ Σόλωνος νόμος καὶ τοὺς βόλιτον ὑφελομένους κολάζει.
DUNG SUIT: [a proverb] coined for those who face justice just because of trifles. For the law of Solon punishes also those who have stolen dung.

Those fragments suggest that the laws of Solon apparently went to the point of embracing minutiae such as those involving rights concerning natural fertilisers or animal waste. The term βόλιτον designates specifically cow-dung (Poll. V. 91), and therefore the regulation might have been aimed at those who owned or took care of cattle of this kind. At any rate, the low value of the goods under dispute seem to have inspired the creation of a proverb referred to by the expression βολίτου δίκη (literally 'dung suit'), applied to penalties resulting from trivial quarrels. It is doubtful whether this regulation could be part of the section on offences against property (see frs. 23–5).

ECONOMIC MATTERS

Measures, weights, [coinage]

†Fr. 64/1a: *Ath. Pol.* 10. i–ii

πρὸ δὲ τῆς νομοθεσίας ποιῆσαι τὴν τῶν χρεῶν ἀποκοπὴν (cf. fr. 67), καὶ μετὰ ταῦτα τήν τε τῶν μέτρων καὶ σταθμῶν καὶ τὴν τοῦ νομίσματος αὔξησιν. ἐπ' ἐκείνου γὰρ ἐγένετο καὶ τὰ μέτρα μείζω τῶν Φειδωνείων, καὶ ἡ μνᾶ πρότερον ἔχουσα σταθμὸν ἑβδομήκοντα δραχμὰς ἀνεπληρώθη ταῖς ἑκατόν, ἦν δ' ὁ ἀρχαῖος χαρακτὴρ δίδραχμον. ἐποίησε δὲ καὶ σταθμὰ πρὸς τὸ νόμισμα τρεῖς καὶ ἑξήκοντα μνᾶς τὸ τάλαντον ἀγούσας, καὶ ἐπιδιενεμήθησαν αἱ τρεῖς μναῖ τῷ στατῆρι καὶ τοῖς ἄλλοις σταθμοῖς.

Before this legislation he made the cancellation of debts, and after that the increase in the measures, weights and coinage. For under him the measures were made larger than the Pheidonean; and the mina, which previously had a weight of seventy drachmae, was filled up with the hundred; and the old standard coin was the two-drachmae. He made weights with regard to the coins at sixty-three minas to the talent, and the three minas were apportioned to the stater and the other weights.

†Fr. 64/1b: Androtion *FGrH* 324 F 34 *ap.* Plut. *Sol.* 15. iii–iv

... καὶ τὴν ἅμα τούτῳ γενομένην τῶν τε μέτρων ἐπαύξησιν καὶ τοῦ νομίσματος τιμῆς. ἑκατὸν γὰρ ἐποίησε δραχμῶν τὴν μνᾶν, πρότερον ἑβδομήκοντ' ἄγουσαν, ὥστ' ἀριθμῷ μὲν ἴσον, δυνάμει δ' ἔλαττον ἀποδιδόντων, ὠφελεῖσθαι μὲν τοὺς ἐκτίνοντας μεγάλα, μηδὲν δὲ βλάπτεσθαι τοὺς κομιζομένους.

ἑβδομήκοντ' ἄγουσαν T. Reinach: ἑβδομήκοντα καὶ τριῶν οὐσῶν MSS.

... and the increase in the measures and value of the currency which accompanied this [reduction in interest]. For he made the mina consist of a hundred drachmae, where it had previously consisted of seventy, so that repayments were the same in number but less in value, and those paying were greatly helped but those receiving were not harmed.

See Rhodes, *Comm. Ath. Pol*, on 10. i–ii, who on the meaning of that text follows C. M. Kraay, 'An Interpretation of *Ath. Pol.* Ch. 10', in *Essays* . . . *S. Robinson*, 1–9; Harding, *Androtion and the Atthis*, 129–33 on F34. Androtion / Plutarch differs from *Ath. Pol.* in applying the change in the ratio of drachma and mina to coinage, and in implying that the drachma was made lighter whereas *Ath. Pol.* implies that the mina was made heavier (though Harding argues that if *Ath. Pol.* were consciously disagreeing with Androtion that disagreement would have been made explicit). It now seems likely that Athens had no coinage until the middle of the sixth century, but for a time before that made some use of standard weights of silver (cf. Rhodes, *Comm. Ath. Pol.* 152–3; J. H. Kroll, 'Silver in Solon's Laws', in *Studies in Greek Numismatics* . . . *M. J. Price*, 225–32; G. E. M. de Ste. Croix, *Athenian Democratic Origins*, 38). However, G. Davis, 'Dating the Drachmas in Solon's Laws', *Historia* lxi 2012, 127–58, rejects that use of silver. It is true that the standard coins in Athens' first series, the *Wappenmünzen*, were of two drachmae but the subsequent 'owls' were of four drachmae (see e.g. C. M. Kraay, *Archaic and Classical Greek Coins*, 56–60). Because coins were named after their weights, it would be easy for later Greeks to suppose that a change in the drachma and mina was a change in the coinage.

Ath. Pol. and Androtion / Plutarch believed that Solon had changed Athens' quantitative standards, and there have been attempts to explain that in terms of a realignment of Athens in the Greek world for commercial advantage (e.g. F. E. Adcock, *C.A.H.*[1] iv [1926], 39–40). More probably Solon legislated for the use of existing standards, measures of capacity which were larger than the 'Pheidonean' (named after Pheidon of Argos) measures with the same names, and weights on a scale in which there were not seventy drachmae to the mina (as in the Aeginetan system) but a hundred. J. H. Kroll, 'Two Inscribed Corinthian Bronze Weights', in *Stephanèphoros* . . . *R. Descat*, 111–6, suggests that there was already a scale of weights applicable to silver which was different from the ordinary commercial weights. Androtion / Plutarch seems to have thought that Solon did not do anything so revolutionary as to cancel debts but merely used a device to reduce repayments (which of course would have harmed the creditors); but Harding, while stressing that the explanation is economic nonsense, does not accept that this was an attempt to distance Solon from revolutionary views.

Exports

Fr. 65: Plut. *Sol.* 24. i
τῶν δὲ γιγνομένων διάθεσιν πρὸς ξένους ἐλαίου μόνον ἔδωκεν, ἄλλα δ' ἐξάγειν ἐκώλυσε. καὶ κατὰ τῶν ἐξαγόντων ἀρὰς τὸν ἄρχοντα ποιεῖσθαι προσέταξεν, ἢ τίνειν αὐτὸν ἑκατὸν δραχμὰς εἰς τὸ δημόσιον. καὶ πρῶτος ἄξων ἐστὶν ὁ τοῦτον περιέχων τὸν νόμον.

Of natural products Solon allowed disposal to foreigners only of olive oil, and forbade the export of others. He also instructed the archon to pronounce curses against those who exported, failing which he should himself pay a hundred drachmae to the public treasury. It is the first *axon* that contains this law.

In the classical period Athens was dependent, at least in bad years and probably to some extent in all years, on imported grain. For a minimising view of this dependence see P. D. A. Garnsey, 'Grain for Athens', in *Crux* ... *G. E M. de Ste. Croix*, 62–75 = his *Cities, Peasants and Food in Classical Greece*, 183–95(–200); for a response see M. Whitby, 'The Grain Trade of Athens in the Fourth Century B.C.', in Parkins & Smith (edd.), *Trade, Traders and the Ancient City*, 102–28. This law can be seen as an attempt to prevent the export of home-grown grain which might sometimes sell for higher prices elsewhere and / or as an attempt to encourage a move from aspirations to self-sufficiency towards concentrating on what grew well in Attica and being willing to import other foodstuffs.

Papazarkadas, *Sacred and Public Land in Ancient Athens*, 272–3, discusses the inconsistency between this law and that mentioned by schol. Pind. *Nem.* x. 64b, that only victors in the games could export olive oil from Athens, and suggests that our law may be authentically Solonian but no longer in force in the classical period.

In Solon's laws a fine of a hundred drachmae is found also for raping a free woman (fr. 26), and other attested fines range between that and 5 dr. (fr. 32a): see Ruschenbusch, *Untersuchungen*, 11–15 esp. 11–12 = his *Kleine Schriften*, 77–80 esp. 77. It now seems likely that Athens had no coinage until the middle of the sixth century, but for a time before that made some use of standard weights of silver (cf. on Fr. 64/1). However, G. Davis, 'Dating the Drachmas in Solon's Laws', *Historia* lxi 2012, 127–58, who rejects that use of silver, argues that all specifications of value in terms of drachmae must be post-Solonian. Second-order penalties, for officials who fail to enforce a first-order law, are found often in Athens and in other Greek states: e.g., again with a hundred-drachmae fine, Athens' 'Hekatompedon inscription', *IG* i³ 4. B. 15–17 (485/4).

Limit to land acquisition

Fr. 66: see fr. 149/1

Fr. 66/1a (fr. 78a Ruschenbusch): Hdt. II. 177. ii

νόμον δὲ Αἰγυπτίοισι τόνδε Ἄμασίς ἐστι ὁ καταστήσας, ἀποδεικνύναι ἔτεος ἑκάστου τῷ νομάρχῃ πάντα τινὰ Αἰγυπτίων ὅθεν βιοῦται· μὴ δὲ ποιεῦντα ταῦτα μηδὲ ἀποφαίνοντα δικαίην ζόην ἰθύνεσθαι θανάτῳ. Σόλων δὲ ὁ Ἀθηναῖος λαβὼν ἐξ Αἰγύπτου τοῦτον τὸν νόμον Ἀθηναίοισι ἔθετο. τῷ ἐκεῖνοι ἐς αἰεὶ χρέωνται ἐόντι ἀμώμῳ νόμῳ.

It is Amasis who established this law for the Egyptians, that each of the Egyptians should declare each year to the nomarch his source of livelihood; if he did not do this or disclose a just means of life, he should be punished with death. Solon the Athenian took this law from Egypt and enacted it for the Athenians — and they should use it for all time, as it is an excellent law.

Fr. 66/1b (fr. 78b Ruschenbusch): Diod. Sic. I. 77. v
προσετέτακτο δὲ καὶ πᾶσι τοῖς Αἰγυπτίοις ἀπογράφεσθαι πρὸς τοὺς ἄρχοντας ἀπὸ τίνων ἕκαστος πορίζεται τὸν βίον, καὶ τὸν ἐν τούτοις ψευσάμενον ἢ πόρον ἄδικον ἐπιτελοῦντα θανάτῳ περιπίπτειν ἦν ἀναγκαῖον. λέγεται δὲ τοῦτον τὸν νόμον ὑπὸ Σόλωνος παραβαλόντος εἰς Αἴγυπτον εἰς τὰς Ἀθήνας μετενεχθῆναι.
It was prescribed for all the Egyptians that they should report to the officials what the source of each man's livelihood was, and anybody who lied in this or enjoyed unjust means was bound to be sentenced to death. It is said that Solon after crossing to Egypt transferred this law to Athens.

Fr. 66/1c (frs. 78c and 148e Ruschenbusch): Plut. *Sol.* 22. iii
Σόλων δὲ τοῖς πράγμασι τοὺς νόμους μᾶλλον ἢ τὰ πράγματα τοῖς νόμοις προσαρμόζων, καὶ τῆς χώρας τὴν φύσιν ὁρῶν γλίσχρως τοῖς γεωργοῦσι διαρκοῦσαν, ἀργὸν δὲ καὶ σχολαστὴν ὄχλον οὐ δυναμένην τρέφειν, ταῖς τέχναις ἀξίωμα περιέθηκε καὶ τὴν ἐξ Ἀρείου πάγου βουλὴν ἔταξεν ἐπισκοπεῖν ὅθεν ἕκαστος ἔχει τὰ ἐπιτήδεια, καὶ τοὺς ἀργοὺς κολάζειν.
Solon fitted his laws to the facts rather than the facts to his laws, and, when he saw that the nature of the land was barely adequate for the farmers, and could not sustain an idle and unoccupied mob, he set a value on crafts and appointed the council of the Areopagus to examine the source of each man's provisions and to punish the idle.

Fr. 66/1d (fr. 148a Ruschenbusch): Plut. *Sol.* 31. v
ὡς δ' ὁ Θεόφραστος (fr. 99 Wimmer) ἱστόρηκε, καὶ τὸν τῆς ἀργίας νόμον οὐ Σόλων ἔθηκεν ἀλλὰ Πεισίστρατος, ᾧ τήν τε χώραν ἐνεργοτέραν καὶ τὴν πόλιν ἡρεμαιοτέραν ἐποίησεν.
As Theophrastus has recorded, it was also not Solon who enacted the law on idleness but Pisistratus, who thereby made the land more active and the city more calm.

Fr. 66/1e (fr. 148b Ruschenbusch): Diog. Laert. I. 55 (part of **fr. 104b**)
καὶ ὁ ἀργὸς ὑπεύθυνος ἔστω παντὶ τῷ βουλομένῳ γράφεσθαι. Λυσίας ἐν τῷ κατὰ Νικίδου (fr. 246 Carey) Δράκοντά φησι γεγραφέναι τὸν νόμον.
Ruschenbusch made the following words, Σόλωνα δὲ τεθηκέναι, part of this sentence; but see fr. 104b.

And the idle man can be called to account by anybody who wishes to prosecute. Lysias in the speech against Nicides says that it was Draco who wrote this law.

Fr. 66/1f (fr. 148c Ruschenbusch): *Lex. Rhet. Cant.* (72. 3–6 *Lexica Graeca Minora*)
ΑΡΓΙΑΣ ΔΙΚΗ· Λυσίας ἐν τῷ κατὰ Ἀρίστωνός (fr. 40b Carey) φησιν ὅτι Δράκων ἦν ὁ θεὶς τὸν νόμον [sc. ἀργίας], αὖθις δὲ Σόλων ἐχρήσατο, θάνατον οὐχ ὁρίσας ὥσπερ ἐκεῖνος ἀλλ' ἀτιμίαν ἐάν τις ἁλῷ τρίς, ἐὰν δ' ἅπαξ ζημιοῦθαι δραχμὰς ἑκατόν.
τρίς, ἐὰν Dobree: τίσαι· ἂν MS., τρὶς ἁλῷη τις, ἐὰν Houtsma.   δραχμὰς: δραχμαῖς Houtsma.

ARGIAS DIKE ['private suit for idleness']: Lysias in the speech against Ariston says that it was Draco who enacted the law and Solon again used it, not stipulating death as Draco did but *atimia* if a man was convicted three times, or if once a penalty of a hundred drachmae.

Fr. 66/1g (fr. 148d Ruschenbusch): Poll. VIII. 42
τῆς δὲ ἀργίας ἐπὶ μὲν Δράκοντος ἀτιμία ἦν τὸ τίμημα· ἐπὶ δὲ Σόλωνος, εἰ τρίς τις ἁλῴη ἠτιμοῦτο.

For idleness the assessment was *atimia* under Draco, under Solon if a man was convicted three times he was made *atimos*.

Ruschenbusch saw behind his frs. 77 and 78 a census, repeated at intervals (cf. Arist. *Pol.* V. 1308 A 35 – B 6, Pl. *Leg.* XII. 955 D–E, and note Anthemion's change of class in *Ath. Pol.* 7. iv), to assign men correctly to their property classes (but he suspected that the mention of the Areopagus in fr. 77c was a product of fourth-century speculation about the earlier role of the Areopagus); and he distinguished from that the law against idleness, which he included among the spurious laws as fr. 148. Rhodes doubts whether the assignment to classes was based on a full review of each man's livelihood (cf. on fr. 77 = 80/2), and suspects that generally a man will have been asked on relevant occasions which class he belonged to, and that his answer will have been accepted unless somebody challenged it. Fr. 77 = 80/2 concerns not the Solonian classes but sacrificial offerings, and fr. 78 = 66/1 concerns not the Solonian classes but the alleged law of idleness.

Is that law, and the Areopagus' role in enforcing it, an authentic law and Solonian? It is defended as a law of Solon by Wallace, *The Areopagos Council*, 62–4, who sees it as a precaution against theft, on the assumption that men without an honest means of livelihood might turn to stealing. Whether or not that is the right explanation, the mention of the law by Herodotus, before debates about the traditional constitution had begun, encourages acceptance, and Solon is more likely than Draco or Pisistratus to have enacted such a law, but it is unlikely that Solon copied this or any other law from Egypt, and impossible that he should have copied a law of Amasis, who ruled 570–526, after Solon's archonship in 594/3. If it is authentic, we should perhaps think of a possibility of denouncing alleged offenders to the Areopagus, rather than an inquisition from time to time, or even once, into the livelihood of each of the citizens (cf. fr. 66/1e). Different penalties under Draco and Solon will be an embroidery on the original debate over who was the author of the law.

Seisachtheia

Fr. 67: Poll. VII. 151
ἐπίμορτος δὲ γῆ παρὰ Σόλωνι ἡ ἐπὶ μέρει γεωργουμένη, καὶ μόρτη τὸ μέρος τὸ ἀπὸ τῶν γεωργῶν.
ἐπίμορτος: ἐπιμοργός II.   μόρτη: μοργή II.   Cf. Hesych. ε 4985 Latte *et al.* ἐπίμορτος.
Epimortos land in Solon is that farmed for a portion, and *morte* is the portion paid by the farmers.

While there has been debate over how the *hektemoroi* came into existence, and they are now often seen as men in a quasi-feudal state of dependence rather than as formerly free men who had fallen into debt once and were being given a second chance on special terms, it is generally though not universally agreed that among the beneficiaries of the *seisachtheia* were the *hektemoroi* (glossed as *pelatai* by *Ath. Pol.*; *hektemorioi*, glossed as *thetes*, by Plutarch), so named because they had to pay a sixth of their produce to an overlord (*Ath. Pol.* 2. ii, Plut. *Sol.* 13. iv–v: see the reviews of modern theories by Rhodes, *Comm. Ath. Pol.* 89–97; Leão, *Sólon: Ética e política*, 230–8). If this is so, it is likely that Pollux' *epimortos ge* was the land which these men farmed and *morte* was the payment which they were required to make. The land will have belonged to these men, and will have been passed to their heirs, as long as they made their payments, but if they were unable to make their payments the overlord might take over their land and enslave them. Solon claimed to have freed the land by uprooting the *horoi* planted in it (fr. 36. 6–10 West *ap. Ath. Pol.* 12. iv), and it is credible that the overlords should have set up *horoi* to mark *epimortos ge* on which they had a claim. What *Ath. Pol.* and Plutarch see as a cancellation of debts will have been primarily the abolition of the obligations of the *hektemoroi*, who thereby became the unencumbered owners of their land. To prevent the continuation or revival of this system, Solon may well have enacted a law which mentioned *epimortos ge* and the *morte*.

However, M. Faraguna in another review ('*Hektemoroi, isomoiria, seisachtheia*: ricerche recenti sulle riforme economiche di Solone', *Dike* xv 2012, 171–93), while agreeing that the problem was an agrarian problem, argues that the *hektemoroi* retained only one sixth; he thinks of additional land brought under cultivation, and sees this as land improperly annexed by the overlords, the *hektemoroi* as labourers paid to work it, whose harsh conditions might force them into debt, and the *seisachtheia* as a 'liberation' of the wrongly annexed land, coupled with easier terms for the *hektemoroi*.

Rate of interest

Fr. 68: Lys. X. *Theomnestus* 18 (part of **fr. 23c**)
(15 καί μοι ἀνάγνωθι τούτους τοὺς νόμους τοὺς Σόλωνος τοὺς παλαίους.)
"τὸ ἀργύριον στάσιμον εἶναι ἐφ' ὁπόσῳ ἂν βούληται ὁ δανείζων."
τὸ στάσιμον τοῦτό ἐστιν, ὦ βέλτιστε, οὐ ζύγῳ ἱστάναι ἀλλὰ τόκον πράττεσθαι ὁπόσον ἂν βούληται.
εἶναι: θεῖναι Francken, τιθέναι Zakas.
(15 And read for me these ancient laws of Solon.)
'The silver is to be placed on the basis of whatever amount the lender wishes.' 'Placed', my good fellow, means not weighed on a balance, but let out at whatever rate of interest he wishes.

This is part of a series of examples intended to show that the Athenians act on the meaning of the laws rather than limiting themselves to the precise wording (§§6–20). The law will be certainly archaic and probably a law of Solon. Millett, *Lending and Borrowing in Ancient Athens*, 50, notes in support of this that στάσιμον is found with the meaning 'lent' only here.

Ban on enslavement for debt

Fr. 69a: *Ath. Pol.* 9. i (part of **fr. 39/1a**)
δοκεῖ δὲ τῆς Σόλωνος πολιτείας τρία ταῦτ' εἶναι τὰ δημοτικώτατα· πρῶτον μὲν καὶ μέγιστον τὸ μὴ δανείζειν ἐπὶ τοῖς σώμασιν.
These seem to be the most democratic features of Solon's constitution: first and greatest, that there should be no loans on the security of the person.

Fr. 69b: *Ath. Pol.* 6. i
κύριος δὲ γενόμενος τῶν πραγμάτων Σόλων τόν τε δῆμον ἠλευθέρωσε καὶ ἐν τῷ παρόντι καὶ εἰς τὸ μέλλον, κωλύσας δανείζειν ἐπὶ τοῖς σώμασιν· καὶ νόμους ἔθηκε· καὶ χρεῶν ἀποκοπὰς ἐποίησε καὶ τῶν ἰδίων καὶ τῶν δημοσίων.
Having gained control of affairs Solon liberated the people both in the present and for the future, by forbidding loans on the security of the person; and he enacted laws; and he made a cancellation of debts both public and private.

Fr. 69c: Plut. *Sol.* 15. ii
γράψας τὰ μὲν ὑπάρχοντα τῶν χρεῶν ἀνεῖσθαι, πρὸς δὲ τὸ λοιπὸν ἐπὶ τοῖς σώμασιν μηδένα δανείζειν.
He wrote that existing debts should be annulled, and for the future that nobody should lend on the security of the person.

Ath. Pol. and later texts interpreted as a cancellation of all debts what was probably in essence an abolition of the obligations and of the status of the *hektemoroi*: they had been liable to enslavement and loss of their land if they defaulted on their obligations, and with the removal of their obligations that liability was removed too (cf. on fr. 67). Solon claims to have brought back many Athenians serving abroad as slaves ('some unjustly, some justly') and also to have liberated many serving as slaves in Attica, unless the latter is a metaphorical statement of his liberation of the *hektemoroi* (fr. 36. 11–18 West *ap. Ath. Pol.* 12. iv). It is possible — but we cannot be sure — that he cancelled some debts in addition to the obligations of the *hektemoroi*, and that he rescued and liberated some slaves in addition to defaulting *hektemoroi*, but is doubtful whether many outside Attica were rescued, since slave-owners outside Attica would have no obligation to respect a liberation proclaimed in Athens. Cf. Rhodes, *Comm. Ath. Pol.* 125–7.

What Solon did not do was abolish all forms of debt bondage: it is clear that in the classical period an Athenian could be bound to a creditor until his debt was discharged (e.g. Ar. *Plut.* 147–8, Men. *Her.* 18–38), and men with overdue debts to the state could be imprisoned until their debts had been paid (e.g. *Ath. Pol.* 48. i). What he did abolish was the outright and permanent enslavement of defaulting debtors. See E. M. Harris, 'Did Solon Abolish Debt-Bondage?', CQ^2 lii 2002, 415–30 = his *Democracy and the Rule of Law*, 249–69.

Amnesty for *atimoi*

Fr. 70: see fr. 22/1

SUMPTUARY LAWS

Dowry restrictions

Fr. 71a: Plut. *Sol.* 20. vi
τῶν δ' ἄλλων γάμων ἀφεῖλε τὰς φερνάς, ἱμάτια τρία καὶ σκεύη μικροῦ τιμήματος ἄξια κελεύσας, ἕτερον δὲ μηδέν, ἐπιφέρεσθαι τὴν γαμουμένην.
In all other marriages, he banned dowries, prescribing that the bride could take with her three garments, household stuff of little value and nothing else.

Fr. 71b: Poll. I. 246
Σόλων δὲ καὶ τὰς νύμφας ἰούσας ἐπὶ τὸν γάμον ἐκέλευσε φρύγετρον φέρειν σημεῖον ἀλφιτουργίας.
Solon prescribed that brides going to their wedding should take a vessel for roasting barley as a symbol of the household obligations.

Those laws deal with practices adopted in regular marriage ceremonies, therefore not with the special case of *epikleroi* (see frs. 51–2 with commentary). The controversy aroused by them concerns the interpretation of the expression τὰς φερνάς in fr. 71a. If it is understood as 'dowries', then Solon was probably intending to restrain the giving of excessive dowries to daughters in order to prevent the diminution of the paternal possessions that would be transmitted to the male son. However, the value of the goods prescribed by the regulation is much less significant than those involved in dowries by the time of the orators, although this does not preclude a different situation in Solon's days. See Sondhaus, *De Solonis Legibus*, 29; Harrison, *L.A.* i. 45–7. On the other hand, *pherne* could be interpreted simply as 'bridal gifts', thus providing this regulation with a flavour of sumptuary purposes that would be in accordance with a strategy of reducing unessential costs, in order not to harm a fragile economy and also to avoid increasing social tensions (see frs. 72a–d with commentary). For a synopsis of the main lines of argumentation, see Manfredini & Piccirilli, *Plutarco. La vita di Solone*[5], 229–30.

Funeral restrictions

Fr. 72a: Cic. *Leg.* II. 63–6

Nam et Athenis iam ille mos a Cecrope, ut aiunt, permansit corpus terra humandi, quod quom proximi fecerant obductaque terra erat, frugibus obserebatur, ut sinus et gremium quasi matris mortuo tribueretur, solum autem frugibus expiatum ut vivis redderetur. Sequebantur epulae, quas inibant propinqui coronati, apud quos de mortui laude quom si quid veri erat praedicatum — nam mentiri nefas habebatur — iusta confecta erant. (64) *Postea quam, ut scribit Phalereus, sumptuosa fieri funera et lamentabilia coepissent, Solonis lege sublata sunt. — quam legem eisdem prope verbis nostri X viri in decimam tabulam coniecerunt. Nam de tribus reciniis et pleraque illa Solonis sunt. De lamentis vero expressa verbis sunt 'mulieres genas ne radunto neve lessum funeris ergo habento'. — de sepulcris autem nihil est apud Solonem amplius quam ne quis ea deleat neve alienum inferat, poenaque est, si quis bustum — nam id puto appellari* τύμβον *— aut monimentum, inquit, aut columnam violauerit, iacerit, fregerit. Sed post aliquanto propter has amplitudines sepulcrorum, quas in Ceramico videmus, lege sanctum est, ne quis sepulcrum faceret operosius quam quod decem homines effecerint triduo,* (65) *neque id opere tectorio exornari, nec hermas hos, quos vocant, licebat inponi, nec de mortui laude nisi in publicis sepulturis, nec ab alio, nisi qui publice ad eam rem constitutus esset, dici licebat. Sublata etiam erat celebritas virorum ac mulierum, quo lamentatio minueretur; auget enim luctum concursus hominum.* (66) *Quocirca Pittacus omnino accedere quemquam vetat in funus aliorum. Sed ait rursus idem Demetrius increbuisse eam funerum sepulcrorumque magnificentiam, quae nunc fere Romae est. Quam consuetudinem lege minuit ipse . . . sumptum minuit non solum poena, sed etiam tempore: ante lucem enim iussit efferri. Sepulcris autem novis finivit modum; nam super terrae tumulum noluit quicquam statui, nisi columellam tribus cubitis ne altiorem aut mensam aut labellum, et huic procurationi certum magistratum praefecerat.*

§66 *quicquam* Lambinus: *quod* MSS.

In fact, they say that, in Athens, the tradition to bury the dead in the earth began in the time of Cecrops. When the next of kin had done that and the earth was cast over the dead, then vegetable seeds were sown on the grave, as if they were a kind of maternal womb and bosom given to the deceased, so that, through the expiation of the seeds, the land could again bear fruit for the living. Then followed a feast, attended by the near relatives crowned with garlands, during which the praise of the dead was pronounced, if his virtues were truly worthy of praise — it was in fact considered wicked to lie on such moments — and the proper ceremonies were performed. (64) In later times, according to Demetrius of Phalerum, when funerals became sumptuous and extravagant mournings grew up, Solon abolished those excesses by law — a law that our decemvirs included almost word for word in the Tenth Table. In effect, the clauses regarding the three veils and most of the other regulations come from Solon. In what respects mourning, they clearly follow his exact words: 'Women shall not tear their cheeks nor indulge in weeping at funerals.' However Solon has no other regulations concerning graves, with the exception of the one that forbids causing injury to them or putting the body of a stranger in them, and he punishes anyone who violates, casts down or breaks a sepulchral mound — for I think this is what *tymbos* means — or a funeral monument or a column. But some time afterwards, because of the extravangance of these tombs which we can observe in the Ceramicus, a law was enacted prescribing that no one should build a tomb more elaborate than one which ten men could complete during the period of three days, (65) and also that it should not be decorated with plaster covering, and that no herms, as they call them, should be set on them; nor was it permitted to praise the dead except in public funerals, and by no one else except the man who had officially been appointed for that operation. Also the gathering of men and women was forbidden, in order to restrain the expressions of mourning; in effect, the assembling of people tends to stimulate their lamentations. (66) This is the reason why Pittacus expressly forbade anyone who was a stranger to the family to attend the funeral. But the same Demetrius maintains that the majesty of funerals and sepulchres had increased again, almost to the level of those taking place now in Rome. Demetrius limited this custom also by law. . . . He limited lavishness not only by the penalty but also by the restriction of time: in fact, the funeral had to take place before daybreak. He also defined a rule of contention for all the new tombs, because he did not allow any construction over the site, with the exception of a small column, not bigger than three cubits high, a small altar or a basin. And he assigned a regular magistrate to supervise these rules.

Fr. 72b: Cic. *Leg.* II. 59

Iam cetera in XII minuendi sumptus sunt lamentationisque funeris, translata de Solonis fere legibus. 'Hoc plus', inquit, 'ne facito: rogum ascea ne polito.' Nostis quae sequuntur, discebamus enim pueri XII, ut carmen necessarium, quas iam nemo discit. 'Extenuato igitur sumptu tribus reciniis et tunicula purpurea et decem tibicinibus.' Tollit etiam lamentationem: 'Mulieres genas ne radunto neve lessum funeris ergo habento'. Hoc veteres interpretes, Sex. Aelius, L. Acilius, non satis se intellegere dixerunt, sed suspicari uestimenti aliquod genus funebris, L. Aelius lessum quasi lugubrem eiulationem, ut vox ipsa significat. quod eo magis iudico verum esse, quia lex Solonis id ipsum vetat.

There are also other regulations in the Twelve Tables that contribute to the limitation of expenditure and mourning at funerals, which are, for the most part, taken from the laws of Solon. The disposition says: 'Do no more than that: do not polish the pyre with an axe.' You know what comes after, for we have learned the Twelve Tables, as an indispensable lesson, even if no one learns them these days. 'Therefore let expenditure be limited to three veils, a purple tunic and ten flute-players.' He limited also the expression of mourning: 'Women shall not tear their cheeks nor indulge in weeping (*lessum*) at funerals.' Those ancient interpreters of our laws, Sextus Aelius and Lucius Acilius, admitted that they did not entirely understand this regulation, although they suspected that it concerned some sort of funeral garment. Lucius Aelius considered that the *lessus* was a kind of mournful lamentation, because that seemed to be the very meaning of the word. This latter interpretation is to my reasoning more probable, since Solon's law forbids exactly that behaviour.

Fr. 72c: Plut. *Sol.* 21. v–vii

ἐπέστησε δὲ καὶ ταῖς ἐξόδοις τῶν γυναικῶν καὶ τοῖς πένθεσι καὶ ταῖς ἑορταῖς νόμον ἀπείργοντα τὸ ἄτακτον καὶ ἀκόλαστον, ἐξιέναι μὲν ἱματίων τριῶν μὴ πλέον ἔχουσαν κελεύσας, μηδὲ βρωτὸν ἢ ποτὸν πλείονος ἢ ὀβολοῦ φερομένην, μηδὲ κάνητα πηχυαίου μείζονα, μηδὲ νύκτωρ πορεύεσθαι πλὴν ἁμάξῃ κομιζομένην λύχνου προφαίνοντος. ἀμυχὰς δὲ κοπτομένων καὶ τὸ θρηνεῖν πεποιημένα καὶ τὸ κωκύειν ἄλλον ἐν ταφαῖς ἑτέρων ἀφεῖλεν. ἐναγίζειν δὲ βοῦν οὐκ εἴασεν, οὐδὲ συντιθέναι πλέον ἱματίων τριῶν, οὐδ' ἐπ' ἀλλότρια μνήματα βαδίζειν χωρὶς ἐκκομιδῆς. ὧν τὰ πλεῖστα κἀν τοῖς ἡμετέροις νόμοις ἀπηγόρευται· πρόσκειται δὲ τοῖς ἡμετέροις ζημιοῦσθαι τοὺς τὰ τοιαῦτα ποιοῦντας ὑπὸ τῶν γυναικονόμων, ὡς ἀνάνδροις καὶ γυναικώδεσι τοῖς περὶ τὰ πένθη πάθεσι καὶ ἁμαρτήμασιν ἐνεχομένους.

Also with respect to the public appearances of women, their expressions of mourning and participation in festivals, [Solon] established a law preventing disorder and licence: he prescribed that they were not go out with more than three garments, were not to carry food or drink costing more than an obol, nor a basket larger than a cubit long, were not to travel at night, except in a wagon with a lamp to light the road. He forbade self-laceration of mourners, the singing of dirges and the weeping of someone at the funeral ceremonies of others. He did not permit the sacrifice of an ox to the deceased, or the burial of the dead with more than three pieces of grave gift clothing, or visiting the tombs of others outside the family, except on the day of the funeral. Most of those practices are also banned in our laws, but our regulations add that men who behave like this shall be punished by the *gynaikonomoi*, because they do wrong by indulging in such unmanly and effeminate attitudes of mourning.

These funerary regulations attributed to Solon by Cicero and Plutarch deal with the way a funeral celebration should be carried out, including the participation of women in the ceremonies, the way mourning and other manifestations of sorrow (like the singing of dirges) should be conducted, and also the offering of sacrifices and other grave-gifts in honour of the deceased. However, the interpretation of their purpose has prompted many different approaches, which could be summarised: (*a*) as restrictive laws, directed against the prerogatives of certain groups (especially the aristocrats) whose economic power and social influence Solon wanted to control by limiting their luxurious manifestations of mourning, and consequently those regulations could be interpreted as sumptuary laws; (*b*) as regulations intended to control women, not only in what concerned their participation in burial rites, but also in what concerned their liberty of movement; (*c*) as dispositions that illustrated a new attitude towards death and burial, connected with the fear of pollution; or, finally, (*d*) as a variant of the previous interpretation, which sees those laws as regulating relations between the living and the dead. For an outline of the main arguments and studies dealing with each of these perspectives, see J. H. Blok, 'Solon's Funerary Laws: Questions of Authenticity and Function', in Blok & Lardinois (edd.), *Solon of Athens*, 197–247, esp. 197–9, who considers that the first two interpretations are based mainly on historical studies that give preference to the written sources, while the last two are based mainly on archaeological material. She discusses both kinds of evidence, even if they belong to different periods and come from other *poleis* than Athens, and thus do not all have direct relevance to Solon's time (200–26). They show, nevertheless, that Solon's regulations had parallels in documentation from Delphi, Iulis or Gortyn, thus reinforcing their authenticity. Plutarch (*Sol.* 12. vii–ix) maintains that Epimenides of Crete inspired Solon's funeral legistation. Some Solonian religious dispositions were said to have been directly influenced by Cretan rites (see frs. 85a–c with commentary).

In one of his poems (fr. 21 West), Solon states that he does not want his death to be 'tearless' (ἄκλαυτος θάνατος μόλοι) and that he expects his decease to cause grief and wailing (καλλείποιμι θανὼν ἄλγεα καὶ στοναχάς) among his friends. This statement does not need to be interpreted as if it were contradicting the spriritof the law to restrain manifestations of sorrow. In the poem, Solon is most probably thinking in terms of private grief (the intensity of the relation with his *philoi*) and not in terms of how grief should be expressed in public. See Noussia-Fantuzzi, *Solon the Athenian: The Poetic Fragments*, 407.

Cicero (frs. 72a–b) compares Solon's regulations and those of the Roman Twelve Tables, deriving his information from Demetrius of Phalerum, who took inspiration from the laws of Solon (and theoretically from those of the time of Cecrops) for his own legislation on sober funerary monuments, possibly using Aristotle's commentaries on Solon's legislation. See Ruschenbusch, *Nomoi*, 40–2. Both Cicero and Plutarch (fr. 72c) combine the quotation of Solon's laws with their own comments particularly on expressions of mourning and limiting funeral costs, but this does not put in question the authenticity of those fragments. The prescription respecting night travels (μηδὲ νύκτωρ πορεύεσθαι πλὴν ἁμάξῃ κομιζομένην λύχνου προφαίνοντος) is not necessarily connected directly with funerals, and may be understood also as a more general statement dealing with the safety of women.

Fr. 72/d (fr. 109 Ruschenbusch): Dem. XLIII. *Macartatus* 62–3

ἔτι δὲ σαφέστερον γνώσεσθε, ὦ ἄνδρες δικασταί, καὶ ἐκ τοῦδε τοῦ νόμου, ὅτι Σόλων ὁ νομοθέτης σπουδάζει περὶ τοὺς οἰκείους καὶ οὐ μόνον δίδωσι τὰ καταλειφθέντα ἀλλὰ καὶ προστάγματα ποιεῖται τὰ δυσχερῆ ἅπαντα τοῖς προσήκουσι. λέγε τὸν νόμον. ΝΟΜΟΣ· "τὸν ἀποθανόντα προτίθεσθαι ἔνδον, ὅπως ἂν βούληται. ἐκφέρειν δὲ τὸν ἀποθανόντα τῇ ὑστεραίᾳ ᾗ ἂν προθῶνται, πρὶν ἥλιον ἐξέχειν. βαδίζειν δὲ τοὺς ἄνδρας πρόσθεν, ὅταν ἐκφέρωνται, τὰς δὲ γυναῖκας ὄπισθεν. γυναῖκα δὲ μὴ ἐξεῖναι εἰσιέναι εἰς τὰ τοῦ ἀποθανόντος μηδ' ἀκολουθεῖν ἀποθανόντι, ὅταν εἰς τὰ σήματα ἄγηται, ἐντὸς ἑξήκοντ' ἐτῶν γεγονυῖαν, πλὴν ὅσαι ἐντὸς ἀνεψιαδῶν εἰσι. μηδ' εἰς τὰ τοῦ ἀποθανόντος εἰσιέναι, ἐπειδὰν ἐξενεχθῇ ὁ νέκυς, γυναῖκα μηδεμίαν, πλὴν ὅσαι ἐντὸς ἀνεψιαδῶν εἰσιν." οὐκ ἐᾷ εἰσιέναι οὗ ἂν ᾖ ὁ τετελευτηκώς, οὐδεμίαν γυναῖκα ἄλλην ἢ τὰς προσηκούσας μέχρι ἀνεψιότητος, καὶ πρὸς τὸ μνῆμα ἀκολουθεῖν τὰς αὐτὰς ταύτας.

You will learn even more clearly, men of the jury, from this law as well, that Solon the lawgiver is serious about the relatives, and not only gives them the possessions that are left but also imposes all the tiresome obligations on the relatives. Read the law. LAW: 'The deceased shall be laid out inside [*sc.* the house], however one wishes. The deceased shall be carried forth on the day after he is laid out, before the sun rises. The men shall walk in front when they carry him forth, and the women behind. It shall not be permitted to a woman to enter into the house of the deceased, or to follow the deceased when he is carried to the tomb, if she is less than sixty years old, apart from those within the degree of cousins' children; nor shall any woman go into the house of the deceased when the body is brought forth, apart from those within the degree of cousins' children.' The law does not allow any woman to enter where the deceased is apart from those within the degree of cousinhood, and only these same to follow to the memorial.

For laying out on the day after the death and carrying forth to the tomb on the day after that cf. Antiph. VI. *Chorus Member* 34; and see Kurtz & Boardman, *Greek Burial Customs*, 143–6. Ruschenbusch printed Cicero's and Plutarch's accounts of Solon's funeral laws among the genuine fragments, but Demosthenes' among the spurious. What Demosthenes quotes is no doubt the law current in his own time: there may have been changes after Solon, but we should expect to find conservatism rather than innovation in such matters, and nothing here is obviously late, so we have added Demosthenes' account to the genuine fragments. For detailed laws on funerals from other places see *IG* XII. v 593 = Buck 8 = *LSCG* 97 (Iulis), *C. Delphes* i 9 = Buck 52 = Rhodes & Osborne 1. *C.* 19 sqq. (Labyadae at Delphi). J. H. Blok, 'Solon's Funerary Laws: Questions of Authenticity and Function', in Blok & Lardinois (edd.), *Solon of Athens*, 197–247, defends the attribution to Solon of fr. 72/d, and sees in it a religious purpose, fixing relations between the living and the dead, rather than a political or sumptuary purpose.

Ban on the trade in perfumes

Fr. 73a: Ath. XV. 687 A
Σόλων τε ὁ σοφὸς διὰ τῶν νόμων κεκώλυκε τοὺς ἄνδρας μυροπωλεῖν.
Solon the wise man in his laws prevented men from trading in perfumes.

Fr. 73b: Ath. XIII. 612 A
Σόλωνος δὲ τοῦ νομοθέτου οὐδ' ἐπιτρέποντος ἀνδρὶ τοιαύτης προΐστασθαι τέχνης [sc. τῆς μυρεψικῆς].

Solon the lawgiver did not allow a man to devote himself to professions of this kind [*sc.* trading in perfumes].

This ban on the trade in perfumes may have a merely educational intent, in the sense of discouraging involvement in tasks appropriate to women rather than men. Immediately after the statement of fr. 73b, Athenaeus quotes a passage from Pherecrates that favours this interpretation, by mocking the way the perfumer's trade stimulates gossip (τοῖς μειρακίοις ἐλλαλεῖν δι' ἡμέρας) and arguing that there is no such thing as a 'female cook' (μαγείραινα) or a 'fishwoman' (ἰχθυοπώλαινα). He even concludes that each *genos* should practice the *techne* that is best suited to each case (ἑκάστῳ γὰρ γένει ἁρμόζοντα δεῖν εἶναι καὶ τὰ τῆς τέχνης). However, there still might be an economic motivation for the ban, since it would require vast extents of land to grow enough flowers for the making of perfumes, thus creating further difficulties for basic food provision, because less land would be available for the production of grain. Sondhaus, *De Solonis Legibus*, 58–9, favours the first interpretation; Ruschenbusch, *Gesetzeswerk*, 142, the latter.

On Solon's regulations concerning the teaching of a *techne* to children, see fr. 56 with commentary. See also fr. 65, for the prohibition on exporting natural products except olive oil.

Paederasty

Fr. 74a: Hermias Alexandrinus on Pl. *Phdr.* 231 E
ὁ δὲ Σόλων ἐν τοῖς νόμοις καὶ πόσους πήχεις ἀπέχοντα ἀκολουθεῖν δεῖ τὸν ἐραστὴν τῷ ἐρωμένῳ δεδήλωκε, καὶ τοῖς ἐλευθέροις τὸ ἐπιτήδευμα τετήρηκε, δοῦλον κωλύσας ἐρᾶν ξηραλοιφεῖν τε, καὶ τὸν ἀστράτευτον καὶ τὸν λιπόντα τὴν τάξιν καὶ τὸν μὴ θρέψαντα τοὺς γονεῖς μηδὲ θάψαντα καὶ τὸν φρούριον προδεδωκότα.
Solon in his laws has indicated how many cubits behind a lover must follow his beloved, and he reserved this habit for free men only, and forbade a slave to be lover [of a free boy] and to rub dry with oil, and [he forbade it] also to the man who had never been in service, who left his rank in battle, who did not support or bury his parents, who deserted his guard.

Fr. 74b: Plut. *Sol.* 1. vi
ὅτι δὲ πρὸς τοὺς καλοὺς οὐκ ἦν ἐχυρὸς ὁ Σόλων οὐδ' ἔρωτι θαρραλέος ἀντανιαστῆναι "πύκτης ὅπως ἐς χεῖρας" (Soph. *Trach.* 442), ἔκ τε τῶν ποιημάτων αὐτοῦ λαβεῖν ἔστι, καὶ νόμον ἔγραψε διαγορεύοντα δούλῳ μὴ ξηραλοιφεῖν μηδὲ παιδεραστεῖν, εἰς τὴν τῶν καλῶν μερίδα καὶ σεμνῶν ἐπιτηδευμάτων τιθέμενος τὸ πρᾶγμα.

That Solon was not proof against beautiful youths, nor was he valiant enough to resist passion, 'like a boxer, hand to hand', can be inferred from his own poems. He passed also a law forbidding a slave to rub dry with oil and to be a lover of [free] boys, thus ranging this practice among the beautiful and honourable habits.

Fr. 74c: Plut. *Conv. Sept. Sap.* 152 D
"σὺ γάρ", ἔφη ὁ Αἴσωπος, "οὔπω γέγραφας ὅ τι ὅμοιον ἦν, οἰκέτας μὴ μεθύειν, ὡς ἔγραψας Ἀθήνησιν οἰκέτας μὴ ἐρᾶν μηδὲ ξηραλοιφεῖν."
'You indeed', said Aesop, 'have not yet written a law that forbids slaves to get drunk, similar to the one that you have passed in Athens, which does not allow slaves to be the lover [of a free boy] or to rub dry with oil.'

Fr. 74d: Plut. *Amat.* 751 B
ὡς καὶ Σόλων κατέβαλε· δούλοις μὲν γὰρ ἐρᾶν ἀρρένων παίδων ἀπεῖπε καὶ ξηραλοιφεῖν.
As Solon also set down: for he forbade slaves to be lovers of free boys and to rub dry with oil.

Fr. 74e: Aeschin. I. *Timarchus* 138–9
οἱ γὰρ πατέρες ἡμῶν, ὅθ' ὑπὲρ τῶν ἐπιτηδευμάτων καὶ τῶν ἐκ φύσεως ἀναγκαίων ἐνομοθέτουν, ἃ τοῖς ἐλευθέροις ἡγοῦντο εἶναι πρακτέα, ταῦτα τοῖς δούλοις ἀπεῖπον μὴ ποιεῖν. "δοῦλον", φησὶν ὁ νόμος, "μὴ γυμνάζεσθαι μηδὲ ξηραλοιφεῖν ἐν ταῖς παλαίστραις."
... πάλιν ὁ αὐτὸς εἶπε νομοθέτης· "δοῦλον ἐλευθέρου παιδὸς μήτ' ἐρᾶν μήτ' ἐπακολουθεῖν, ἢ τύπτεσθαι τῇ δημοσίᾳ μάστιγι πεντήκοντα πληγάς."
Our forefathers, when they were enacting laws to regulate men's habits and the necessities of nature, forbade slaves to engage in those activities that they considered exclusive to free men. 'A slave', says the law, 'is not to practise gymnastic exercises, nor to rub dry with oil in wrestling spaces.' ... Again the same lawgiver said: 'A slave shall not be the lover of a free boy, nor shall he pursue him, otherwise he shall receive fifty lashes with the public whip.'

†**Fr. 74/f:** Joannes Chrysostomus, *In epistulam ad Romanos* (Migne, *Patrologia Graeca*, lx. 418–9)

ἐπεὶ τό γε παλαιὸν καὶ νόμος εἶναι τὸ πρᾶγμα ἐδόκει, καὶ νομοθέτης τις παρ' αὐτοῖς οἰκέτας ἐκέλευσε μήτε ξηραλοιφεῖν μήτε παιδεραστεῖν, τοῖς ἐλευθέροις τῆς προεδρείας παραχωρήσας ταύτης, μᾶλλον δὲ τῆς ἀσχημοσύνης. ἀλλ' ὅμως οὐκ ἐνόμισαν ἀσχημοσύνην εἶναι τὸ πρᾶγμα, ἀλλ' ὡς σεμνὸν καὶ μεῖζον ἢ κατ' οἰκετῶν ἀξίωμα, τοῖς ἐλευθέροις ἐπέτρεψαν· καὶ τοῦτο ὁ σοφώτατος τῶν Ἀθηναίων δῆμος, καὶ ὁ μέγας παρ' αὐτοῖς Σόλων.

However in antiquity this matter seems even to have been a law, and a certain lawgiver among them determined that slaves were not allowed to rub dry with oil or to be lovers of [free] boys, conceding to free men this privilege, or rather disgrace. Nevertheless they did not consider this practice to be disgraceful, but on the contrary honourable and of too great value for slaves, the reason why it was entrusted to free men only. And this was the thinking of the Athenians, the wisest people, and also of Solon, who was great among them.

†**Fr. 74/g:** Joannes Chrysostomus, *In epistulam ad Titum* (Migne, *Patrologia Graeca*, lxii. 693)

ἐπαιδεράστουν· καὶ παρ' αὐτοῖς φιλόσοφός τις ἐνομοθέτει, δούλῳ ἐξεῖναι μήτε παιδεραστεῖν, μήτε ξηραλοιφεῖν, ὡς ἐναρέτου τοῦ πράγματος ὄντος καὶ πολλὴν ἔχοντος τιμήν.

They were lovers of boys: and a philosopher among them enacted a law that a slave was not allowed to be a lover of [free] boys or to rub dry with oil, as if it was a virtuous practice and a thing of great honour.

Prohibiting slaves to exercise (γυμνάζεσθαι) and to rub dry with oil (ξηραλοιφεῖν) at the *palaistra* is easily understood as a disposition motivated by a social preoccupation: those activities were distinctive of free men (connected, in particular, to the lifestyle of the aristocrats), and therefore slaves could not have equal access to them, as is made very clear by Aeschines (fr. 74e). Despite the moralizing intent of Chrysostom, frs. 74f–g also underline the honour (προεδρεία, τιμή) attached to those leisure and training activities, as does Plutarch (fr. 74b). All the passages use the term ξηραλοιφεῖν, a rare verb and possibly archaic, thus reinforcing the authenticity of the law. Classical sources often approach the question how slaves and free citizens differ in their daily conditions of life. Xenophon (*Symp.* ii. 4) is particularly illuminating on this topic, arguing, through the mouth of Socrates, that olive oil is enough to make a man's odour pleasant, as long as his body is well exercised, while perfume makes free men and slaves smell alike. See Fisher, *Aeschines: Against Timarchos*, 283–4.

The ban on having slaves as *erastai* of free boys should also be understood as expressing the same concern in preserving status distinctions. Moreover, the passive role of a free *eromenos* before a slave *erastes* could be interpreted as an act of *hybris* concerning his dignity as future citizen. Gagarin, *Early Greek Law*, 67–8, argues that this regulation was intended to strengthen the capacity of the *kyrios* to control the members of the household.

The last provisions in fr. 74a (καὶ τὸν ἀστράτευτον ... προδεδωκότα) most probably are not part of the same law. As is implied by fr. 74b (see also the context of fr. 74d), some of Solon's poems reflect homoerotic love (e.g. frs. 24.5–6, 25 West), as an expression of those 'necessities of nature' (τῶν ἐκ φύσεως ἀναγκαίων) that, according to Aeschines (fr. 74e), were one of the reasons for passing a law of this kind.

CONSTITUTION, INSTITUTIONS

Rights of citizens

†Fr. 74/1a: *Ath. Pol.* 7. iii–iv
τιμήματι διεῖλεν εἰς τέτταρα τέλη, καθάπερ διῄρητο καὶ πρότερον, εἰς πεντακοσιομέδιμνον καὶ ἱππέα καὶ ζευγίτην καὶ θῆτα. καὶ τὰς μεγάλας ἀρχὰς ἀπένειμεν ἄρχειν ἐκ πεντακοσιομεδίμνων καὶ ἱππέων καὶ ζευγιτῶν, τοὺς ἐννέα ἄρχοντας καὶ τοὺς ταμίας καὶ τοὺς πωλητὰς καὶ τοὺς ἕνδεκα καὶ τοὺς κωλακρέτας, ἑκάστοις ἀνάλογον τῷ μεγέθει τοῦ τιμήματος ἀποδιδοὺς τὴν ἀρχήν. τοῖς δὲ τὸ θητικὸν τελοῦσιν ἐκκλησίας καὶ δικαστηρίων μετέδωκε μόνον. ἔδει δὲ τελεῖν πεντακοσιομέδιμνον μὲν ὃς ἂν ἐκ τῆς οἰκείας ποιῇ πεντακόσια μέτρα τὰ συνάμφω ξηρὰ καὶ ὑγρά, ἱππάδα δὲ τοὺς τριακόσια ποιοῦντας, ὡς δ' ἔνιοί φασι τοὺς ἱπποτροφεῖν δυναμένους. ... ζευγίσιον δὲ τελεῖν τοὺς διακόσια τὰ συνάμφω ποιοῦντας· τοὺς δ' ἄλλους θητικόν, οὐδεμιᾶς μετέχοντας ἀρχῆς.

μεγάλας read by Chambers, με[γάλ]ας Fritz & Kapp: μὲ[ν ἄλλ]ας Diels, accepted by Kenyon.

He divided them by assessment into four classes, as they had been divided previously also: *pentakosiomedimnos*, *hippeus*, *zeugites* and *thes*. The great offices he assigned to be held by the *pentakosiomedimnoi*, *hippeis* and *zeugitai*: the nine archons, the treasurers, the *poletai* and the *kolakretai*, giving to each an office corresponding to the size of his assessment. To those in the thetic class he gave only a share in the assembly and the lawcourts. A man was to belong to the class of *pentakosiomedimnoi* who from his own estate produced five hundred measures wet and dry together; to the class of *hippeis* three hundred, or as some say those able to maintain a horse. ... Those were to belong to the class of *zeugitai* who produced two hundred measures of the two kinds; the others to the class of *thetes*, who had no share in office-holding.

†**Fr. 74/1b:** Plut. *Sol.* 18. i–ii
δεύτερον δὲ Σόλων τὰς μὲν ἀρχὰς ἁπάσας ὥσπερ ἦσαν τοῖς εὐπόροις ἀπολιπεῖν βουλόμενος, τὴν δ' ἄλλην μεῖξαι πολιτείαν, ἧς ὁ δῆμος οὐ μετεῖχεν, ἔλαβε τὰ τιμήματα τῶν πολιτῶν, καὶ τοὺς μὲν ἐν ξηροῖς ὁμοῦ καὶ ὑγροῖς μέτρα πεντακόσια ποιοῦντας πρώτους ἔταξε καὶ πεντακοσιομεδίμνους προσηγόρευσε· δευτέρους δὲ τοὺς ἵππον τρεφεῖν δυναμένους ἢ μέτρα ποιεῖν τριακόσια, καὶ τούτους ἱππάδα τελοῦντας ἐκάλουν· ζευγῖται δ' οἱ τοῦ τρίτου τιμήματος ὠνομάσθησαν, ὃ μέτρων ἦν συναμφοτέρων διακοσίων. οἱ δὲ λοιποὶ πάντες ἐκαλοῦντο θῆτες, οἷς οὐδεμίαν ἄρχειν ἔδωκεν ἀρχήν, ἀλλὰ τῷ συνεκκλησιάζειν καὶ δικάζειν μόνον μετεῖχον τῆς πολιτείας.

Secondly, Solon wanted to leave all the offices for the rich, as they were, but to mix the rest of the constitution, in which the *demos* did not participate; so he took the assessments of the citizens. Those who produced five hundred measures of wet and dry crops together he placed first and called *pentakosiomedimnoi*; second those able to maintain a horse or produce three hundred measures, and these were called the class of *hippeis*; the name *zeugitai* was given to those of the third level of assessment, whose measure was two hundred of the two kinds; all the rest were called *thetes*, and he did not allow them to hold any office, but they participated in the constitution only by joining in the assembly and serving as jurors.

†**Fr. 74/1c:** Arist. *Pol.* II. 1274 A 15–21
... ἐπεὶ Σόλων γε ἔοικε τὴν ἀναγκαιοτάτην ἀποδιδόναι τῷ δήμῳ δύναμιν, τὸ τὰς ἀρχὰς αἱρεῖσθαι καὶ εὐθύνειν (μηδὲ γὰρ τούτου κύριος ὢν ὁ δῆμος δοῦλος ἂν εἴη καὶ πολέμιος), τὰς δ' ἀρχὰς ἐκ τῶν γνωρίμων καὶ τῶν εὐπόρων κατέστησε πάσας, ἐκ τῶν πεντακοσιομεδίμνων καὶ ζευγιτῶν καὶ τρίτου τέλους τῆς καλουμένης ἱππάδος· τὸ δὲ τέταρτον τὸ θητικόν, οἷς οὐδεμιᾶς ἀρχῆς μετῆν.

... since Solon seems to have given the *demos* the minimum necessary power, to elect and hold to account the officials (for without power over that the *demos* would be a slave and an enemy), but he had all the officials appointed from the distinguished and the rich, from the *pentakosiomedimnoi*, the *zeugitai* and the third class, called that of the *hippeis*; the fourth class was that of the *thetes*, with no share in any office.

See Rhodes, *Comm. Ath. Pol.* on 7. iii–iv; de Ste. Croix, *Athenian Democratic Origins*, 5–72. Arist. *Pol.* has the second and third classes in the wrong order; the 'Draconian constitution' in *Ath. Pol.* 4. iii mentions the three highest classes. It is likely that the three lower classes existed in some sense before Solon, and that he filtered out a separate highest class and defined political rights in terms of the four classes. *Hippeis* and *zeugitai* are more probably military categories, cavalry and hoplites, than agricultural, owners of a horse and of a yoke of oxen (cf. Rhodes; and D. Whitehead, 'The Archaic Athenian ζευγῖται', *CQ* xxxi 1981, 282–6). The best explanation of the 'wet and dry' measures is that crops of other kinds were given an equivalent value in terms of barley (de Ste. Croix, 33–40); 1 Athenian *medimnos* = 52.4 litres. It has been argued that if the figures here are right even the *zeugitai* will have been part of a rich minority (L. Foxhall, 'A View from the Top: Evaluating the Solonian Property Classes', in Mitchell & Rhodes (edd.), *The Development of the Polis in Archaic Greece*, 113–36; H, van Wees, 'Mass and Elite in Solon's Athens: The Property Classes Revisited', in Blok & Lardinois [edd.], *Solon of Athens*, 351–89), but the best response to that is that probably only the *pentakosiomedimnoi* had a qualification defined in terms of produce and the figures for *hippeis* and *zeugitai* are later guesses (Rhodes, in Mitchell & Rhodes, 4; de Ste. Croix, 46–51).

Previously appointments were made ἀριστίνδην καὶ πλουτίνδην, on the basis of birth and wealth (*Ath. Pol.* 3. vi), i.e. limited to a circle of leading families. Using wealth as the sole criterion of eligibility suggests that there was now in Athens a significant body of rich men outside the leading families, who claimed and to whom Solon wanted to give a share in political leadership.

†Fr. 74/2: *Ath. Pol.* 8. i

τὰς δ' ἀρχὰς ἐποίησε κληρωτὰς ἐκ προκρίτων, οὓς ἑκάστη προκρίνειε τῶν φυλῶν. προύκρινεν δ' εἰς τοὺς ἐννέα ἄρχοντας ἑκάστη δέκα, καὶ τούτους ἐκλήρουν.

τού[τους ἐκ]ληρουν Kenyon originally, τούτους ἐκλήρουν Chambers: <ἐκ> τού[των ἐκλ]ήρουν Kaibel & Wilamowitz, afterwards accepted by Kenyon.

He had the archons appointed by lot from men pre-elected by each of the tribes: for the nine archons each tribe pre-elected ten men, and they performed the allotment on these.

See Rhodes, *Comm. Ath. Pol.*, ad loc. Direct election was later restored, probably under the tyrants, since *Ath. Pol.* 22. v reports the revival of a two-stage process in 487/6. Appointment by the Areopagus before Solon, in *Ath. Pol.* 8. ii, is probably a guess. Arist. *Pol.* II. 1273 B 35 – 1274 A 17, III. 1281 B 25–31, claims that Solon left unchanged the 'aristocratic' practice of election, but *Ath. Pol.* is probably better informed. If Solon wanted to provide an opportunity for rich men outside the leading families, election in the first stage would exclude men palpably unsuitable while allotment in the second would improve the chances of these outsiders.

Fr. 74/3a (fr. 150a Ruschenbusch): *Ath. Pol.* 8. i
σημεῖον δ' ὅτι κληρωτὰς ἐποίησεν ἐκ τῶν τιμημάτων ὁ περὶ τῶν ταμιῶν νόμος, ᾧ χρώμενοι διατελοῦσιν ἔτι καὶ νῦν· κελεύει γὰρ κληροῦν τοὺς ταμίας ἐκ πεντακοσιομεδίμνων.

The proof that he made appointment to offices by lot on the basis of the assessments is the law concerning the treasurers of Athena, which they continue to use even now. It prescribes that the treasurers are to be appointed by lot from the *pentakosiomedimnoi*.

Fr. 74/3b (fr. 150b Ruschenbusch): *Ath. Pol.* 47. i
οἱ ταμίαι τῆς Ἀθηνᾶς εἰσὶ μὲν δέκα, κληροῦται δ' εἷς ἐκ τῆς φυλῆς, ἐκ πεντακοσιομεδίμνων κατὰ τὸν Σόλωνος νόμ[ον (ἔτι γὰρ ὁ] νόμος κύριός ἐστιν), ἄρχει δ' ὁ λαχὼν κἂν πάνυ πένης ᾖ.

The treasurers of Athena are ten in number, one appointed by lot from each tribe, from the *pentakosiomedimnoi*, according to the law of Solon (for the law is still in force), and the man to whom the lot falls holds office even if he is very poor.

Rhodes, *Comm. Ath. Pol.*, 148 and 551, thinks that there is no reason to doubt that in the fourth century the law still in force prescribing that the treasurers of Athena should be appointed from the *pentakosiomedimnoi* was Solonian — but Solon's law will have been modified, at any rate to provide for one treasurer from each of Cleisthenes' ten tribes, and perhaps to substitute allotment for election. The end of *Ath. Pol.* 7. iv (διὸ καὶ νῦν ἐπειδὰν ἔρηται τὸν μέλλοντα κληροῦσθαί τιν' ἀρχήν, ποῖον τέλος τέλει, οὐδ' ἂν εἷς εἴποι θητικόν) and the last clause of fr. 74/3b (κἂν πάνυ πένης ᾖ) suggest that by the fourth century requirements based on the property classes were no longer enforced.

Areopagus and Council of four hundred

†Fr. 74/4a: *Ath. Pol.* 8. iv
τὴν δὲ τῶν Ἀρεοπαγιτῶν [sc. βουλὴν] ἔταξεν ἐπὶ τὸ νομοφυλακεῖν, ὥσπερ ὑπῆρχεν καὶ πρότερον ἐπίσκοπος οὖσα τῆς πολιτείας, καὶ τά τε ἄλλα τὰ πλεῖστα καὶ τὰ μέγιστα τῶν πολιτ<ικ>ῶν διετήρει, καὶ τοὺς ἁμαρτάνοντας ηὔθυνεν κυρία οὖσα καὶ ζημιοῦν καὶ κολάζειν, καὶ τὰς ἐκτίσεις ἀνέφερεν εἰς πόλιν, οὐκ ἐπιγράφουσα τὴν πρόφασιν †δ[ιὰ] τὸ [ε]ὐθύ[ν]εσθαι†. (**Fr. 37b** follows.)

πολιτ<ικ>ῶν H. Richards.   †δ[ιὰ] τὸ [ε]ὐθύ[ν]εσθαι† read by Wilcken and deleted Kaibel & Wilamowitz, read and obelised Chambers: δι' ὃ [τὸ ἐ]κτ[ίν]εσθαι Kenyon as doubtful reading.

The council of the Areopagites he appointed to guard the laws, just as previously it had been overseer of the constitution; and in general it kept watch over most and the greatest of the city's affairs, and it held offenders to account, with full power to penalise and punish, and it took up the payments to the acropolis, without recording the reason for the punishment (?).

†Fr. 74/4b: Plut. *Sol.* 19. i–ii
συστησάμενος δὲ τὴν ἐν Ἀρείῳ πάγῳ βουλὴν ἐκ τῶν κατ' ἐνιαυτὸν ἀρχόντων ... **(fr. 74/5b)** τὴν δ' ἄνω βουλὴν ἐπίσκοπον πάντων καὶ φύλακα τῶν νόμων ἐκάθισεν.

After he had established the council of the Areopagus from those serving as archons year by year ... he appointed the upper council to be overseer of all and guardian of the laws.

See Rhodes, *Comm. Ath. Pol.* on 8. iv. It is plausible that when Solon created the new council of four hundred (fr. 74/5) he should have specified that the old was to continue in existence. He may well have specified its membership, men who had held one of the nine archonships (cf. *Ath. Pol.* 3. vi, 60. iii). The Areopagus is guardian of the constitution or the laws in *Ath. Pol.* 3. vi, [4. iv, the 'constitution of Draco'], and 8. iv, and in 25. ii it is deprived of that function by Ephialtes in 462/1. Rhodes has suggested that the description was ancient, and that it was perhaps used as a basis for the Areopagus' acting in different ways at different times without explicit authorisation (*Comm. Ath. Pol.* 107, 315–7); and it is plausible that a law of Solon should have stated that the Areopagus was to be guardian of the laws as before. For the Areopagus' power of punishment cf. again *Ath. Pol.* 3. vi, [4. iv]: this is less likely to have been spelled out in a law of Solon. There were perhaps records of penalties which did not state the reason, but this does not mean that the Areopagus could or did impose penalties arbitrarily without giving a reason.

†Fr. 74/5a: *Ath. Pol.* 8. iv
βουλὴν δ' ἐποίησε τετρακοσίους, ἑκατὸν ἐξ ἑκάστης φυλῆς. (**Fr. 74/4a** follows.)

He instituted a council of four hundred, one hundred from each tribe.

†Fr. 74/5b: Plut. *Sol.* 19. i–ii
συστησάμενος δὲ τὴν ἐν Ἀρείῳ πάγῳ βουλὴν ... (**fr. 74/4b**), ἔτι δ' ὁρῶν τὸν δῆμον οἰδοῦντα καὶ θρασυνόμενον τῇ τῶν

χρεῶν ἀφέσει, δευτέραν προσκατένειμε βουλήν, ἀπὸ φυλῆς ἑκάστης (τεσσάρων οὐσῶν) ἑκατὸν ἄνδρας ἐπιλεξάμενος, οὓς προβουλεύειν ἔταξε τοῦ δήμου καὶ μηδὲν ἐᾶν ἀπροβούλευτον εἰς ἐκκλησίαν εἰσφέρεσθαι ... (fr. 74/4b) οἰόμενος ἐπὶ δυσὶ βουλαῖς ὥσπερ ἀγκύραις ὁρμοῦσαν ἧττον ἐν σάλῳ τὴν πόλιν ἔσεσθαι καὶ μᾶλλον ἀτρεμοῦντα τὸν δῆμον παρέξειν.

After he had established the council of the Areopagus ... , seeing that the *demos* was becoming swollen and bold because of its release from debts, he provided a second council in addition, enrolling a hundred men from each of the tribes, which were four in number, who were given the duty of deliberating in advance of the *demos* and not allowing anything without advance deliberation to be introduced to the assembly ... thinking that the city, moored with two councils as with anchors, would be less tossed by the waves and the people would be kept calmer.

See Rhodes, *Comm. Ath. Pol.* on 8. iv. Some have doubted the existence of Solon's second council, but without sufficient reason; and, since the Areopagus would for some time continue to be dominated by the old leading families, a separate body to prepare the assembly's business would contribute to the weakening of those leading families. Preparing the assembly's business was a duty of the later council of five hundred (*Ath. Pol.* 43. ii–vi and, with wording close to Plutarch's, 45. iv), and we need not doubt that it was the duty of Solon's four hundred. It may be that, as in the Great Rhetra at Sparta (Plut. *Lyc.* 6. ii), the creation of this probouleutic council was accompanied by provision for regular meetings of the assembly. The reference to the two councils as two anchors is possibly derived from one of Solon's poems (e.g. Freeman, *The Work and Life of Solon*, 79 with n. 1, cf. earlier Grote, *History of Greece*, 12-volume ed. iii. 122 = 10-volume ed. ii. 490), but not certainly (editors of Solon's poetic fragments do not include it).

Grants of citizenship

Fr. 75: Plut. *Sol.* 24. iv
παρέχει δ' ἀπορίαν καὶ ὁ τῶν δημοποιήτων νόμος, ὅτι γενέσθαι πολίτας οὐ δίδωσι πλὴν τοῖς φεύγουσιν ἀειφυγίᾳ τὴν ἑαυτῶν ἢ πανεστίοις Ἀθήναζε μετοικιζομένοις ἐπὶ τέχνῃ. τοῦτο δὲ ποιῆσαί φασιν αὐτὸν οὐχ οὕτως ἀπελαύνοντα τοὺς ἄλλους ὡς κατακαλούμενον Ἀθήναζε τούτους ἐπὶ βεβαίῳ τῷ μεθέξειν τῆς

πολιτείας, καὶ ἅμα πιστοὺς νομίζοντα τοὺς μὲν ἀποβεβληκότας τὴν ἑαυτῶν διὰ τὴν ἀνάγκην, τοὺς δ' ἀπολελοιπότας διὰ τὴν γνώμην. Problematic also is the law about men granted citizenship, because it does not give the right to become citizens except to those in permanent exile from their own land or to those who migrate to Athens with their whole household to ply a craft. They say that he did this not so much to drive the others away as to invite these to come to Athens for a secure share in the citizenship, and at the same time that he thought these would be reliable, in the one case because they had forsaken their own land out of necessity, in the other because they had left it by choice.

The explanation which 'they say' is probably correct: Solon's law is likely to have stated that the two categories of men mentioned here could be granted citizenship — and to have specified a procedure for approving candidates and making the grant — but not to have stated that men outside these categories could not be granted citizenship. An offer of citizenship to men exiled from their own state, perhaps for homicide or for involvement in political strife (cf. the categories excluded from the amnesty in fr. 22/1) can be seen as a secular equivalent of showing pity to suppliants; encouragement of men coming to ply a craft (frs. 56/a–b) can be seen as an economic measure to make Athens more diverse than a community of subsistence farmers (cf. fr. 65).

Associations

Fr. 76a: *Dig.* XLVII. 22. iv
Gaius libro quarto ad legem XII tabularum. Sodales sunt qui eiusdem collegii sunt, quam Graeci ἑταιρείαν *vocant. His autem potestatem facit lex pactionem quam velint sibi ferre, dum ne quid ex publica lege corrumpant. Sed haec lex videtur ex lege Solonis tralata esse. Nam illuc ita est:* "ἐὰν δὲ δῆμος ἢ φράτορες ἢ †ἱερῶν ὀργιῶν ἢ ναῦται† ἢ σύσσιτοι ἢ ὁμόταφοι ἢ θιασῶται ἢ ἐπὶ λείαν οἰχόμενοι ἢ εἰς ἐμπορίαν, ὅτι ἂν διαθῶνται πρὸς ἀλλήλους κύριον εἶναι, ἐὰν μὴ ἀπαγορεύσῃ δημόσια γράμματα."
ἱερῶν ὀργιῶν ἢ ναῦται: ὀργεῶνες ἢ γεννῆται Wilamowitz, ἡρώων ὀργεῶνες ἢ γεννῆται Ferguson, ἢ ναυκραρίαι Lambert.

Gaius in the fourth book on the law of the Twelve Tables: *Sodales* are members of the same association, which the Greeks call *hetaireia*. The law gives them the power to make any agreement they wish, as long as they do not contravene anything in the public law. But this law seems to be copied from a law of Solon. For there it reads: 'If a *demos* or *phratriai* or *orgeones* of heroes or *naukrariai* (?) or those who eat together or those who are buried together or *thiasotai* or those who go off for plunder or for trade, whatever they agree with one another shall be valid unless it is forbidden by public documents.'

Fr. 76b: Phot. o 439 Theodoridis, *Suda* o 511 Adler
ΟΡΓΕΩΝΕΣ· . . . Σέλευκος (*FGrH* 341 F 1) δ' ἐν τῷ ὑπομνήματι τῶν Σόλωνος ἀξόνων ὀργεῶνάς φησι καλεῖσθαι τοὺς συλλόγους ἔχοντας περί τινας ἥρωας ἢ θεούς.
συλλόγους *Suda*: συνόλους Phot. MS, συνόδους Coraes.

ORGEONES: . . . Seleucus in his commentary on Solon's *axones* says that the name *orgeones* is given to those who hold sessions with regard to certain heroes and gods.

Unfortunately fr. 76a is grammatically incoherent, and part of its list of associations is corrupt; 76b belongs with 76a only if *orgeones* are correctly restored in that corrupt passage. It probably gives a mixture of Solonian and later material. For discussion see particularly W. S. Ferguson, 'The Attic Orgeones', *HTR* xxxvii 1944, 61–140 at 64–8; Lambert, *The Phratries of Attica*, 250 with n. 27; Jones, *The Associations of Classical Athens*, 33–7, 311–20.

Demos is most easily interpreted as meaning one of the local units given a formal standing by Cleisthenes, in which case this element cannot be Solonian (though some including Jones have thought of pre-Cleisthenic villages). *Phratriai* are kinship groups, fictitious as regards their origin but hereditary, to one of which each citizen belonged (Lambert; Parker, *Athenian Religion*, 104–8). *Orgeones* are groups of men who celebrate rites, at least some of them hereditary units within *phratriai* (Ferguson; Parker, 109–11). For *naukrariai* see frs. 79–80; the alternative *gennetai* are now understood to be members of hereditary *gene* from which priests and priestesses were drawn, and which had connections with particular festivals (Parker, 56–66). There were various groups of men in Athens who ate together, but no equivalent is known of the *syssitia* of Sparta and Crete (e.g. Arist. *Pol.* II. 1274 A 1–4), though Jones considers it possible that there were such messes in Solonian Athens. *Thiasotai* were members of *thiasoi*, commonly groups of worshippers, and in Athens sub-groups within *phratriai*. Pirates and traders are surprising components of the list, and what is most remarkable is the recognition of pirates, more likely in early than in classical Athens. It has been generally accepted that the final clause, referring to *demosia grammata*, is most unlikely to give the wording of Solon's law.

Beyond the details the significance of this, as remarked by Lambert, is that it asserts the priority of prescriptions of the whole state (however that may have been expressed originally) over decisions of bodies within the state.

Assessment and property classes

Fr. 77: see fr. 80/2

Fr. 78: see fr. 66/1

Naukrariai

Fr. 79a: *Ath. Pol.* 8. iii
ἦν δ' ἐπὶ τῶν ναυκραριῶν ἀρχὴ καθεστηκυῖα ναύκραροι, τεταγμένη πρός τε τὰς εἰσφορὰς καὶ τὰς δαπάνας τὰς γιγνομένας· διὸ καὶ ἐν τοῖς νόμοις τοῖς Σόλωνος οἷς οὐκέτι χρῶνται πολλαχοῦ γέγραπται "τοὺς ναυκράρους εἰσπράττειν" καὶ "ἀναλίσκειν ἐκ τοῦ ναυκραρικοῦ ἀργυρίου".

The *naukraroi* were officers set over the *naukrariai*, given charge over revenue and expenditure which occurred. Therefore also in the laws of Solon which are no longer in use there is written in many places 'The *naukraroi* shall exact' and 'Disburse from the naucraric silver'.

†Fr. 79/b (*testimonium* to fr. 79 Ruschenbusch): Androtion *FGrH* 324 F 36 *ap.* schol. Ar. *Av.* 1541
Ἀνδροτίων γράφει οὕτως· "τοῖς δὲ ἰοῦσι Πυθῶδε θεωροῖς τοὺς κωλακρέτας διδόναι ἐκ τῶν ναυκραρικῶν ἐφόδιον ἀργύρια, καὶ εἰς ἄλλο ὅ τι ἂν δέῃ ἀναλῶσαι".

Androtion writes as follows: 'To the *theoroi* going to Delphi the *kolakretai* shall give silver from the naucraric funds for their travelling expenses, and for anything else which they need to spend'.

Fr. 80: Phot. ν 40 Theodoridis
ΝΑΥΚΡΑΡΙΑ· ... ναυκραρία μὲν ὁποῖόν τι ἡ συμμορία καὶ ὁ δῆμος, ναύκραρος δὲ ὁποῖόν τι ὁ δήμαρχος, Σόλωνος οὕτως ὀνομάσαντος, ὡς καὶ Ἀριστοτέλης φησί (*Ath. Pol.* 8. iii, 21. v), καὶ ἐν τοῖς νόμοις δὲ "ἄν τις ναυκραρίας ἀμφισβητῇ" καὶ "τοὺς ναυκράρους τοὺς κατὰ τὴν ναυκραρίαν".

NAUKRARIA: ... A *naukraria* is the same kind of thing as a *symmoria* and a deme, and a *naukraros* the same kind of thing as a demarch, given this name by Solon, as Aristotle says. And in the laws it says, 'If anybody disputes over a *naukraria*' and 'The *naukraroi* in the *naukraria*'.

The *naukrariai* and their *naukraroi* are mysterious entities, about which what is most certain is that they no longer existed in the classical period: *Ath. Pol.* 21. v claims that Cleisthenes replaced them with demes and demarchs, but Clidemus *FGrH* 323 F 8 states that Cleisthenes subdivided his ten tribes into fifty *naukrariai* — in which case they will have been abolished early in the fifth century. Though other derivations have been suggested, the most likely is from *naus* and **kraros*, 'ship' and 'chief' (cf. *Anecd. Bekk.* i. 283. 20–1, Poll. VIII. 108; inconclusive discussion by V. Gabrielsen, 'The Naukrariai and the Athenian Navy', *C&M* xxxvi 1985, 21–51), but the laws quoted in frs. 79–80 suggest that they had responsibilities beyond the provision of ships. For a reconstruction of early Athenian finance which accepts this derivation and gives them an important role see van Wees, *Ships and Silver, Taxes and Tribute*, 44–61.

The laws quoted here encourage the view that Athens in the time of Solon, although it did not yet have coins, did use standard weights of silver as a medium for payment (cf. on fr. 65: G. Davis rejects the attribution of these laws to Solon). The fact that *Ath. Pol.* can quote from 'the laws of Solon which are no longer in use' confirms that in the fourth century, while the orators tended to attribute all current laws to Solon, it was possible to distinguish between laws of Solon and current laws.

Assembly

†Fr. 80/1a: Aeschin. I. *Timarchus* 22–3
(ὁ σκέψασθε γάρ, ὦ ἄνδρες, ὅσην πρόνοιαν περὶ σωφροσύνης ἐποιήσατο ὁ Σόλων ἐκεῖνος, ὁ παλαιὸς νομοθέτης, καὶ ὁ Δράκων καὶ οἱ κατὰ τοὺς χρόνους ἐκείνους νομοθέται.)
ἀπαλλαγεὶς γὰρ τῶν νόμων τούτων, ἐσκέψατο τίνα χρὴ τρόπον συλλεγομένους ἡμᾶς εἰς τὰς ἐκκλησίας βουλεύεσθαι περὶ τῶν σπουδαιοτάτων πραγμάτων. καὶ πόθεν ἄρχεται; ΝΟΜΟΙ, φησί, ΠΕΡΙ ΕΥΚΟΣΜΙΑΣ. ἀπὸ σωφροσύνης πρῶτον ἤρξατο, ὡς, ὅπου πλεῖστα εὐκοσμία ἐστί, ταύτην ἄριστα τὴν πόλιν οἰκουμένην. καὶ πῶς κελεύει τοὺς προέδρους χρηματίζειν; ἐπειδὰν τὸ καθάρσιον περιενεχθῇ καὶ ὁ κῆρυξ τὰς πατρίους εὐχὰς εὔξηται, προχειροτονεῖν κελεύει τοὺς προέδρους περὶ ἱερῶν

τῶν πατρίων καὶ κήρυξι καὶ πρεσβείαις καὶ ὁσίων, καὶ μετὰ ταῦτα ἐπερωτᾷ ὁ κῆρυξ, "τίς ἀγορεύειν βούλεται τῶν ὑπὲρ πεντήκοντα ἔτη γεγονότων;" ἐπειδὰν δὲ οὗτοι πάντες εἴπωσι, τότ' ἤδη κελεύει λέγειν τῶν ἄλλων Ἀθηναίων τὸν βουλόμενον οἷς ἔξεστιν.

(6 Consider, men, what forethought concerning modesty that man Solon, the ancient lawgiver, had, and Draco and the lawgivers in those times.) For when he had finished with these laws he considered in what way we ought to gather in the assemblies and deliberate about the most serious affairs. Where does he begin? LAWS, he says, ABOUT GOOD ORDER. He started first from modesty, since, where there is the greatest good order, that city would be the best run. And how does he order the *proedroi* to conduct the business? When the purifying sacrifice has been carried round and the herald has uttered the traditional prayers, he orders the *proedroi* to hold a preliminary vote [*procheirotonia*] on traditional religion, for heralds, for embassies and on secular matters, and after this the herald asks, 'Who wishes to speak of those over fifty years old?' When all of these have spoken, then he orders whoever wishes of the other Athenians to speak, of those who are entitled to do so.

Fr. 80/1b (fr. 101 Ruschenbusch): Aeschin. III. *Ctesiphon* 2–3
ἐβουλόμην μὲν οὖν, ὦ ἄνδρες Ἀθηναῖοι, καὶ τὴν βουλὴν τοὺς πεντακοσίους καὶ τὰς ἐκκλησίας ὑπὸ τῶν ἐφεστηκότων ὀρθῶς διοικεῖσθαι, καὶ τοὺς νόμους οὓς ἐνομοθέτησε ὁ Σόλων περὶ τῆς τῶν ῥητόρων εὐκοσμίας ἰσχύειν, ἵνα ἐξῆν πρῶτον μὲν τῷ πρεσβυτάτῳ τῶν πολιτῶν, ὥσπερ οἱ νόμοι προστάττουσι, σωφρόνως ἐπὶ τὸ βῆμα παρελθόντι ἄνευ θορύβου καὶ ταραχῆς ἐξ ἐμπειρίας τὰ βέλτιστα τῇ πόλει συμβουλεύειν, δεύτερον δ' ἤδη καὶ τῶν ἄλλων πολιτῶν τὸν βουλόμενον καθ' ἡλικίαν χωρὶς καὶ ἐν μέρει περὶ ἑκάστου γνώμην ἀποφαίνεσθαι. οὕτω γὰρ ἄν μοι δοκεῖ ἥ τε πόλις ἄριστα διοικεῖσθαι αἵ τε κρίσεις ἐλάχισται γίγνεσθαι. ἐπειδὴ δὲ πάντα τὰ πρότερον ὡμολογημένα καλῶς ἔχειν νυνὶ καταλέλυται, ...

I wished, men of Athens, that the council of five hundred and the assemblies were rightly administered by those set over them, and that the laws enacted by Solon about the good order of speakers were in force, so that it would be possible first for the oldest of the citizens, as the laws prescribe, to come forward modestly to the platform and without uproar and confusion advise from his experience what is best for the city, and then secondly whoever wished of the other citizens, in accordance with this age, separately and in his turn to reveal his opinion on each matter. In this way I think the city would be best administered and the fewest court cases would arise. But since all that was previously agreed to be a good arrangement has now been abolished, . . .

The sacrifice and prayers at the beginning of the assembly were presumably ancient. The four subject areas appear in the same order and with the same mixture of cases in *Ath. Pol.* 43. vi (cf. the 'future constitution' of 411 in 30. v), and were presumably prescribed by law not later than the late fifth century; *Ath. Pol.* 43. vi mentions the *procheirotonia* only to say that it is sometimes omitted (Hansen, *The Athenian Ecclesia* <I>, 123–30, argued that it was used to decide whether a proposal could be accepted immediately or required debate), so fr. 80/1a at any rate contains some early material.

No other texts mention a law giving priority in the assembly to older speakers, and we can be confident that in the classical period no such law was in force. Three solutions have been proposed: Hansen, *The Athenian Assembly*, 171 n. 581, supposed that the prior invitation was never formally abolished but its use was discontinued between 346/5 (Aeschin. I) and 330 (Aeschin. III); K. Kapparis, 'The Law on the Age of Speakers in the Athenian Assembly', *RM²* cxli 1998, 255–9, suggested that it was a Solonian institution, discontinued by 462/1 if not earlier; R. Lane Fox, 'Aeschines and Athenian Democracy', in *Ritual, Finance, Politics . . . D. Lewis*, 135–55 at 147–9, argued that Aeschines misremembered preference for older men in other contexts or had simply invented this.

RELIGION

Regulations for offerings

Fr. 80/2 (fr. 77 Ruschenbusch): Plut. *Sol.* 23. iii
εἰς μέν γε τὰ τιμήματα τῶν θυσιῶν λογίζεται πρόβατον καὶ δραχμὴν ἀντὶ μεδίμνου.
θυσιῶν: οὐσιῶν Wilcken.
For the valuations of sacrifices he reckons a sheep and a drachma as equivalent to a *medimnos* [*sc.* of barley].

U. Wilcken ('Zu Solons Schatzungsklassen', *Hermes* lxiii 1928, 236–8) changed 'sacrifices' to 'property' to make this relevant to the basis of Solon's four property classes. However, the manuscripts' 'sacrifices' is convincingly defended by C. M. A. van den Oudenrijn, 'Solon's System of Property-Classes Once More', *Mnemosyne*[4] v 1952, 19–27; de Ste. Croix, *Athenian Democratic Origins*, 45–6 cf. 39–40. There is no other evidence that Solon's classes were based on any form of wealth except agricultural produce (and indeed Rhodes suspects that only the *pentakosiomedimnoi* were defined even in that way, and that the figures for the lower classes in *Ath. Pol.* 7. iv and elsewhere are due simply to fourth-century reconstruction: cf. on fr. 74/1). With the manuscripts' text, this passage like the sentence which follows it (fr. 81) is concerned with the value of sacrificial offerings. K. H. Waters, 'Solon's "Price-Equalisation"', *JHS* lxxx 1960, 181–90 at 185–8, finds the passage problematic but offers no solutions. G. Davis, arguing that references to drachmae must be post-Solonian (cf. on fr. 65), notes that, whatever its significance, this passage envisages *medimnoi* of barley as primary.

Fr. 81: Plut. *Sol.* 23. iii–iv
λύκον δὲ τῷ κομίσαντι πέντε δραχμάς, λυκιδέα δὲ μίαν, ὧν φησιν ὁ Φαληρεὺς Δημήτριος (fr. 147 Wehrli) τὸ μὲν βοὸς εἶναι, τὸ δὲ προβάτου τιμήν **(fr. 92)**. ἃς γὰρ ἐν τῷ ἑκκαιδεκάτῳ τῶν ἀξόνων ὁρίζει τιμὰς τῶν ἐκκρίτων ἱερείων, εἰκὸς μὲν εἶναι πολλαπλασίας, ἄλλως δὲ κἀκεῖναι πρὸς τὰς νῦν εὐτελεῖς εἰσιν. ἀρχαῖον δὲ τοῖς Ἀθηναίοις τὸ πολεμεῖν τοῖς λύκοις, βελτίονα νέμειν ἢ γεωργεῖν χώραν ἔχουσι.
The man who caught a wolf [was given] five drachmae, and one drachma if he caught a wolf's cub. According to Demetrius of Phalerum, those prices were equivalent respectively to that of an ox

and that of a goat. Although the prices Solon sets in the sixteenth *axon* are for selected victims, and probably many times higher than the average ones, they are still moderate compared to present prices. It is an old practice among the Athenians to make war on wolves, because their land is better for pasture than for farming.

Fr. 82: Poll. I. 29
Σόλων δὲ τὰ <μηδὲ> ἔμπηρα καὶ ἀφελῆ ὠνόμασε.
Ruschenbusch, *Gesetzeswerk* 152, suggests emending ἔμπηρα to ἄπηρα. Another possibility would be <μηδὲ> ἔμπηρα: in the previous sentence Pollux uses both ἄπηρα and μηδὲ ἔμπηρα.
Solon names the unmaimed [victims] also as 'unaffected'.

The regulations dealing with offerings show that Solon's laws dealt also with religious practices. This does not imply necessarily that he should be credited with the foundation of a state religion, as suggested by Jacoby, *Atthis*, 23. As remarked already by Parker, *Athenian Religion*, 54, laws regulating religious issues are present in any community, and thus it should be expected that Solon contemplated also this area in his legislation. It is more plausible that he simply organised already existing practices, mainly in what concerns festivals and sacrifices, perhaps in order to strengthen the control of the *polis* over these events. At any rate, his intervention cannot be compared with the reforms of the Panathenaea and the City Dionysia undertaken by Pisistratus, despite the fact that Diogenes Laertius (I. 57 = frs. 123c, 149) states that Solon did more for Homer than Pisistratus did (cf. Gagarin, *Early Greek Law*, 70).

According to Plutarch, Solon listed prices for choice victims in the sixteenth *axon*. Aristophanes of Byzantium (cf. *Etymologicum Gudianum* 164. ii Reitz = *Nomoi* T 2) maintained instead that the *axones* contained the laws (*nomoi*) and that the *kyrbeis* dealt specifically with sacrifices (*thysiai*), but this statement is contradicted by other sources, in which the term *kyrbeis* is used to mention all the legislation. See Ruschenbusch, *Nomoi*, 17–18; Leão, *Sólon. Ética e política*, 334–6. Besides listing the prices of choice victims, Solon seems to have forbidden the use in sacrifices of physically damaged animals (fr. 82). See Plutarch (*De Def. Or.* 437 A–B) for an example of comparable practices regarding the oracle of Apollo in Delphi. On the equivalence between oxen, goats and drachmae, see fr. 92 (and commentary on fr. 65).

Calendar of sacrifices

Fr. 83: Steph. Byz. *Ethn.*
ΑΓΝΟΥΣ· τὸ τοπικὸν Ἁγνουντόθεν, καὶ ἐν τόπῳ Ἁγνοῦντι· ἐν τοῖς ἄξοσιν "ἐπειδὴ Ἁγνοῦντι θυσία ἐστὶ τῷ Λεῷ". εἰς τόπον Ἁγνοῦντάδε.
HAGNOUS: The designations of place are *Hagnountothen* ('from Hagnous') and at the place, *Hagnounti* ('at Hagnous'); in the *axones*

[is stated] 'when the sacrifice takes place at Hagnous (*Hagnounti*) to Leos.' To the place, *Hagnountade*.

Fr. 84: *Anecd. Bekk.* i. 86. 20
ΓΕΝΕΣΙΑ: οὔσης τε ἑορτῆς δημοτελοῦς Ἀθήναις, Βοηδρομιῶνος πέμπτης, γενέσια καλουμένης, καθότι φησὶ Φιλόχορος (FGrH 328 F 168) καὶ Σόλων ἐν τοῖς ἄξοσι.
GENESIA: a festival organized at public expense in Athens, on the fifth of Boedromion, named *Genesia*, as stated by Philochorus and by Solon in his *axones*.

Fr. 85a: Theophr. *De Piet.* apud Porph. *Abstin.* II. 20–1
διὰ πολλῶν δὲ ὁ Θεόφραστος <ἐκ> τῶν παρ' ἑκάστοις πατρίων ἐπιδείξας, ὅτι τὸ παλαιὸν τῶν θυσιῶν διὰ τῶν καρπῶν ἦν ἔτ' εἰπὼν πρότερον τῆς πόας λαμβανομένης, καὶ τὰ τῶν σπονδῶν ἐξηγεῖται τοῦτον τὸν τρόπον. τὰ μὲν ἀρχαῖα τῶν ἱερῶν νηφάλια παρὰ πολλοῖς ἦν, νηφάλια δ' ἐστὶν τὰ ὑδρόσπονδα, τὰ δὲ μετὰ ταῦτα μελίσπονδα· τοῦτον γὰρ ἕτοιμον παρὰ μελιττῶν πρῶτον ἐλάβομεν τὸν ὑγρὸν καρπόν· εἶτ' ἐλαιόσπονδα· τέλος δ' ἐπὶ πᾶσιν τὰ ὕστερον γεγονότα οἰνόσπονδα. μαρτυρεῖται δὲ ταῦτα οὐ μόνον ὑπὸ τῶν κύρβεων, αἳ τῶν Κρήτηθέν εἰσι Κορυβαντικῶν ἱερῶν οἷον ἀντίγραφα ἄττα πρὸς ἀλήθειαν.
Theophrastus demonstrates, by mentioning many ancestral rites from other places, that in ancient times sacrifices were made from fruits, adding that previously there were even offerings of grass. He approaches the question of libations in this manner: 'Sacrifices in ancient times were for the most part made with sobriety. They were sober because libations were made with water, but afterwards they started to be made with honey. In fact, we received this liquid fruit prepared beforehand by the bees. Then libations were made of oil, and finally, in later times, libations of wine became general.' These things are attested not only by the *kyrbeis*, which correspond to a faithful copy of the Corybantic rites from Crete.

Fr. 85b: Phot. κ 1234 Theodoridis
ΚΥΡΒΕΙΣ· … Θεόφραστος δὲ ἀπὸ τῶν Κρητικῶν Κορυβάντων· τῶν γὰρ Κορυβαντικῶν ἱερῶν οἷον ἀντίγραφα αὐτοὺς εἶναι.

KYRBEIS: ... Theophrastus says that they derive from the Cretan Corybantes. He maintains in fact that they correspond to a copy of the Corybantic rites.

Fr. 85c: Schol. Ar. *Av.* 1354
ΕΝ ΤΑΙΣ ΤΩΝ ΠΕΛΑΡΓΩΝ ΚΥΡΒΕΣΙΝ **(cf. fr. 55a)**· ἀπὸ τῶν κορυβάντων. ἐκείνων γὰρ εὕρημα, ὥς φησι Θεόφραστος ἐν τῷ περὶ εὐσεβείας.
IN THE *KYRBEIS* OF THE STORKS: from the Corybantes. The invention is theirs, as Theophrastus says in his *On Piety*.

Fr. 86: Lys. XXX. *Nicomachus* 17–18
θαυμάζω δὲ εἰ μὴ ἐνθυμεῖται, ὅταν ἐμὲ φάσκῃ ἀσεβεῖν λέγοντα ὡς χρὴ θύειν τὰς θυσίας τὰς ἐκ τῶν κύρβεων καὶ τῶν στηλῶν κατὰ τὰς συγγραφάς, ὅτι καὶ τῆς πόλεως κατηγορεῖ· ταῦτα γὰρ ὑμεῖς ἐψηφίσασθε. ... οἱ τοίνυν πρόγονοι τὰ ἐκ τῶν κύρβεων θύοντες μεγίστην καὶ εὐδαιμονεστάτην τῶν Ἑλληνίδων τὴν πόλιν παρέδοσαν.
καὶ τῶν στηλῶν Taylor: εὔπλων X, ὅπλων Af, καὶ οὐ πλείω M. Nelson, *CQ*² lvi 2006, 309–12.
I am surprised that he does not realise that, when he accuses me of impiety for saying that it is necessary to perform the sacrifices from the *kyrbeis* and the *stelai* in accordance with the schedule, he is accusing the city also: those regulations were in fact decreed by you. ... Our ancestors, indeed, by performing the sacrifices according to the *kyrbeis*, have handed down to us the greatest and most prosperous city in Greece.

Even if we do not know the exact degree of Solon's originality in the regulations dealing religion, he is usually credited with the organisation of an official calendar of sacrifices (frs. 83–4). For an attempt to reconstruct the shape of this calendar, see Parker, *Athenian Religion*, 43–55, although the analysis relies mainly on the revised version of those regulations inscribed around the years 403–399, as part of a more extensive legislative revision (see below).

The public festival called *Genesia* (fr. 84) has attracted special attention because of the political implications usually attached to it. Probably before Solon the *Genesia* was an aristocratic private cult in honour of the dead, but by turning it into a public festival with a fixed date in the calendar, he intended to foster the role of the state and to control the action of certain groups, such as phratries and family associations. Jacoby, *Atthis*, 36–41, strongly supports this idea. Parker, *Athenian Religion*, 48–9, accepts it as possible, although he underlines that it cannot be shown with certainty that Solon was the creator of those festivals. Further details in Leão, *Sólon: Ética e política*, 99–100 and 394; J. H. Blok, 'Solon's Funerary Laws: Questions of Authenticity and Function', in Blok & Lardinois (edd.), *Solon of Athens*, 197–247, at 235–7. For other Solonian laws dealing with the control of honours given to the deceased and public manifestations of mourning, see frs. 72a–d with commentary. Stroud, *Axones and Kyrbeis*, 18, accepts Jacoby's conjecture that the source of fr. 84 may be Aristophanes of Byzantium, although the reference goes back to the Atthidographer Philochorus. Frs. 85a–c suggest that these regulations were a 'copy' of the Corybantic rites from Crete. Elsewhere, Plutarch (*Sol.* 12. vii-ix) maintains that Epimenides of Crete inspired Solon's funerary legistation.

Fr. 86 is sometimes evoked as a basis for the suggestion that the *kyrbeis* (as opposed to the *axones*) contained explicitly the laws about sacrifices (see fr. 81 with commentary). However, the expression τὰς θυσίας τὰς ἐκ τῶν κύρβεων has most probably a broader meaning, covering the entire Solonian legislation (and up to a certain point also Draco's laws) and not simply the regulations on religious issues. If Taylor's emendation, generally accepted, is right, along with the ancient *kyrbeis* Lysias states that there was additional legislation concerning sacrifices, which had been published on supplementary *stelai* (καὶ τῶν στηλῶν) over time. Nicomachus and the commission of *anagrapheis* who were responsible for producing the new official calendar of sacrifices had at their disposal this kind of material, but allegedly did not limit themselves to revising the regulations, adding new sacrifices also. On the behaviour of Nicomachus regarding this *dossier*, see Hansen, *The Athenian Democracy*, 163–4, 245.

Irrespective of the possible misconduct of the *anagrapheis*, frs. 83–6 make it clear that there were ancient dispositions regarding religious matters, although the sources do not allow us to decide clearly whether Solon enacted them for the first time or simply systematised already existing regulations.

Parasitein / eating at public expense

Fr. 87: Plut. *Sol.* 24. v
ἴδιον δὲ τοῦ Σόλωνος καὶ τὸ περὶ τῆς ἐν δημοσίῳ σιτήσεως, ὅπερ αὐτὸς παρασιτεῖν κέκληκε. τὸν γὰρ αὐτὸν οὐκ ἐᾷ σιτεῖσθαι πολλάκις, ἐὰν δ' ᾧ καθήκει μὴ βούληται, κολάζει, τὸ μὲν ἡγούμενος πλεονεξίαν, τὸ δ' ὑπεροψίαν τῶν κοινῶν.
Distinctive also is the law of Solon regarding the right to eat at the public table, a practice to which he gave the designation *parasitein*. He did not allow the same person to eat there often, but he punished the man who had the right to take seat there and refused, because he considered greediness the conduct of the first, and disrespect to the community that of the latter.

Fr. 88: Ath. VI. 234 E–F
ἐν δὲ τοῖς κύρβεσι τοῖς περὶ τῶν Δηλιαστῶν οὕτως γέγραπται· "καὶ τὼ κήρυκε ἐκ τοῦ γένους τῶν Κηρύκων τοῦ τῆς μυστηριώτιδος. τούτους δὲ παρασιτεῖν ἐν τῷ Δηλίῳ ἐνιαυτόν."

In the *kyrbeis* respecting the Deliastai is written the following: 'Also the two heralds of the *genos* Kerykes, that of the mysteries: they have the right to eat at the public table (*parasitein*) at the Delium for a year'.

Plutarch maintains that Solon coined the term *parasitein* (literally 'eat with') to name the honour of receiving the right to eat at the public table. According to him, Solon prescribed that the privilege should be used with moderation and as a sign of respect towards the community, but this may simply express Plutarch's own interpretation. The law mentioned by Athenaeus (fr. 88) gives support to the authenticity of the regulation. He is quoting from Polemon, who probably copied the information directly from inscribed physical objects. The privileges granted to members of the *genos* of the Kerykes concern the sanctuary of Delian Apollo at Marathon. See Freeman, *The Work and Life of Solon*, 114; Stroud, *Axones and Kyrbeis*, 24–5 and 36.

Fr. 89: Ath. IV. 137 E
Σόλων δὲ τοῖς ἐν πρυτανείῳ σιτουμένοις μᾶζαν παρέχειν κελεύει, ἄρτον δὲ ταῖς ἑορταῖς προσπαρατιθέναι, μιμούμενος τὸν Ὅμηρον (Hom. *Od*. XVII. 343, XVIII. 120).
Solon prescribes that a barley cake should be provided to those eating in the *prytaneion* but that a wheat loaf should be added at festivals, imitating Homer.

The context in Homer suggests that Telemachus is giving a wheat loaf (ἄρτος) to Odysseus (*Od*. XVII. 343) because he is disguised as a very poor *xeinos*, and the same is implied on the part of the suitors (XVIII. 120), who take Odysseus as a pitiable *xeinos*. The implication may be that to provide an extra wheat loaf at festivals to those eating at the *prytaneion* would be a way of symbolically reinforcing links of *xenia*.

Rewards for victors in games

Fr. 89/1a (= fr. 143a Ruschenbusch): Plut. *Sol*. 23. iii
τῷ δ' Ἴσθμια νικήσαντι δραχμὰς ἑκατὸν ἔταξε δίδοσθαι, τῷ δ' Ὀλυμπιονίκῃ πεντακοσίας.
He determined that one hundred drachmae were to be given to a winner at the Isthmian games, and five hundred to an Olympic victor.

Fr. 89/1b (= fr. 143b Ruschenbusch): Diog. Laert. I. 55–6
συνέστειλε δὲ καὶ τὰς τιμὰς τῶν ἐν ἀγῶσιν ἀθλητῶν, Ὀλυμπιονίκῃ μὲν τάξας πεντακοσίας δραχμάς, Ἰσθμιονίκῃ δὲ ἑκατόν, καὶ ἀνὰ

λόγον ἐπὶ τῶν ἄλλων· ἀπειρόκαλον γὰρ τὸ ἐξαίρειν τὰς τούτων τιμάς, ἀλλὰ μόνων ἐκείνων τῶν ἐν πολέμοις τελευτησάντων (**fr. 144c**), ὧν καὶ τοὺς υἱοὺς δημοσίᾳ τρέφεσθαι καὶ παιδεύεσθαι (**fr. 145**). ὅθεν καὶ ἐζήλουν πολλοὶ καλοὶ κἀγαθοὶ γίνεσθαι κατὰ πόλεμον· ὡς Πολύζηλος, ὡς Κυνέγειρος, ὡς Καλλίμαχος, ὡς σύμπαντες οἱ Μαραθωνομάχαι· ἔτι δ' Ἁρμόδιος καὶ Ἀριστογείτων καὶ Μιλτιάδης καὶ μυρίοι ὅσοι. ἀθληταὶ δὲ καὶ ἀσκούμενοι πολυδάπανοι, καὶ νικῶντες ἐπιζήμιοι· καὶ στεφανοῦνται κατὰ τῆς πατρίδος μᾶλλον ἢ κατὰ τῶν ἀνταγωνιστῶν. γέροντές τε γενόμενοι κατὰ τὸν Εὐριπίδην (fr. 282. 12 Nauck) "τρίβωνες ἐκλιπόντες οἴχονται κρόκας". ὅπερ συνιδὼν ὁ Σόλων μετρίως αὐτοὺς ἀπεδέξατο.

Also he curtailed the honours paid to the athletes participating in games, assigning five hundred drachmae to an Olympic victor, one hundred to an Isthmian victor, and in proportion for the others. He argued that it would be tasteless to praise those men with such great honours, which ought to be given only to those who had fallen in battle, and whose children were to be reared and educated at public expense. Because of this, many men were eager to be fine and good in war: this was the case of Polyzelus, of Cynegirus, of Callimachus, and of all the men who fought at Marathon; also of Harmodius, of Aristogiton, of Miltiades, and of countless others. As for athletes, their training is very expensive and their victories detrimental, but they receive crowns as if they have beaten their country and not simply their competitors. And when they become old, as Euripides says, 'they are like worn-out cloaks that have lost their nap'. Solon realised this, and treated them with moderation.

Fr. 89/1c (= fr. 143c Ruschenbusch): Diod. Sic. IX. 2. v
ὅτι ὁ Σόλων ἡγεῖτο τοὺς μὲν πύκτας καὶ σταδιεῖς καὶ τοὺς ἄλλους ἀθλητὰς μηδὲν ἀξιόλογον συμβάλλεσθαι ταῖς πόλεσι πρὸς σωτηρίαν, τοὺς δὲ φρονήσει καὶ ἀρετῇ διαφέροντας μόνους δύνασθαι τὰς πατρίδας ἐν τοῖς κινδύνοις διαφυλάττειν.

Solon thought that pugilists, stadium runners and other athletes made no important contribution to the salvation of their cities, and that only those who were renowned for their wisdom and virtue were able to provide protection to the fatherland in times of danger.

Plutarch and Diogenes agree on the amount of the award that was to be given by the city of Athens to victors at the Olympic and Isthmian games, as a sign of public recognition, but they differ on an essential point: the first says that Solon created that law, and the latter maintains that he reduced the value of the prizes, implying that the practice already existed. Diogenes adds that the decision covered all the games, and also (frs. 144c–145) that it would be more appropriate to pay those honours to soldiers who died in battle, thus making a substantial contribution to the salvation of the city. This reasoning, like the arguments used by Diodorus, corresponds probably just to moralising rhetorical expressions directed against the excessive importance given to athletes. Ruschenbusch, *Nomoi*, 43 and 123, ranks these norms among the spurious laws, on the ground that the rewards are too high for Solon's time. This is correct, but need not be fatal to the authenticity of the law, because Solon may have prescribed a lower value (for a similar case see fr. 51/1 with commentary). Nevertheless, the penalty for raping a free woman (fr. 26) was one hundred drachmae, the same amount to be given to an Isthmian victor. Elsewhere (fr. 87), Solon is said to have coined the term *parasitein* ('eating at public expense'), an honour attached also to the awards given to athletes in Athens (cf. Pl. *Ap.* 36 D). Sondhaus, *De Solonis Legibus*, 70-1; I. Weiler, 'Einige Bemerkungen zu Solons Olympionikengesetz', in Händel *et al.* (edd.), *Festschrift für Robert Muth*, 573–82, consider that the law may be Solonian. Though cautiously, that possibility is also envisaged by Leão, 'Os honorários dos atletas vencedores (a propósito de Plutarco, *Sol.* 23.3)', in Oliveira (ed.), *O espírito olímpico no novo milénio*, 73–83. That such rewards were given to athletes as early as the sixth century is confirmed by Xenophanes, DK 21 B 2. 8.

Varia

Fr. 90/a: Poll. V. 36
Σόλων δὲ καὶ στοιχάδας τινὰς ἐλάας ἐκάλεσε, ταῖς μορίαις ἀντιτιθείς, ἴσως τὰς κατὰ στοῖχον πεφυτευμένας.
Solon called some olive trees *stoichades* ('planted in rows'), in contrast to the *moriai* ('sacred olives'), and he perhaps means by this the olive trees planted in rows (*stoichos*).

†**Fr. 90/b:** Harp. π 63 Keaney, cf. *Suda* π 1313 Adler, Phot. π 776 Theodoridis
ΠΕΡΙΣΤΟΙΧΟΙ· ... Δίδυμος δέ τι γένος ἐλαῶν περιστοίχους καλεῖ, ἃς Φιλόχορος (FGrH 328 F 180) στοιχάδας προσηγόρευσεν.
PERISTOICHOI: ... Didymus calls a kind of olive trees *peristoichoi* ('set round in rows'), while Philochorus named them *stoichades*.

Fr. 90/a states that Solon gave a technical designation to the ordinary olive trees (*stoichades*), distinguishing them from the sacred ones (*moriai*). The information provided by

Pollux might derive from Solon's legislation about agriculture or from the norms dealing with religion, because the act of damaging a *moria* was considered a serious crime (e.g. Lysias VII. *Sacred Olive* 2, 41). The name *stoichades* applied to ordinary olive trees, as those planted in rows (*stoichos*), intended perhaps to underline the idea that they were the result of human labour, thus differing from the divine origin of the *moriai*. Philochorus' use of the term *stoichades* (fr. 90/b) probably derives from Solon's laws (cf. fr. 84 for a similar use of a word common to Solon and Philochorus). For Didymus' 'round' cf. Ar. *Ach.* 998. For other regulations dealing with olive trees, see frs. 60a–b with commentary. See also Sondhaus, *De Solonis Legibus*, 34.

Fr. 91: Phot. α 808 Theodoridis
ΑΚΟΥΣΑΙ ΟΡΓΩ· . . . ὀργάδες καλοῦνται πάντα τὰ ἀνειμένα εἰς ὕλην καὶ ἀνημέρωτα καὶ ἀργά, ὡς καὶ Σόλων φησίν.
I AM PASSIONATE TO HEAR: . . . The term *orgades* is attributed to all kinds of wild, untilled and uncultivated land devoted to forest, as Solon says.

Since the term *orgades* applies to uncultivated fertile land, it could theoretically occur in the legislation about agriculture. However, the same word also denoted specifically a piece of land, located between Athens and Megara, and dedicated to the two Eleusinian godesses Demeter and Persephone (Plut. *Per.* 30; Paus. III. 4. ii.), and any violation of sacred land was a serious offence. Therefore this regulation fits better a religious context. See Stadter, *A Commentary on Plutarch's Pericles*, 277.

Fr. 92: Plut. *Sol.* 23. iii (part of **fr. 81**)
λύκον δὲ τῷ κομίσαντι πέντε δραχμάς, λυκιδέα δὲ μίαν, ὧν φησιν ὁ Φαληρεὺς Δημήτριος (fr. 147 Wehrli) τὸ μὲν βοὸς εἶναι, τὸ δὲ προβάτου τιμήν.
The man who caught a wolf [was given] five drachmae, and one drachma if he caught a wolf's cub. According to Demetrius of Phalerum, those prices were equivalent respectively to that of an ox and that of a sheep.

Plutarch mentions the kind of reward that was to be given to a man who brought in a wolf (five drachmae) or a wolf's cub (one drachma). The amount is quite high, if compared to the penalty of a hundred drachmae for raping a free woman (fr. 26) and of twenty drachmae for procuring a free woman (fr. 30a). These rewards are also significant when compared to the value of choice victims, because they were equivalent to the price of an ox and of a goat, respectively, as maintained by Demetrius. Plutarch is probably correct when he establishes a connection between the hunting of wolves and the importance of pasture activitites in Athens. On the question of coinage in Solon's time see fr. 65 with commentary. See also frs. 81–2 for other regulations concerning offerings.

ENTRENCHMENT OF THE LAWS

Fr. 93a: Dio Chrys. *Or.* LXXX. 6
καὶ τὴν ἀράν ἣν Ἀθηναῖοι περὶ τῶν Σόλωνος ἔθεντο νόμων τοῖς ἐπιχειροῦσι καταλύειν, ἀγνοεῖτε κυριωτέραν οὖσαν ἐπὶ τοῖς ἐκείνου νόμοις. πᾶσα γὰρ ἀνάγκη τὸν συγχέοντα τὸν θεσμὸν ἄτιμον ὑπάρχειν, πλὴν παῖδας καὶ γένος οὐκ ἐπέξεισιν, ὡς ἐκεῖ, τῶν ἁμαρτανόντων, ἀλλ' ἕκαστος αὐτῷ γίγνεται τῆς ἀτυχίας αἴτιος.
συγχέοντα Casaubon: συνέχοντα MSS.   ἄτιμον ὑπάρχειν Emperius: Ἀθηναῖον ἐπάρχειν MSS., ἀραῖον ὑπάρχειν von Arnim.   αὐτῷ Reiske: αὐτῶν MSS.

Besides, the curse that the Athenians established regarding those who attempted to overthrow Solon's laws, though you fail to see it, is even more authoritative when it regards the laws of him [Zeus]. In fact, any person who tries to overturn the law [of Zeus] will inevitably become *atimos* — with the difference that children and family of those who have transgressed will not be prosecuted, as happened there [i.e. in Athens]: on the contary, each one is responsible for his own misfortunes.

Fr. 93b: Gell. *N.A.* II. 12. i
In legibus Solonis illis antiquissimis, quae Athenis axibus ligneis incisae sunt quasque latas ab eo Athenienses, ut sempiternae manerent, poenis et religionibus sanxerunt.
In those most ancient laws of Solon, which were engraved in Athens on wooden axles and were enacted by him, and which the Athenians made everlasting by the threat of legal and religious punishments.

Both passages maintain that the Athenians reinforced the laws of Solon by threatening legal and religious penalties for those who tried to overthrow or change them. This kind of entrenchment clause was quite frequent in legal documents, because they were seen by the Greeks as a way of preventing the risk of disorder. As suggested in fr. 93a, entrenchment clauses usually extended their effects to the family and property of the transgressor. For a similar clause regarding Draco's law, see fr. 22 with commentary. In general see D. M. Lewis, 'Entrenchment-Clauses in Attic Decrees', in φόρος . . . *B. D. Meritt*, 81–9 = his *Selected Papers in Greek and Near Eastern History*, 136–49, not mentioning fr. 22 or this fragment; E. M. Harris,

'Solon and the Spirit of the Laws in Archaic and Classical Greece', in Blok & Lardinois (edd.), *Solon of Athens*, 290–318 at 309–12 = his *Democracy and the Rule of Law*, 22–4.

Herodotus (I. 29. i), *Ath. Pol.* (11. i) and Plutarch (*Sol.* 25. vi) maintain that Solon left Athens for ten years after having finished his activity as legislator. The real motivation for the travel must have been, as implied by the sources, to avoid pressure from his fellow citizens to introduce changes into the recently enacted code. Herodotus is most probably correct in linking this period of time with the ten years during which the laws of Solon were to remain unchanged. *Ath. Pol.* (7. ii) and Plutarch (*Sol.* 25. i) have the laws safeguarded for a hundred years, a number that could be interpreted as equivalent to the idea that they were intended to have an unlimited duration. This is in fact the perspective presented in Gellius (*ut sempiternae manerent*). For a review of the main lines of interpretation regarding this question, see Rhodes, *Comm. Ath. Pol.*, 136, 169–70; Leão, *Sólon. Ética e política*, 275–7.

UNUSABLE, DOUBTFUL, SPURIOUS

From the orators

Fr. 94: Andoc. I. *Myst.* 95-9

Ἐπιχάρης δ' οὑτοσί ... οὗτος γὰρ ἐβούλευεν ἐπὶ τῶν τριάκοντα. ὁ δὲ νόμος τί κελεύει, ὃς ἐν τῇ στήλῃ ἔμπροσθέν ἐστι τοῦ βουλευτηρίου; "ὃς ἂν ἄρξῃ ἐν τῇ πόλει τῆς δημοκρατίας καταλυθείσης, νηποινεὶ τεθνάναι, καὶ τὸν ἀποκτείναντα ὅσιον εἶναι καὶ τὰ χρήματα ἔχειν τοῦ ἀποθανόντος." ἄλλο τι οὖν, ὦ Ἐπίχαρες, ἢ νῦν ὁ ἀποκτείνας σε καθαρὸς τὰς χεῖρας ἔσται, κατά γε τὸν Σόλωνος νόμον; (96) καί μοι ἀνάγνωθι τὸν νόμον τὸν ἐκ τῆς στήλης.

ΝΟΜΟΣ· "ἔδοξε τῇ βουλῇ καὶ τῷ δήμῳ. Αἰαντὶς ἐπρυτάνευε· Κλειγένης ἐγραμμάτευε· Βοηθὸς ἐπεστάτει. τάδε Δημόφαντος συνέγραψεν. ἄρχει χρόνος τοῦδε τοῦ ψηφίσματος ἡ βουλὴ οἱ πεντακόσιοι λαχόντες τῷ κυάμῳ, οἷς Κλειγένης πρῶτος ἐγραμμάτευεν. ἐάν τις δημοκρατίαν καταλύῃ τὴν Ἀθήνησιν ἢ ἀρχήν τινα ἄρχῃ καταλελυμένης τῆς δημοκρατίας, πολέμιος ἔστω Ἀθηναίων καὶ νηποινεὶ τεθνάτω καὶ τὰ χρήματα δημόσια ἔστω καὶ τῆς θεοῦ τὸ ἐπιδέκατον. ὁ δὲ ἀποκτείνας τὸν ταῦτα ποιήσαντα καὶ ὁ συμβουλεύσας ὅσιος ἔστω καὶ εὐαγής. (97) ὀμόσαι δ' Ἀθηναίους ἅπαντας καθ' ἱερῶν τελείων κατὰ φυλὰς καὶ κατὰ δήμους ἀποκτενεῖν τὸν ταῦτα ποιήσαντα. ὁ δὲ ὅρκος ἔστω ὅδε· 'κτενῶ <καὶ λόγῳ καὶ ἔργῳ καὶ ψήφῳ καὶ> τῇ ἐμαυτῷ χειρί, ἂν δύνατος ὦ, ὃς ἂν καταλύσῃ τὴν δημοκρατίαν τὴν Ἀθήνησι, καὶ ἐάν τις ἄρξῃ τιν' ἀρχὴν καταλελυμένης τῆς δημοκρατίας τὸ λοιπόν, καὶ ἐάν τις τυραννεῖν ἐπαναστῇ ἢ τὸν τύραννον συγκαταστήσῃ. καὶ ἐάν τις ἄλλος ἀποκτείνῃ, ὅσιον αὐτὸν νομιῶ εἶναι καὶ πρὸς θεῶν καὶ δαιμόνων ὡς πολέμιον κτείναντα τῶν Ἀθηναίων καὶ τὰ κτήματα τοῦ ἀποθανόντος πάντα ἀποδόμενος ἀποδώσω τὰ ἡμίσεα τῷ ἀποκτείναντι {καὶ λόγῳ καὶ ἔργῳ καὶ ψήφῳ} καὶ οὐκ ἀποστερήσω οὐδέν. (98) ἐὰν δέ τις κτείνων τινὰ τούτων ἀποθάνῃ ἢ ἐπιχειρῶν, εὖ ποιήσω αὐτόν τε καὶ τοὺς παῖδας τοὺς ἐκείνου καθάπερ Ἁρμόδιόν τε καὶ Ἀριστογείτονα καὶ τοὺς ἀπογόνους αὐτῶν. ὁπόσοι δὲ ὅρκοι ὀμώμονται Ἀθήνησιν ἢ ἐν τῷ στρατοπέδῳ ἢ ἄλλοθί που ἐνάντιοι τῷ δήμῳ τῷ Ἀθηναίων, λύω καὶ ἀφίημι.' ταῦτα δὲ ὀμοσάντων Ἀθηναῖοι πάντες καθ' ἱερῶν τελείων, τὸν νόμιμον ὅρκον, πρὸ Διονυσίων. καὶ ἐπεύχεσθαι εὐορκοῦντι μὲν εἶναι πολλὰ καὶ ἀγαθά, ἐπιορκοῦντι δ' ἐξώλη αὐτὸν εἶναι καὶ γένος."

(99) πότερον, ὦ συκοφάντα καὶ ἐπίτριπτον κίναδος, κύριος ὁ νόμος ὅδε ἐστὶν ἢ οὐ κύριος; διὰ τοῦτο δ' οἶμαι γεγένηται ἄκυρος, ὅτι τοῖς νόμοις δεῖ χρῆσθαι ἀπ' Εὐκλείδου ἄρχοντος.

καὶ λόγῳ καὶ ἔργῳ καὶ ψήφῳ καὶ inserted at beginning of oath and (without final καὶ) deleted at end of §97 Sauppe.

This man Epichares ... for he was a member of the council under the Thirty. What is commanded by the law on the *stele* in front of the council house? 'Whoever holds office in the city when the democracy has been abolished may be killed with impunity, and the man who kills him shall be free from guilt and shall have the property of the deceased.' Will it not be the case now, Epichares, that the man who kills you will have undefiled hands, at any rate in accordance with Solon's law? (96) *Read me the law from the* stele.

LAW: 'Resolved by the council and the people. Aiantis was the prytany; Cleigenes was the secretary; Boethus was the chairman. The following was drafted by Demophantus. The time of this decree begins from the council of five hundred appointed by lot, for which Cleigenes was first to serve as secretary. If anybody overthrows the democracy at Athens, or holds any office when the democracy has been overthrown, he shall be an enemy of the Athenians and may be killed with impunity, and his property shall be public, a tithe going to the goddess. Anybody who kills a man who has acted thus or has joined in planning to do so shall be free from guilt and pure. (97) All the Athenians shall swear over perfect victims, by tribes and by demes, to kill a man who acts thus. The oath shall be as follows: 'I shall kill <by word and deed and vote and> by my own hand, if I am able, whoever overthrows the democracy at Athens, and if anybody holds any office afterwards when the democracy has been overthrown, and if anybody rises up to be a tyrant or joins in establishing a tyrant. And if anybody else kills him I shall consider that man free from guilt before the gods and *daimones*, for having killed an enemy of the Athenians, and I shall sell all the possessions of the deceased, giving half to the killer {by word and deed and vote}, and shall not hold anything back. (98) And if anybody is killed while killing or attempting to kill any of these men, I shall act well by him and his children, as by Harmodius and Aristogeiton and their descendants. Whatever oaths have been sworn at Athens or in the forces or anywhere else which are opposed to the *demos* of Athens I annul and cancel.' This oath is to be sworn by all the Athenians over perfect victims, the customary oath, before the Dionysia. And they shall pray for many good things for those who keep the oath, but for those who break it destruction for themselves and their descendants.'

(99) You sycophant and damned fox, is this law valid or is it not? For this reason I think it has become invalid, that the laws are to be applied from the archonship of Euclides (403/2).

Andocides refers to a law of Solon on a *stele* in front of the council house. However, the laws of Solon were inscribed on a set of *axones*, whereas the oldest known council house was not built before the end of the sixth century, and that was superseded by a new council house nearby about the time of this speech, at the end of the fifth century (see Camp, *The Athenian Agora: Site Guide*[5], 58–63); a surviving *stele* is not likely to have been set up earlier than the rebuilding of Athens after the Persian Wars. The text then quoted purports to be a decree of Demophantus enacted in 410/09, when the democracy was restored after the régimes of the Four Hundred and the Five Thousand. Demophantus is not named in Andocides' own text, but his decree is cited by Dem. XX. *Leptines* 159, Lyc. *Leocrates* 124–7 (the latter dating it to 403). The authenticity of this text and of others inserted in this speech is challenged by M. Canevaro & E. M. Harris, 'The Documents in Andocides' *On the Mysteries*', *CQ*[2] lxii 2012, 98–129; but this text is defended as an authentic decree (though not the text which ought to have been inserted at that point) by A. H. Sommerstein, 'The Authenticity of the Demophantus Decree', *CQ*[2] lxiv 2014, 49–57. It seems to us not obviously false as the other documents do seem; if it is authentic, it is manifestly not a law of Solon; if it is not, the decree which Andocides did cite from a *stele* is unlikely to have been a law of Solon (and this will be one of the earliest surviving instances of the attribution to Solon of a later law). For other laws against tyranny see on fr. 37c.

The meaning of what Andocides says at the end of this extract is made clear by §§87–9: the laws are to be enforced with regard to acts committed in and after 403/2, and the law quoted by Andocides is *akyros* not because it is invalid absolutely — he would not undermine his own argument in that way — but in that it cannot be enforced against Epichares because his service under the Thirty preceded 403/2.

Fr. 95: Andoc. I. *Myst.* 111
ἐπειδὴ γὰρ ἤλθομεν Ἐλευσινόθεν καὶ ἡ ἔνδειξις ἐγεγένητο, προσῄει ὁ βασιλεὺς περὶ τῶν γεγενημένων Ἐλευσῖνι κατὰ τὴν τελευτήν,

ὥσπερ ἔθος ἐστίν, οἱ δὲ πρυτάνεις προσάξειν ἔφασαν αὐτὸν πρὸς τὴν βουλὴν ἐπαγγεῖλαί τ' ἐκέλευον ἐμοί τε καὶ Κηφισίῳ παρεῖναι εἰς τὸ Ἐλευσίνιον. ἡ γὰρ βουλὴ ἐκεῖ καθεδεῖσθαι ἔμελλε κατὰ τὸν Σόλωνος νόμον ὃς κελεύει τῇ ὑστεραίᾳ τῶν μυστηρίων ἕδραν ποιεῖν ἐν τῷ Ἐλευσινίῳ.

ἐπαγγεῖλαι Bekker: ἀπαγγεῖλαι cod.

When we came from Eleusis and the *endeixis* had been made, the *basileus* stepped forward about what had happened in the rites at Eleusis, as is customary. The *prytaneis* said they would bring him before the council, and they told him to summon me and Cephisius to attend at the Eleusinium. (The council was going to meet there in accordance with the law of Solon which orders it to hold a session there on the day after the Mysteries.)

We believe in the existence of the council of four hundred attributed to Solon (*Ath. Pol.* 8. iv, Plut. *Sol.* 19. i–ii); but Cleisthenes' council of five hundred acquired much more business than Solon's council is likely ever to have had, and it is not probable that a law requiring the council to hold a special meeting to review the Mysteries is Solonian.

Fr. 95/1 (fr. 15b Ruschenbusch): Lys. X. *Theomnestus i*. 16–17 (part of **fr. 23c**)
(15 καί μοι ἀνάγνωθι τούτους τοὺς νόμους τοὺς Σόλωνος τοὺς παλαιούς.)
λέγε ἕτερον νόμον. ΝΟΜΟΣ· "ἐπεγγυᾶν δ' ἐπιορκήσαντα τὸν Ἀπόλλω. δεδιότα δὲ δίκης ἕνεκα δρασκάζειν." τοῦτο τὸ ἐπιορκήσαντα ὀμόσαντά ἐστι, τό τε δρασκάζειν ὃ νῦν ἀποδιδράσκειν ὀνομάζομεν.

δίκης ἕνεκα <μὴ> δρασκάζειν Hillgruber.

(15 And read for me these ancient laws of Solon.)
Read another law. LAW: 'He shall give a guarantee after oath-taking by Apollo. If he is afraid because of justice, he shall abscond.' 'Oath-taking' means swearing, and 'abscond' is what we call run away.

This passage quotes among examples of archaic language in laws *epiorkesanta* as meaning swearing (as it presumably did in that context, though in all other surviving instances the compound verb means to swear falsely), and *draskazein* as meaning run away. Probably the two sentences are from the same law. Ruschenbusch took them to be consecutive sentences of that law, took 'abscond' to refer to the right to withdraw of a man accused of homicide (cf. fr. 15a), and therefore to confirm the antiquity of that right, though he believed the two pairs of speeches, after the first of which the accused could withdraw, were not introduced until *c.* 430 (*Gesetzeswerk*, 21–2), and the oath and guarantee to be connected with the accused's undertaking to leave Attica. He then identified the oath with that of *Anecd. Bekk.* i. 239. 23–30 (but on that see MacDowell, *Athenian Homicide Law*, 97–8).

However, as remarked by Todd *ad loc.*, Ruschenbusch's confidence was misplaced. The two sentences are not necessarily consecutive sentences of the law, and it is not obvious that 'run away' must refer to the right to withdraw of a man accused of homicide, in which case the archaic language here does not confirm that that right was present already in Draco's law. If the two sentences are consecutive, Todd thought that the purpose of the oath and guarantee would be to ensure the defendant's appearance in court on some charge, in which case with Hillgruber, *Die zehnte Rede des Lysias*, 71–7, we should read <μὴ> δρασκάζειν. Hillgruber considered frs. 95/1, 25 and 68 all to be from the same law, concerned with theft, but that seems improbable.

Fr. 96a: Dem. XXIV. *Timocrates* 144–8

ἵνα δὲ καὶ περὶ ἐκείνου εἴπω τοῦ νόμου, ὦ ἄνδρες δικασταί, ᾧ ἀκούω μέλλειν παραδείγματι χρῆσθαι τοῦτον καὶ φήσειν ἀκολουθὸν αὐτῷ τεθημέναι, ἐν ᾧ ἔνι "οὐδὲ δήσω Ἀθηναίων οὐδένα ὃς ἂν ἐγγυητὰς τρεῖς καθιστῇ τὸ αὐτὸ τέλος τελοῦντας, πλὴν ἐάν τις ἐπὶ προδοσίᾳ τῆς πόλεως ἢ ἐπὶ καταλύσει τοῦ δήμου συνιὼν ἁλῷ, ἢ τέλος πριάμενος ἢ ἐγγυησάμενος ἢ ἐκλέγων μὴ καταβάλῃ", ἀκούσατέ μου καὶ περὶ τούτου. . . . (147) ἔπειτα δ', ὦ ἄνδρες δικασταί, τοῦτο τὸ γράμμα αὐτὸ μὲν καθ' αὑτὸ οὔκ ἐστι νόμος, τὸ "οὐδὲ δήσω Ἀθηναίων οὐδένα", ἐν δὲ τῷ ὅρκῳ τῷ βουλευτικῷ γέγραπται, ἵνα μὴ συνιστάμενοι οἱ ῥήτορες οἱ ἐν τῇ βουλῇ δεσμὸν κατά τινος τῶν πολιτῶν λέγοιεν. ἄκυρον οὖν τοῦ δῆσαι τὴν βουλὴν ποιῶν ὁ Σόλων τοῦτο πρὸς τὸν ὅρκον τὸν βουλευτικὸν προσέγραψεν, ἀλλ' οὐ πρὸς τὸν ὑμέτερον.

So that I may speak about that law, men of the jury, which I hear this man is going to use as an example and say he followed in his law, in which it is stated, 'I shall not imprison any of the Athenians who provides three guarantors of the same [*sc.* Solonian] class, except any convicted of betraying the city or combining to overthrow the people, or taking a contract for taxes or guaranteeing one or collecting and failing to pay', hear me about this. . . . (147) Then, men of the jury, this text, 'I shall not imprison any of the Athenians', is not itself a law, but it has been written in the councillors' oath, so that the politicians in the council shall not combine to propose imprisonment for any of the citizens. Solon, then, made the council powerless to imprison, and he added this to the councillors' oath, but not to yours [*sc.* the jurors'].

Ath. Pol. 22. ii states that in (probably) 501/0 'they instituted for the council of five hundred the oath which they still swear now'. In fact we know of subsequent additions to that oath (see Rhodes, *The Athenian Boule*, 194–9), while we know nothing of the oath sworn by Solon's council if there was one. The oath to which Demosthenes is alluding is the current version of the oath instituted for the five hundred, and this clause will not have been added before the council acquired judicial powers, probably through Ephialtes' reform of 462/1 (*Ath. Pol.* 25. ii): the attribution of this to Solon is a fiction like the attribution of the current laws to Solon.

Fr. 96b: Stob. *Flor.* (iv. 72 Meineke)
καὶ δὴ παρίσταταί μοι μάρτυς τῶν λεγομένων Ἀθηναῖος Σόλων νομοθετήσας μήτε ἄρχειν τὸν σφόδρα νέον μήτε ξυμβουλεύειν, εἰ καὶ ἄριστα δοκοίη γνώμης ἔχειν.
And let Solon the Athenian stand as a witness of what I have said, who enacted a law that a man who was very young should not hold office or join in the council, even if he seemed excellent in judgment.

Ruschenbusch placed this fragment here because he thought it might have been derived from the councillors' oath, which is possible but not necessary. We do not know when age requirements for holding office were first specified in Athenian law.

Fr. 97a: Dem. XXIV. *Timocrates* 148–51
(cf. fr. 96a) ἄκυρον οὖν τοῦ δῆσαι τὴν βουλὴν ποιῶν ὁ Σόλων τοῦτο πρὸς τὸν ὅρκον τὸν βουλευτικὸν προσέγραψεν, ἀλλ' οὐ πρὸς τὸν ὑμέτερον· ἁπάντων γὰρ κυριώτατον ᾤετο δεῖν εἶναι τὸ δικαστήριον, καὶ ὅ τι γνοίη τοῦτο πάσχειν τὸν ἁλόντα. ἀναγνώσται δ' ὑμῖν αὐτοῦ τούτου ἕνεκα τὸν τῶν ἡλιαστῶν ὅρκον. λέγε σύ.
(149) ΟΡΚΟΣ ΗΛΙΑΣΤΩΝ· "ψηφιοῦμαι κατὰ τοὺς νόμους καὶ τὰ ψηφίσματα τοῦ δήμου τοῦ Ἀθηναίων καὶ τῆς βουλῆς τῶν πεντακοσίων. καὶ τύραννον οὐ ψηφιοῦμαι εἶναι οὐδ' ὀλιγαρχίαν. οὐδ' ἐάν τις καταλύῃ τὸν δῆμον τὸν Ἀθηναίων ἢ λέγῃ ἢ ἐπιψηφίζῃ παρὰ ταῦτα, οὐ πείσομαι. οὐδὲ τῶν χρεῶν τῶν ἰδίων ἀποκοπὰς οὐδὲ γῆς ἀναδασμὸν τῆς Ἀθηναίων οὐδ' οἰκιῶν. οὐδὲ τοὺς φεύγοντας κατάξω, οὐδὲ ὧν θάνατος κατέγνωσται, οὐδὲ τοὺς μένοντας ἐξελῶ παρὰ τοὺς νόμους τοὺς κειμένους καὶ τὰ ψηφίσματα τοῦ δήμου τοῦ Ἀθηναίων καὶ τῆς βουλῆς, οὔτ' αὐτὸς ἐγὼ οὔτ' ἄλλον οὐδένα ἐάσω. (150) οὐδ' ἀρχὴν καταστήσω ὥστ' ἄρχειν ὑπεύθυνον ὄντα ἑτέρας ἀρχῆς, καὶ τῶν ἐννέα ἀρχόντων καὶ τοῦ ἱερομνήμονος καὶ ὅσοι μετὰ τῶν ἐννέα ἀρχόντων κυαμεύονται ταύτῃ τῇ ἡμέρᾳ καὶ κήρυκος καὶ

πρεσβείας καὶ συνέδρων· οὐδὲ δὶς τὴν αὐτὴν ἀρχὴν τὸν αὐτὸν ἄνδρα, οὐδὲ δύο ἀρχὰς ἄρξαι τὸν αὐτὸν ἐν τῷ ἐνιαυτῷ. οὐδὲ δῶρα δέξομαι τῆς ἡλιάσεως ἕνεκα, οὔτ' αὐτὸς ἐγὼ οὔτ' ἄλλος ἐμοὶ οὔτ' ἄλλη εἰδότος ἐμοῦ, οὔτε τέχνῃ οὔτε μηχανῇ οὐδεμιᾷ. (151) καὶ γέγονα οὐκ ἔλαττον ἢ τριάκοντα ἔτη. καὶ ἀκροάσομαι τοῦ τε κατηγόρου καὶ τοῦ ἀπολογουμένου ὁμοίως ἀμφοῖν, καὶ διαψηφιοῦμαι περὶ αὐτοῦ οὗ ἂν ἡ δίωξις ᾖ." ἐπομνύναι Δία, Ποσειδῶ, Δήμητρα, καὶ ἐπαρᾶσθαι ἐξώλειαν ἑαυτῷ καὶ οἰκίᾳ τῇ ἑαυτοῦ εἴ τι τούτων παραβαίνοι, εὐορκοῦντι δὲ πολλὰ κἀγαθὰ εἶναι.

ἐνταῦθ' οὐκ ἔνι, ὦ ἄνδρες Ἀθηναῖοι, "οὐδὲ δήσω Ἀθηναίων οὐδένα".

Solon, then, made the council powerless to imprison, and he added this to the councillors' oath, but not to yours [*sc.* the jurors']. For he thought the *dikasterion* ought to be the most authoritative of all, and that what it decided the man convicted should suffer. For this very reason the oath of the *eliastai* will be read to you. Read the oath.

(149) ELIASTS' OATH: 'I shall vote in accordance with the laws and decrees of the people of Athens and the council of five hundred. I shall not vote for the existence of a tyrant or oligarchy. Nor, if anybody overthrows the *demos* of Athens or speaks or puts a proposal to the vote contrary to that shall I obey. Nor cancellation of private debts or redistribution of the land of Athens or houses. Nor shall I restore exiles or men condemned to death, or drive out men remaining here contrary to the established laws and the decrees of the people of Athens and the council, neither I myself nor shall I allow anybody else. (150) Nor shall I appoint anybody to hold any office while he is accountable for another office, the offices of the nine archons and the *hieromnemon* and those who are allotted with the nine archons on that day, and the herald and embassy and *synedroi*. Nor shall I allow the same man to hold the same office twice, or the same man to hold two offices in the same year. Nor shall I accept bribes for my eliastic service, neither I myself nor any other man or woman for me with my knowledge, by any craft or contrivance. (151) I am not less than thirty years old. I shall listen to the prosecutor and defendant, the two alike, and I shall vote on the issue on which the prosecution is made.' One must swear by Zeus, Poseidon and Demeter, and invoke destruction

on oneself and one's household if one contravenes any of these, but if one keeps the oath there shall be many benefits for him.

This does not contain, men of Athens, 'Nor shall I imprison any Athenian'.

Fr. 97b: Dem. XVIII. *Crown* 6
ἀξιῶ καὶ δέομαι πάντων ὁμοίως ὑμῶν ἀκοῦσαί μου περὶ τῶν κατηγορημένων ἀπολογουμένου δικαίως, ὥσπερ οἱ νόμοι κελεύουσιν οὓς ὁ τιθεὶς ἐξ ἀρχῆς Σόλων, εὔνους ὢν ὑμῖν καὶ δημοτικός, οὐ μόνον τῷ γράψαι κυρίους ᾤετο δεῖν εἶναι ἀλλὰ καὶ τῷ τοὺς δικάζοντας ὀμωμοκέναι, οὐκ ἀπιστῶν ὑμῖν, ὥς γ' ἐμοὶ φαίνεται, ἀλλ' ὁρῶν ὅτι τὰς αἰτίας καὶ διαβολὰς αἷς ἐκ τοῦ πρότερος λέγειν ὁ διώκων ἰσχύει οὐκ ἔνι τῷ φεύγοντι παρελθεῖν, εἰ μὴ τῶν δικαζόντων ἕκαστος ὑμῶν τὴν πρὸς τοὺς θεοὺς εὐσέβειαν φυλάττων καὶ τὰ τοῦ λέγοντος ὑστέρου δίκαια εὐνοϊκῶς προσδέξεται, καὶ παρασχὼν αὑτὸν ἴσον καὶ κοινὸν ἀμφοτέροις ἀκροατήν, οὕτω τὴν διάγνωσιν ποιήσεται περὶ ἁπάντων.

I demand and beg you all alike to listen to me as I reply to the accusations, justly, as is commanded by the laws enacted from the beginning by Solon, who was well disposed to you and democratic, and thought that they should be made effective not only by his writing them but by the jurors' swearing them, not because he distrusted you, I judge, but because he saw that the accusations and slanders in which the prosecutor has the advantage of speaking first cannot be circumvented by the defendant unless each of you jurors keeps his piety towards the gods and receives the claims to justice of the second speaker with good will, offering himself as an equal and common listener to each, and in that way makes his decision about everything.

Fr. 97c: Lib. *Decl.* I. 9
ταῦτα γὰρ δήπου καὶ ὁ Σόλων εἰδὼς καὶ νομίζων τῶν ἀγωνιουμένων τοὺς μὲν ἐν φίλοις τοῖς δικάζουσι δώσειν λόγον, τοὺς δὲ ἐν χαλεπῶς ἔχουσιν, ἵνα μηδετέρωθεν καταβλάπτοιτο τὸ δίκαιον, ὅρκον ἔταξεν οὐκ ἐῶντα χάριν ἢ δυσμένειαν ἤ τινα πρόφασιν ἄλλην ἄδικον ἐνοχλῆσαι τῇ κρίσει.

Solon knew this and thought that some of those about to contend would make their speech to friendly jurors and others to harsh jurors. So that justice should not be damaged from either side, he appointed an oath which did not allow any favour or ill will or other unjust pretext to make trouble for the judgment.

Fr. 97d: Lucian *Cal.* 8
ἐσχάτης ἀδικίας τὸ τοιοῦτον, ὡς φαῖεν ἂν καὶ οἱ ἄριστοι τῶν νομοθετῶν, οἷον ὁ Σόλων καὶ ὁ Δράκων, ἔνορκον ποιησάμενοι τοῖς δικασταῖς τὸ ὁμοίως ἀμφοῖν ἀκροᾶσθαι καὶ τὸ τὴν εὔνοιαν ἴσην τοῖς κρινομένοις ἀπονέμειν, ἄχρι ἂν ὁ τοῦ δευτέρου λόγος παρατεθεὶς θατέρου χείρων ἢ ἀμείνων φανῇ· πρὶν δέ γε ἀνεξετάσαι τὴν ἀπολογίαν τῇ κατηγορίᾳ παντελῶς ἀσεβῆ καὶ ἀνόσιον ἡγήσαντο ἔσεσθαι τὴν κρίσιν.

This kind of thing [*sc.* listening to slander but not to the reply] is extreme injustice, as would be said by the best of the lawgivers, such as Solon and Draco, making it an element in their oath for the jurors to listen to each party alike and to assign equal good will to [*sc.* each of] those being judged, until the argument of the second has been presented and appears worse or better than the other: until the defence has been examined in response to the accusation they thought it utterly impious and unrighteous to make a judgment.

What kind of body Solon's *eliaia* was remains uncertain (cf. on fr. 23c), so we do not know whether it was a body with defined membership to which an oath could be administered; but since Solon was credited with the creation of the *eliaia* it was easy for the oath to be attributed to him too. The oath for which we have evidence is the oath sworn in the era of the orators, and we have no good evidence for the same or a different oath earlier. It has long been believed that fr. 97a is a later compilation from material found in various places (e.g. Bonner & Smith, *Administration of Justice*, ii. 152–6), cf. Canevaro, who shows that it is one of the documents in Dem. XXIV which are not included in the stichometry and which seem as a group to be unreliable, and stresses the various problematic features of this document (*The Documents in the Attic Orators*, 173–80). Frs. 97b–d concentrate on the obligation to give an equal hearing to each side. Other texts, omitted by Ruschenbusch because they do not name Solon, add an undertaking to vote in accordance with the laws, 'and on matters on which there are no laws to judge with the most just opinion' (καὶ περὶ ὧν ἂν νόμοι μὴ ὦσι γνώμῃ τῇ δικαιοτάτῃ κρινεῖν: Dem. XX. *Leptines* 118, cf. XXIII. *Aristocrates* 96, XXXIX. *Boeotus i.* 40, LVII. *Eubulides* 63, Aeschin. III. *Ctesiphon* 6).

Fr. 98a: Dem. XX. *Leptines* 89–94

ὁ παλαιός, ὃν οὗτος παρέβη, νόμος οὕτω κελεύει νομοθετεῖν, γράφεσθαι μέν, ἄν τίς τινα τῶν ὑπαρχόντων νόμων μὴ καλὸν ἔχειν ἡγῆται, παρεισφέρειν δ' αὐτὸν ἄλλον, ὃν ἂν τιθῇ λύων ἐκεῖνον, ὑμᾶς δ' ἀκούσαντες ἑλέσθαι τὸν κρείττω. (90) οὐ γὰρ ᾤετο δεῖν ὁ Σόλων, ὁ τοῦτον τὸν νόμον προστάξας νομοθετεῖν, τοὺς μὲν θεσμοθέτας τοὺς ἐπὶ τοὺς νόμους κληρουμένους δὶς δοκιμασθέντες ἄρχειν, ἔν τε τῇ βουλῇ καὶ παρ' ὑμῖν ἐν τῷ δικαστηρίῳ, τοὺς δὲ νόμους αὐτούς, καθ' οὓς καὶ τούτοις ἄρχειν καὶ πᾶσι τοῖς ἄλλοις πολιτεύεσθαι προσήκει, ἐπὶ καιροῦ τεθέντας, ὅπως ἔτυχον, μὴ δοκιμασθέντας κυρίους εἶναι. . . . (92) ἵν' οὖν μὴ λόγον λέγω μόνον, ἀλλὰ καὶ τὸν νόμον αὐτόν, ὅν φημί, δείξω, λαβέ μοι τὸν νόμον καθ' ὃν ἦσαν οἱ πρότερον νομοθέται. λέγε. ΝΟΜΟΣ [deest]. *(93)* συνίεθ' ὃν τρόπον, ὦ ἄνδρες Ἀθηναῖοι, ὁ Σόλων τοὺς νόμους ὡς καλῶς κελεύει τιθέναι, πρῶτον μὲν παρ' ὑμῖν, ἐν τοῖς ὀμωμοκόσιν, παρ' οἷσπερ καὶ τἆλλα κυροῦται, ἔπειτα λύοντα τοὺς ἐναντίους, ἵν' εἷς ᾖ περὶ τῶν ὄντων ἑκάστου νόμος. . . . (94) καὶ πρὸ τούτων γ' ἐπέταξεν ἐκθεῖναι πρόσθε τῶν ἐπωνύμων καὶ τῷ γραμματεῖ παραδοῦναι, τοῦτον δ' ἐν ταῖς ἐκκλησίαις ἀναγιγνώσκειν, ἵν' ἕκαστος ὑμῶν ἀκούσας πολλάκις, καὶ κατὰ σχολὴν σκεψάμενος ἃ ἂν ᾖ καὶ δίκαια καὶ συμφέροντα, ταῦτα νομοθετῇ.

The old law, which this man has transgressed, orders that laws should be enacted in this way: one should prosecute, if anybody thinks any of the existing laws is not in a good condition, and propose beside it another which one would enact when one annuls that, and you should listen and choose the better. (90) For Solon, who thought that laws should be enacted in this way, did not think that whereas the *thesmothetai* who are allotted to take charge of the laws should hold office after undergoing two *dokimasiai*, in the council and among you in the lawcourt, nevertheless the laws themselves, in accordance with which it is proper for them to hold office and for all of you to engage in political life, should be enacted *ad hoc*, in any casual way, and be valid without undergoing a *dokimasia*. . . . (92) So that I may not only speak but demonstrate the law which I mentioned, take for me the law in accordance with which the *nomothetai* previously served, and read it. LAW [*text not inserted*]. (93) You see, men of Athens, the way in which Solon orders the laws to be enacted well: first among you, who have sworn the oath, and among whom other things are validated; then by annulling the laws opposed to them, so that there may be one law on each subject. ... (94) And before this he ordered [*sc.* the new proposal] to be displayed in front of the eponymous heroes and given to the secretary, and read by him in the assemblies, so that each of you may hear several times and consider at leisure, and, what is just and advantageous, enact that.

Fr. 98b: Schol. Dem. XX. *Leptines* 88 (196 Dilts)
ΑΝΑΓΝΩΣΕΤΑΙ ΤΟΝ ΝΟΜΟΝ ΥΜΙΝ· ὁ Σόλων προσέταξε τὸν λύοντά τινα τῶν κυρίων νόμων τιθέναι ἕτερον· ὅπου μὲν οὖν κύριος, ἀντεισφέρειν δεῖ, ὅπου δὲ οὔ, λύειν μόνον.
HE WILL READ THE LAW TO YOU: Solon appointed that anybody who annulled one of the valid laws should enact another; where it is [*sc.* to remain?] valid, he should make an alternative proposal; where it is not, he should simply annul it.

†Fr. 98/c: Aeschin. III. *Ctesiphon* 38–9
οὔτε ἠμέληται περὶ τῶν τοιούτων τῷ νομοθέτῃ τῷ τὴν δημοκρατίαν καταστήσαντι, ἀλλὰ διαρρήδην προστέτακται τοῖς θεσμοθέταις καθ' ἕκαστον ἐνιαυτὸν διορθοῦν ἐν τῷ δήμῳ τοὺς νόμους, ἀκριβῶς ἐξετάσαντας καὶ σκεψαμένους εἴ τις ἀναγέγραπται νόμος ἐναντίος ἑτέρῳ νόμῳ, ἢ ἄκυρος ἐν τοῖς κυρίοις, ἢ εἴ που εἰσὶ νόμοι πλείους ἑνὸς ἀναγεγραμμένοι περὶ ἑκάστης πράξεως. κἄν τι τοιοῦτον εὑρίσκωσιν, ἀναγεγραφότας ἐν σανίσιν ἐκτιθέναι κελεύει πρόσθεν τῶν ἐπωνύμων, τοὺς δὲ πρυτάνεις ποιεῖν ἐκκλησίαν ἐπιγράψαντας ΝΟΜΟΘΕΤΑΙΣ, τὸν δ' ἐπιστάτην τῶν προέδρων διαχειροτονίαν διδόναι {τῷ δήμῳ, καὶ} τοὺς μὲν ἀναιρεῖν τῶν νόμων, τοὺς δὲ καταλείπειν, ὅπως ἂν εἷς ᾖ νόμος καὶ μὴ πλείους περὶ ἑκάστης πράξεως. καί μοι λέγε τοὺς νόμους. ΝΟΜΟΙ [*desunt*].
ΝΟΜΟΘΕΤΑΙΣ Dobree; ΝΟΜΟΘΕΤΑΣ MSS.   τῷ δήμῳ deleted Schöll, καὶ deleted Kaibel.
Neither was there neglect of such matters by the lawgiver who established the democracy, but he explicitly made it the duty of the *thesmothetai* each year to correct the laws in the assembly, examining precisely and considering whether any law has been written up which is opposed to another law, or any invalid law among the valid,

or whether anywhere more than one law has been written up about each act. If they find anything of that kind he orders them to be written up on tablets and displayed in front of the eponymous heroes, and the *prytaneis* are to convene an assembly, writing the heading, FOR NOMOTHETAI, and the chairman of the *proedroi* is to call for a vote to annul some of the laws and leave others, so that there shall be one law and not several about each act. Read the laws for me. LAWS [*text not inserted*].

Fr. 98 is concerned with the fourth-century procedure for the enactment of *nomoi* (laws), at a time when *nomoi* enacted by boards of *nomothetai* were distinct from and ranked above *psephismata* (decrees) of the assembly (cf. fr. 99); and for mention of the *proedroi* cf. on fr. 80/1. Ruschenbusch added as *testimonia* the document EPICHEIROTONIA NOMON ('vote of confidence in the laws') *ap*. Dem. XXIV. *Timocrates* 20–3 and a law *ap*. §33 which requires the annulment of any law to be accompanied by the proposal of a new law to replace it. He omitted our fr. 98c. Attempts to reconstruct the procedure(s) on the basis of all these texts have been made by D. M. MacDowell, 'Law-Making at Athens in the Fourth Century B.C.', *JHS* xcv 1975, 62–74; P. J. Rhodes, 'Nomothesia in Fourth-Century Athens', *CQ²* xxxv 1985, 55–60; M. H. Hansen, 'Athenian *Nomothesia*', *GRBS* xxvi 1985, 345–71. However, M. Canevaro has shown that the documents printed as Ruschenbusch's *testimonia* are suspect, both because they are hard to reconcile with the orators' own words and because they are among those not included in the stichometry of Dem. XXIV, and that a reconstruction of Athens' fourth-century procedures should be based on the orators' words alone (*The Documents in the Attic Orators*; 'Nomothesia in Classical Athens: What Sources should we Believe?', *CQ²* lxiii 2013, 139–60). That exercise does not need to be performed here.

In fr. 98a 'prosecute' seems to result from a confusion, perhaps deliberate, of the procedure for *nomothesia* with the *graphai paranomon* and *nomon me epitedeion theinai* against newly proposed or enacted decrees and laws. The possibility envisaged by the scholiast in fr. 98b, that a law might simply be annulled without being replaced, seems not to have been envisaged in the fourth century.

†Fr. 98/1: Dem. XXI. *Midias* 47

ΝΟΜΟΣ· ἐάν τις ὑβρίζῃ εἴς τινα, ἢ παῖδα ἢ γυναῖκα ἢ ἄνδρα, τῶν ἐλευθέρων ἢ τῶν δούλων, ἢ παράνομόν τι ποιήσῃ εἰς τούτων τινά, γραφέσθω πρὸς τοὺς θεσμοθέτας ὁ βουλόμενος τῶν Ἀθηναίων οἷς ἔξεστιν, οἱ δὲ θεσμοθέται εἰσαγόντων εἰς τὴν ἡλιαίαν τριάκοντα ἡμερῶν ἀφ' ἧς ἂν ἡ γραφή, ἐὰν μή τι δημόσιον κωλύῃ, εἰ δὲ μή, ὅταν ᾖ πρῶτον οἷόν τε. ὅτου δ' ἂν καταγνῷ ἡ ἡλιαία, τιμάτω περὶ αὐτοῦ παραχρῆμα ὅτου ἂν δοκῇ ἄξιος εἶναι παθεῖν ἢ ἀποτεῖσαι. ὅσοι δ' ἂν γράφωνται γραφὰς ἰδίας κατὰ τὸν νόμον, ἐάν τις μὴ

ἐπεξέλθῃ ἢ ἐπεξιὼν μὴ μεταλάβῃ τὸ πέμπτον μέρος τῶν ψήφων, ἀποτεισάτω χιλίας δραχμὰς τῷ δημοσίῳ. ἐὰν δὲ ἀργυρίου τιμηθῇ τῆς ὕβρεως, δεδέσθω, ἐὰν {δὲ} ἐλεύθερον ὑβρίσῃ, μέχρι ἂν ἐκτείσῃ.
γραφὰς ἰδίας deleted MacDowell.   τῆς ὕβρεως: deleted Taylor, τις ὑβρίσας Westermann, τῆς ὕβρεως <τῷ αἰτίῳ> Weil.   {δὲ} deleted Oporinus.

LAW: If anybody commits *hybris* against anybody, whether child or woman or man, whether free or slave, or commits any unlawful act against any of these, a *graphe* (public suit) may be entered with the *thesmothetai* by whoever wishes of the Athenians who are entitled to do so, and the *thesmothetai* shall introduce it into the *eliaia* within thirty days from the entering of the suit, unless some public business prevents, or failing that whenever it is first possible. Whoever is convicted by the *eliaia*, there shall be an assessment about him immediately, of what he is judged to deserve to suffer or pay. Whichever men enter private *graphai* in accordance with the law, if anybody fails to follow it through or after following it through does not gain a fifth part of the votes, he shall pay a thousand drachmae to the public treasury. If [the offender] is assessed for money for the *hybris*, he shall be imprisoned, if he committed *hybris* against a free man, until he has paid.

For the law on *hybris* see fr. 30/1. We add here for completeness' sake a text on *hybris* which is not to be accepted as authentic.

The documents inserted in Dem. XXI. *Midias* are not included in the stichometry. MacDowell has defended the authenticity of four of the five laws, including fr. 98/1, and of the oracles, but not of the law in §94 or the witness statements (*Demosthenes, Against Meidias*, 43–7 and *ad locc.*); but E. M. Harris (in reviewing MacDowell, *CP* lxxxvii 1992, 71–80 at 75–8; and in Canevaro, *The Documents in the Attic Orators*, 208–36) argues that all the documents including this one are spurious. *Inter alia*, agreement with Aeschines is a sign of authenticity for MacDowell, a sign that the compiler has drawn on Aeschines for Harris; 'private *graphai*', which cannot be right, is deleted as an interpolation by MacDowell, seen as a sign of falsehood by Harris. The work of Canevaro has given good reason to believe in general that documents not included in the stichometry of the speeches are not genuine, and fr. 98/1 is better discarded. Demosthenes' elucidation in §§46–9 stresses that the law forbids *hybris* even against slaves.

Fr. 99: Hyp. III. *Athenogenes* 22
(after **fr. 119**) [σὺ δὲ τὸν] νόμον ἀφεὶς περὶ συνθ[ηκῶν παραβαινο]-μένων διαλέγῃ. καὶ ὁ [μὲν Σόλων οὐδ' ὃ] δικαίως ἔγραφεν

ψήφ[ισμά τις τοῦ νόμου] οἴεται δεῖν κυριώ[τ]ε[ρον εἶναι· σὺ δὲ καὶ τ]ὰς ἀδίκους συνθ[ήκας ἀξιοῖς κρατεῖν πάντων] τῶν νόμων.

You are neglecting the law and talking about a broken contract. Solon did not think that even a decree, justly drafted by somebody, should have more validity than the law; but you are claiming that even unjust contracts should prevail over all the laws.

Ruschenbusch cites as *testimonia* a law *ap.* Andoc. I. *Myst.* 87 (confirmed by the text of §89), attributed to 403, and a law *ap.* Dem. XXIII. *Aristocrates* 87 (elucidated in the text which follows), not attributed to Solon or dated (cf. §218 and Dem. XXIV. *Timocrates* 30). This cannot have been enacted before the distinction between laws and decrees was made, as a result of the revision of the law code and the creation of a new procedure for *nomothesia* in 410–399.

Fr. 100a: Aristid. III. *Quattuor* 630
καὶ ὁ μὲν τοῦ Σόλωνος νόμος οὐδὲ νόμον ἐπ' ἀνδρὶ γράφειν ἐᾷ.

Solon does not allow the proposal of a law aimed at an individual.

Fr. 100b: Aeneas of Gaza, *Theophrastus* (22. 19–20 Colonna)
εἶθ' ὁ μὲν τοῦ Σόλωνος οὐκ ἐᾷ νόμον ἐπ' ἀνδρὶ τιθέναι ἀλλ' ἢ τὸν αὐτὸν ἐπὶ πᾶσιν ἀνθρώποις τίθεσθαι.

Then Solon's [law] does not allow the enactment of a law aimed at an individual rather than the same law aimed at all people.

Ruschenbusch cites texts not referring to Solon: law *ap.* Andoc. I. *Myst.* 87, allowing as an exception a law approved by a quorum of six thousand in a secret ballot and attributed to 403 (the basic rule but not the exception is confirmed in §89); law *ap.* Dem. XXIV. *Timocrates* 59, the same law, in the manuscripts' text requiring a quorum of six thousand and a secret ballot for all laws, but restored by Petit to give the exception of Andoc. I. 87 (and again with the basic rule but not the supplement / exception confirmed in the text which follows), cf. law *ap.* §§45–6, banning the restoration of *atimoi* and debtors without a vote of immunity and a secret ballot of six thousand (confirmed by Demosthenes, but apparently envisaging a decree of the assembly); he omits Dem. XXIII. *Aristocrates* 86 cf. 218, where the exception appears neither in the inserted law nor in Demosthenes' own words. When the distinction between laws and decrees was instituted, it was based on the assumption that laws should be both permanent and applicable to all, and that matters which did not satisfy both of those requirements should be dealt with by decrees (e.g. Hansen, *The Athenian Democracy*, 171). The rule requiring general application probably belongs in or near 403, the context in which it is mentioned by Andocides. The supplement / exception, in inserted laws but not confirmed by the words of Andocides or Demosthenes, ought not to be authentic, but was probably fabricated later by somebody who was aware of such passages as Dem. XXIV. 46 and of the requirement of a vote by a quorum of six thousand to ratify grants of citizenship from *c.* 385 onwards (cf. [Dem.] LIX.

Neaera 89–90, *IG* ii² 103. 33–6, with Osborne, *Naturalization in Athens*, ii. 56–9, iii–iv. 161–4). Rhodes, *CQ*² xxxv 1985, 59, suggested that the exception was enacted at first when the new system was still uncertain but was never acted on. Canevaro, *The Documents in the Attic Orators*, 145–50, rejects the whole document in Dem. XXIV. 59 as a forgery.

Fr. 101: see fr. 80/1b

Fr. 102: Aeschin. I *Timarchus* 6–7

σκέψασθε γάρ, ὦ ἄνδρες, ὅσην πρόνοιαν περὶ σωφροσύνης ἐποιήσατο ὁ Σόλων ἐκεῖνος, ὁ παλαιὸς νομοθέτης, καὶ ὁ Δράκων καὶ οἱ κατὰ τοὺς χρόνους ἐκείνους νομοθέται. πρῶτον μὲν γὰρ περὶ τῆς σωφροσύνης τῶν παίδων τῶν ἡμετέρων ἐνομοθέτησαν καὶ διαρρήδην ἀπέδειξαν ἃ χρὴ τὸν παῖδα τὸν ἐλεύθερον ἐπιτηδεύειν καὶ ὡς δεῖ αὐτὸν τραφῆναι, ἔπειτα δεύτερον περὶ τῶν μειρακίων, τρίτον δ' ἐφεξῆς περὶ τῶν ἄλλων ἡλικιῶν οὐ μόνον περὶ τῶν ἰδιωτῶν ἀλλὰ καὶ περὶ τῶν ῥητόρων. καὶ τούτους τοὺς νόμους ἀναγράψαντες ὑμῖν παρακατέθεντο, καὶ ὑμᾶς αὐτῶν ἐπέστησαν φύλακας.

Consider, men, what forethought concerning modesty that man Solon, the ancient lawgiver, had, and Draco and the lawgivers in those times. First of all they enacted laws about the modesty of our children, and they set out explicitly what practices a free child should follow and how he ought to be brought up; then secondly about the youths, and thirdly in turn about the other age groups, and not only about private citizens but also about public speakers. They wrote up these laws, left them on trust to you, and appointed you as the guardians of them.

This is a *testimonium* rather than a fragment, and an introduction to the laws which are to follow: it is followed by a series of laws, including frs. 30/c, 30/1a, 103, 80/1a, 104a.

Fr. 103: Aeschin. I. *Timarchus* 19–20

(6 σκέψασθε γάρ, ὦ ἄνδρες, ὅσην πρόνοιαν περὶ σωφροσύνης ἐποιήσατο ὁ Σόλων ἐκεῖνος, ὁ παλαιὸς νομοθέτης, καὶ ὁ Δράκων καὶ οἱ κατὰ τοὺς χρόνους ἐκείνους νομοθέται.)
ἐάν τις Ἀθηναίων, φησίν, ἑταιρήσῃ, μὴ ἐξέστω αὐτῷ τῶν ἐννέα ἀρχόντων γενέσθαι, ὅτι, οἶμαι, στεφανηφόρος ἡ ἀρχή, μηδ' ἱερωσύνην ἱερώσασθαι, ὡς οὐδὲ καθαρῷ {διαλέγεται} τῷ σώματι, μηδὲ συνδικῆσαι τῷ δημοσίῳ· μηδὲ ἀρξάτω, φησι, ἀρχὴν μηδεμίαν μηδέποτε, μήτ' ἔνδημον μήτε ὑπερόριον, μήτε κληρωτὴν μήτε

χειροτονητήν· (20) μηδὲ κηρυκευσάτω, μηδὲ πρεσβευσάτω, μηδὲ πρεσβεύσαντας κρινέτω, μηδὲ συκοφαντείτω μισθωθείς, μηδὲ γνώμην εἰπάτω μηδέποτε μήτε ἐν τῇ βουλῇ μήτε ἐν τῷ δήμῳ, μηδ' ἂν δεινότατος ᾖ λέγειν. ἐὰν δέ τις παρὰ ταῦτα πράττῃ, γραφὰς ἑταιρήσεως πεποίηκε καὶ τὰ μέγιστα ἐπιτίμια ἐπέθηκεν.

καθαρῷ {διαλέγεται}: {διαλέγεται} deleted Martin, καθαρεύοντι Franke.

(6 Consider, men, what forethought concerning modesty that man Solon, the ancient lawgiver, had, and Draco and the lawgivers in those times.) If any of the Athenians, he says, acts as a prostitute, he shall not be permitted to become one of the nine archons (because, I think, this is a crown-wearing office), nor hold any priesthood (because he is not pure in his body) nor become an advocate for the public, nor (he says) is he to hold any office at any time, whether internal or external, whether allotted or elected; (20) nor may he be a herald or an envoy (nor may he prosecute those who have served as envoys, nor may he be a hired *sykophantes*); nor may he ever express his opinion in the council or the assembly (even if he is a very clever speaker). If anybody acts contrary to this, he has created *graphai* (public suits) *hetaireseos* and has imposed the greatest penalties.

In contrast to other laws cited at the beginning of this speech, the details here do not suit the time of Solon (and the passages which we place in parentheses in the translation are likely to be Aeschines' own glosses on the law). The contrast between internal and external offices is not likely to be earlier than the time of the Delian League, when Athens first had a large number of external offices (cf. *Ath. Pol.* 24. iii), and the contrast between allotted and elected offices likewise seems more at home in the fifth or fourth century. *Sykophantai*, men who prosecuted or threatened to prosecute in public suits in the hope of making money, are again a feature of Athens' developed judicial system (cf. Ar. *Ach.* 860–958, *Ath. Pol.* 35. ii). Attempts to control speakers in the council and assembly belong particularly to the late fifth and the fourth century, when leading politicians were frequently not office-holders who could be held to account in that capacity. Advocates (*syndikoi*) for the public are puzzling: *syndikoi* and *synegoroi* are found most often as supporting speakers for individual litigants (cf. Rubinstein, *Litigation and Cooperation*), but there were occasions when the state or a subdivision of it appointed advocates (e.g. *Ath. Pol.* 42. i, 54. ii); it is not clear what is envisaged here. It is possible that material has been added to a Solonian core, but much of what Aeschines quotes seems later, Fisher *ad loc.* doubts whether there was a Solonian version of this law at all, and we retain this fragment in this part of the collection.

Fr. 104a: Aeschin. I. *Timarchus* 27–33
ἃ συνιδὼν ὁ νομοθέτης διαρρήδην ἀπέδειξεν οὓς χρὴ δημηγορεῖν καὶ οὓς οὐ δεῖ λέγειν ἐν τῷ δήμῳ, καὶ οὐκ ἀπελαύνει ἀπὸ τοῦ βήματος

εἴ τις μὴ προγόνων ἐστὶν ἐστρατηγηκότων οὐδέ γε εἰ τέχνην τινὰ ἐργάζεται ἐπικουρῶν τῇ ἀναγκαίᾳ τροφῇ, ἀλλὰ τούτους καὶ μάλιστα ἀσπάζεται, καὶ διὰ τοῦτο πολλάκις ἐπερωτᾷ τίς ἀγορεύειν βούλεται. (28) τίνας δ' οὐκ ᾤετο δεῖν λέγειν; τοὺς αἰσχρῶς βεβειωκότας τούτους οὐκ ἐᾷ δημηγορεῖν. καὶ ποῦ τοῦτο δηλοῖ; "ΔΟΚΙΜΑΣΙΑ", φησί, "ΡΗΤΟΡΩΝ· ἐάν τις λέγῃ ἐν τῷ δήμῳ τὸν πατέρα τύπτων ἢ τὴν μητέρα, ἢ μὴ τρέφων ἢ μὴ παρέχων οἴκησιν"· τοῦτον οὐκ ἐᾷ λέγειν. ... καὶ τίσι δεύτερον ἀπεῖπε μὴ λέγειν; (29) "ἢ τὰς στρατείας", φησί, "μὴ ἐστρατευμένος ὅσαι ἂν αὐτῷ προσταχθῶσιν, ἢ τὴν ἀσπίδα ἀποβεβληκώς." ... τρίτον τίσι διαλέγεται; "ἢ πεπορνευμένος", φησίν, "ἢ ἡταιρηκώς." ... τέταρτον τίσι διαλέγεται; (30) "ἢ τὰ πατρῷα", φησί, "κατεδηδοκὼς ἢ ὧν ἂν κληρόνομος γένηται." ... (32) τούτους οὖν ἐξείργει ἀπὸ τοῦ βήματος, τούτους ἀπαγορεύει δημηγορεῖν. ἐὰν δέ τις παρὰ ταῦτα μὴ μόνον λέγῃ ἀλλὰ καὶ συκοφαντῇ καὶ ἀσελγαίνῃ, καὶ μηκέτι τὸν τοιοῦτον ἄνθρωπον δύνηται φέρειν ἡ πόλις, "δοκιμασίαν μέν", φησίν, "ἐπαγγειλάτω Ἀθηναίων ὁ βουλόμενος οἷς ἔξεστιν", ὑμᾶς δ' ἤδη κελεύει περὶ τούτων ἐν τῷ δικαστηρίῳ διαγιγνώσκειν. ... (33) ταῦτα μὲν οὖν πάλαι νενομοθέτηται. καὶ νῦν ἐγὼ κατὰ τοῦτον τὸν νόμον ἥκω πρὸς ὑμᾶς.

[In §§25–6 Aeschines contrasted the decorum of Solon and other earlier leaders with the disgraceful manner of Timarchus when speaking in the assembly.] Seeing this the lawgiver set out explicitly which men ought to speak and which men ought not to speak in public. He did not drive from the platform a man who lacked ancestors who had served as generals, or who plies some craft to support the necessities of his maintenance, but he particularly welcomes these, and for this reason he frequently asks, 'Who wishes to speak?' (28) But who does he think ought not to speak? Those who have lived disgracefully. These he does not allow to speak in public. And where does he show this? 'VETTING', he says, 'OF SPEAKERS. If anybody speaks in the assembly who beats his father or mother, or does not maintain them or provide a home for them', this man he does not allow to speak. ... And whom secondly does he forbid to speak? (29) 'Or', he says, 'has not served on the military campaigns which have been prescribed for him, or has thrown away his shield.' ... Whom does he mention third? 'Or anybody who has been a prostitute or escort.' ... Whom does he mention fourth? (30) 'Or has eaten up his family property or what he has inherited.' ... (32) These, then, he excludes from the platform, these he forbids to speak in public. If anybody in contravention of this not merely speaks but plays the *sykophantes* and behaves outrageously, and the city can no longer bear such a person, he says, 'Let whoever wishes of the Athenians who are entitled to do so challenge him to *dokimasia*', and he then orders you to decide about these men in a lawcourt. ... (33) This was enacted into law long ago, and I have now come before you in accordance with this law.

Fr. 104b: Diog. Laert. I. 55
δοκεῖ δὲ καὶ κάλλιστα νομοθετῆσαι· ἐάν τις μὴ τρέφῃ τοὺς γονέας, ἄτιμος ἔστω· ἀλλὰ καὶ ὁ τὰ πατρῷα κατεδηδοκὼς ὁμοίως· (καὶ ὁ ἀργὸς ὑπεύθυνος ἔστω παντὶ τῷ βουλομένῳ γράφεσθαι. Λυσίας δ' ἐν τῷ κατὰ Νικίδου Δράκοντά φησι γεγραφέναι τὸν νόμον (**fr. 66/1e**). Σόλωνα δὲ τεθηκέναι τόν τι ἡταιρηκότα εἴργειν τοῦ βήματος.
τι Lapini: τε MSS.

He seems to have legislated very well: 'If anybody does not maintain his parents, he shall be *atimos*; and the man who has eaten up his family property likewise.' (And the idle man can be called to account by anybody who wishes to prosecute. Lysias in the speech against Nicides says that it was Draco who wrote this law.) And Solon enacted the law to exclude from the platform the man who had commited some act of prostitution.

Fr. 104c: Dem. XXII. *Androtion* 30–1
ἄξιον τοίνυν, ὦ ἄνδρες Ἀθηναῖοι, καὶ τὸν θέντα τὸν νόμον ἐξετάσαι Σόλωνα, καὶ θεάσασθαι ὅσην πρόνοιαν ἐποιεῖτο ἐν ἅπασιν οἷς ἐτίθει νόμοις τῆς πολιτείας καὶ ὅσῳ περὶ τούτου μᾶλλον ἐσπούδαζεν ἢ περὶ τοῦ πράγματος οὗ τιθείη τὸν νόμον. πολλαχόθεν μὲν οὖν ἄν τις ἴδοι τοῦτο, οὐχ ἥκιστα δ' ἐκ τούτου τοῦ νόμου, "μήτε λέγειν μήτε γράφειν ἐξεῖναι τοῖς ἡταιρηκόσιν". ... ᾔδει γάρ, ᾔδει τοῖς αἰσχρῶς βεβιωκόσιν ἁπασῶν οὖσαν ἐναντιωτάτην πολιτείαν ἐν ᾗ πᾶσιν ἔξεστι λέγειν τἀκείνων ὀνείδη. ἔστι δ' αὕτη τις; δημοκρατία.

It is right, men of Athens, to examine Solon who enacted this law and see what forethought for the constitution he had in all the laws which he enacted, and how much more he was concerned for this than for the act about which he enacted the law. One could see this in many places, and not least in this law, 'Those who have been prostitutes shall not speak or make proposals.' ... For he knew, he knew the constitution which most of all is opposed to those who have lived shamefully, in which it is possible for all to speak in reproach of them. What is this? Democracy.

Some or all of the offences mentioned by Aeschines (in what may well be a selection from the full list to suit his prosecution of Timarchus) occur in other contexts, and may well have been dealt with in earlier laws: cf. frs. 26–30/1, Lys. X. *Theomnestus i* (with Todd, *The Shape of Athenian Law*, 258–62), Dem. LVII. *Eubulides* 30. However, the *dokimasia rhetoron* is likely to have been instituted about the late fifth century, as one of the attempts to control speakers who were not office-holders (cf. on fr. 103). It was perhaps used for Lysitheus' prosecution of Theomnestus mentioned in Lys. X. *Theomnestus i*. 1 (where the manuscripts' verb is εἰσήγγελλε but Gernet suggested ἐπήγγελλε), and was mentioned by Lycurgus (fr. 18 Conomis); Lane Fox, in *Ritual, Finance, Politics* ... *D. Lewis*, 135–55 at 149–51, expressed doubts; Fisher *ad loc.* suggested that it was introduced by the late fifth century.

Fr. 105: [Dem.] XXVI. *Aristogeiton ii*. 4
τὰς τιμωρίας ὁ Σόλων τοῖς μὲν ἰδιώταις ἐποίησε βραδείας, ταῖς δ' ἀρχαῖς καὶ τοῖς δημαγωγοῖς ταχείας, ὑπολαμβάνων τοῖς μὲν ἐνδέχεσθαι καὶ παρὰ τὸν χρόνον τὸ δίκαιον λαβεῖν, τοῖς δ' οὐκ ἐνεῖναι παραμεῖναι· τὸ γὰρ τιμωρησόμενον οὐχ ὑπέσται τῆς πολιτείας καταλυθείσης.
Solon instituted slow punishments for private citizens but quick for officials and politicians, assuming that justice can be obtained for the former even after a lapse of time but it is not possible to wait for the latter; for there will not be a possibility of punishment if the constitution has been overthrown.

Solon has been brought into a rhetorical commonplace; there is no reason to think that his laws did reflect the distinction alleged here.

Fr. 106: Dem. XXII. *Androtion* 25–7
καὶ μὴν κἀκεῖνό γε δεῖ μαθεῖν ὑμᾶς, ὅτι τοὺς νόμους ὁ τιθεὶς τούτους Σόλων καὶ τῶν ἄλλων τοὺς πολλοὺς οὐδὲν ὅμοιος ὢν τούτῳ νομοθέτης, οὐχ ἑνὶ ἔδωκε τρόπῳ περὶ τῶν ἀδικημάτων ἑκάστων λαμβάνειν δίκην τοῖς βουλομένοις παρὰ τῶν ἀδικούντων ἀλλὰ πολλαχῶς. ᾔδει γάρ, οἶμαι, τοῦθ', ὅτι τοὺς ἐν τῇ πόλει γενέσθαι

πάντας ὁμοίως ἢ δεινοὺς ἢ θρασεῖς ἢ μετρίους οὐκ ἂν εἴη. εἰ μὲν οὖν, ὡς τοῖς μετρίοις δίκην ἐξαρκέσει λαβεῖν, οὕτω τοὺς νόμους θήσει, μήτ' ἀδείας ἔσεσθαι πολλοὺς πονηροὺς ἡγεῖτο· εἰ δ' ὡς τοῖς θρασέσιν καὶ δυνατοῖς λέγειν, τοὺς ἰδιώτας οὐ δυνήσεσθαι τὸν αὐτὸν τούτοις τρόπον λαμβάνειν δίκην. (26) δεῖν δ' ᾤετο μηδέν' ἀποστερεῖσθαι τοῦ δίκης τυχεῖν, ὡς ἕκαστος δύναται. πῶς οὖν ἔσται τοῦτο; ἐὰν πολλοὺς ὁδοὺς δῷ διὰ τῶν νόμων ἐπὶ τοὺς ἠδικηκότας οἷον τῆς κλοπῆς. ἔρρωσαι καὶ σαυτῷ πιστεύεις· ἄπαγε· ἐν χιλίοις ὁ κίνδυνος. ἀσθενέστερος εἶ· τοῖς ἄρχουσι ἐφηγοῦ· τοῦτο ποιήσουσι ἐκεῖνοι. φοβεῖ καὶ τοῦτο· γράφου. (27) καταμέμφει σεαυτὸν καὶ πένης ὢν οὐκ ἂν ἔχοις χιλίας ἐκτεῖσαι· δικάζου κλοπῆς πρὸς διαιτητὴν καὶ οὐ κινδυνεύσεις. τούτων οὐδέν ἐστι ταὐτό. τῆς ἀσεβείας κατὰ ταὔτ' ἐστιν ἀπάγειν, γράφεσθαι, δικάζεσθαι πρὸς Εὐμολπίδας, φαίνειν πρὸς τὸν βασιλέα. περὶ τῶν ἄλλων ἁπάντων τὸν αὐτὸν τρόπον σχεδόν.

φαίνειν Weil cf. schol. (84 Dilts): φράζειν codd.

And moreover you need to learn this, that Solon, who enacted these laws and the majority of the others, was a lawgiver not at all like this one: he provided not a single way for those who wished to exact justice for each offence from the offenders but many. He knew this, I think, that it is not possible for all the men in the city to be equally clever, bold or moderate. If he had enacted his laws in such a way as was sufficient for the moderate to obtain justice, he thought that many criminals would enjoy immunity; but if he enacted them for the bold and capable speakers, then ordinary citizens would not be able to obtain justice in the same way as these. (26) He thought nobody ought to be deprived of finding justice as each is able. How will this be? If he gave many routes through the laws, as in the case of theft. You are strong and trust in yourself: make an *apagoge*; the risk is a thousand [*sc.* drachmae]. You are weaker: make an *ephegesis* to the officials; they will do this [*sc.* make the arrest]. You are afraid even of this: enter a *graphe* [public suit]. (27) You have a low opinion of yourself, and are poor and could not pay a thousand: enter a *dike* [private suit] for theft before an arbitrator and you will run no risk. None of these is the same. For impiety in the same way it is possible to make an *apagoge*, enter a *graphe*, undertake a *dike* before the Eumolpidae, make a *phasis* ['demonstration'] before the *basileus*. And in all the other cases in more or less the same way.

What Demosthenes here attributes to Solon is the range of procedures for theft and impiety available in his own time. We do not know when the different procedures for theft and for impiety were instituted: Solon was credited with the original distinction between *graphai* and *dikai* (cf. on fr. 40), and *apagoge, endeixis* and presumably *ephegesis* seem to have existed in his time (cf. on fr. 16). On the significance of the range of possibilities see especially R. G. Osborne, 'Law in Action in Classical Athens', *JHS* cv 1985, 40–58; C. Carey, 'Offence and Procedure in Athenian Law', in Harris & Rubinstein (edd.), *The Law and the Courts in Ancient Greece*, 111–36. Demosthenes' account needs qualification: not all procedures were available in all circumstances (cf. below); there were many offences for which there was not a comparable range of procedures; and the choice of procedure had different consequences for the defendant if convicted as well as for the prosecutor if unsuccessful.

As for the details, *apagoge* (haling the offender before the authorities) and *ephegesis* (bringing the authorities to the offender) were available only when the offender was caught *ep' autophoroi* (manifestly guilty, but not necessarily caught in the act: E. M. Harris, ' "In the Act" or "Red-Handed"? *Apagoge* to the Eleven and *Furtum Manifestum*', in *Symposion 1993* [*AGR* x 1994], 129–46 = his *Democracy and the Rule of Law*, 373–89[–90]). The thousand drachmae were a penalty for a prosecutor who failed to obtain a fifth of the votes (e.g. Dem. XXIV. *Timocrates* 7: cf. Harrison, *L.A.* ii. 83). A *graphe* may have been available only for theft of public property (cf. on fr. 23). A *dike* could be brought only by the injured party (cf. on fr. 40); and *dikai* were handled by *diaitetai*, men in their last year on the military registers serving as arbitrators, only from 399/8 or slightly earlier (*Ath. Pol.* 53. ii–v: date D. M. MacDowell, 'The Chronology of Athenian Speeches and Legal Innovations in 401–398 B.C.', *RIDA*³ xviii 1971, 267–73, D. Whitehead, 'Athenian Laws and Lawsuits in the Late Fifth Century B.C.', *MH* lix 2002, 71–96. For impiety we have no further evidence on *dikai* before the Eumolpidae (one of the two *gene* supplying officials of the Eleusinian cult, perhaps handling only cases concerning that cult: Parker, *Athenian Religion*, 296), or on *phasis* to the *basileus*.

Fr. 107: Dem. XLII. *Phaenippus* 1
πολλὰ κἀγαθὰ γένοιτο, ὦ ἄνδρες δικασταί, πρῶτον μὲν ὑμῖν ἅπασιν, ἔπειτα δὲ καὶ Σόλωνι τῷ νομοθετήσαντι τὸν περὶ τῶν ἀντιδόσεων νόμων. εἰ μὴ γὰρ οὗτος ἡμῖν σαφῶς διώρισεν τί πρῶτον δεῖ ποιεῖν τοὺς ἀντιδεδωκότας καὶ τί δεύτερον καὶ τἆλλα δ' ἐφεξῆς, οὐκ οἶδ' ὅποι προῆλθεν ἂν ἡ τουτουὶ Φαινίππου τόλμα, ὅπου γε καὶ νῦν ἅπαντα ταῦτα προλέγοντος ἡμῖν τοῦ νόμου ὅμως οὐδὲν φροντίσας τῶν ἐν αὐτῷ γεγραμμένων δικαίων ἀντὶ μὲν τοῦ τριῶν ἡμερῶν, ἀφ' ἧς ὤμοσε τὴν ἀπόφασιν δοῦναί μοι τῆς οὐσίας τῆς αὑτοῦ κατὰ τὸν νόμον, ἤ, εἰ μὴ τότ' ἐβούλετο, τῇ γ' ἕκτῃ <φθίνοντος> δοῦναι τοῦ Βοηδρομιῶνος μηνός, ἣν δεηθείς μου ἔθετο καὶ ἐν ᾗ ὡμολόγησε δώσειν τὴν ἀπόφασιν, οὐδέτερα τούτων ἐποίησεν.
<φθίνοντος> Thalheim cf. §12.

May there be many blessings, men of the jury, first on all of you, and then also on Solon, who enacted the law about *antidoseis*. If he had not clearly defined what must be done first by those who have offered an *antidosis*, and what second and the rest in order, I do not know how far the daring of this man Phaenippus would have gone, when even now, while the law prescribes all these things, he has cared nothing about the just things written in it, but instead of giving me the declaration of his property within three days from when he swore the oath, in accordance with the law, or, if he was not willing to do that, at any rate to give it on the 25th (or 24th) of the month Boedromion, which he fixed at my request and on which he agreed to give his declaration, he has not done either of these things.

Antidosis was a procedure by which a man on whom a liturgy (a public duty to be performed at his own expense) was imposed could identify a man who had been passed over but whom he believed to be richer, and challenge that man either to perform the liturgy or to exchange property with him (cf. Harrison, *L.A.* ii. 236–8, MacDowell, *L.C.A.* 162–4). Liturgies if they had existed earlier at any rate became more numerous in the fifth century, with more to be performed in connection with festivals and with the trierarchy used to fund Athens' large navy, and it is doubtful if the procedure of *antidosis* existed before the institution of the trierarchic system.

Fr. 108: Dem. XXXVI. *For Phormio* 25–7
λάβε δή μοι καὶ τὸν τῆς προθεσμίας νόμον. ΝΟΜΟΣ [*deest*]. ὁ μὲν τοίνυν νόμος, ὦ ἄνδρες Ἀθηναῖοι, σαφῶς οὑτωσὶ τὸν χρόνον ὥρισεν. Ἀπολλόδωρος δ' οὑτοσὶ παρεληλυθότων ἐτῶν πλέον ἢ εἴκοσι τὴν ἑαυτοῦ συκοφαντίαν ἀξιοῖ περὶ πλείονος ὑμᾶς ποιήσασθαι τῶν νόμων, καθ' οὓς ὀμωμοκότες δικάζετε. καίτοι πᾶσι μὲν τοῖς νόμοις προσέχειν εἰκός ἐσθ' ὑμᾶς, οὐχ ἥκιστα δὲ τούτῳ, ὦ ἄνδρες Ἀθηναῖοι. δοκεῖ γάρ μοι καὶ ὁ Σόλων οὐδενὸς ἄλλου ἕνεκα θεῖναι αὐτὸν ἢ τοῦ μὴ συκοφαντεῖσθαι ὑμᾶς. τοῖς μὲν γὰρ ἀδικουμένοις τὰ πέντ' ἔτη ἱκανὸν ἡγήσατ' εἶναι εἰσπράξασθαι, κατὰ δὲ τῶν ψευδομένων τὸν χρόνον ἐνόμισε σαφέστατον ἔλεγχον ἔσεσθαι.
Take and read for me the law about *prothesmia* [fixed times]. LAW [*text not inserted*]. The law, men of Athens, has clearly defined the time in this way. But this man Apollodorus, though more than twenty years have passed, claims that you should regard his vexatious prosecution as worth more than the laws, in accordance with which you swore to judge. Yet it is right that you should give attention to all the laws, and not least to this, men

of Athens. For it seems to me that Solon enacted it for no other purpose than to save you from vexatious prosecutions. For those who are wronged he thought the five years sufficient to exact [*sc.* what is their due], while against those who lie he thought the time would be the clearest proof.

Some cases were not subject to a time limit (Lys. VII. *Olive Stump* 17, XIII. *Agoratus* 83). Probably for those which were there was not one overall time limit but there were different limits in different cases (H. J. Wolff, 'Verjährung von Ansprüches nach attischem Recht', in *Eranion . . . G. S. Maridakis*, 87–109); the five years (after the death of the original *kleronomos*) for cases relating to a guardianship are confirmed by Isae. III. *Pyrrhus* 58 and Dem. XXXVIII. *Nausimachus & Xenopithes* 17–18, and for an unknown case by Lys. fr. 228 Carey *ap.* Harp. π 94 Keaney προθεσμίας νόμος. Pl. *Leg.* XII. 954 c–e recommended different limits with regard to different categories of property. See Charles, *Statutes of Limitation at Athens*, 53–9. Rules of this kind are more likely to belong to the later than to the earlier stages in the history of Athenian law, and probably the attribution to Solon is simply conventional.

Fr. 109: see fr. 72/d

Fr. 110/a: Aeschin. III. *Ctesiphon* 175–6
ὁ γὰρ Σόλων ὁ παλαιὸς νομοθέτης ἐν τοῖς αὐτοῖς ἐπιτιμίοις ᾤετο δεῖν ἐνέχεσθαι τὸν ἀστράτευτον καὶ τὸν λελοιπότα τὴν τάξιν καὶ τὸν δειλὸν ὁμοίως. εἰσὶ γὰρ καὶ δειλίας γραφαί. καίτοι θαυμάσειεν ἄν τις ὑμῶν εἴ εἰσι φύσεως γραφαί· εἰσίν. τίνος ἕνεκα; ἵν' ἕκαστος ἡμῶν τὰς ἐκ τῶν νόμων ζημίας φοβούμενος μᾶλλον ἢ τοὺς πολεμίους ἀμείνων ἀγωνιστὴς ὑπὲρ τῆς πατρίδος ὑπάρχῃ. ὁ μὲν τοίνυν νομοθέτης τὸν ἀστράτευτον καὶ τὸν δειλὸν καὶ τὸν λιπόντα τὴν τάξιν ἔξω τῶν περιρραντηρίων τῆς ἀγορᾶς ἐξείργει καὶ οὐκ ἐᾷ στεφανοῦσθαι οὐδ' εἰσιέναι εἰς τὰ ἱερὰ τὰ δημοτελῆ.

Solon the ancient lawgiver thought that the same penalties should apply to the man who shirked military service, the man who left his rank and the coward alike. For there are *graphai deilias* [public suits for cowardice]. One of you might be surprised that there are *graphai* for natural characteristics. There are. Why? So that each of us should fear the penalties from the laws more than the enemy, and so be a better contender for our fatherland. The lawgiver excludes from the sprinkled area of the agora the shirker and the coward and the man who abandoned his shield, and does not allow him to wear a crown or enter into the publicly-funded rites.

†**Fr. 110/b:** Aeschin. I. *Timarchus* 29
(extract from ΔΟΚΙΜΑΣΙΑ ΡΗΤΟΡΩΝ, **fr. 104a**) καὶ τίσι δεύτερον ἀπεῖπε μὴ λέγειν; "ἢ τὰς στρατείας", φησί, "μὴ ἐστρατευμένος ὅσαι ἂν αὐτῷ προσταχθῶσιν, ἢ τὴν ἀσπίδα ἀποβεβληκώς."
And whom secondly does he forbid to speak? 'Or', he says, 'has not served on the military campaigns which have been prescribed for him, or has thrown away his shield.'

There are various other references to these related offences, shirking military service when called up, deserting one's position in the rank (*lipotaxion*) and abandoning one's shield to run away (*deilia*, 'cowardice', is a collective term applicable to all three): see Andoc. I. *Myst.* 74, Lys. XIV. *Alcibiades i.* 5–6, Dem. XV. *Liberty of Rhodians* 32, XXI. *Midias* 103, XXXIX. *Boeotus i.* 16–17, [Dem.] LIX. *Neaera* 27, and MacDowell, *L.C.A.* 160. Apart from the two passages printed here, and fr. 111, below, none invokes the name of Solon, and these procedures were probably instituted at some time after Cleisthenes' institution of the ten annual generals (*Ath. Pol.* 22. ii).

Frs. 111–4: Dem. XXIV. *Timocrates* 103–6, 112–14
λεγόντων γὰρ τῶν νόμων οὓς ἔθηκε Σόλων, οὐδὲν ὅμοιος ὢν τούτῳ νομοθέτης, "ἐάν τις ἁλῷ κλοπῆς καὶ μὴ τιμηθῇ θανάτου, προστιμᾶν αὐτῷ δεσμόν (**fr. 112** cf. **fr. 23d**), καὶ ἐάν τις ἁλοὺς τῆς κακώσεως τῶν γονέων εἰς τὴν ἀγορὰν ἐμβάλλῃ, δεδέσθαι, κἂν ἀστρατείας τις ὄφλῃ καί τι τῶν αὐτῶν τοῖς ἐπιτίμοις ποιῇ, καὶ τοῦτον δεδέσθαι (**fr. 111**), Τιμοκράτης ἅπασι τούτοις ἄδειαν ποιεῖ, τῇ καταστήσει τῶν ἐγγυητῶν τὸν δεσμὸν ἀφαιρῶν. (104) . . . ἀνάγνωθι δὲ καὶ τούτους τοὺς νόμους. ΝΟΜΟΙ ΚΛΟΠΗΣ, ΚΑΚΩΣΕΩΣ ΓΟΝΕΩΝ, ΑΣΤΡΑΤΕΙΑΣ· (105) "ὅ τι ἄν τις ἀπολέσῃ, ἐὰν μὲν ἀπολάβῃ, τὴν διπλασίαν καταδικάζειν, ἐὰν δὲ μή, τὴν δεκαπλασίαν πρὸς τοῖς ἐπαιτίοις. δεδέσθαι δ' ἐν τῇ ποδοκάκκῃ τὸν πόδα πενθ' ἡμέρας καὶ νύκτας ὅσας, ἐὰν προστιμήσῃ ἡ ἡλιαία· προστιμᾶσθαι δὲ τὸν βουλόμενον, ὅταν περὶ τοῦ τιμήματος ᾖ (**fr. 23d**). ἐὰν δέ τις ἀπαχθῇ τῶν γονέων κακώσεως ἑαλωκὼς ἢ ἀστρατείας ἢ προειρημένον αὐτῷ τῶν νομίμων εἴργεσθαι, εἰσιὼν ὅποι μὴ χρή, δησάντων αὐτὸν οἱ ἕνδεκα καὶ εἰσαγόντων εἰς τὴν ἡλιαίαν, κατηγορείτω δὲ ὁ βουλόμενος οἷς ἔξεστιν. ἐὰν δ' ἁλῷ, τιμάτω ἡ ἡλιαία ὅ τι χρὴ παθεῖν αὐτὸν ἢ ἀποτεῖσαι. ἐὰν δ' ἀργυρίου τιμηθῇ, δεδέσθω τέως ἂν ἐκτείσῃ (**fr. 111**)." (106) ὅμοιός γ', οὐ γάρ, ὦ ἄνδρες Ἀθηναῖοι Σόλων νομοθέτης καὶ Τιμοκράτης; . . .

(112) εἰ δέ τινες πρέσβεις αἱρεθέντες ὑπὸ τοῦ δήμου, πλούσιοι ὄντες, ὑφείλοντο χρήματα πολλὰ τὰ μὲν ἱερὰ τὰ δ᾽ ὅσια καὶ εἶχον χρόνον πολύν, τούτοις, ὅπως μηδὲν πείσονται μήθ᾽ ὧν οἱ νόμοι μήθ᾽ ὧν τὰ ψησίσματα προστάττει, μαλ᾽ ἀκριβῶς εὗρεν [sc. ὁ Τιμοκράτης]. (113) καίτοι γ᾽ ὁ Σόλων, ὦ ἄνδρες δικασταί, ᾧ οὐδ᾽ ἂν αὐτὸς Τιμοκράτης φήσειεν ὅμοιος νομοθέτης εἶναι, οὐχ ὅπως ἀσφαλῶς κακουργήσουσι φαίνεται παρασκευάζων τοῖς τοιούτοις ἀλλ᾽ ὅπως ἢ μὴ ἀδικήσουσι ἢ δώσουσι δίκην ἀξίαν, καὶ νόμον εἰσήνεγκεν, εἰ μέν τις μεθ᾽ ἡμέραν ὑπὲρ πεντήκοντα δραχμὰς κλέπτοι, ἀπαγωγὴν πρὸς τοὺς ἕνδεκ᾽ εἶναι, εἰ δέ τις νύκτωρ ὁτιοῦν κλέπτοι, τοῦτον ἐξεῖναι καὶ ἀποκτεῖναι καὶ τρῶσαι διώκοντα καὶ ἀπαγαγεῖν τοῖς ἕνδεκα, εἰ βούλοιτο. τῷ δ᾽ ἁλόντι, ὧν αἱ ἀπαγωγαί εἰσιν, οὐκ ἐγγυητὰς καταστήσαντι ἔκτισιν εἶναι τῶν κλεμμάτων, ἀλλὰ θάνατον τὴν ζημίαν (**fr. 113 = fr. 23/1**). (114) καὶ εἴ τίς γ᾽ ἐκ Λυκείου ἢ ἐξ Ἀκαδημείας ἢ ἐκ Κυνοσάργους ἱμάτιον ἢ ληκύθιον ἢ ἄλλο τι φαυλότατον, ἢ εἰ τῶν σκευῶν τι τῶν ἐκ τῶν γυμνασίων ὑφέλοιτο ἢ ἐκ τῶν λιμένων ὑπὲρ δέκα δραχμάς, καὶ τούτοις θάνατον ἐνομοθέτησεν εἶναι τὴν ζημίαν (**fr. 114**). εἰ δέ τις ἰδίαν δίκην κλοπῆς ἁλοίη, ὑπάρχειν μὲν αὐτῷ διπλάσιον ἀποτεῖσαι τὸ τιμηθέν, προστιμῆσαι δ᾽ ἐξεῖναι τῷ δικαστηρίῳ πρὸς τῷ ἀργυρίῳ δεσμὸν τῷ κλέπτῃ, πένθ᾽ ἡμέρας καὶ νύκτας ἴσας, ὅπως ὁρῷεν ἅπαντες αὐτὸν δεδεμένον (**fr. 112 cf. fr. 23d**).

δεκαπλασίαν codd.: διπλασίαν Heraldus, cf. §§114, 115. See commentary on fr. 23d.

For the laws enacted by Solon, a lawgiver in no way like this one, say that if a man is convicted of theft and the death penalty is not assessed he may be subjected to the additional assessment of being bound, and if anybody convicted of maltreating his parents intrudes into the agora he too is to be bound, and if anybody is sentenced for shirking military service and does any of the same things as those with full rights he too is to be bound. But Timocrates creates immunity for all of these, and does away with being bound if guarantors are appointed. (104) . . . Read also these laws. LAWS ON THEFT, MALTREATMENT OF PARENTS, SHIRKING MILITARY SERVICE: (105) 'When a man has lost something, if he has recovered it, [the thief] shall be sentenced to twofold restitution, but if not, tenfold in addition to the *epaitia* [= the property in question?]. He shall be bound in the foot-clasp by his foot for five days and as many nights, if the *eliaia* makes that additional assessment; whoever wishes may propose the additional assessment, when the assessment is being considered. If anybody is subjected to *apagoge* when he has been convicted of maltreating his parents or shirking military service, or has been placed under orders of exclusion from the places specified in the laws and enters where he ought not, the Eleven shall bind him and bring him to the *eliaia*, and he shall be prosecuted by whoever wishes of those who are entitled to do so. If he is convicted, the *eliaia* shall assess what he is to suffer or pay; if a monetary penalty is assessed, he shall be imprisoned until he pays.' (106) Men of Athens, Solon and Timocrates are similar lawgivers, are they not? . . .

(112) If envoys elected by the people, rich men, have embezzled sacred and secular monies and have retained them for a long time, [Timocrates] has scrupulously devised for them ways to avoid suffering what is prescribed both by the laws and by the decrees. (113) Yet Solon, men of the jury, whom not even Timocrates himself can claim to resemble as a lawgiver, far from enabling them to commit crimes in safety can be seen to have prepared for such men that they should either not do wrong or pay a worthy penalty. He introduced a law that if anybody by day steals more than fifty drachmae he may be brought by *apagoge* to the Eleven, and if anybody by night steals anything at all one may pursue him and kill or wound him, or bring him by *apagoge* to the Eleven if he wishes. The man convicted of offences which are subject to *apagoge* is not allowed to present guarantors for the repayment of what is stolen, but the punishment is death. (114) And if anybody stole a cloak or an oil-flask, or something else absolutely trivial, from the Lyceum or Academy or Cynosarges, or any of the equipment from the gymnasia or the harbours worth over ten drachmae, he made it the law that death should be the penalty for these too. But if a man was convicted of theft in a private suit, he was liable to repay the assessed amount twofold, and it was possible for the court in addition to the money to make an additional assessment of being bound for the thief, for five days and the same number of nights, so that all should see him bound.

The laws inserted here are not to be accepted as genuine: see on fr. 23d. If we limit ourselves to Demosthenes' own words, fr. 111 prescribes imprisonment (probably arrest pending trial before the Eleven) for men convicted of maltreatment of parents or shirking military service who fail to comply with the restrictions imposed on them; fr. 112 makes the additional penalty of confinement for five days, we believe in the stocks, available for men convicted of theft; fr. 113 allows *apagoge* and the death penalty for the theft of more than fifty drachmae by day and any theft by night, and allows direct action against nocturnal thieves; fr. 114 prescribes the death penalty for thefts from gymnasia or harbours.

If fr. 110 is post-Solonian, then fr. 111, at least in so far as it refers to men convicted of military offences, must be post-Solonian too. Fr. 23c (from Lysias X. *Theomnestus i*) quotes an ancient, and probably Solonian, law, which is not in itself obviously about theft but could be about theft and by being associated with fr. 23d has been assumed to be so by Ruschenbusch and generally. We therefore need to ask how much of the laws about theft in frs. 23d/112, 113 and 114 is likely to be Solonian. Confinement in the stocks as an additional penalty looks likely to be early rather than late, so we do accept fr. 23d/112 as Solonian whether the confinement in the stocks of fr. 23c is for theft or not. We accept the procedure of *apagoge* as Solonian (cf. fr. 16) so fr. 113 becomes our fr. 23/1. The three gymnasia are thought to have been founded in the sixth century (Travlos, *Pictorial Dictionary of Ancient Athens*, 345), the best evidence being for the Academy (*Suda* τ 733 Adler τὸ Ἱππάρχου τειχίον attributes a circuit wall to Pisistratus' son Hipparchus, and a boundary stone reading [hό]ρος τες hεκαδεμίας, *IG* i³ 1091, is dated *c.* 500). Harbours became more important after the enlargement of the Athenian navy in the late 480's. The law of fr. 114, with special penalties for theft from the gymnasia and harbours, is probably post-Solonian.

Fr. 115/a: Aeschin. I. *Timarchus* 183
ὁ δὲ Σόλων ὁ τῶν νομοθετῶν ἐνδοξότατος γέγραφεν ἀρχαίως καὶ σεμνῶς περὶ τῆς γυναικῶν εὐκοσμίας. τὴν γὰρ γυναῖκα ἐφ' ᾗ ἂν ἁλῷ μοιχὸς οὐκ ἐᾷ κοσμεῖσθαι οὐδὲ εἰς τὰ δημοτελῆ ἱερὰ εἰσιέναι, ἵνα μὴ τὰς ἀναμαρτήτους τῶν γυναικῶν ἀναμειγνυμένη διαφθείρῃ, ἐὰν δ' εἰσίῃ ἢ κοσμῆται, τὸν ἐντυχόντα κελεύει καταρρηγνύναι τὰ ἱμάτια καὶ τὸν κόσμον ἀφαιρεῖσθαι καὶ τύπτειν, εἰργόμενον θανάτου καὶ τοῦ ἀνάπηρον ποιῆσαι, ἀτιμῶν τὴν τοιαύτην γυναῖκα καὶ τὸν βίον ἀβίωτον αὐτῇ παρασκευάζων.
(Fr. 30/d [116 Ruschenbusch] follows.)
Solon, the most distinguished of the lawgivers, has written in an archaic and solemn way about the good order of women. For the woman with whom an adulterer has been caught he does not allow to adorn herself or to enter publicly-funded rites, to prevent her from corrupting the innocent women by mixing with them. If she does enter or adorn herself, he orders anybody who encounters her to tear off her clothes, remove her adornment and beat her, short of killing or maiming her, in order to shame such a woman and make her life not worth living.

†**Fr. /115b:** [Dem.] LIX. *Neaera* 86–7 (Ruschenbusch printed the inserted law as a *testimonium*)
ἀλλὰ μόναις ταύταις ἀπαγορεύουσιν οἱ νόμοι ταῖς γυναιξὶ μὴ εἰσιέναι εἰς τὰ ἱερὰ τὰ δημοτελῆ, ἐφ' ᾗ ἂν μοιχὸς ἁλῷ· ἐὰν δ' εἰσίωσι καὶ παρανομῶσι, νηποινεὶ πάσχειν ὑπὸ τοῦ βουλομένου ὅ τι ἂν πάσχῃ, πλὴν θανάτου, καὶ ἔδωκεν ὁ νόμος τὴν τιμωρίαν ὑπὲρ αὐτῶν τῷ ἐντυχόντι. ... (87) καὶ ὅτι ταῦτα οὕτως ἔχει, τοῦ νόμου αὐτοῦ ἀκούσαντες ἀναγνωσθέντος εἴσεσθε. καί μοι λάβε. ΝΟΜΟΣ ΜΟΙΧΕΙΑΣ· "ἐπειδὰν δὲ ἕλῃ τὸν μοιχόν, μὴ ἐξέστω τῷ ἑλόντι συνοικεῖν τῇ γυναικί· ἐὰν δὲ συνοικῇ, ἄτιμος ἔστω. μηδὲ τῇ γυναικὶ ἐξέστω εἰσιέναι εἰς τὰ ἱερὰ τὰ δημοτελῆ, ἐφ' ᾗ ἂν μοιχὸς ἁλῷ· ἐὰν δ' εἰσίῃ, νηποινεὶ πασχέτω ὅ τι ἂν πάσχῃ, πλὴν θανάτου."
But these are the only women whom the laws forbid to enter publicly-funded rites, one on whom an adulterer has been caught; if she breaks the law and enters, she may suffer anything that whoever wishes may inflict on her except death, and the law has given the right of punishment to anybody who encounters them. ... (87) You will know that this is the case by hearing the actual law read. Take it for me. LAW OF ADULTERY: 'When he has caught the adulterer, it shall not be permitted to the man who has caught him to live in wedlock with his wife; if he does live with her he shall be *atimos*. Nor shall it be permitted to the woman on whom an adulterer has been caught to enter any of the publicly-funded rites: if she does enter, she shall suffer with impunity [*sc.* for the one who inflicts it] whatever she may suffer except death.'

Commentators suggest that the law of fr. 115 is later than the mid fifth century, when Pericles' citizenship law of 451/0 (*Ath. Pol.* 26. iv) made Athenian parentage on both sides essential for citizenship and doubts about the parentage of sons therefore more serious: K. Kapparis, 'When Were the Athenian Adultery Laws Introduced?', *RIDA*[3] xlii 1995, 97–122 at 117–9; Fisher on fr. 115a. The law inserted in fr. 115b is not included in the stichometry of [Dem.] LIX: Canevaro argues that it is a later forgery, and that the requirement for the husband to divorce his wife, not attested elsewhere, was not part of the authentic law (*The Documents in the Attic Orators*, 190–6).

Fr. 116: see fr. 30/d

Fr. 117: Dem. LVII. *Eubulides* 30–2
οὐ μόνον παρὰ τὸ ψήφισμα τὰ περὶ τὴν ἀγορὰν διέβαλλεν ἡμᾶς Εὐβουλίδης, ἀλλὰ καὶ παρὰ τοὺς νόμους, οἳ κελεύουσιν ἔνοχον εἶναι

τῇ κακηγορίᾳ τὸν τὴν ἐργασίαν τὴν ἐν τῇ ἀγορᾷ ἢ τῶν πολιτῶν ἢ τῶν πολιτίδων ὀνειδίζοντά τινι. ἡμεῖς δ' ὁμολογοῦμεν καὶ ταινίας πωλεῖν καὶ ζῆν οὐχ ὅντινα τρόπον βουλόμεθα. καὶ εἴ σοί ἐστιν τοῦτο σημεῖον, ὦ Εὐβουλίδη, τοῦ μὴ Ἀθηναίους εἶναι ἡμᾶς, ἐγώ σοι τούτου ὅλως τοὐναντίον ἐπιδείξω, ὅτι οὐκ ἔξεστιν ξένῳ ἐν τῇ ἀγορᾷ ἐργάζεσθαι. καί μοι λαβὼν ἀνάγνωθι πρῶτον τὸν Σόλωνος νόμον. ΝΟΜΟΣ [deest]. λάβε δὲ καὶ τὸν Ἀριστοφῶντος· οὕτω γάρ, ὦ ἄνδρες Ἀθηναῖοι, τοῦτον ἔδοξεν ἐκεῖνος καλῶς καὶ δημοτικῶς νομοθετῆσαι ὥστ' ἐψηφίσασθε πάλιν ἀνανεώσασθαι. ΝΟΜΟΣ [deest]. Eubulides' slander against us with regard to the agora is contrary not only to the decree but also to the laws, which say that a man shall be liable for speaking ill if he reproaches any of the citizen men or women for working in the agora. We admit that we sell ribbons and do not live in the way we wish; and if that is a sign for you, Eubulides, that we are not Athenians, I shall demonstrate to you entirely the opposite, that it is not permitted to a foreigner to work in the agora. First take and read for me the law of Solon. LAW [*text not inserted*]. Take also that of Aristophon: for, men of Athens, Solon was judged to have made this such a good and democratic law that you voted again to renew it. LAW [*text not inserted*].

In fact it appears from §34 that a foreigner could work in the agora on payment of a special tax. The law perhaps dated from before the Peloponnesian War, was allowed to lapse during the war, and was reaffirmed after the war (according to one text, Carystius fr. 11 Müller *ap*. Ath. XIII. 577 B–C, it was Aristophon who was responsible for the reaffirmation of Pericles' citizenship law of 451/0 after the war, but Eumelus, *FGrH* 77 F 2, names Nicomenes): see MacDowell, *L.C.A.* 156. However, the law is more likely to have been enacted after the Athenians became more protective of their citizenship, in the middle of the fifth century (cf. on fr. 115) than before.

Fr. 118a: Dem. XX. *Leptines* 104

καὶ μὴν κἀκεῖνος τῶν καλῶς δοκούντων ἔχειν νόμων Σόλωνός ἐστι, μὴ λέγειν κακῶς τὸν τεθνεῶτα, μηδ' ἂν ὑπὸ τῶν ἐκείνου τις ἀκούῃ παίδων αὐτός. σὺ δὲ ποιεῖς, οὐ λέγεις, κακῶς τοὺς τετελευτηκότας, τῷ δεῖνι μεμφόμενος καὶ τὸν δεῖν' ἀνάξιον εἶναι φάσκων, ὧν οὐδὲν ἐκείνοις προσῆκεν. ἆρ' οὐ πολὺ τοῦ Σόλωνος ἀποστατεῖς τῇ γνώμῃ;

And this also is one of those laws of Solon which are judged good, that one should not speak ill of the dead, even if one is spoken ill of by the dead man's sons. You are not merely speaking but acting ill with regard to the dead, blaming this man and saying that that man is unworthy, when none of this has anything to do with them. Have you not departed far from the intention of Solon?

Fr. 118b: Schol. Dem. XX. *Leptines* 104 (239b Dilts)
ὁ Σόλωνος νόμος ἀπηγόρευσε τοὺς τεθνεῶτας ἅπαντας λέγειν κακῶς, κἂν ἐρεθίζηταί τις ὑπὸ τῶν παίδων τοῦ τεθνηκότος ὑβριζόμενος.
Solon's law forbade all to speak ill of the dead, even if somebody is provoked by *hybris* from the dead man's sons.

Fr. 118c: Aristid. III. *Quattuor* 646
ἐνθυμηθῶμεν δὴ καὶ τὸν τοῦ Σόλωνος νόμον ὡς ἥμερος, μὴ λέγειν κακῶς τὸν τελευτήσαντα, μηδ' ἂν αὐτὸς ἀκούσῃ ὑπὸ τῶν αὐτοῦ παίδων.
Let us take to heart also how civilised the law of Solon is, that one should not speak ill of the man who has died, even if one is oneself spoken ill of by his sons.

For a law of Solon which forbade speaking ill of the dead see fr. 32a = 33a. The texts printed here add the qualification, even if one is ill spoken of by the dead man's sons: that may have been a comment attributed to Solon, but it is not likely to have been formally included in his law.

Fr. 119: see fr. 34/c

Fr. 120: see fr. 50/c

Frs. 121a–c: see frs. 49/e–g

Fr. 122: [Gal.] *An Animal Sit* 5 (xix. 179–80 Kühn)
οἱ οὖν τούτων [sc. τῶν θεῶν] μαθηταὶ νομοθέται Λυκοῦργος καὶ Σόλων βεβαίως ἡμῖν, δι' ὧν προεῖπον κεφαλαίων δύο, τὴν ὑπὲρ τῶν ἐμβρύων ἀναμφισβήτητον παρέσχον ὑπόθεσιν. εἰ γὰρ {ὅταν} μὴ ζῷα ἦν, οὐκ ἂν ἐκόλασαν τοῖς νόμοις φανερῶς τιμωρησάμενοι τοὺς αἰτίους ἐξαμβλώσεως, ἐπειδὴ δὲ ἔφασαν ζῷα εἶναι, τὴν τιμωρίαν ἐπήγαγον.
ὅταν omitted Ruschenbusch, cf. Kapparis p. 210.

The disciples of these [*sc.* gods], the lawgivers Lycurgus and Solon, as I have said in the two chapters above, made the position with regard to embryos firm and beyond dispute. For if they were not living creatures, they would not have censured [*sc.* abortion] in their laws by openly punishing those responsible for an abortion; but since they did say these were living creatures they did impose the punishment.

See especially Kapparis, *Abortion in the Ancient World*, 169–94, and 201–13 (introduction to, translation of and commentary on this work).

Some scholars have believed that abortion in some circumstances was illegal in classical Athens, on the basis of Lys. frs. 19–24 Carey: e.g. Harrison, *L.A.* i. 72–3, Carey *ad loc.* However, it is better to see there a prosecution for homicide, undertaken because there was no law against abortion: e.g. Kapparis, 185–93. Miscarriage and abortion were regarded as polluting, but not to the same degree as homicide (cf. Parker, *Miasma*, 50 n. 67, 325, 346, 354–6; Kapparis, 169–74), and abortion, or at any rate early abortion, was not always condemned in the Greek world (e.g. Arist. *Pol.* VII. 1335 B 22–6; *Hist. An.* VII. 583 B 11–23 says that most abortions take place within the first forty days). Most probably abortion was not illegal anywhere in the Graeco-Roman world before the third century A.D.; certainly this attribution of a law to Lycurgus and Solon is a late invention (Kapparis, cf. earlier C. Brecht, *RE* xviii. 2046–8; Glotz, *La Solidarité de la famille*, 351–5).

From comedy

Fr. 123a: Ar. *Nub.* 1178–95

ΦΕΙ. φοβεῖ δὲ δὴ τί;
ΣΤΡ. τὴν ἕνην τε καὶ νέαν.
ΦΕΙ. ἕνη γάρ ἐστι καὶ νέα τις ἡμέρα;
ΣΤΡ. εἰς ἥν γε θήσειν τὰ πρυτανεῖά φασί μοι.
ΦΕΙ. ἀπολοῦσ' ἄρ' αὔθ' οἱ θέντες. οὐ γάρ ἐσθ' ὅπως
μί' ἡμέρα γένοιτ' ἂν ἡμέραι δύο.
ΣΤΡ. οὐκ ἂν γένοιτο;
ΦΕΙ. πῶς γάρ; εἰ μή περ γ' ἅμα
αὐτὴ γένοιτ' ἂν γραῦς τε καὶ νέα γυνή.
ΣΤΡ. καὶ μὴν νενόμισταί γ'.
ΦΕΙ. οὐ γὰρ οἶμαι τὸν νόμον
ἴσασιν ὀρθῶς ὅτι νοεῖ.
ΣΤΡ. νοεῖ δὲ τί;

ΦΕΙ. ὁ Σόλων ὁ παλαιὸς ἦν φιλόδημος τὴν φύσιν.
ΣΤΡ. τουτὶ μὲν οὐδέν πω πρὸς ἕνην τε καὶ νέαν.
ΦΕΙ. ἐκεῖνος οὖν τὴν κλῆσιν εἰς δύ' ἡμέρας
ἔθηκεν, εἴς γε τὴν ἕνην τε καὶ νέαν,
ἵν' αἱ θέσεις γίγνοιντο τῇ νουμηνίᾳ.
ΣΤΡ. ἵνα δὴ τί τὴν ἕνην προσέθηκεν;
ΦΕΙ. ἵν', ὦ μέλε,
παρόντες οἱ φεύγοντες ἡμέρᾳ μιᾷ
πρότερον ἀπαλλάττοινθ' ἑκόντες· εἰ δὲ μή,
ἕωθεν ὑπανιῷντο τῇ νουμηνίᾳ.

PHEI. What then do you fear?
STR. The old and new day.
PHEI. Is there a day which is old and new?
STR. Yes, that on which they say they will file the deposits [for a lawsuit] against me.
PHEI. They will waste their deposits by doing this. In fact, it is not possible to turn a day into two days.
STR. It is not?
PHEI. How could it be? Unless the very same woman could be old and young at the same time.
STR. But that is what the law says.
PHEI. I think that they are not properly interpreting the law's intention.
STR. What is its intention, then?
PHEI. Solon, that man of antiquity, was by nature a friend of the people.
STR. This has absolutely nothing to do with the old and new day.
PHEI. It was he who established the summonses for two days, the old and the new, so that the deposits might be made in the new month [*sc.* in the first day of the month].
STR. For what reason then did he add the old day?
PHEI. With the purpose, my friend, that the defendants, by being present a day in advance, could settle the case voluntarily; otherwise, they would be distressed in the new month.

Fr. 123b: Plut. *Sol.* 25. iv–v
συνιδὼν δὲ τοῦ μηνὸς τὴν ἀνωμαλίαν, καὶ τὴν κίνησιν τῆς σελήνης
οὔτε δυομένῳ τῷ ἡλίῳ πάντως οὔτ' ἀνίσχοντι συμφερομένην,

ἀλλὰ πολλάκις τῆς αὐτῆς ἡμέρας καὶ καταλαμβάνουσαν καὶ παρερχομένην τὸν ἥλιον, αὐτὴν μὲν ἔταξε ταύτην ἕνην καὶ νέαν καλεῖσθαι, τὸ μὲν πρὸ συνόδου μόριον αὐτῆς τῷ παυομένῳ μηνί, τὸ δὲ λοιπὸν ἤδη τῷ ἀρχομένῳ προσήκειν ἡγούμενος, πρῶτος ὡς ἔοικεν ὀρθῶς ἀκούσας Ὁμήρου (Od. XIV. 162; XIX. 307) λέγοντος· "τοῦ μὲν φθίνοντος μηνός, τοῦ δ' ἱσταμένοιο." τὴν δ' ἐφεξῆς ἡμέραν νουμηνίαν ἐκάλεσε. τὰς δ' ἀπ' εἰκάδος οὐ προστιθείς, ἀλλ' ἀφαιρῶν καὶ ἀναλύων, ὥσπερ τὰ φῶτα τῆς σελήνης ἑώρα, μέχρι τριακάδος ἠρίθμησεν.

He perceived the irregularity of the month and that the motion of the moon did not always coincide with the setting and the rising of the sun, but that often it overtook and surpassed the sun on the same day. He then determined that that day ought to be called the old and the new, having decided to ascribe to the month that was ending the part of it that preceded the conjunction, and the remaining part to the one that was beginning. He seems therefore to have been the first to understand correctly the verse of Homer that says, 'when a month ends and another one begins'. And the day following that one he called the first of the month. Instead of counting the days by adding them after the twentieth, he subtracted them from the thirtieth, in a descending order, the same way as he saw happening with the fading of the moon.

Fr. 123c: Diog. Laert. I. 57–8
τά τε Ὁμήρου ἐξ ὑποβολῆς γέγραφε ῥαψῳδεῖσθαι, οἷον ὅπου ὁ πρῶτος ἔληξεν, ἐκεῖθεν ἄρχεσθαι τὸν ἐχόμενον. (**fr. 149**) μᾶλλον οὖν Σόλων Ὅμηρον ἐφώτισεν ἢ Πεισίστρατος < ... >, ὥς φησι Διευχίδας ἐν πέμπτῳ Μεγαρικῶν (FGrH 485 F 6). ἦν δὲ μάλιστα τὰ ἔπη ταυτί· "οἳ δ' ἄρ' Ἀθήνας εἶχον" καὶ τὰ ἑξῆς (Il. II. 546). πρῶτος δὲ Σόλων τὴν τριακάδα ἕνην καὶ νέαν ἐκάλεσεν.
<ὃς ἔπη τινὰ ἐνέβαλε εἰς τὴν ποίησιν αὐτοῦ> Jacoby.   ἕνην Ruschenbusch: ἔνην MSS.

He wrote that Homer's verses ought to be recited in sequence, in the sense that at the point where the first reciter stopped, there the next one should start. Therefore Solon shed more light on Homer than Pisistratus did < ... >, as Dieuchidas says in the fifth book of his *History of Megara*. This concerns particularly the following line, 'those men who occupied Athens', and what follows. Solon was the first to call the thirtieth day [of the month] old and new.

†Fr. 123d: *Lex. Rhet. Cant.* (75. 11–12 *Lexica Graeca Minora*)
ΕΝΗ ΚΑΙ ΝΕΑ· παρ' Ἀθηναίοις ἡ τριακάς· φασὶ δὲ οὕτω Σόλωνα αὐτὴν ὀνομάσαι.
OLD AND NEW: thirtieth day [of the month], among the Athenians. They say that the name was given by Solon.

This group of fragments deals with the understanding of ἕνη τε καὶ νέα, in fact a current expression that Aristophanes' Phidippides pretends to be a legal archaism, in order to argue that it thereby requires (his) authoritative interpretation. Although Plutarch, Diogenes and others — see Martina, *Solon: Testimonia Veterum*, 185–9, for other sources — took it to be an expression coined by Solon, possibly as part of his reform of the Attic calendar, Ruschenbusch, *Nomoi*, 46, is probably correct in seeing the attribution as a simple comic invention. See also Sommerstein, *Aristophanes, Clouds*, 218; Manfredini & Piccirilli, *Plutarco, La vita di Solone*[5], 262–3.

Frs. 123c and 149 imply that it was Solon and not Pisistratus who started the official practice in Athens of reciting the Homeric poems. This is highly implausible, but Diogenes may be correct in seeing as the probable source for this tradition the Megarian historian Dieuchidas. If we take this together with the information provided by Plutarch (*Sol.* 10. i–ii) that Solon interpolated a line in the *Iliad* (II. 558), a reasonable conclusion is that the anecdote was motivated within the context of the Megarian dispute over Salamis (cf. also Diogenes I. 48). On Solon's regulations concerning festivities and sacrifices, see commentary on frs. 81–2.

Fr. 124: Comoedus Incertus (Ribbeck, *Scaenicae Romanorum Poesis Fragmenta*, ii. 2-8)
Athenis Megaram vesperi advenit Simo;
ubi advenit Megaram, insidias fecit virgini;
insidias postquam fecit, vim in loco attulit.
In Venere sapere didicit ni mirum Solon,
qui lege cauit, uitia uti transcenderent
auctoris poenae: nulla poena acerbior
excogitari potuit uxoris malis.
In Venere Ribbeck: *in ventrem* Charis.

In the evening, Simo arrived at Megara from Athens; when he arrived at Megara, he laid a trap for a girl, and after having trapped her he subjected her to violence there. In love affairs, Solon taught not surprisingly that one should be prudent, safeguarding by law that punishment of the offender should exceed the fault, and no harsher punishment could be devised for the misfortunes of a woman.

Ruschenbusch does not include the first three lines, but they may provide a suitable context for the fragment, implying probably the rape of a free woman. If this is the case, this fragment could be evocative of Solon's laws dealing with moral offences, especially those respecting rape (cf. frs. 26–7). At any rate, this supposition is not enough to turn this into credible evidence for a law of Solon.

Fr. 125: Philemon, fr. 3. 1–9 Kassel & Austin *ap.* Ath. XIII. 569 D–E
καὶ Φιλήμων δὲ ἐν Ἀδελφοῖς προσιστορῶν ὅτι πρῶτος Σόλων διὰ τὴν τῶν νέων ἀκμὴν ἔστησεν ἐπὶ οἰκημάτων γύναια πριάμενος, καθὰ καὶ Νίκανδρος ὁ Κολοφώνιος ἱστορεῖ ἐν τρίτῳ Κολοφωνιακῶν (*FGrH* 271/2 F 10) φάσκων αὐτὸν καὶ πανδήμου Ἀφροδίτης ἱερὸν πρῶτον ἱδρύσασθαι ἀφ' ὧν ἠργυρίσαντο αἱ προστᾶσαι τῶν οἰκημάτων. ἀλλ' ὅ γε Φιλήμων οὕτως φησί·
σὺ δ' εἰς ἅπαντας εὗρες ἀνθρώπους, Σόλων·
σὲ γὰρ λέγουσιν τοῦτ' ἰδεῖν πρῶτον, μόνον
δημοτικόν, ὦ Ζεῦ, πρᾶγμα καὶ σωτήριον
(καί μοι λέγειν τοῦτ' ἐστὶν ἁρμοστόν, Σόλων)
μεστὴν ὁρῶντα τὴν πόλιν νεωτέρων
τούτους τ' ἔχοντας τὴν ἀναγκαίαν φύσιν
ἁμαρτάνοντάς τ' εἰς ὃ μὴ προσῆκον ἦν,
στῆσαι πριάμενόν τοι γυναῖκας κατὰ τόπους
κοινὰς ἅπασι καὶ κατεσκευασμένας.

And Philemon, in his *Brothers*, narrates moreover that Solon first, because of the uncontrolled passions of the young, purchased women and established them in brothels, as Nicander of Colophon states also, in the third book of his *History of Colophon*, maintaining that he established the first sanctuary of Aphrodite *Pandemos*, with the money he obtained from the women who presided over these brothels. Philemon however talks about this as follows:
'You found the solution for all men, Solon: they say, in fact, that you were the first to perceive this, by Zeus, the one democratic and saving matter (and it befits me well to proclaim this, Solon); seeing that the city was full of young men, and that they were possessed of their natural appetites, and erring where it was not appropriate for them, you purchased women and placed them at certain places, making them common and available to all.

Although Solon forbade the procuring (*proagogeia*) of free women, prescribing a fine of twenty drachmae for the wrongdoers, he did not forbid voluntary prostitution (cf. frs. 29–30 with commentary). This is, however, very different from maintaining that Solon created brothels for the first time in Athens, purchasing women for that purpose, as implied by fr. 125, which clearly cannot be considered a genuine Solonian law. It has been suggested that Philemon's intent was perhaps to underline that democracy did not exist so long as access to sexual pleasure remained a privilege of a few, but this connection with democratic sociology only increases the difficulties in the attribution to Solon. See Hartmann, *Heirat, Hetärentum und Konkubinat im klassischen Athen*, 248–9; A. Grazebook, '*Porneion*: Prostitution in Athenian Civic Space', in Grazebrook *et al.* (edd.), *Greek Prostitutes in the Ancient Mediterranean, 800 B.C.E.–200 C.E.*, 53. S. Lape, 'Solon and the Institution of the "Democratic" Family Form', *CJ* xcviii 2002/3, 117–39 at 134, although suggesting that the passage could parodically show the theoretical association between democratic ideology and prostitution, recognises nevertheless that it 'may reflect a democratic fantasy rather than the historical reality'.

Fr. 126a: see fr. 51/2

Fr. 126b: see fr. 51/3

Fr. 126c: see fr. 71a

***Testimonium* to frs. 126a-c: see fr. 51/1**

Fr. 127a: Plut. *Sol.* 20. iii–iv (part of **fr. 52a**)
εὖ δ' ἔχει καὶ τὸ μὴ πᾶσιν, ἀλλὰ τῶν συγγενῶν τοῦ ἀνδρὸς ᾧ βούλεται διαλέγεσθαι τὴν ἐπίκληρον, ὅπως οἰκεῖον ᾖ καὶ μετέχον τοῦ γένους τὸ τικτόμενον. εἰς τοῦτο δὲ συντελεῖ καὶ τὸ τὴν νύμφην τῷ νυμφίῳ συγκαθείργνυσθαι μήλου κυδωνίου {συγ}κατα- τραγοῦσαν.
{συγ}κατατραγοῦσαν Coraes, cf. fr. 127b.

It is also a good disposition that the *epikleros* may not choose her consort from all, but that she should choose the man she prefers from among the kinsmen of her husband, so that the offspring is kept within the family and the same lineage. To that purpose also contributes the requirement that a bride should be shut up in a chamber with the bridegroom, after having eaten a quince.

Fr. 127b: Plut. *Coni. Praec.* 138 D
ὁ Σόλων ἐκέλευε τὴν νύμφην τῷ νυμφίῳ συγκατακλίνεσθαι μήλου κυδωνίου κατατραγοῦσαν.

Solon prescribed that the bride should get into bed with the bridegroom after having eaten a quince.

Fr. 127c: Plut. *Quaest. Graec.* 279 F
ὁ Σόλων ἔγραψε μήλου κυδωνίου τὴν νύμφην ἐντραγοῦσαν εἰς τὸν θάλαμον βαδίζειν.
Solon wrote that the bride should go to the bedroom after having eaten a quince.

When dealing with the regular sexual encounters that an *epikleros* should have with her husband (fr. 52a), Plutarch mentions a norm connected with fertility rites (fr. 127a), but it is probably not Solonian, even if it might be appropriate in a context dealing with sexual impotence. The context of frs. 127b–c suggests that the idea is to make more pleasant and tender the first intimate contact between husband and wife. For other instances of the practice of eating a quince in such contexts, see frs. 51–2 with commentary.

From Solon's poetry (?)

Fr. 128: Phot. κ 701 Theodoridis, *Suda* κ 1585 Adler
ΚΙΓΧΑΝΕΙΝ· τὸ ἐπεξιέναι οἱ περὶ Σόλωνα.
οὕτως Σόλων Phot.: οἱ περὶ Σόλωνα Suda.
TO HIT: to prosecute, [used by] Solon.

There is a law *ap.* Dem. XLIII. *Macartatus* 71 where the verb ἐπεξιέναι occurs: ὀφειλέτω δὲ καὶ τῷ ἰδιώτῃ τῷ ἐπεξιόντι ἑκατὸν δραχμὰς καθ' ἑκάστην ἐλάαν ('he must pay to the private citizen who prosecutes him one hundred drachmae for each olive tree'). Among Solon's laws there were several regulations dealing with olive trees (see frs. 60a–b, 90/a–b with commentary). The verb κιγχάνειν is used in fr. 20 West of Solon's poems: ὀγδωκονταέτη μοῖρα κίχοι θανάτου ('may the time of death hit me at the age of eighty'), and in an equivalent poem of Mimnermus (fr. 6 West: ἑξηκονταέτη μοῖρα κίχοι θανάτου 'may the time of death hit me at the age of sixty') to which Solon is responding. Sondhaus, *De Solonis Legibus*, 34–5, calls attention to the law in Demosthenes; Ruschenbusch, *Nomoi*, 121, prints Solon fr. 20 as a *testimonium*. At any rate, the context of the quotation is too fragmentary for us to decide whether this is derived from a law or a poem of Solon.

Fr. 129: Phot. ρ 162 Theodoridis
ΡΟΥΝ· τὸ ἥδυσμα· Σόλων.
SUMACH: a sauce. Solon.

The word ῥοῦν may be a gloss taken from the laws of Solon, or perhaps from his poetry (= fr. 41 West). Noussia-Fantuzzi, *Solon the Athenian: The Poetic Fragments*, 511, interprets the term as sumach, a product known for its astringent qualities in the making of leather (ῥοῦς βυρσοδεψική), although it may also be used in food. Therefore the text is usually taken as transmitting a Solonian word, even if its interpretation is not clear. The word is in the accusative, as the object of a verb meaning perhaps 'crush' or something of the kind.

Fr. 130: *Anecd. Bekk.* i. 340. 16
ΑΓΡΕΥΜΑΤΑ· τὰ ἐπὶ τῆς ἀγροικίας κτήματα Σόλων εἶπε. σημαίνει δὲ καὶ σκῦλα.
PREY: rustic possessions, as Solon says. It also designates animal's skin.

ἀγρεύματα is a relatively rare word that may have occurred in Solon's poetry or even in his laws. In fr. 81 (Plut. *Sol.* 23. iii–iv) there are regulations concerning the kind of reward that was to be given to someone who caught a wolf. In fr. 36. 26–7 West Solon compares himself to a wolf surrounded by dogs.

Confusion with other legislators

Frs. 131–5: Diog. Laert. I. 56–7
κάλλιστον δὲ κἀκεῖνο· τὸν ἐπίτροπον τῇ τῶν ὀρφανῶν μητρὶ μὴ συνοικεῖν, μηδ' ἐπιτροπεύειν, εἰς ὃν ἡ οὐσία ἔρχεται τῶν ὀρφανῶν τελευτησάντων (**fr. 131**). κἀκεῖνο· δακτυλιογλύφῳ μὴ ἐξεῖναι σφραγῖδα φυλάττειν τοῦ πραθέντος δακτυλίου (**fr. 132**). καὶ ἐὰν ἕνα ὀφθαλμὸν ἔχοντος ἐκκόψῃ τις, ἀντεκκόπτειν τοὺς δύο (**fr. 133**). ἃ μὴ ἔθου, μὴ ἀνέλῃ· εἰ δὲ μή, θάνατος ἡ ζημία (**fr. 134**). τῷ ἄρχοντι, ἐὰν μεθύων ληφθῇ, θάνατον εἶναι τὴν ζημίαν (**fr. 135**).

This is also another excellent regulation: a guardian was not allowed to marry the mother of the orphans [under his care], and no man could be nominated guardian, if the property of the orphans would come to him in the event that they died. And another one: a seal engraver is not allowed to keep the impression of a ring that he has already sold. And if a person knocks out the eye of someone who had only one, that person shall lose both eyes in turn. What you did not deposit, do not redeem, or the penalty shall be death. If an official is caught drunk, he shall face the death penalty.

Fr. 131 implies that there was a Solonian law forbidding the marriage of a guardian to the mother of the orphans under his care, but this regulation is probably spurious. H. F. Jolowicz, 'The Wicked Guardian', *JHS* xxxvii 1947, 82-90, compares this regulation with that attributed to Charondas by Diodorus (XII. 15. i–ii), concluding that the alleged law of Solon is surely false. See also Harrison, *L.A.* i. 24.

Fr. 134 mentions the death penalty for a man who claims a deposit not belonging to him, but Aelian maintains (III. 46: Σταγειριτῶν νόμος οὗτος καὶ πάντη Ἑλληνικός) that this regulation was universally valid throughout Greece, not attributing its creation to anyone in particular. Fr. 133 respects the so-called *lex talionis* ('eye for an eye'), but it is usually attributed to Zaleucus and Charondas, not to Solon. The death penalty prescribed for an official caught drunk (fr. 135) is perhaps inspired by Pittacus' regulations about drunkenness. See Gagarin, *Early Greek Law*, 64–7, for an outline of the sources dealing with these earlier legislators. The disposition on the obligations of seal engravers (fr. 132) could theoretically be Solonian, although the many confusions made by Diogenes among this set of laws do not justify confidence in asserting its authenticity, as remarked already by Sondhaus, *De Solonis Legibus*, 56.

Misinterpretation of laws

Fr. 136: see fr. 4/d

Fr. 137: Poll. VIII. 53
χίλιοι δὲ κατὰ μὲν τὸν Σόλωνα τὰς εἰσαγγελίας ἔκρινον, κατὰ δὲ τὸν Φαληρέα (fr. 141a Wehrli, *FGrH* 228 F 12b) καὶ πρὸς πεντακόσιοι.
With Solon, a thousand [men] decided disputes concerning *eisangeliai*, and with [Demetrius] of Phalerum it was before five hundred.

For Solon's law of *eisangelia* see fr. 37: we do not know what the basis for Pollux's erroneous statement is.

Fr. 138a: see fr. 39/1b

Fr. 138b: see fr. 39/1c

Unusable collective quotations

Fr. 139: Plut. *De Amore Prolis* 493 E
ὅρα περὶ τοὺς γάμους ὅσον ἐστὶν ἐν τοῖς ζῴοις τὸ κατὰ φύσιν· πρῶτον οὐκ ἀναμένει νόμους ἀγαμίου καὶ ὀψιγαμίου, καθάπερ οἱ Λυκούργου πολῖται καὶ Σόλωνος, οὐδ' ἀτιμίας ἀτέκνων δέδοικεν, οὐδὲ τιμὰς διώκει τριπαιδίας, ὡς Ῥωμαίων πολλοὶ γαμοῦσι καὶ γεννῶσιν, οὐχ ἵνα κληρονόμους ἔχωσιν ἀλλ' ἵνα κληρονομεῖν δύνωνται.
Take notice how, with regard to marriage, among animals, things are disposed according to nature: in the first place, they do not wait

until laws are passed against celibacy and late marriages, as the fellow citizens of Lycurgus and Solon did; they are not anxious about the possibility of experiencing the disgrace (*atimiai*) of those who are childless, nor are they chasing the honour (*timai*) of having three children, like many Romans, who marry and produce children, not to have heirs, but rather to inherit themselves.

I. Calero Secall, 'Plutarco y su interpretación de leyes griegas concernientes a la familia y propiedad', in Ferreira *et al.* (edd.), *Nomos, Kosmos and Dike in Plutarch*, 54–5, envisages, even if cautiously, the possibility that this law may be Solonian, establishing a parallel with the laws on *epikleroi*, as a way of promoting the generation of children, although Plutarch himself does not mention such a regulation in his life of Solon. Nevertheless Plutarch does state that Lycurgus determined (*Lyc.* 15. i–ii) that men who remained unmarried (*agamoi*) would suffer some degree of *atimia*. In his poetry (fr. 27. 9-10 West) Solon mentions the fifth hebdomad (πέμπτη δ' ὥριον) as the appropriate time for marriage and for having children (i.e after the age of 35 years). Solon is not far from Hesiod (*Op.* 695–7), who suggests roughly the same age for marriage (μήτε τριηκόντων ἐτέων μάλα πόλλ' ἀπολείπων). They both share the idea that submission to the requirements of temporality is to be in accord with nature, thereby marrying and having children at the right time or season (ὥρα and therefore ὡραῖος, ὥριος). See Noussia-Fantuzzi, *Solon the Athenian: The Poetic Fragments*, 383. At any rate, this does not imply that Solon passed a law punishing with *atimia* those who did not behave κατὰ φύσιν in this area.

Fr. 140: Alciphron II. 38. iii
μέμφομαι τῷ Σόλωνι καὶ τῷ Δράκοντι, οἳ τοὺς μὲν κλέπτοντας σταφυλὰς θανάτῳ ζημιοῦν ἐδικαίωσαν, τοὺς δὲ ἀνδραποδίζοντας ἀπὸ τοῦ φρονεῖν τοὺς νέους ἀθῴους εἶναι τιμωρίας ἀπέλιπον.
I blame Solon and Draco, who deemed it right to punish with death those who had stolen a bunch of grapes, but left those who enslaved the will of young boys to remain unpunished and without reprisal.

Fr. 141: Xen. *Oec.* xiv. 4–5
καίτοι τὰ μὲν καὶ ἐκ τῶν Δράκοντος νόμων, τὰ δὲ καὶ ἐκ τῶν Σόλωνος πειρῶμαι, ἔφη, λαμβάνων ἐμβιβάζειν εἰς τὴν δικαιοσύνην τοὺς οἰκέτας. δοκοῦσι γάρ μοι, ἔφη, καὶ οὗτοι οἱ ἄνδρες θεῖναι πολλοὺς τῶν νόμων ἐπὶ δικαιοσύνης τῆς τοιαύτης διδασκαλίᾳ. γέγραπται γὰρ ζημιοῦσθαι ἐπὶ τοῖς κλέμμασι καὶ δεδέσθαι ἄν τις ἁλῷ ποιῶν καὶ θανατοῦσθαι τοὺς ἐγχειροῦντας.
I shall take now some directives from the laws of Draco and some from those of Solon, he said, and try to direct my household slaves

into the path of righteousness. Indeed it seems to me, he continued, that those men enacted many of their laws aiming expressly at the teaching of this kind of righteousness. It is in fact written that a man shall be punished for theft, and those who make the attempt shall be imprisoned, and put to death if a man is caught in the act.

The passage in Alciphron corresponds probably to a simple rhetorical use of the traditional severity of Draco's laws (here extended to Solon) respecting lesser crimes punished by the death penalty, thus establishing a sharp contrast with their leniency concerning the corruption of the young. Xenophon reports the penalty for theft in *Mem.* I. ii. 62 also, without naming Draco or Solon. Whether there were laws of Draco on matters other than homicide we consider uncertain (cf. on fr. 1, and for idleness fr. 66/1). Even if there was a law of Draco on theft, it will have been changed by Solon, at least in respect of the penalty. Cf. frs. 1, 16 and 23 with commentary.

Fr. 142: Dion. Hal. *Ant. Rom.* II. 26. ii–iii
οἱ μὲν γὰρ τὰς Ἑλληνικὰς καταστησάμενοι πολιτείας βραχύν τινα κομιδῇ χρόνον ἔταξαν ἄρχεσθαι τοὺς παῖδας ὑπὸ τῶν πατέρων, οἱ μὲν ἕως τρίτον ἐκπληρώσωσιν ἀφ' ἥβης ἔτος, οἱ δὲ ὅσον ἂν χρόνον ἠίθεοι μένωσιν, οἱ δὲ μέχρι τῆς εἰς τὰ ἀρχεῖα τὰ δημόσια ἐγγραφῆς, ὡς ἐκ τῆς Σόλωνος καὶ Πιττακοῦ καὶ Χαρώνδου νομοθεσίας ἔμαθον, οἷς πολλὴ μαρτυρεῖται σοφία· τιμωρίας τε κατὰ τῶν παίδων ἔταξαν, ἐὰν ἀπειθῶσι τοῖς πατράσιν, οὐ βαρείας, ἐξελάσαι τῆς οἰκίας ἐπιτρέψαντες αὐτοὺς καὶ χρήματα μὴ καταλιπεῖν, περαιτέρω δὲ οὐδέν.
In fact, those who established the constitutions for the Greeks determined quite a short time for sons to be under the rule of their fathers: some until they reach the third year after puberty, others during the time they remain unmarried, and others until they enrol their names in the public records, as I learned from the legislation of Solon, Pittacus, and Charondas, in whom much wisdom is shown. They determined punishments for the children, in the case they disobey their fathers, but not very heavy: they allow [the fathers] to expel them from their home and to exclude them from their inheritance, but nothing beyond that.

Dionysius intends to emphasise the distinctiveness of the Roman *paterfamilias*, making a comparison with Greek practices respecting relations between a father and his children. Solon is mentioned along with Pittacus and Chaerondas, so these norms are not directly attributed to him. Solon made laws concerning the obligation of a father to teach a *techne* to his children (fr. 56) and on principles of reciprocity (like *paidotrophia* and *gerotrophia*) binding fathers and sons (frs. 55–7). For differences and similarities between Greek and Roman practice, see Strauss, *Fathers and Sons in Athens*, 62–5.

Varia

Fr. 143a: see fr. 89/1a

Fr. 143b: see fr. 89/1b

Fr. 143c: see fr. 89/1c

Fr. 144a: Schol. Thuc. II. 35. i
ΟΙ ΜΕΝ ΠΟΛΛΟΙ· οἱ μὲν πολλοί, φησί, τῶν ἐνθάδε ἤδη εἰρηκότων ἐπαινοῦσι τὸν νομοθέτην τὸν προσθέντα ἐν τῷ αὐτοῦ νόμῳ τὸν λόγον τὸν κελεύοντα λέγεσθαι τὸν ἐπιτάφιον ἐπὶ τοῖς θαπτομένοις δημοσίᾳ.
ΤΟΝ ΠΡΟΣΘΕΝΤΑ· τὸν νομοθέτην, τὸν Σόλωνα.
ΤΩΙ ΝΟΜΩΙ ΤΟΝ ΛΟΓΟΝ· νόμος, ὅτι δεῖ τοὺς ἐκ τῆς πόλεως ἀνῃρημένους δημοσίᾳ ταφῆς ἀξιοῦν. προστιθέασι δὲ τῷ τοιούτῳ νόμῳ τὸ δεῖν καὶ ἐπιταφίους ἐπαίνους εἰς αὐτοὺς λέγειν, ὃ δὴ καὶ λόγον ὁ ῥήτωρ ἐνταῦθα καλεῖ καὶ προσθήκην νόμου προσαγορεύει.
THE MAJORITY: the majority, he says, of those who have already spoken on this occasion praise the legislator who introduced this principle into his law, determining that the funeral oration should be pronounced in honour of those who had a burial at the public expense.
THE ONE WHO INTRODUCED: the legislator, Solon.
THIS PRINCIPLE INTO THE LAW: the law that those from the *polis* who died are worthy of burial at public expense. They add to such a law the obligation also of pronouncing a funeral oration in honour of them, and here the orator invokes that principle and speaks of an addition to the law.

Fr. 144b: Plut. *Publ.* 9. ix
λέγεται δὲ καὶ τῶν Ἑλληνικῶν ἐπιταφίων ἐκεῖνος γενέσθαι πρεσβύτερος, εἴ γε μὴ καὶ τοῦτο Σόλωνός ἐστιν, ὡς Ἀναξιμένης ὁ ῥήτωρ (*FGrH* 72 F 24) ἱστόρηκεν.

And it is said that this funeral oration was pronounced earlier than those of the Greeks, unless it is actually an institution of Solon, as is stated by the orator Anaximenes.

Frs. 144c, 145: Diog. Laert. I. 55
ἀπειρόκαλον γὰρ τὸ ἐξαίρειν τὰς τούτων τιμάς, ἀλλὰ μόνων ἐκείνων τῶν ἐν πολέμοις τελευτησάντων (**fr. 144c**), ὧν καὶ τοὺς υἱοὺς δημοσίᾳ τρέφεσθαι καὶ παιδεύεσθαι (**fr. 145**).
He argued that it would be tasteless to praise those men with such great honours, which ought to be given only to those who had fallen in battle, and whose children were to be reared and educated at public expense.

For the context of frs. 144c and 145, see frs. 143a–c with commentary. Frs. 144a–b suggest that Athens' *epitaphioi logoi* were instituted by Solon, but the public funeral and the speech which accompanied it were certainly instituted later, probably in the late sixth or early fifth century. On the institution of the public funeral see Ruschenbusch, *Nomoi*, 9–10; A. C. Scafuro, 'Identifying Solonian laws', in Blok & Lardinois (edd.), *Solon of Athens*, 179; and, among many discussions, F. Jacoby, '*Patrios Nomos*: State Burial in Athens and the Public Cemetery in the Kerameikos', *JHS* lxiv 1944, 37–66 = his *Abhandlungen zur griechischen Geschichtschreibung*, 260–315; Stupperich, *Staatsbegräbnis und Privatgrabmal im klassischen Athen*, 206–24; Pritchett, *The Greek State at War*, iv, 106–24. Diod. Sic. XI. 33. iii dates the oration and the games 479, which could be right; Dion. Hal. *Ant. Rom.* V. 17. iii–iv claims that the earliest instance in Rome was in 507, before the earliest instance in Athens.

Fr. 146: Plut. *Sol.* 31. iii–iv
καὶ νόμους αὐτὸς ἑτέρους ἔγραψεν, ὧν ἐστι καὶ ὁ τοὺς πηρωθέντας ἐν πολέμῳ δημοσίᾳ τρέφεσθαι κελεύων. τοῦτο δέ φησιν Ἡρακλείδης (fr. 149 Wehrli) καὶ πρότερον ἐπὶ Θερσίππῳ πηρωθέντι τοῦ Σόλωνος ψηφισαμένου μιμήσασθαι τὸν Πεισίστρατον.
He [*sc.* Pisistratus] wrote also other laws himself, among which is the one prescribing that those mutilated in war should be maintained at public expense. However Heraclides says that before that Solon passed a decree for Thersippus, who was mutilated, and that Pisistratus followed his example.

Fr. 147: Schol. Aeschin. I. *Timarchus*. 103 (223 Dilts)
ΜΙΣΘΟΦΟΡΟΥΝΤΑ· ἀντὶ τοῦ "μισθὸν δεχόμενον ἐν τῷ καταλόγῳ τῶν λελωβημένων καὶ ἀδυνάτων". νόμος γὰρ ἦν Σόλωνος ὁ κελεύων τοὺς τοιούτους ἐκ τῶν δημοσίων τρέφεσθαι.

TAKING PAYMENT: meaning 'receiving payment on account of enrolment in the list of those mutilated and disabled'. It was in fact a law of Solon which prescribed that such men should be maintained at public expense.

It may be true that illustrious invalids received grants of *sitesis* at the time of Solon and Pisistratus, as implied by fr. 146, although most probably not on a regular basis. Solon was credited with the creation of the term *parasitein* ('eating at the public expense', fr. 87), but dispositions regarding the care of war orphans are doubtful (fr. 89/1b). The institution ascribed to Solon in fr. 147 must be a creation of the Periclean or post-Periclean democracy. See Rhodes, *Comm. Ath. Pol.* 579; Manfredini & Piccirilli, *Plutarco. La vita di Solone*[5], 278–9.

Fr. 148a: see fr. 66/1d

Fr. 148b: see fr. 66/1e

Fr. 148c: see fr. 66/1f

Fr. 148d: see fr. 66/1g

Fr. 148e: see fr. 66/1c

Fr. 149: Diog. Laert. I. 57 (part of **fr. 123c**)
τά τε Ὁμήρου ἐξ ὑποβολῆς γέγραφε ῥαψῳδεῖσθαι, οἷον ὅπου ὁ πρῶτος ἔληξεν, ἐκεῖθεν ἄρχεσθαι τὸν ἐχόμενον.
He wrote that Homer's verses ought to be recited in sequence, in the sense that at the point where the first reciter stopped, there the next one should start.

For commentary, see fr. 123c.

Fr. 149/1 (fr. 66 Ruschenbusch): Arist. *Pol.* II. 1266 B 14–18
διότι μὲν οὖν ἔχει τινὰ δύναμιν εἰς τὴν πολιτικὴν κοινωνίαν ἡ τῆς οὐσίας ὁμαλότης, καὶ τῶν πάλαι τινὲς φαίνονται διεγνωκότες, οἷον καὶ Σόλων ἐνομοθέτησεν, καὶ παρ' ἄλλοις ἐστὶ νόμος, ὃς κωλύει κτᾶσθαι γῆν ὁπόσην βούληταί τις.

That evenness in property has some force with a view to political community was clearly recognised by some of the ancients also: for example Solon legislated, and there is a law among others which forbids men to acquire as much land as they like.

Ruschenbusch assumed that this was based on the Aristotelian school's work on Solon's *axones* (T 1 in *Nomoi*), and that the law was connected with the *seisachtheia*. He felt unable to decide whether the law remained in force in the classical period, but noted that the largest attested Athenian estates are of 300 *plethra* (*c.* 260,000 m².) (Lys. XIX. *Property of Aristophanes* 29, Pl. *Alc. i.* 123 c). Others have been less confident, even in a law of Solon (e.g. Harrison, *L.A.* i. 237, citing Dem. XIII. *Syntaxis* 30, XXIII. *Aristocrates* 208, as pointing to the absence of restrictions in the fourth century; A. Andrewes, in *C.A.H.*² III. iii. 384). Mention of Solon in Aristotle's *Politics* was not necessarily always based on good evidence (cf. Rhodes, *Comm. Ath. Pol.* 60–1), and we too are inclined to reject this as a fiction.

Fr. 150a: see fr. 74/3a

Fr. 150b: see fr. 74/3b

Fr. 151: Ael. *N.A.* II. 42

νεκρὸν δὲ ἄνθρωπον ἰδὼν ἱέραξ, ὡς λόγος, πάντως ἐπιβάλλει γῆς τῷ ἀτάφῳ (καὶ τοῦτο μὲν αὐτῷ οὐ κελεύει Σόλων), οὐδὲ σώματος ἅψεται.
Seeing a dead man, the hawk — so it is told — invariably starts spreading earth over the unburied person (and it was not Solon who prescribed this), without touching the corpse.

Fr. 152: Ael. *N.A.* VI. 61

ἐπαΐουσι γοῦν τὸ τῶν ἐλεφάντων γένος, ὦ Λυκοῦργοί τε καὶ Σόλωνες καὶ Ζάλευκοι καὶ Χαρῶνδαι, ὦνπερ οὖν ὑμεῖς νομοθετεῖτε οὐδὲ τὴν ἀρχήν, καὶ ὅμως δρῶσι τοιαῦτα, καὶ τροφῆς ἀφίστανται τοῖς πρεσβυτέροις οἱ νέοι, καὶ γήρᾳ παρειμένους θεραπεύουσιν αὐτούς. ... ποῦ δαὶ ἠλόησε πληγαῖς πατέρα ἐλέφας;
The race of elephants perceives this without what you have not even begun to legislate about — you Lycurgi, Solones, Zaleuci and Charondae — and follows such practices: the young give way to the elder for nourishment, and they take good care of those weakened by old age. ... When did an elephant assail his father with blows?

Those two passages make a rhetorical and moralising use of laws with a remote Solonian flavour, such as those concerning burial and customary funeral rites, and the reciprocal obligations of *paidotrophia* and *gerotrophia* (cf. especially frs. 55–7 with commentary).

Fr. /153 (fr. 7 Ruschenbusch): Schol. Hom. *Il.* II. 665

Ἑλληνικόν ἐστι τὸ μὴ φόνῳ φόνον λύειν, φυγαδεύειν δὲ τὸν ἅπαντα χρόνον· ὅθεν Σόλων ἔτη πέντε ὥρισεν.

The Greek practice is not to recompense killing with killing but to exile [*sc.* the killer] for all time: whence Solon fixed a period of five years.

Ruschenbusch, *Gesetzeswerk*, rejected this as a false generalisation from fr. 108; Heitsch, *Aidesis*, 5–8, noted the clear statement of Dem. XXIII. *Aristocrates* 72 that the exile was permanent unless / until reconciliation was agreed, discussed the various texts which mention a time limit, and produced strong arguments against this text. Pl. *Leg.* IX. 869 E proposed one year's exile for unwilling homicide, there are texts which claim that that was the limit (e.g. Hesych. α 5977 Latte *et al.* ἀπενιαυτισμός, *Anecd. Bekk.* i. 421. 18–22 — but Pl. *Leg.* IX. 868 C uses *apeniautein* generically, to refer to a period of more than one year), and Heitsch thought that might be a minimum for unwilling killers. There is no good evidence for a fixed period of exile in Athenian homicide cases.

Fr. /154 (fr. 9 Ruschenbusch): Harp. υ 13 Keaney

ΥΠΟΦΟΝΙΑ· τὰ ἐπὶ φόνῳ διδόμενα χρήματα τοῖς οἰκείοις τοῦ φονευθέντος ἵνα μὴ ἐπεξίωσιν· Δείναρχος ἐν τῷ κατὰ Καλλισθένους (fr. XIX. 13 Conomis) καὶ ἐν τῷ κατὰ Φορμισίου (fr. X. 5 Conomis) , Θεόφραστος Νόμων ις΄ (fr. 12 Szegedy-Maszak).

HYPOPHONIA: Money paid for homicide to the relatives of the one killed to prevent them from prosecuting. Dinarchus in the speeches against Callisthenes and against Phormisius, Theophrastus in *Laws* XVI.

Ruschenbusch, *Gesetzeswerk*, rightly sees here the fourth-century practice of bribing the next of kin to refrain from prosecuting (e.g. [Dem.] LVIII. *Theocrines* 28–9), not a reference to payment of blood money leading to reconciliation.

BIBLIOGRAPHY

(*Festschriften* are listed under the name of the honorand, after the honorand's own works.)

Arnaoutoglou, I., *Ancient Greek Laws: A Sourcebook* (London: Routledge, 1998).
Balogh, E., with Heichelheim, F. M., *Political Refugees in Ancient Greece* (Witwatersrand University Press, 1943).
Beloch, K. J., *Griechische Geschichte* (Strassburg: Trübner → Berlin & Leipzig: de Gruyter, ²1912–27).
Bertrand, J.-M. (ed.), *La Violence dans les mondes grec et romain* (Paris: Publications de la Sorbonne, 2005).
Biscardi, A., *Diritto greco antico* (Varese: Giuffrè, 1982).
Blok, J. H., & Lardinois, A. P. M. H. (edd.), *Solon of Athens: New Historical and Philological Approaches* (*Mnemosyne* Supp. cclxxii 2006).
Boegehold, A. L., *The Athenian Agora*, xxviii. *The Lawcourts at Athens* (Princeton: Am. Sch. Class. Stud. Ath., 1995).
Bonner, R. J., & Smith, G., *The Administration of Justice from Homer to Aristotle* (University of Chicago Press, 1930–8).
Camp, J. M., II, *The Athenian Agora: Site Guide* (Princeton: A.S.C.S.A., ⁵2010).
Canevaro, M., *The Documents in the Attic Orators: Laws and Decrees in the Public Speeches of the Demosthenic Corpus* (Oxford University Press, 2013).
Charles, J. F., *Statutes of Limitation at Athens* (University of Chicago Press, 1938).
Cohen, D., *Law, Sexuality, and Society: The Enforcement of Morals in Classical Athens* (Cambridge University Press, 1991).
—— *Theft in Athenian Law* (Munich: Beck, 1983).
Coulson, W. D. E., *et al.* (edd.), *The Archaeology of Athens and Attica under the Democracy* (Oxford: Oxbow, 1994).
de Ste. Croix, G. E. M., *Athenian Democratic Origins and Other Essays* (edd. F. D. Harvey & R. C. T. Parker. Oxford University Press, 2004).
—— *Crux: Essays Presented to G. E M. de Ste. Croix* (*History of Political Thought* VI. ii 1985 / London: Duckworth, 1985).

Descat, R., *Stephanèphoros: De L'économie antique à l'Asie Mineure: Hommages à R. Descat* (Bordeaux: Ausonius Éditions, Mémoires xxviii, 2012).

Dillon, M., & Garland, L., *Ancient Greece: Social and Historical Documents from Archaic Times to the Death of Socrates* (London: Routledge, 2000).

Dover, K. J., *Greek Popular Morality in the Time of Plato and Aristotle* (Oxford: Blackwell, 1974).

—— *Owls for Athens: Essays on Classical Subjects for Sir K. Dover* (Oxford University Press, 1990).

Ferreira, J. R., Leão, D. F., & Jesus, C. (edd.), *Nomos, Kosmos and Dike in Plutarch* (Coimbra: Imprensa da Universidade, 2012).

Ferreira, J. R., Stockt, L. van der, & Fialho, M. do Céu (edd.), *Philosophy in Society. Virtues and Values in Plutarch* (Leuven: Katholieke Universiteit & Coimbra: Imprensa da Universidade, 2008).

Fisher, N. R. E., *Aeschines, Against Timarchos: Introduction, Translation and Commentary* (Oxford University Press, 2001).

—— *Hybris; A Study of the Values of Honour and Shame in Ancient Greece* (Warminster: Aris & Phillips, 1992).

—— *Sociable Man: Essays on Ancient Greek Social Behaviour in Honour of N. Fisher* (Swansea: Classical Press of Wales, 2011).

Freeman, K., *The Work and Life of Solon* (Cardiff: University of Wales Press, 1926).

Gagarin, M., *Drakon and Early Athenian Homicide Law* (Yale University Press, 1981).

—— *Early Greek Law* (University of California Press, 1986).

—— *Writing Greek Law* (Cambridge University Press, 2008).

Gagarin, M., & Cohen, D. (edd.), *The Cambridge Companion to Ancient Greek Law* (Cambridge University Press, 2005).

Garnsey, P. D. A., *Cities, Peasants and Food in Classical Greece* (Cambridge University Press, 1998).

Gauthier, P., *Symbola: Les Étrangers et la justice dans les cités grecques* (Nancy: Annales de l'Est, Mém. xlii 1972).

Glotz, G., *La Solidarité de la famille dans le droit criminel en Grèce* (Paris: Fontemoing, 1904).

Grazebrook, A., & Henry, M. M. (edd.), *Greek Prostitutes in the Ancient Mediterranean, 800 B.C.E.-200 C.E.* (Madison: University of Wisconsin Press, 2011).

Grote, G., *A History of Greece* (London: Murray, 'new edition' in 12 volumes, 1869/84; in 10 volumes, 1888).

Hansen, M. H., *Apagoge, Endeixis and Ephegesis against Kakourgoi, Atimoi and Pheugontes* (Odense University Press, 1976).

—— *Eisangelia: The Sovereignty of the People's Court in Athens in the Fourth Century B.C. and the Impeachment of Generals and Politicians* (Odense University Press, 1975).

—— *The Athenian Assembly in the Age of Demosthenes* (Oxford: Blackwell, 1987).

—— *The Athenian Democracy in the Age of Demosthenes* (trans J. A. Crook. Bristol Classical Paperbacks. London: Duckworth, ²1999)

—— *The Athenian Ecclesia <I>* (Copenhagen: Museum Tusculanum Press, 1983).

Harding, P. E., *Androtion and the Atthis* (Oxford University Press, 1994).

Harris, E. M., *Democracy and the Rule of Law in Classical Athens* (Cambridge University Press, 2006).

——— *The Rule of Law in Action in Democratic Athens* (Oxford University Press, 2013).
Harris, E. M., Leão, D. F., & Rhodes, P. J. (edd.), *Law and Drama in Ancient Greece* (London: Duckworth, 2010).
Harris, E. M., & Rubinstein, L. (edd.), *The Law and the Courts in Ancient Greece* (London: Duckworth, 2004).
Harrison, A. R. W., *The Law of Athens* (Oxford University Press, 1968–71).
Hartmann, E., *Heirat, Hetärentum und Konkubinat im klassischen Athen* (Frankfurt: Campus, 2002).
Heitsch, E., *Aidesis im attischen Strafrecht* (*Abh. Mainz* 1984. i).
Hignett, C., *A History of the Athenian Constitution to the End of the Fifth Century B.C.* (Oxford University Press, 1952).
Hillgruber, M., *Die zehnte Rede des Lysias* (Berlin: de Gruyter, 1988).
Jacoby, F., *Abhandlungen zur griechischen Geschichtschreibung* (Leiden: Brill, 1956).
——— *Atthis: The Local Chronicles of Ancient Athens* (Oxford University Press, 1949).
Jones, N. F., *The Associations of Classical Athens: The Response to Democracy* (Oxford University Press, 1999).
Kapparis, K., *Abortion in the Ancient World* (London: Duckworth, 2002).
Karabélias, E., *L'Épiclérat attique* (Athens: Academy of Athens, 2002).
——— *Études d'histoire juridique et sociale de la Grèce ancienne* (Athens: Academy of Athens, 2005).
Knox, B. M. W., *Arktouros: Hellenic Studies Presented to B. M. W. Knox* (Berlin: de Gruyter, 1979)
Kraay, C. M., *Archaic and Classical Greek Coins* (London: Methuen, 1976).
Kurtz, D. C., & Boardman, J., *Greek Burial Customs* (London: Thames & Hudson, 1971).
Lambert, S. D., *The Phratries of Attica* (University of Michigan Press, 1993).
Leão, D. F., *Sólon: Ética e política* (Lisbon: Fundação Calouste Gulbenkian, 2001).
Leão, D. F., Rossetti, L., & Fialho, M. do Céu G. Z. (edd.), *Nomos: Direito e sociedade na Antiguidade Clássica* (U. of Coimbra P. & Madrid: Ediciones Clásicas, 2004).
Lewis, D. M., *Selected Papers in Greek and Near Eastern History* (ed. P. J. Rhodes. Cambridge University Press, 1997).
Lipsius, J. H., *Das attische Recht und Rechtsverfahren* (Leipzig: Reisland, 1905–15).
MacDowell, D. M., *Athenian Homicide Law in the Age of the Orators* (Manchester University Press, 1963).
——— *Demosthenes, Against Meidias (Oration 21)* (Oxford University Press, 1990).
——— *Demosthenes the Orator* (Oxford University Press, 2009).
——— *Spartan Law* (Edinburgh: Scottish Academic Press, 1986).
——— *The Law in Classical Athens* (London: Thames and Hudson, 1978).
——— *Law, Rhetoric and Comedy in Classical Athens: Essays in Honour of D. M. MacDowell* (Swansea: Class. Press of Wales, 2004).
Maddoli, G. (ed.), *L'Athenaion Politeia di Aristotele, 1891–1991: Per un bilancio di cento anni di studi* (Naples: Edizioni Scientifiche Italiane, 1994).

Manfredini, M., & Piccirilli, L., *Plutarco. La vita di Solone* (Milan: Mondadori for Fondazione Lorenzo Valla, ⁵1998).
Maridakis, G. S., *Eranion in Honorem Georgii S. Maridakis* (Athens: Kleisiounes, 1963–4).
Martina, A., *Solon: Testimonia Veterum* (Roma, Edizioni dell'Ateneo, 1968).
Mattingly, H. B., Ἀθηναίων ἐπίσκοπος: *Studies in Honour of H. B. Mattingly* (Athens: Greek Epigraphic Society, 2014).
Meiggs, R., *The Athenian Empire* (Oxford University Press, 1972).
Meritt, B. D., φόρος: *Tribute to Benjamin Dean Meritt* (Locust Valley: Augustin, 1974).
Millett, P. C., *Lending and Borrowing in Ancient Athens* (Cambridge University Press, 1991).
Mitchell, L. G., & Rhodes, P. J. (edd.), *The Development of the Polis in Archaic Greece* (London: Routledge, 1997).
Muth, R., *Festschrift für Robert Muth* (Innsbruck: Institut für Sprachwissenschaft der Universität, 1983).
Noussia-Fantuzzi, M., *Solon the Athenian: The Poetic Fragments* (Leiden: Brill, 2010).
Oliveira, F. (ed.), *O espírito olímpico no novo milénio* (Coimbra: Imprensa da Universidade, 2000).
Osborne, M. J., *Naturalization in Athens* (Brussels: Royal Academy, 1981–3).
Ostwald, M., *Nomodeiktes: Greek Studies in Honor of M, Ostwald* (University of Michigan Press, 1993).
Papazarkadas, N., *Sacred and Public Land in Ancient Athens* (Oxford University Press, 2011).
Parker, R. C. T., *Athenian Religion: A History* (Oxford University Press, 1996).
—— *Miasma: Pollution and Purification in Early Greek Religion* (Oxford University Press, 1983).
Parkins, H., & Smith, C. (edd.), *Trade, Traders and the Ancient City* (London: Routledge, 1998).
Pepe, L., *Phonos: L'omicidio da Draconte all'età degli oratori* (Milan: Giuffrè for the University of Milan, 2012).
Price. M. J., *Studies in Greek Numismatics in Memory of M. J. Price* (London: Spink, 1998).
Pritchett, W. K., *The Greek State at War* (University of California Press, 1974–91).
Raaflaub, K. A. (ed.), *Social Struggles in Archaic Rome* (Oxford: Blackwell, ²2005).
Rhodes, P. J., *Aristotle, The Athenian Constitution* (Harmondsworth: Penguin, 1984).
—— *A Commentary on the Aristotelian Athenaion Politeia* (Oxford University Press, 1981; reissued with addenda, 1993).
—— *The Athenian Boule* (Oxford University Press, 1972; reissued with addenda, 1985).
Rickert, G. A., ἑκών *and* ἄκων *in Early Greek Thought* (Atlanta: Scholars Press, 1989).
Robinson, E. S. G., *Essays in Greek Coinage Presented to S. Robinson* (Oxford University Press, 1968).
Rose, V., *Aristotelis Qui Ferebantur Librorum Fragmenta* (Leipzig: Teubner, 1886).
Rubinstein, L., *Adoption in IV. Century Athens* (Copenhagen: Museum Tusculanum Press, 1993).
—— *Litigation and Cooperation: Supporting Speakers in the Courts of Classical Athens* (Historia Einzelschriften cxlvii 2000).

Ruschenbusch, E., *Kleine Schriften zur griechischen Rechtsgeschichte* (Philippika x. Wiesbaden: Harrassowitz, 2005).

—— *Solon: das Gesetzeswerk — Fragmente: Übersetzung und Kommentar* (ed. K. Bringmann. *Historia* Einzelschriften ccxv 2010).

—— Σόλωνος νόμοι: *Die Fragmente des solonischen Gesetzeswerkes mit einer Text- und Überlieferungsgeschichte* (*Historia* Einzelschriften ix 1966).

—— *Untersuchungen zur Geschichte des athenischen Strafrechts* (Köln & Graz: Böhlau, 1968).

Sealey, R., *Essays in Greek Politics* (New York: Manyland, 1967).

Shear, J. L., *Polis and Revolution: Responding to Oligarchy in Classical Athens* (Cambridge University Press, 2011).

Sommerstein, A. H., *Aristophanes, Clouds* (Warminster: Aris & Phillips, 1982).

Sondhaus, C., *De Solonis Legibus* (Jena: Nevenhahn, 1909).

Sourvinou-Inwood, C., *Athenian Myths and Festivals: Aglauros, Erechtheus, Plynteria, Panathenaia, Dionysia* (ed. R. C. T. Parker. Oxford University Press, 2011).

—— *'Reading' Greek Death, to the End of the Classical Period* (Oxford University Press, 1995).

Stadter, P. A., *A Commentary on Plutarch's Pericles* (University of North Carolina Press, 1986).

Steiner, D. T., *The Tyrant's Writ* (Princeton University Press, 1994).

Strauss, B. S., *Fathers and Sons in Athens: Ideology and Society in the Era of the Peloponnesian War* (London: Routledge, 1993).

Stroud, R. S., *Drakon's Law on Homicide* (University of California Pub. Cl. Stud. iii 1968).

—— *The Axones and Kyrbeis of Drakon and Solon* (University of California Pub. Cl. Stud. xix 1979).

Stupperich, R., *Staatsbegräbnis und Privatgrabmal im klassischen Athen* (University of Münster, 1977).

Todd, S. C., *A Commentary on Lysias, Speeches 1–11* (Oxford University Press, 2007).

—— *The Shape of Athenian Law* (Oxford University Press, 1993).

Travlos, J., *Pictorial Dictionary of Ancient Athens* (London: Thames & Hudson, 1967).

Wade-Gery, H. T., *Essays in Greek History* (Oxford: Blackwell. 1958).

Wallace, R. W., *The Areopagos Council, to 307 B.C.* (Johns Hopkins University Press, 1989).

Walter, U., *An der Polis teilhaben: Bürgerstaat und Zugehörigkeit im archaischen Griechenland* (Stuttgart: Steiner, 1993).

Wees, H. van, *Ships and Silver, Taxes and Tribute: A Fiscal History of Archaic Athens* (London: I.B.Tauris, 2013).

INDEX OF FRAGMENTS

Fr. 1a: *Ath. Pol.* 7. i (11–13)
Fr. 1b: Plut. *Sol.* 17. i (11–13)
*Fr. 1c: Ael. *V.H.* VIII. 10 (11–13)
*Fr. 1d: Georgius Cedrenus, Historiarum Compendium (i. 145. 18–20 Bekker) (12–13)
Fr. 2: Plut. *Sol.* 19. iii (13–14)
Fr. 3: Phot. α 1753 Theodoridis (14)
Fr. 4a: Diog. Laert. I. 59 (14–15)
Fr. 4b: Cic. *Rosc. Am.* 70 (14–15)
Fr. 4c: Orosius, V. 16. xxiii–xxiv (15)
Fr. 4/d: Sext. Emp. *Pyr.* III. 211 (15)
†Fr. 4/1a: Dem. XXIII. *Aristocrates* 22 (15–17)
†Fr. 4/1b: *Ath. Pol.* 57. iii–iv (16–17)
Fr. 5a: *IG* i³ 104 (17–24)
Fr. 5b: law *ap.* Dem. XLIII. *Macartatus* 57 (20–4)
Fr. 5c: *Anecd. Bekk.* i. 401. 18–24 (21–4)
Fr. 5d: Poll. III. 28 (21–4)
†Fr. 5/e: *Ath. Pol.* 57. iii (part of fr. 4/1b) (21–4)
Fr. 6: Dem. XXIII. *Aristocrates* 72 (24)
Fr. 7: see fr. 153
Fr. 8: *Anecd. Bekk.* i. 82. 17–18 (25)
Fr. 9: see fr. 154
Fr. 10: Poll. IX. 61 (25)
Fr. 11: Phot. π 1009 Theodoridis (25–6)
Fr. 12: *Anecd. Bekk.* i. 428. 9–10, Suda α 3716 Adler (25–6)
Fr. 13: Dem. XXIII. *Aristocrates* 82 (26)
Fr. 14: Dem. XX. *Leptines* 158 (26–7)
Fr. 15a: Dem. XXIII. *Aristocrates* 69 (27)
Fr. 15b: see fr. 95/1
Fr. 16/a: Dem. XXIII. *Aristocrates* 28 (27–8)
†Fr. /16b: law *ap.* Dem. XXIII. *Aristocrates* 51 (28)

Fr. 17: Dem. XXIII. *Aristocrates* 44 (28–9)
Fr. 18a: *IG* i³ 104. 26–9 (part of fr. 5a) (29)
Fr. 18b: law *ap.* Dem. XXIII. *Aristocrates* 37 (29)
Fr. 19a: *IG* i³ 104. 37–8 (part of fr. 5a) (29–30)
Fr. 19b: Dem. XXIII. *Aristocrates* 60 (30–2)
Fr. 20: law *ap.* Dem. XXIII. *Aristocrates* 53 (30–2)
Fr. 21: Dem. IX. *Philippic iii.* 43–4 (30–2)
†Fr. 21/1: *Ath. Pol.* 57. iii (part of fr. 4/1b) (31–2)
*Fr. 21a: Dem. XXIII. *Aristocrates* 76 (32–4)
*Fr. 21b: *Ath. Pol.* 57. iv (part of fr. 4/1b) (33–4)
*Fr. 21c: Poll. VIII. 120 (33–4)
*Fr. 21d: *Lexicon Patmense ad* Dem. XXIII. *Aristocrates* 76 (149. 1–7 *Lexica Graeca Minora*) (33–4)
†Fr. 21/2a: Dem. XXIII. *Aristocrates* 77–8 (34–5)
†Fr. 21/2b: *Ath. Pol.* 57. iii (part of fr. 4/1b) (34–5)
Fr. 22: law *ap.* Dem. XXIII. *Aristocrates* 62 (35)
Fr. 22/1: Plut. *Sol.* 19. iv (35–6)
Fr. 23a: Gell. *N.A.* XI. 18. v (37)
Fr. 23b: Poll. VIII. 22 (37)
Fr. 23c: Lys. X. *Theomnestus i*, 15–20 (37–9)
Fr. 23d: Dem. XXIV. *Timocrates* 105 (part of frs. 111–4) (39–40)
Fr. 23/1: Dem. XXIV. *Timocrates* 113 (part of frs. 111–4) (40–1)
Fr. 24: Poll. VIII. 34 (41)
Fr. 25: Lys. X. *Theomnestus i*, 17 (part of fr. 23c) (41)

Fr. 26: Plut. *Sol.* 23. i (42)
Fr. 27 (= fr. 52b): Hesych. β 466 Latte *et al.* (42)
Fr. 28a: Plut. *Sol.* 23. i (42–4)
Fr. 28b: *Dig.* XLVIII. 5. xxiv (43–4)
Fr. 28c: Lucian *Eunuchus* 10 (43–4)
Fr. 29a: [Dem.] LIX. *Against Neaera* 67 (44–5)
Fr. 29b: Lys. X. *Theomnestus i.* 19 (part of fr. 23c) (44–5)
Fr. 30a: Plut. *Sol.* 23. i (45)
Fr. 30b = fr. 29b
†Fr. 30/c: Aeschin. I. *Timarchus* 13–14 (45–7)
Fr. 30/d: Aeschin. I. *Timarchus* 183 (46–7)
†Fr. 30/1a: Aeschin. I. *Timarchus* 15 (47–8)
Fr. 31a: Plut. *Sol.* 23. ii (48–9)
Fr. 31b: Plut. *Sol.* 13. iv–v (48–9)
Fr. 32a: Plut. *Sol.* 21. i–ii (49–53)
Fr. 32b: Lys. X. *Theomnestus i.* 6–12 (50–3)
†Fr. 32c: Dem. XXI. *Midias* 32 (51–3)
Fr. 33a: Plut. *Sol.* 21. i (part of fr. 32a) (51–3)
Fr. 33b: *Lex. Rhet. Cant.* (78. 18–23 *Lexica Graeca Minora*) (51–3)
Fr. 34a: Lys. X. *Theomnestus i.* 19 (part of fr. 23c) (53–5)
Fr. 34b: Ammon. *Diff.* 345 (53–5)
Fr. 34/c: Hyp. III. *Athenogenes* 21 (53–5)
Fr. 35: Plut. *Sol.* 24. iii (54–5)
Fr. 36a: Schol. Hom. *Il.* XXI. 282 (55–6)
Fr. 36b: *P. Oxy.* ii. 221 (Schol. Hom. *Il.*) col. xiv. 9–16 (*ad Il.* XXI. 282, ἐρχθέντ' ἐν μεγάλῳ) (56)
Fr. 37a: *Ath. Pol.* 16. x (57–8)
Fr. 37b: *Ath. Pol.* 8. iv (57–9)
Fr. 37c: Plut. *Comp. Sol. Publ.* 2. iv (58–9)
Fr. 38a: *Ath. Pol.* 8. v (59–66)
Fr. 38b: Gell. *N.A.* II. 12. i (59–66)
Fr. 38c: Cic. *Att.* X. 1. ii (60–6)
Fr. 38d: Plut. *Sol.* 20. i (60–6)
Fr. 38e: Plut. *De Sera* 550 C (60–6)
Fr. 38f: Plut. *Praec. Ger. Reip.* 823 F (61–6)
Fr. 38g: Diog. Laert. I. 58 (61–6)
*Fr. 38h: Alexander of Aphrodisias *in Arist. Top.* II. 109 B 13 (*Comm. in Arist. Graeca* II. ii, p. 139. 33) (61–6)
*Fr. 38i: Nicephorus Gregoras, *Historia Byzantina* IX. 7 (i, p. 427. 4 Schopen) (*Corpus Scriptorum Historiae Byzantinae*, XXV. i) (62–6)
*Fr. 38j: Cantacuzenus, *Historia* IV. 13 (iii, p. 87 Schopen) (*Corpus Scriptorum Historiae Byzantinae* II. iii) (62–6)
*Fr. 38k: Plut. *De Soll. An.* 965 E (62)
†Fr. 38/l: Plut. *De Soll. An.* 965 D (62–6)
†Fr. 38/m: Lysias XXXI. *Philon* 27 (62–6)
Fr. 39: Lib. *Decl.* XIX. 7 (67–8)
†Fr. 39/1a: *Ath. Pol.* 9. i (67–8)
†Fr. 39/1b: Plut. *Sol.* 18. ii–iii (68)
†Fr. 39/1c: Plut. *Comp. Sol. Publ.* 2. ii (68)
Fr. 40a: *Ath. Pol.* 9. i (part of fr. 39/1a) (69–70)
Fr. 40b: Plut. *Sol.* 18. vi–vii (69–70)
Fr. 41a: Gal. *Linguarum Hippocratis Explicatio, prooemium* (xix. 66 Kuhn) (70–3)
Fr. 41b: Phot. ι 36 Theodoridis (71–3)
Fr. 41c: Eustathius *ad Hom. Il.* XVIII. 501 (1158. 23) (71–3)
Fr. 42: *Anecd. Bekk.* i. 242. 19–22 (71–3)
Fr. 43: Hesych. α 907 Latte *et al.* (71–3)
Fr. 44a: Hesych. τ 1298 Latte *et al.* (71–3)
Fr. 44b: Poll. VIII. 142 (71–3)
†Fr. 44/1: [Dem.] XLVI. *Stephanus ii.* 7–8 (72–3)
†Fr. 44/2: [Dem.] XLVI. *Stephanus ii.* 9–10 (72–3)
Fr. 45: Schol. Hom. *Il.* XXI. 260 (73)
Fr. 46: Hesych. τ 1437 Latte *et al.* (73–4)
*Fr. 47a: *Ath. Pol.* 9. ii (75)
Fr. 47b: Philo, *De Specialibus Legibus* III. 22 (75–6)
Fr. 48a: Poll. III. 33 (76–8)
Fr. 48b: law *ap.* [Dem.] XLVI. *Stephanus ii.* 18 (76–8)
Fr. 49a: law *ap.* [Dem.] XLVI. *Stephanus ii.* 14 (78–83)
Fr. 49b: Plut. *Sol.* 21. iii–iv (78–83)
Fr. 49c: Plut. *Quaest. Rom.* 265 E (79–83)
Fr. 49d: *Ath. Pol.* 35. ii (79–83)
Fr. 49/e = fr. 58/c: [Dem.] XLIV. *Leochares* 67 (80–3, 98–9)
Fr. 49/f: Dem. XLVIII. *Olympiodorus* 56 (80–3)
Fr. 49/g: Dem. XX. *Leptines* 102 (81–3)
†Fr. 49/h: Phot. α 2316 Theodoridis (81–3)
Fr. 50a: Ar. *Av.* 1660–4 (83–5)
Fr. 50b: Dem. XLIII. *Macartatus* 51 (83–5)
Fr. 50/c: Dem. XLIII. *Macartatus* 78 (84–5)
Fr. 51a: Plut. *Sol.* 20. iv (85–91)

Fr. 51b: Plut. *Amat.* 769 A (85–91)
†Fr. 51/c: Dem. XLIII. *Macartatus* 75 (85–91)
†Fr. 51/d: *Ath. Pol.* 56. vii (86–91)
Fr. 51/1: Dem. XLIII. *Macartatus* 54 (86–91)
Fr. 51/2: Eustathius *ad Hom. Il.* XXI. 450 (1246.13) (87–91)
Fr. 51/3: Diod. Sic. XII. 18. iii (88–91)
Fr. 52a: Plut. *Sol.* 20. ii–vi (88–91)
Fr. 52b (= fr. 27): Hesych. β 466 Latte *et al.* (89–91)
Fr. 52c: Gal. *Linguarum Hippocratis Explicatio, prooemium* (xix. 66 Kuhn) (part of fr. 41a) (89–91)
Fr 53: [Dem.] XLVI. *Stephanus ii.* 20 (91–2)
Fr. 54: Harp. σ 18 Keaney, cf. *Suda* σ 502 Adler, Phot. σ 248 Theodoridis (92)
Fr. 55a: Ar. *Av.* 1353–7 (92–7)
Fr. 55b: Lib. *Decl.* XI. 14 (93–7)
Fr. 55c: Ael. *N.A.* IX. 1 (93–7)
Fr. 56/a: Plut. *Sol.* 22. i (94–7)
†Fr. 56/b: Vitr. *De Arch.* VI. *praefatio* 3–4 (94–7)
†Fr. 56/c: Gal. *Adhortatio ad Artes Addiscendas*, 8. i (i. 15 Kuhn) (95–7)
Fr. 57/a: Plut. *Sol.* 22. iv (95–7)
†Fr. 57/b: Aeschin. I. *Timarchus* 13 (part of fr. 30/c) (95–7)
Fr. 58a: Harp. o 43 Keaney (97–9)
Fr. 58b: [Dem.] XLIV. *Leochares* 64 (98–9)
Fr. 58/c = fr. 49/e: Dem. XLIV. *Leochares* 67 (80–3, 98–9)
Fr. 59: Poll. VI. 156 (101)
*Fr. 59a: *Anecd. Oxon.* iii 193 (101)
Fr. 60a: *Dig.* X. 1. xiii (103–5)
Fr. 60b: Plut. *Sol.* 23. vii–viii (103–5)
Fr. 60c: *Anecd. Bekk.* i. 85. 1 (104–5)
Fr. 61: Hesych. π 3643 Latte *et al.* (104–5)
Fr. 62: Plut. *Sol.* 23. viii (104–5)
Fr. 63: Plut. *Sol.* 23. vi (105–6)
Fr. 64a: *Paroemiogr. Appendix* I. 58 (i. 388) (106)
Fr. 64b: Schol. Ar. *Eq.* 658, *Suda* β 367 (106)
†Fr. 64/1a: *Ath. Pol.* 10. i–ii (107–8)
†Fr. 64/1b: Androtion *FGrH* 324 F 34 *ap.* Plut. *Sol.* 15. iii–iv (107–8)
Fr. 65: Plut. *Sol.* 24. i (108–9)
Fr. 66: see fr. 149/1
Fr. 66/1a: Hdt. II. 177. ii (109–12)
Fr. 66/1b: Diod. Sic. I. 77. v (110–12)
Fr. 66/1c: Plut. *Sol.* 22. iii (110–12)

Fr. 66/1d: Plut. *Sol.* 31. v (110–12)
Fr. 66/1e: Diog. Laert. I. 55 (part of fr. 104b) (111–12)
Fr. 66/1f: *Lex. Rhet. Cant.* (72. 3–6 *Lexica Graeca Minora*) (111–12)
Fr. 66/1g: Poll. VIII. 42 (111–12)
Fr. 67: Poll. VII. 151 (112)
Fr. 68: Lys. X. *Theomnestus* 18 (part of fr. 23c) (113)
Fr. 69a: *Ath. Pol.* 9. i (part of fr. 39/1a) (113–14)
Fr. 69b: *Ath. Pol.* 6. i (113–14)
Fr. 69c: Plut. *Sol.* 15. ii (114)
Fr. 70: see fr. 22/1
Fr. 71a: Plut. *Sol.* 20. vi (115)
Fr. 71b: Poll. I. 246 (115)
Fr. 72a: Cic. *Leg.* II. 63–6 (116–20)
Fr. 72b: Cic. *Leg.* II. 59 (118–20)
Fr. 72c: Plut. *Sol.* 21. v–vii (118–20)
Fr. 72/d: Dem. XLIII. *Macartatus* 62–3 (120–1)
Fr. 73a: Ath. XV. 687 A (121–2)
Fr. 73b: Ath. XIII. 612 A (120–1)
Fr. 74a: Hermias Alexandrinus on Pl. *Phdr.* 231 E (122–5)
Fr. 74b: Plut. *Sol.* 1. vi (122–5)
Fr. 74c: Plut. *Conv. Sept. Sap.* 152 D (123–5)
Fr. 74d: Plut. *Amat.* 751 B (123–5)
Fr. 74e: Aeschin. I. *Timarchus* 138–9 (123–5)
†Fr. 74/f: Joannes Chrysostomus, *In epistulam ad Romanos* (Migne, *Patrologia Graeca*, lx. 418–9) (124–5)
†Fr. 74/g: Joannes Chrysostomus, *In epistulam ad Titum* (Migne, *Patrologia Graeca*, lxii. 693) (124–5)
†Fr. 74/1a: *Ath. Pol.* 7. iii–iv (127–9)
†Fr. 74/1b: Plut. *Sol.* 18. i–ii (128–9)
†Fr. 74/1c: Arist. *Pol.* II. 1274 A 15–21 (128–9)
†Fr. 74/2: *Ath. Pol.* 8. i (129)
Fr. 74/3a: *Ath. Pol.* 8. i (130)
Fr. 74/3b: *Ath. Pol.* 47. i (130)
†Fr. 74/4a: *Ath. Pol.* 8. iv (130–1)
†Fr. 74/4b: Plut. *Sol.* 19. i–ii (131)
†Fr. 74/5a: *Ath. Pol.* 8. iv (131–2)
†Fr. 74/5b: Plut. *Sol.* 19. i–ii (131–2)
Fr. 75: Plut. *Sol.* 24. iv (132–3)
Fr. 76a: *Dig.* XLVII. 22. iv (133–4)
Fr. 76b: Phot. o 439 Theodoridis, *Suda* o 511 Adler (134)

INDEX OF FRAGMENTS 205

Fr. 77: see fr. 80/2
Fr. 78: see fr. 66/1
Fr. 79a: *Ath. Pol.* 8. iii (135–6)
†Fr. 79/b: Androtion *FGrH* 324 F 36 *ap.* schol. Ar. *Av.* 1541 (135–6)
Fr. 80: Phot. v 40 Theodoridis (135–6)
†Fr. 80/1a: Aeschin. I. *Timarchus* 22–3 (136–8)
Fr. 80/1b: Aeschin. III. *Ctesiphon* 2–3 (137–8)
Fr. 80/2: Plut. *Sol.* 23. iii (139–40)
Fr. 81: Plut. *Sol.* 23. iii–iv (139–40)
Fr. 82: Poll. I. 29 (140)
Fr. 83: Steph. Byz. *Ethn.* (140–3)
Fr. 84: *Anecd. Bekk.* i. 86. 20 (141–3)
Fr. 85a: Theophr. *De Piet.* apud Porph. *Abstin.* II. 20–1 (141–3)
Fr. 85b: Phot. κ 1234 Theodoridis (141–3)
Fr. 85c: Schol. Ar. *Av.* 1354 (142–3)
Fr. 86: Lys. XXX. *Nicomachus* 17–18 (142–3)
Fr. 87: Plut. *Sol.* 24. v (143–4)
Fr. 88: Ath. VI. 234 E–F (143–4)
Fr. 89: Ath. IV. 137 E (144)
Fr. 89/1a: Plut. *Sol.* 23. iii (144–6)
Fr. 89/1b: Diog. Laert. I. 55–6 (144–6)
Fr. 89/1c: Diod. Sic. IX. 2. v (145–6)
Fr. 90/a: Poll. V. 36 (146–7)
†Fr. 90/b: Harp. ϖ 63 Keaney, cf. *Suda* ϖ 1313 Adler, Phot. π 776 Theodoridis (146–7)
Fr. 91: Phot. α 808 Theodoridis (147)
Fr. 92: Plut. *Sol.* 23. iii (part of fr. 81) (147)
Fr. 93a: Dio Chrys. *Or.* LXXX. 6 (149–50)
Fr. 93b: Gell. *N.A.* II. 12. i (149–50)
Fr. 94: Andoc. I. *Myst.* 95–9 (151–3)
Fr. 95: Andoc. I. *Myst.* 111 (153–4)
Fr. 95/1: Lys. X. *Theomnestus i.* 16–17 (part of fr. 23c) (154–5)
Fr. 96a: Dem. XXIV. *Timocrates* 144–8 (155–6)
Fr. 96b: Stob. *Flor.* (iv. 72 Meineke) (156)
Fr. 97a: Dem. XXIV. *Timocrates* 148–51 (156–9)
Fr. 97b: Dem. XVIII. *Crown* 6 (158–9)
Fr. 97c: Lib. *Decl.* I. 9 (158–9)
Fr. 97d: Lucian *Cal.* 8 (159)
Fr. 98a: Dem. XX. *Leptines* 89–94 (160–2)
Fr. 98b: Schol. Dem. XX. *Leptines* 88 (196 Dilts) (161–2)
†Fr. 98/c: Aeschin. III. *Ctesiphon* 38–9 (161–2)
†Fr. 98/1: Dem. XXI. *Midias* 47 (162–3)
Fr. 99: Hyp. III. *Athenogenes* 22 (163–4)

Fr. 100a: Aristid. III. *Quattuor* 630 (164–5)
Fr. 100b: Aeneas of Gaza, *Theophrastus* (22. 19–20 Colonna) (164–5)
Fr. 101: see fr. 80/1b
Fr. 102: Aeschin. I *Timarchus* 6–7 (165)
Fr. 103: Aeschin. I. *Timarchus* 19–20 (165–6)
Fr. 104a: Aeschin. I. *Timarchus* 27–33 (166–9)
Fr. 104b: Diog. Laert. I. 55 (168–9)
Fr. 104c: Dem. XXII. *Androtion* 30–1 (168–9)
Fr. 105: [Dem.] XXVI. *Aristogeiton ii.* 4 (169)
Fr. 106: Dem. XXII. *Androtion* 25–7 (169–71)
Fr. 107: Dem. XLII. *Phaenippus* 1 (171–2)
Fr. 108: Dem. XXXVI. *For Phormio* 25–7 (172–3)
Fr. 109: see fr. 72/d
Fr. 110/a: Aeschin. III. *Ctesiphon* 175–6 (173–4)
†Fr. 110/b: Aeschin. I. *Timarchus* 29 (174)
Frs. 111–4: Dem. XXIV. *Timocrates* 103–6, 112–14 (174–7)
Fr. 115/a: Aeschin. I. *Timarchus* 183 (177–8)
†Fr. /115b: [Dem.] LIX. *Neaera* 86–7 (178)
Fr. 116: see fr. 30/d
Fr. 117: Dem. LVII. *Eubulides* 30–2 (178–9)
Fr. 118a: Dem. XX. *Leptines* 104 (179–80)
Fr. 118b: Schol. Dem. XX. *Leptines* 104 (239b Dilts) (180)
Fr. 118c: Aristid. III. *Quattuor* 646 (180)
Fr. 119: see fr. 34/c
Fr. 120: see fr. 50/c
Frs. 121a–c: see frs. 49/e–g
Fr. 122: [Gal.] *An Animal Sit* 5 (xix. 179–80 Kühn) (180–1)
Fr. 123a: Ar. *Nub.* 1178–95 (181–4)
Fr. 123b: Plut. *Sol.* 25. iv–v (182–4)
Fr. 123c: Diog. Laert. I. 57–8 (183–4)
†Fr. 123d: *Lex. Rhet. Cant.* (75. 11–12 *Lexica Graeca Minora*) (184)
Fr. 124: Comoedus Incertus (Ribbeck, *Scaenicae Romanorum Poesis Fragmenta,* ii. 2-8) (184–45)
Fr. 125: Philemon, fr. 3. 1–9 Kassel & Austin *ap.* Ath. XIII. 569 D–E (185–6)
Fr. 126a: see fr. 51/2
Fr. 126b: see fr. 51/3
Fr. 126c: see fr. 71a
Fr. 127a: Plut. *Sol.* 20. iii–iv (part of fr. 52a) (186–7)
Fr. 127b: Plut. *Coni. Praec.* 138 D (186–7)

Fr. 127c: Plut. *Quaest. Graec.* 279 F (187)
Fr. 128: Phot. κ 701 Theodoridis, *Suda* κ 1585 Adler (187)
Fr. 129: Phot. ρ 162 Theodoridis (187–8)
Fr. 130: *Anecd. Bekk.* i. 340. 16 (188)
Frs. 131–5: Diog. Laert. I. 56–7 (188–9)
Fr. 136: see fr. 4/d
Fr. 137: Poll. VIII. 53 (189)
Fr. 138a: see fr. 39/1b
Fr. 138b: see fr. 39/1c
Fr. 139: Plut. *De Amore Prolis* 493 E (189–90)
Fr. 140: Alciphron II. 38. iii (190–1)
Fr. 141: Xen. *Oec.* xiv. 4–5 (190–1)
Fr. 142: Dion. Hal. *Ant. Rom.* II. 26. ii–iii (191–2)
Fr. 143a: see fr. 89/1a
Fr. 143b: see fr. 89/1b
Fr. 143c: see fr. 89/1c
Fr. 144a: Schol. Thuc. II. 35. i (192–3)
Fr. 144b: Plut. *Publ.* 9. ix (192–3)
Frs. 144c, 145: Diog. Laert. I. 55 (193)
Fr. 146: Plut. *Sol.* 31. iii–iv (193–4)
Fr. 147: Schol. Aeschin. I. *Timarchus.* 103 (223 Dilts) (193–4)
Fr. 148a: see fr. 66/1d
Fr. 148b: see fr. 66/1e
Fr. 148c: see fr. 66/1f
Fr. 148d: see fr. 66/1g
Fr. 148e: see fr. 66/1c
Fr. 149: Diog. Laert. I. 57 (part of fr. 123c) (194)
Fr. 149/1: Arist. *Pol.* II. 1266 B 14–18 (194–5)
Fr. 150a: see fr. 74/3a
Fr. 150b: see fr. 74/3b
Fr. 151: Ael. *N.A.* II. 42 (195–6)
Fr. 152: Ael. *N.A.* VI. 61 (195–6)
Fr. /153: Schol. Hom. *Il.* II. 665 (196)
Fr. /154: Harp. υ 13 Keaney (196)

INDEX OF SOURCE TEXTS

[Works attributed to an author but probably not by him are marked with an asterisk.]

Ael. *N.A.* II. 42: Fr. 151 (195–6)
— VI. 61: Fr. 152 (195–6)
— IX. 1: Fr. 55c (93–7)
— *V.H.* VIII. 10: *Fr. 1c (11–13)
Aeneas of Gaza, *Theophrastus* (22. 19–20 Colonna): Fr. 100b (164–5)
Aeschin. I *Timarchus* 6–7: Fr. 102 (165)
— — 13 (part of fr. 30/c): †Fr. 57/b (95–7)
— — 13–14: †Fr. 30/c (45–7)
— —15: †Fr. 30/1a (47–8)
— — 19–20: Fr. 103 (165–6)
— — 22–3: †Fr. 80/1a (136–8)
— —27–33: Fr. 104a (166–9)
— — 29: †Fr. 110/b (174)
— — 138–9: Fr. 74e (123–5)
— — 183: Fr. 30/d (46–7)
— — 183: Fr. 115/a (177–8)
— III. *Ctesiphon* 2–3: Fr. 80/1b (137–8)
— — 38–9: †Fr. 98/c (161–2)
— — 175–6: Fr. 110/a (173–4)
Alciphron II. 38. iii: Fr. 140 (190–1)
Alexander of Aphrodisias *in Arist. Top.* II. 109 B 13 (*Comm. in Arist. Graeca* II. ii, p. 139. 33): *Fr. 38h (61–6)
Ammon. *Diff.* 345: Fr. 34b (53–5)
Andoc. I. *Myst.* 95–9: Fr. 94 (151–3)
— — 111: Fr. 95 (153–4)
Androtion *FGrH* 324 F 34: †Fr. 64/1b (107–8)
— — F 36: †Fr. 79/b (135–6)
Anecd. Bekk. i. 82. 17–18: Fr. 8 (25)
— — 85. 1: Fr. 60c (104–5)
— — 86. 20: Fr. 84 (141–3)
— — 242. 19–22: Fr. 42 (71–3)
— — 340. 16: Fr. 130 (188)

Anecd. Bekk. i. 401. 18–24: Fr. 5c (21–4)
— — 428. 9–10: Fr. 12 (25–6)
Anecd. Oxon. iii 193: *Fr. 59a (101)
Ar. *Av.* 1353–7: Fr. 55a (92–7)
— — 1660–4: Fr. 50a (83–5)
— *Nub.* 1178–95: Fr. 123a (181–4)

Arist. *Pol.* II. 1266 B 14–18: Fr. 149/1 (194–5)
— — 1274 A 15–21: †Fr. 74/1c (128–9)
Aristid. III. *Quattuor* 630: Fr. 100a (164–5)
— — 646: Fr. 118c (180)
Ath. IV. 137 E: Fr. 89 (144)
— VI. 234 E–F: Fr. 88 (143–4)
— XIII. 612 A: Fr. 73b (120–1)
— XV. 687 A: Fr. 73a (120–1)
Ath. Pol. 6. i: Fr. 69b (113–14)
— 7. i: Fr. 1a (11–13)
— 7. iii–iv: †Fr. 74/1a (127–9)
— 8. i: †Fr. 74/2 (129)
— 8. i: Fr. 74/3a (130)
— 8. iii: Fr. 79a (135–6)
— 8. iv: Fr. 37b (57–9)
— 8. iv: †Fr. 74/4a (130–1)
— 8. iv: †Fr. 74/5a (131–2)
— 8. v: Fr. 38a (59–66)
— 9. i: †Fr. 39/1a (67–8)
— 9. i (part of fr. 39/1a): Fr. 40a (69–70)
— 9. i (part of fr. 39/1a): Fr. 69a (113–14)
— 9. ii: *Fr. 47a (75)
— 10. i–ii: †Fr. 64/1a (107–8)
— 16. x: Fr. 37a (57–8)
— 35. ii: Fr. 49d (79–83)
— 47. i: Fr. 74/3b (130)
— 56. vii: †Fr. 51/d (86–91)
— 57. iii (part of fr. 4/1b): †Fr. 5/e (21–4)

Ath. Pol. 57. iii (part of fr. 4/1b): †Fr. 21/1 (31–2)
— 57. iii (part of fr. 4/1b): †Fr. 21/2b (34–5)
— 57. iii–iv: †Fr. 4/1b (16–17)
— 57. iv (part of fr. 4/1b): *Fr. 21b (33–4)

Cantacuzenus, *Historia* IV. 13 (iii, p. 87 Schopen) (*Corpus Scriptorum Historiae Byzantinae* II. iii): *Fr. 38j (62–6)
Cic. *Att.* X. 1. ii: Fr. 38c (60–6)
— *Leg.* II. 59: Fr. 72b (118–20)
— — II. 63–6: Fr. 72a (116–20)
Cic. *Rosc. Am.* 70: Fr. 4b (14–15)
Comoedus Incertus (Ribbeck, *Scaenicae Romanorum Poesis Fragmenta*, ii. 2-8): Fr. 124 (184–45)

Dem. IX. *Philippic iii.* 43–4: Fr. 21 (30–2)
— XVIII. *Crown* 6: Fr. 97b (158–9)
— XX. *Leptines* 89–94: Fr. 98a (160–2)
— — 102: Fr. 49/g (81–3)
— — 104: Fr. 118a (179–80)
— — 158: Fr. 14 (26–7)
— XXI. *Midias* 32: †Fr. 32c (51–3)
— — 47: †Fr. 98/1 (162–3)
— XXII. *Androtion* 25–7: Fr. 106 (169–71)
— — *Androtion* 30–1: Fr. 104c (168–9)
— XXIII. *Aristocrates* 22: †Fr. 4/1a (15–17)
— — 28: Fr. 16/a (27–8)
— — law *ap.* 37: Fr. 18b (29)
— — 44: Fr. 17 (28–9)
— — law *ap.* 51: †Fr. /16b (28)
— — law *ap.* 53: Fr. 20 (30–2)
— — 60: Fr. 19b (30–2)
— — law *ap.* 62: Fr. 22 (35)
— — 69: Fr. 15a (27)
— — 72: Fr. 6 (24)
— — 76: *Fr. 21a (32–4)
— — 77–8: †Fr. 21/2a (34–5)
— — 82: Fr. 13 (26)
— XXIV. *Timocrates* 103–6, 112–14: Frs. 111–4 (174–7)
— — 105 (part of frs. 111–4): Fr. 23d (39–40)
— — 113 (part of frs. 111–4): Fr. 23/1 (40–1)
— — 144–8: Fr. 96a (155–6)
— — 148–51: Fr. 97a (156–9)
— *XXVI. *Aristogeiton ii.* 4: Fr. 105 (169)

Dem. XXXVI. *For Phormio* 25–7: Fr. 108 (172–3)
— XLII. *Phaenippus* 1: Fr. 107 (171–2)
— XLIII. *Macartatus* 51: Fr. 50b (83–5)
— — 54: Fr. 51/1 (86–91)
— — law *ap.* 57: Fr. 5b (20–4)
— — 62–3: Fr. 72/d (120–1)
— — 75: †Fr. 51/c (85–91)
— — 78: Fr. 50/c (84–5)
— *XLIV. *Leochares* 64: Fr. 58b (98–9)
— — 67: Fr. 49/e = fr. 58/c (80–3, 98–9)
— *XLVI. *Stephanus ii.* 7–8: †Fr. 44/1 (72–3)
— — 9–10: †Fr. 44/2 (72–3)
— — law *ap.* 14: Fr. 49a (78–83)
— — law *ap.* 18: Fr. 48b (76–8)
— — 20: Fr. 53 (91–2)
— XLVIII. *Olympiodorus* 56: Fr. 49/f (80–3)
— LVII. *Eubulides* 30–2: Fr. 117 (178–9)
— *LIX. *Against Neaera* 67: Fr. 29a (44–5)
— — 86–7: †Fr. /115b (178)
Dig. X. 1. xiii: Fr. 60a (103–5)
— XLVII. 22. iv: Fr. 76a (133–4)
— XLVIII. 5. xxiv: Fr. 28b (43–4)
Dio Chrys. *Or.* LXXX. 6: Fr. 93a (149–50)
Diod. Sic. I. 77. v: Fr. 66/1b (110–12)
— IX. 2. v: Fr. 89/1c (145–6)
— XII. 18. iii: Fr. 51/3 (88–91)
Diog. Laert. I. 55 (part of fr. 104b): Fr. 66/1e (111–12)
— — 55: Fr. 104b (168–9)
— — 55: Frs. 144c, 145 (193)
— — 55–6: Fr. 89/1b (144–6)
— — 56–7: Frs. 131–5 (188–9)
— — 57 (part of fr. 123c): Fr. 149 (194)
— — 57–8: Fr. 123c (183–4)
— — 58: Fr. 38g (61–6)
— — 59: Fr. 4a: (14–15)
Dion. Hal. *Ant. Rom.* II. 26. ii–iii: Fr. 142 (191–2)

Eustathius *ad* Hom. *Il.* XVIII. 501 (1158. 23): Fr. 41c (71–3)
— — XXI. 450 (1246.13): Fr. 51/2 (87–91)

Gal. *Adhortatio ad Artes Addiscendas*, 8. i (i. 15 Kuhn): †Fr. 56/c (95–7)
— *An Animal Sit 5 (xix. 179–80 Kühn): Fr. 122 (180–1)
— *Linguarum Hippocratis Explicatio, prooemium* (xix. 66 Kuhn): Fr. 41a (70–73)

INDEX OF FRAGMENTS 209

Gal. *Linguarum Hippocratis Explicatio, prooemium* (xix. 66 Kuhn): Fr. 52c (89–91)
Gell. *N.A.* II. 12. i: Fr. 38b (59–66)
— — 12. i: Fr. 93b (149–50)
— XI. 18. v: Fr. 23a (37)
Georgius Cedrenus, *Historiarum Compendium* (i. 145. 18–20 Bekker): *Fr. 1d (12–13)

Harp. (Keaney) o 43: Fr. 58a (97–9)
— π 63: †Fr. 90/b (146–7)
— σ 18: Fr. 54 (92)
— υ 13: Fr. /154 (196)
Hdt. II. 177. ii: Fr. 66/1a (109–12)
Hermias Alexandrinus on Pl. *Phdr.* 231 E: Fr. 74a (122–5)
Hesych. α 907 Latte *et al.*: Fr. 43 (71–3)
— β 466 Latte *et al.*: Fr. 27 (= fr. 52b) (42)
— β 466 Latte *et al.*: Fr. 52b (= fr. 27) (89–91)
— π 3643 Latte *et al.*: Fr. 61 (104–5)
— τ 1298 Latte *et al.*: Fr. 44a (71–3)
— τ 1437 Latte *et al.*: Fr. 46 (73–4)
Hyp. III. *Athenogenes* 21: Fr. 34/c (53–5)
— — 22: Fr. 99 (163–4)

IG i³ 104: Fr. 5a (17–24)
— — 26–9 (part of fr. 5a): Fr. 18a (29)
— — 37–8 (part of fr. 5a): Fr. 19a (29–30)

Joannes Chrysostomus, *In epistulam ad Romanos* (Migne, *Patrologia Graeca*, lx. 418–9): †Fr. 74/f (124–5)
— *In epistulam ad Titum* (Migne, *Patrologia Graeca*, lxii. 693): †Fr. 74/g (124–5)

Lexicon Patmense ad Dem. XXIII. *Aristocrates* 76 (149. 1–7 *Lexica Graeca Minora*): *Fr. 21d (33–4)
Lex. Rhet. Cant. (72. 3–6 *Lexica Graeca Minora*): Fr. 66/1f (111–12)
— (75. 11–12 *Lexica Graeca Minora*): †Fr. 123d (184)
— (78. 18–23 *Lexica Graeca Minora*): Fr. 33b (51–3)
Lib. *Decl.* I. 9: Fr. 97c (158–9)
— — XI. 14: Fr. 55b (93–7)
— — XIX. 7: Fr. 39 (67–8)
Lucian *Cal.* 8: Fr. 97d (159)
— *Eunuchus* 10: Fr. 28c (43–4)

Lys. X. *Theomnestus i.* 6–12: Fr. 32b (50–3)
— — 15–20: Fr. 23c (37–9)
— — 16–17: (part of fr. 23c) Fr. 95/1 (154–5)
— — 17 (part of fr. 23c): Fr. 25 (41)
— — 18 (part of fr. 23c): Fr. 68 (113)
— — 19 (part of fr. 23c): Fr. 29b (44–5)
— — 19 (part of fr. 23c): Fr. 34a (53–5)
— XXX. *Nicomachus* 17–18: Fr. 86 (142–3)
— XXXI. *Philon* 27: †Fr. 38/m (62–6)

Nicephorus Gregoras, *Historia Byzantina* IX. 7 (i, p. 427. 4 Schopen) (*Corpus Scriptorum Historiae Byzantinae*, XXV. i): *Fr. 38i (62–6)

Orosius, V. 16. xxiii–xxiv: Fr. 4c (15)

P. Oxy. ii. 221 (Schol. Hom. *Il.*) col. xiv. 9–16 (*ad Il.* XXI. 282, ἐρχθέντ' ἐν μεγάλῳ): Fr. 36b (56)
Paroemiogr. Appendix I. 58 (i. 388): Fr. 64a (106)
Philemon, fr. 3. 1–9 Kassel & Austin *ap.* Ath. XIII. 569 D–E: Fr. 125 (185–6)
Philo, *De Specialibus Legibus* III. 22: Fr. 47b (75–6)
Phot. (Theodoridis) α 808: Fr. 91 (147)
— α 1753: Fr. 3 (14)
— α 2316: †Fr. 49/h (81–3)
— ι 36: Fr. 41b (71–3)
— κ 701: Fr. 128 (187)
— κ 1234: Fr. 85b: (141–3)
— ν 40: Fr. 80 (135–6)
— ο 439: Fr. 76b (134)
— π 776: †Fr. 90/b (146–7)
— π 1009: Fr. 11 (25–6)
— ρ 162: Fr. 129 (187–8)
— σ 248: Fr 54 (92)
Plut. *Amat.* 751 B: Fr. 74d (123–5)
— — 769 A: Fr. 51b (85–91)
— *Coni. Praec.* 138 D: Fr. 127b (186–7)
— *Conv. Sept. Sap.* 152 D: Fr. 74c (123–5)
— *De Amore Prolis* 493 E: Fr. 139 (189–90)
— *De Sera* 550 C: Fr. 38e (60–6)
— *De Soll. An.* 965 D: †Fr. 38/l (62–6)
— — 965 E: *Fr. 38k (62)
— *Praec. Ger. Reip.* 823 F: Fr. 38f (61–6)
— *Quaest. Graec.* 279 F: Fr. 127c (187)
— *Quaest. Rom.* 265 E: Fr. 49c (79–83)

Plut. *Publ.* 9. ix: Fr. 144b (192–3)
— *Sol.* 1. vi: Fr. 74b (122–5)
—— 13. iv–v: Fr. 31b (48–9)
—— 15. ii: Fr. 69c (114)
—— 15. iii–iv: †Fr. 64/1b (107–8)
—— 17. i: Fr. 1b (11–13)
—— 18. i–ii: †Fr. 74/1b (128–9)
—— 18. ii–iii: †Fr. 39/1b (68)
—— 18. vi–vii: Fr. 40b (69–70)
—— 19. i–ii: †Fr. 74/4b (131)
—— 19. i–ii: †Fr. 74/5b (131–2)
—— 19. iii: Fr. 2 (13–14)
—— 19. iv: Fr. 22/1 (35–6)
—— 20. i: Fr. 38d (60–6)
—— 20. ii–vi: Fr. 52a (88–91)
—— 20. iii–iv (part of fr. 52a): Fr. 127a (186–7)
—— 20. iv: Fr. 51a (85–91)
—— 20. vi: Fr. 71a (115)
—— 21. i (part of fr. 32a): Fr. 33a (51–3)
—— 21. i–ii: Fr. 32a (49–53)
—— 21. iii–iv: Fr. 49b (78–83)
—— 21. v–vii: Fr. 72c (118–20)
—— 22. i: Fr. 56/a (94–7)
—— 22. iii: Fr. 66/1c (110–12)
—— 22. iv: Fr. 57/a (95–7)
—— 23. i: Fr. 26 (42)
—— 23. i: Fr. 28a (42–4)
—— 23. i: Fr. 30a (45)
—— 23. ii: Fr. 31a (48–9)
—— 23. iii: Fr. 80/2 (139–40)
—— 23. iii: Fr. 89/1a (144–6)
—— 23. iii (part of fr. 81): Fr. 92 (147)
—— 23. iii–iv: Fr. 81 (139–40)
—— 23. vi: Fr. 63 (105–6)
—— 23. vii–viii: Fr. 60b (103–5)
—— 23. viii: Fr. 62 (104–5)
—— 24. i: Fr. 65 (108–9)
—— 24. iii: Fr. 35 (54–5)
—— 24. iv: Fr. 75 (132–3)
—— 24. v: Fr. 87 (143–4)
—— 25. iv–v: Fr. 123b (182–4)
—— 31. iii–iv: Fr. 146 (193–4)
—— 31. v: Fr. 66/1d (110–12)
— *Comp. Sol. Publ.* 2. ii: †Fr. 39/1c (68)
—— 2. iv: Fr. 37c (58–9)
Poll. I. 29: Fr. 82 (140)
—— 246: Fr. 71b (115)
— III. 28: Fr. 5d (21–4)

Poll. III. 33: Fr. 48a (76–8)
— V. 36: Fr. 90/a (146–7)
— VI. 156: Fr. 59 (101)
— VII. 151: Fr. 67 (112)
— VIII. 22: Fr. 23b (37)
—— 34: Fr. 24 (41)
—— 42: Fr. 66/1g (111–12)
—— 53: Fr. 137 (189)
—— 120: *Fr. 21c (33–4)
—— 142: Fr. 44b (71–3)
— IX. 61: Fr. 10 (25)

Schol. Aeschin. I. *Timarchus.* 103 (223 Dilts): Fr. 147 (193–4)
— Ar. *Av.* 1354: Fr. 85c (142–3)
—— 1541: †Fr. 79/b (135–6)
— Ar. *Eq.* 658: Fr. 64b (106)
— Dem. XX. *Leptines* 88 (196 Dilts): Fr. 98b (161–2)
—— 104 (239b Dilts): Fr. 118b (180)
Schol. Hom. *Il.* II. 665: Fr. /153 (196)
—— XXI. 260: Fr. 45 (73)
—— XXI. 282: Fr. 36a (55–6)
— Thuc. II. 35. i: Fr. 144a (192–3)
Sext. Emp. *Pyr.* III. 211: Fr. 4/d (15)
Steph. Byz. *Ethn.*: Fr. 83 (140–3)
Stob. *Flor.* (iv. 72 Meineke): Fr. 96b (156)
Suda (Adler) α 3716: Fr. 12 (25–6)
— β 367: Fr. 64b (106)
— κ 1585: Fr. 128 (187)
— ο 511: Fr. 76b (134)
— π 1313: †Fr. 90/b (146–7)
— σ 502: Fr. 54 (92)

Theophr. *De Piet.* apud Porph. *Abstin.* II. 20–1: Fr. 85a (141–3)

Vitr. *De Arch.* VI. *praefatio* 3–4: †Fr. 56/b (94–7)

Xen. *Oec.* xiv. 4–5: Fr. 141 (190–1)

www.ingramcontent.com/pod-product-compliance
Lightning Source LLC
Chambersburg PA
CBHW061444300426
44114CB00014B/1823